SUDAN

ENERGY POLICY, LAWS AND REGULATION HANDBOOK

STRATEGIC INFORMATION, REGULATIONS, OPPORTUNITIES

International Business Publications, USA
Washington DC, USA - Sudan

SUDAN

ENERGY POLICY, LAWS AND REGULATION HANDBOOK

STRATEGIC INFORMATION, REGULATIONS, OPPORTUNITIES

UPDATED ANNUALLY

We express our sincere appreciation to all government agencies and international organizations which provided information and other materials for this handbook

Cover Design: International Business Publications, USA

2018 Edition Updated Reprint International Business Publications, USA
ISBN 1-4330-7276-9

For additional analytical, business and investment opportunities information, please contact Global Investment & Business Center, USA at (703) 370-8082. Fax: (703) 370-8083. E-mail: ibpusa3@gmail.com Global Business and Investment Info Databank - www.ibpus.com

Printed in the USA

For additional analytical, business and investment opportunities information, please contact Global Investment & Business Center, USA at (703) 370-8082. Fax: (703) 370-8083. E-mail: ibpusa3@gmail.com Global Business and Investment Info Databank - www.ibpus.com

SUDAN

ENERGY POLICY, LAWS AND REGULATION HANDBOOK

STRATEGIC INFORMATION, REGULATIONS, OPPORTUNITIES

TABLE OF CONTENTS

STRATEGIC AND DEVELOPMENT PROFILES

STRATEGIC PROFILE

Capital and largest city	Khartoum 15°38′N 032°32′E
Official languages	• Arabic, English
Religion	Islam
Demonym	Sudanese
Government	Dominant-party federal semi-presidential republic
• President	Omar al-Bashir
• Prime Minister	Bakri Hassan Saleh
• First Vice President	Bakri Hassan Saleh
• Second Vice President	Hassabu Mohamed Abdalrahman
Legislature	National Legislature
• Upper house	Council of States
• Lower house	National Assembly
Formation	
• Nubian kingdoms	3500 BC
• Sennar dynasty	1504
• Unified with Egypt	1820
• Anglo-Egyptian Sudan	1899
• Independence (from the United Kingdom and Egypt)	1 January 1956
• Current constitution	9 January 2005
• Secession of South Sudan	15 January 2011
Area	
• Total	1,886,068 km^2 (728,215 sq mi) (15th)
Population	
• 2015 estimate	40,235,000 (35th)
• 2008 census	30,894,000 (disputed)
• Density	21.3/km^2 (55.2/sq mi)
GDP (PPP)	2017 estimate
• Total	$186.715 billion
• Per capita	$4,578
GDP (nominal)	2017 estimate
• Total	$115.874 billion
• Per capita	$2,841
Gini	35.3 medium
HDI	▲ 0.490 low · 165th
Currency	Sudanese pound (SDG)
Time zone	EAT (UTC+3)
Date format	dd/mm/yyyy
Drives on the	right
Calling code	+249
ISO 3166 code	SD
Internet TLD	.sd, سودان.

Sudan also known as **North Sudan** since South Sudan's independence and officially the **Republic of the Sudan** is a country in Northern Africa. It is bordered by Egypt to the north, the Red Sea, Eritrea, and Ethiopia to the east, South Sudan to the south, the Central African Republic to the southwest, Chad to the west and Libya to the northwest. It is the third largest country in Africa. The River Nile divides the country into eastern and western halves. Before the Sudanese Civil War, South Sudan was part of Sudan but broke away in 2011. Its predominant religion is Islam.

Sudan was home to numerous ancient civilizations, such as the Kingdom of Kush, Kerma, Nobatia, Alodia, Makuria, Meroë and others, most of which flourished along the Nile. During the pre-dynastic period Nubia and Nagadan Upper Egypt were identical, simultaneously evolved systems of pharaonic kingship by 3300 BC. By virtue of its proximity to Egypt, the Sudan participated in the wider history of the Near East inasmuch as it was Christianized by the 6th century, and Islamized in the 15th.

As a result of Christianization, the Old Nubian language stands as the oldest recorded Nilo-Saharan language (earliest records dating to the 9th century). Sudan was the largest country in Africa and the Arab world until 2011, when South Sudan separated into an independent country, following an independence referendum. Sudan is now the third largest country in Africa (after Algeria and the Democratic Republic of the Congo) and also the third largest country in the Arab world (after Algeria and Saudi Arabia).

Sudan is a member of the United Nations, the African Union, the Arab League, the Organisation of Islamic Cooperation and the Non-Aligned Movement, as well as an observer in the World Trade Organization. Its capital is Khartoum, the political, cultural and commercial centre of the nation. It is a presidential representative democratic federal republic. The politics of Sudan are regulated by a parliamentary organization called the National Assembly. The Sudanese legal system is based on Islamic

GEOGRAPHY

Country name:
conventional long form: Republic of the Sudan
conventional short form: Sudan
local long form: Jumhuriyat as-Sudan
local short form: As-Sudan *former:* Anglo-Egyptian Sudan

forests and woodland: 19%
other: 30%

Irrigated land: 19,460 sq km
Natural hazards: dust storms
Environment - current issues: inadequate supplies of potable water; wildlife populations threatened by excessive hunting; soil erosion; desertification
Environment - international agreements:
party to: Biodiversity, Climate Change, Desertification, Endangered Species, Law of the Sea, Nuclear Test Ban, Ozone Layer Protection
signed, but not ratified: none of the selected agreements

Geography - note: largest country in Africa; dominated by the Nile and its tributaries

Location: Northern Africa, bordering the Red Sea, between Egypt and Eritrea

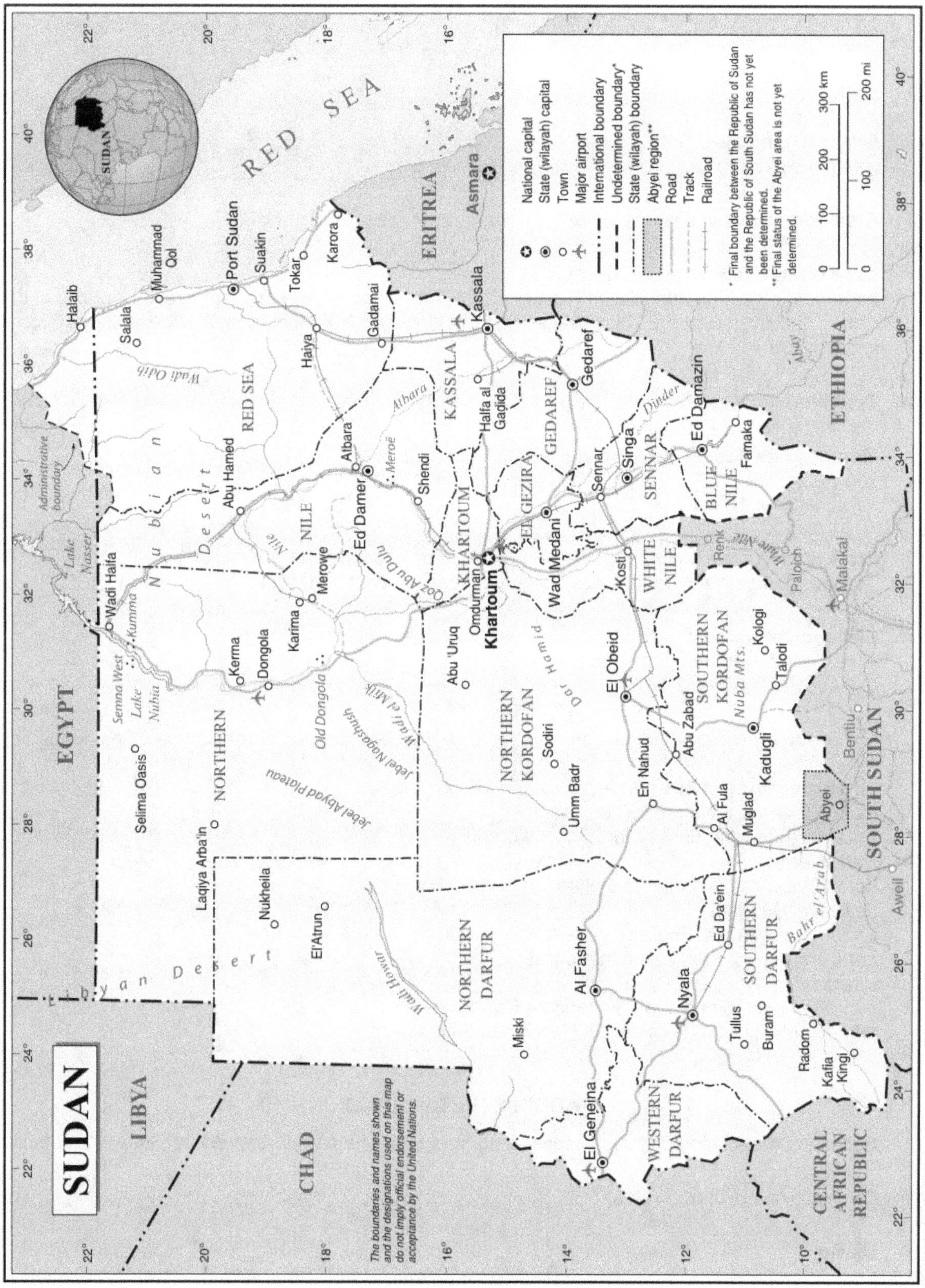

Map No. 4458 UNITED NATIONS
October 2011

Department of Field Support
Cartographic Section

Geographic coordinates: 15 00 N, 30 00 E
Map references: Africa

Area:
total: 2,505,810 sq km
land: 2.376 million sq km
water: 129,810 sq km

Area - comparative: slightly more than one-quarter the size of the US

Land boundaries: *total:* 7,687 km
border countries: Central African Republic 1,165 km, Chad 1,360 km, Democratic Republic of the Congo 628 km, Egypt 1,273 km, Eritrea 605 km, Ethiopia 1,606 km, Kenya 232 km, Libya 383 km, Uganda 435 km

Coastline: 853 km

Maritime claims: *contiguous zone:* 18 nm
continental shelf: 200-m depth or to the depth of exploitation
territorial sea: 12 nm

Climate: tropical in south; arid desert in north; rainy season (April to October)
Terrain: generally flat, featureless plain; mountains in east and west

Elevation extremes:
lowest point: Red Sea 0 m
highest point: Kinyeti 3,187 m

Natural resources: petroleum; small reserves of iron ore, copper, chromium ore, zinc, tungsten, mica, silver, gold, hydropower
Life expectancy at birth: *total population:* 56.55 years
male: 55.49 years *female:* 57.66 years
Total fertility rate: 5.47 children born/woman
Nationality:
noun: Sudanese (singular and plural)
adjective: Sudanese
Sudanic languages, English
note: program of Arabization in process
Literacy:
definition: age 15 and over can read and write
total population: 46.1% *male:* 57.7% *female:* 34.6%

ADMINISTRATIVE DIVISIONS

Sudan is divided into 18 states (*wilayat*, sing. *wilayah*). They are further divided into 133 districts.

Central and northern states

Darfur

Eastern Front

Abyei area

South Kurdufan and Blue Nile states

- Al Jazirah
- Al Qadarif
- Blue Nile
- Central Darfur
- East Darfur
- Kassala
- Khartoum
- North Darfur
- North Kurdufan
- Northern
- Red Sea
- River Nile
- Sennar
- South Darfur
- South Kurdufan
- West Darfur
- West Kurdufan
- White Nile

PEOPLE

Population: 35,079,814

Age structure:
0-14 years: 45% (male 8,064,592; female 7,712,839)
15-64 years: 53% (male 9,300,886; female 9,290,340)
65 years and over: 2% (male 406,034; female 305,123)

Population growth rate: 2.84%
Birth rate: 38.58 births/1,000 population
Death rate: 10.28 deaths/1,000 population
Net migration rate: 0.05 migrant(s)/1,000 population

Sex ratio:
at birth: 1.05 male(s)/female
under 15 years: 1.05 male(s)/female
15-64 years: 1 male(s)/female
65 years and over: 1.33 male(s)/female
total population: 1.03 male(s)/female

Infant mortality rate: 70.21 deaths/1,000 live births
Ethnic groups: black 52%, Arab 39%, Beja 6%, foreigners 2%, other 1%
permanent crops: 0%
permanent pastures: 46% **Religions:** Sunni Muslim 70% (in north), indigenous beliefs 25%, Christian 5% (mostly in south and Khartoum)
Languages: Arabic (official), Nubian, Ta Bedawie, diverse dialects of Nilotic, Nilo-Hamitic,

Data code: SU

Government type: transitional - previously ruling military junta; presidential and National Assembly elections held in March 1996; new constitution drafted by Presidential Committee, went into effect on 30 June 1998 after being approved in nationwide referendum

Capital: Khartoum

Administrative divisions: 26 states (wilayat, singular - wilayah); A'ali an Nil, Al Bahr al Ahmar, Al Buhayrat, Al Jazirah, Al Khartum, Al Qadarif, Al Wahdah, An Nil al Abyad, An Nil al Azraq, Ash

Shamaliyah, Bahr al Jabal, Gharb al Istiwa'iyah, Gharb Bahr al Ghazal, Gharb Darfur, Gharb Kurdufan, Janub Darfur, Janub Kurdufan, Junqali, Kassala, Nahr an Nil, Shamal Bahr al Ghazal, Shamal Darfur, Shamal Kurdufan, Sharq al Istiwa'iyah, Sinnar, Warab

Independence: 1 January 1956 (from Egypt and UK)
National holiday: Independence Day, 1 January (1956)

Constitution: 12 April 1973, suspended following coup of 6 April 1985; interim constitution of 10 October 1985 suspended following coup of 30 June 1989; new constitution implemented on 30 June 1998 partially suspended 12 December 1999 by President BASHIR

Legal system: based on English common law and Islamic law; as of 20 January 1991, the now defunct Revolutionary Command Council imposed Islamic law in the northern states; Islamic law applies to all residents of the northern states regardless of their religion; some separate religious courts; accepts compulsory ICJ jurisdiction, with reservations

Suffrage: NA years of age; universal, but noncompulsory

GOVERNMENT

Executive branch:

chief of state: President Umar Hassan Ahmad al-BASHIR (since 16 October 1993); First Vice President BAKRI Hassan Salih (since 3 December 2013) and prime minister (since 2 March 2017); Second Vice President Hasabu Mohamed ABDEL RAHMIN (since 3 December 2013); note - the president is both chief of state and head of government
head of government: President Umar Hassan Ahmad al-BASHIR (since 16 October 1993); First Vice President BAKRI Hassan Salih (since 3 December 2013) and prime minister (since 2 March 2017); Second Vice President Hasabu Mohamed ABDEL RAHMIN (since 3 December 2013)

cabinet: Council of Ministers appointed by the president; note - the NCP dominates al-BASHIR's cabinet

elections/appointments: president directly elected by absolute majority popular vote in 2 rounds if needed; last held on 13-16 April 2015 (next to be held in 2020); prime minister appointed by the president; note - the position of prime minister was reinstated in December 2016 as a result of the 2015-16 national dialogue process, and President al-BASHIR appointed BAKRI Hassan Salih to the position on 2 March 2017
election results: Umar Hassan Ahmad al-BASHIR reelected president; percent of vote - Umar Hassan Ahmad al-BASHIR (NCP) 94.1%, other (15 candidates) 5.9%

Legislative branch:
description: bicameral National Legislature consists of the Council of States or Majlis al-Wilayat (50 seats; members indirectly elected - 2 each by the 25 state legislatures to serve 6-year terms) and the National Assembly or Majlis Watani (426 seats; 213 members directly elected in single-seat constituencies by simple majority vote, 128 for women only directly elected by proportional representation vote, and 85 directly elected by proportional representation vote; members serve 6-year terms)

elections: last held on 13-15 April 2015 (next to be held in 2021)

election results: National Assembly - percent of vote by party - NA; seats by party - NCP 323, DUP 25, Democratic Unionist Party 15, other 44, independent 19

Judicial branch:
highest court(s): National Supreme Court (consists of 70 judges organized into panels of 3 judges and includes 4 circuits that operate outside the capital); Constitutional Court (consists of 9 justices including the court president); note - the Constitutional Court resides outside the national judiciary

judge selection and term of office: National Supreme Court and Constitutional Court judges appointed by the president of the republic upon the recommendation of the National Judicial Service Commission, an independent body chaired by the chief justice of the republic and members including other judges and judicial and legal officials; Supreme Court judge tenure NA; Constitutional Court judges appointed for 7 years
subordinate courts: Court of Appeal; other national courts; public courts; district, town, and rural courts

Political parties and leaders:
Democratic Unionist Party or DUP [Jalal al-DIGAIR]
Democratic Unionist Party [Muhammad Uthman al-MIRGHANI]
Federal Umma Party [Dr. Ahmed Babikir NAHAR]
Muslim Brotherhood or MB

National Congress Party or NCP [Umar Hassan al-BASHIR]
National Umma Party or NUP [Saddiq al-MAHDI]
Popular Congress Party or PCP [Hassan al-TURABI]
Reform Movement Now [Dr. Ghazi Salahuddin al-ATABANI]
Sudan National Front [Ali Mahmud HASANAYN]
Sudanese Communist Party or SCP [Mohammed Moktar Al-KHATEEB]
Sudanese Congress Party or SCoP [Ibrahim Al-SHEIKH]
Umma Party for Reform and Development
Unionist Movement Party or UMP

Political pressure groups and leaders:
Darfur rebel groups including the Justice and Equality Movement or JEM [Gibril Fidail IBRAHIM], Sudan Liberation Movement or SLM-AW [Abdel Wahid al-NUR, various factional leaders], Sudan Liberation Movement or SLM-MM [Minni Arkou MINAWI]
National Consensus Front or NCF [Farouq ABU ISSA]

Sudan People's Liberation Movement-North or SPLM-N [Yasir ARMAN]

International organization participation:
ABEDA, ACP, AfDB, AFESD, AMF, AU, CAEU, COMESA, FAO, G-77, IAEA, IBRD, ICAO, ICC (NGOs), ICRM, IDA, IDB, IFAD, IFC, IFRCS, IGAD, ILO, IMF, IMO, Interpol, IOC, IOM, IPU, ISO, ITSO, ITU, LAS, MIGA, NAM, OIC, OPCW, PCA, UN, UNCTAD, UNESCO, UNHCR, UNIDO, UNWTO, UPU, WCO, WFTU (NGOs), WHO, WIPO, WMO, WTO (observer)

Diplomatic representation in the US:
chief of mission: Ambassador (vacant); Charge d'Affaires MAOWIA Osman Khalid Mohammed (since 31 January 2014)
chancery: 2210 Massachusetts Avenue NW, Washington, DC 20008
telephone: [1] (202) 338-8565
FAX: [1] (202) 667-2406

Diplomatic representation from the US:
chief of mission: Ambassador (vacant); Charge d'Affaires Steven KOUTSIS (since July 2016)
embassy: Sharia Ali Abdul Latif Street, Khartoum
mailing address: P.O. Box 699, Kilo 10, Soba, Khartoum; APO AE 09829
telephone: [249] (187)-0-(22000)
FAX: [249] (183) 774-137

Flag description:
three equal horizontal bands of red (top), white, and black with a green isosceles triangle based on the hoist side; colors and design based on the Arab Revolt flag of World War I, but the meanings of the colors are expressed as follows: red signifies the struggle for freedom, white is the color of peace, light, and love, black represents the people of Sudan (in Arabic 'Sudan' means black), green is the color of Islam, agriculture, and prosperity

National symbol(s):
secretary bird; national colors: red, white, black, green

National anthem:
name: "Nahnu Djundulla Djundulwatan" (We Are the Army of God and of Our Land)
lyrics/music: Sayed Ahmad Muhammad SALIH/Ahmad MURJAN
note: adopted 1956; originally served as the anthem of the Sudanese military

ECONOMY

Sudan has experienced protracted social conflict, civil war, and, in July 2011, the loss of three-quarters of its oil production due to the secession of South Sudan. The oil sector had driven much of Sudan's GDP growth since 1999. For nearly a decade, the economy boomed on the back of rising oil production, high oil prices, and significant inflows of foreign direct investment. Since the economic shock of South Sudan's secession, Sudan has struggled to stabilize its economy and make up for the loss of foreign exchange earnings.

The interruption of oil production in South Sudan in 2012 for over a year and the consequent loss of oil transit fees further exacerbated the fragile state of Sudan's economy. Ongoing conflicts in Southern Kordofan, Darfur, and the Blue Nile states, lack of basic infrastructure in large areas, and reliance by much of the population on subsistence agriculture, keep close to half of the population at or below the poverty line.

Sudan is also subject to comprehensive US sanctions. Sudan is attempting to develop non-oil sources of revenues, such as gold mining, while carrying out an austerity program to reduce expenditures. The world's largest exporter of gum Arabic, Sudan produces 75-80% of the world's total output. Agriculture continues to employ 80% of the work force.

Sudan introduced a new currency, still called the Sudanese pound, following South Sudan's secession, but the value of the currency has fallen since its introduction. Khartoum devalued the currency in June 2012 and November 2016, in both cases to accompany austerity measures that included gradually repealing fuel subsidies. Sudan also faces high inflation, which reached 20% on an annual basis in October 2016.

GDP (purchasing power parity):

$176.3 billion (2016 est.)
$171.1 billion (2015 est.)
$163.1 billion (est.)
note: data are in 2016 dollars
country comparison to the world: 67

GDP (official exchange rate):
$94.3 billion (2016 est.)

GDP - real growth rate:
3.1% (2016 est.)
4.9% (2015 est.)
1.6% (est.)
country comparison to the world: 92

GDP - per capita (PPP):
$4,500 (2016 est.)
$4,500 (2015 est.)
$4,400 (est.)
note: data are in 2016 dollars
country comparison to the world: 172

Gross national saving:
10.7% of GDP (2016 est.)
9.3% of GDP (2015 est.)
10% of GDP (est.)
country comparison to the world: 150

GDP - composition, by end use:
household consumption: 82.6%
government consumption: 7.4%
investment in fixed capital: 14.1%
investment in inventories: 1.3%
exports of goods and services: 7.1%
imports of goods and services: -12.5% (2016 est.)

GDP - composition, by sector of origin:
agriculture: 27.5%
industry: 20.7%
services: 51.8% (2016 est.)

Agriculture - products:
cotton, groundnuts (peanuts), sorghum, millet, wheat, gum Arabic, sugarcane, cassava (manioc, tapioca), mangoes, papaya, bananas, sweet potatoes, sesame seeds; animal feed, sheep and other livestock

Industries:
oil, cotton ginning, textiles, cement, edible oils, sugar, soap distilling, shoes, petroleum refining, pharmaceuticals, armaments, automobile/light truck assembly, milling

Industrial production growth rate:
2.5% (2016 est.)
country comparison to the world: 93

Labor force:
11.92 million (2007 est.)
country comparison to the world: 49

Labor force - by occupation:
agriculture: 80%
industry: 7%
services: 13% (1998 est.)

Unemployment rate:
13.6% (est.)
14.8% (est.)
country comparison to the world: 147

Population below poverty line:
46.5% (2009 est.)
Household income or consumption by percentage share:
lowest 10%: 2.7%
highest 10%: 26.7% (2009 est.)

Budget:
revenues: $7.301 billion
expenditures: $11.28 billion (2016 est.)

Taxes and other revenues:
7.7% of GDP (2016 est.)
country comparison to the world: 215

Budget surplus (+) or deficit (-):
-4.2% of GDP (2016 est.)
country comparison to the world: 142

Public debt:
68.8% of GDP (2016 est.)
68.9% of GDP (2015 est.)
country comparison to the world: 48

Fiscal year:
calendar year

Inflation rate (consumer prices):
17.6% (2016 est.)
17.3% (2015 est.)
country comparison to the world: 217

Stock of narrow money:
$9.711 billion (31 December 2016 est.)
$9.511 billion (31 December 2015 est.)
country comparison to the world: 83

Stock of broad money:
$15.64 billion (31 December 2016 est.)
$15.42 billion (31 December 2015 est.)
country comparison to the world: 97

Stock of domestic credit:
$17.41 billion (31 December 2016 est.)
$17.34 billion (31 December 2015 est.)
country comparison to the world: 93

Current account balance:
-$5.545 billion (2016 est.)
-$6.386 billion (2015 est.)
country comparison to the world: 172

Exports:
$3.703 billion (2016 est.)
$3.169 billion (2015 est.)
country comparison to the world: 118

Exports - commodities:
gold; oil and petroleum products; cotton, sesame, livestock, peanuts, gum Arabic, sugar

Exports - partners:
UAE 23.4%, Macau 23.3%, Saudi Arabia 20.8%, Egypt 9.6%

Imports:
$9.345 billion (2016 est.)
$8.368 billion (2015 est.)
country comparison to the world: 99

Imports - commodities:
foodstuffs, manufactured goods, refinery and transport equipment, medicines, chemicals, textiles, wheat

Imports - partners:
Macau 22.7%, UAE 8.8%, India 8.4%, Egypt 6%, Saudi Arabia 4.6%, Turkey 4.3 % (2015)
Reserves of foreign exchange and gold:
$167.3 million (31 December 2016 est.)
$173.5 million (31 December 2015 est.)
country comparison to the world: 161
Debt - external:
$51.1 billion (31 December 2016 est.)
$49.42 billion (31 December 2015 est.)
country comparison to the world: 62

Stock of direct foreign investment - at home:
$24.41 billion (31 December 2015 est.)
$24.41 billion (31 December 2015 est.)
country comparison to the world: 72

Exchange rates:
Sudanese pounds (SDG) per US dollar -
6.32 (2016 est.)
6.03 (2015 est.)
6.03 (est.)
5.74 (est.)

3.57 (2012 est.)

ENERGY

Electricity access:
population without electricity: 24,700,000
electrification - total population: 35%
electrification - urban areas: 63%

electrification - rural areas: 21%

Electricity - production:
12 billion kWh (est.)
country comparison to the world: 95

Electricity - consumption:
9.9 billion kWh (est.)
country comparison to the world: 93

Electricity - exports:
0 kWh (est.)
country comparison to the world: 117

Electricity - imports:
0 kWh (est.)
country comparison to the world: 131

Electricity - installed generating capacity:
3.7 million kW (est.)
country comparison to the world: 92
Electricity - from fossil fuels:
30.7% of total installed capacity (2012 est.)
country comparison to the world: 182

Electricity - from nuclear fuels:
0% of total installed capacity (2012 est.)
country comparison to the world: 64

Electricity - from hydroelectric plants:
66.3% of total installed capacity (2012 est.)
country comparison to the world: 31

Electricity - from other renewable sources:
3% of total installed capacity (2012 est.)
country comparison to the world: 72

Crude oil - production:
64,770 bbl/day (est.)
country comparison to the world: 50

Crude oil - exports:
2,060 bbl/day (est.)
country comparison to the world: 74

Crude oil - imports:

0 bbl/day (est.)
country comparison to the world: 109

Crude oil - proved reserves:
5 billion bbl (1 January 2016 es)
country comparison to the world: 25

Refined petroleum products - production:
88,180 bbl/day (est.)
country comparison to the world: 72

Refined petroleum products - consumption:
108,000 bbl/day (est.)
country comparison to the world: 79

Refined petroleum products - exports:
5,984 bbl/day (est.)
country comparison to the world: 92

Refined petroleum products - imports:
24,800 bbl/day (est.)
country comparison to the world: 109

Natural gas - production:
0 cu m (est.)
country comparison to the world: 121
Natural gas - consumption:
0 cu m (est.)
country comparison to the world: 196

Natural gas - exports:
0 cu m (est.)
country comparison to the world: 86

Natural gas - imports:
0 cu m (est.)
country comparison to the world: 176

Natural gas - proved reserves:
21.24 billion cu m (1 January 2016 es)
country comparison to the world: 75

Carbon dioxide emissions from consumption of energy:
14 million Mt (est.)
country comparison to the world: 93

COMMUNICATIONS

Telephones - fixed lines:
total subscriptions: 118,954
subscriptions per 100 inhabitants: less than 1 (July 2015 est.)
country comparison to the world: 102

Telephones - mobile cellular:
total: 27.939 million

subscriptions per 100 inhabitants: 77 (July 2015 est.)
country comparison to the world: 46

Telephone system:
general assessment: well-equipped system by regional standards and being upgraded; cellular communications started in 1996 and have expanded substantially with wide coverage of most major cities
domestic: consists of microwave radio relay, cable, fiber optic, radiotelephone communications, tropospheric scatter, and a domestic satellite system with 14 earth stations

international: country code - 249; linked to the EASSy and FLAG fiber-optic submarine cable systems; satellite earth stations - 1 Intelsat (Atlantic Ocean), 1 Arabsat

Broadcast media:
the Sudanese Government directly controls TV and radio, requiring that both media reflect government policies; TV has a permanent military censor; a private radio station is in operation

Internet country code:
.sd

Internet users:
total: 9.61 million
percent of population: 26.6% (July 2015 est.)
country comparison to the world: 48

TRANSPORTATION

Railways:
total: 5,311 km
narrow gauge: 4,595 km 1.067-m gauge; 716 km 1.6096-m gauge plantation line
note: the main line linking Khartoum to Port Sudan carries over two-thirds of Sudan's rail traffic

Highways:
total: 11,900 km
paved: 4,320 km
unpaved: 7,580 km

Waterways: 5,310 km navigable
Pipelines: refined products 815 km
Ports and harbors: Juba, Khartoum, Kusti, Malakal, Nimule, Port Sudan, Sawakin

Merchant marine:
total: 4 ships (1,000 GRT or over) totaling 38,093 GRT/49,727 DWT
ships by type: cargo 2, roll-on/roll-off 2

Airports: 61
Airports - with paved runways:
total: 12
over 3,047 m: 1
2,438 to 3,047 m: 8
1,524 to 2,437 m: 3

Airports - with unpaved runways:
total: 49
1,524 to 2,437 m: 15
914 to 1,523 m: 24
under 914 m: 10
Heliports: 1

MILITARY

Military branches:
Sudanese Armed Forces (SAF): Land Forces, Navy (includes Marines), Sudanese Air Force (Sikakh al-Jawwiya as-Sudaniya), Rapid Support Forces, Popular Defense Forces (2016)

Military service age and obligation:
18-33 years of age for male and female compulsory or voluntary military service; 1-2 year service obligation; a requirement that completion of national service was mandatory before entering public or private sector employment has been cancelled

TRANSNATIONAL ISSUES

Disputes - international:

the effects of Sudan's almost constant ethnic and rebel militia fighting since the mid-20th century have penetrated all of the neighboring states; Chad wishes to be a helpful mediator in resolving the Darfur conflict, and in 2010 established a joint border monitoring force with Sudan, which has helped to reduce cross-border banditry and violence; as of mid-2013, Chad, Egypt, Ethiopia, Israel, the Central African Republic, and South Sudan provided shelter for more than 600,000 Sudanese refugees; during the same period, Sudan, in turn, hosted about 115,000 Eritreans, 32,000 Chadians, and smaller numbers of Ethiopians and Central Africans; Sudan accuses Eritrea of supporting Sudanese rebel groups; efforts to demarcate the porous boundary with Ethiopia proceed slowly due to civil and ethnic fighting in eastern Sudan; Sudan claims but Egypt de facto administers security and economic development of the Halaib region north of the 22nd parallel boundary; periodic violent skirmishes with Sudanese residents over water and grazing rights persist among related pastoral populations along the border with the Central African Republic; South Sudan-Sudan boundary represents 1 January 1956 alignment, final alignment pending negotiations and demarcation; final sovereignty status of Abyei Area pending negotiations between South Sudan and Sudan

Refugees and internally displaced persons:

refugees (country of origin): 98,676 (Eritrea); 8,894 (Chad) (2015); 375,719 (South Sudan) (2017)

IDPs: 3,218,234 (civil war 1983-2005; ongoing conflict in Darfur region; government and rebel fighting along South Sudan border; inter-tribal clashes) (2016)

Trafficking in persons:

current situation: Sudan is a source, transit, and destination country for men, women, and children who are subjected to forced labor and sex trafficking; Sudanese women and girls, particularly those from rural areas or who are internally displaced, or refugees are vulnerable to domestic servitude in country, as well as domestic servitude and sex trafficking abroad; migrants from East and West Africa, South Sudan, Syria, and Nigeria smuggled into or through Sudan are vulnerable to exploitation; Ethiopian, Eritrean, and Filipina women are subjected to domestic servitude in Sudanese homes, and East African and possibly Thai women are forced into prostitution in Sudan; Sudanese children continue to be recruited and used as combatants by government forces and armed groups

tier rating: Tier 2 Watch List - Sudan does not fully comply with the minimum standards for the elimination of trafficking; however, it is making significant efforts to do so; the government increased its efforts to publically address and prevent trafficking, established a national anti-trafficking council, and began drafting a national action plan against trafficking; the government acknowledges cross-border trafficking but still denies the existence of forced labor, sex trafficking, and the recruitment of child soldiers domestically; law enforcement and judicial officials struggled to apply the national anti-trafficking law, often relying on other statutes with lesser penalties; authorities did not use systematic procedure to identify victims or refer them to care and relied on international organizations and domestic groups to provide protective services; some foreign victims were penalized for unlawful acts committed as a direct result of being trafficked, such as immigration or prostitution violations (2015)

LARGEST SUDANESE CITIES

ATBARA (Atbarah -- The main draw of Atbara is that it's near the Nile's Fifth Cataract. Plan only a few hours there -- enough time to see the cataract and the old steam locomotives that died and are rusting in railyards. 172 mi/277 km northeast of Khartoum.

DINDER NATIONAL PARK -- This medium-sized reserve 16,000 acres/6,475 hectares) is in eastern Sudan, on the border with Ethiopia. Lions, monkeys, giraffes, leopards, bushbucks, kudus, antelope and many kinds of birds can be seen there, but you'll need your own vehicle. The park's main season is January-April. 250 mi/400 km southeast of Khartoum.

DONGOLA (Dunqulah) -- On the Nile in northern Sudan, this town lies in a noted date-growing area. Across the river are the ruins of the Temple of Kawa. Dongola is served by bus and steamer (during winter months only). 284 mi/457 km northeast of Khartoum.

EL OBEID (Al Ubayyid) -- The self-proclaimed "gum arabic capital of the world," El Obeid is a fairly large desert city (pop. 140,000). It has a small history museum, two markets and, interestingly enough, one of the largest cathedrals in Africa (attend a Sunday service, even if you're not particularly religious). Plan one night. 228 mi/367 km southwest of Khartoum.

ERKOWIT -- Located in the beautiful Red Sea Hills, Erkowit was once a cool retreat for the British. There are, however, few original buildings left; it's just a place to go to get out of the heat for a while. The area is reached by private vehicle. 62 mi/100 km south of Port Sudan.

IMATONG MOUNTAINS (Matong) -- When reopened, this area on the border with Uganda will be worth a visit for its cool climate and interesting tribal people. Like Erkowit (see separate paragraph), Matong was also a British hill station. Currently, the region is in rebel territory and considered unsafe to visit. 80 mi/129 km southeast of Juba.

JEBEL MARRA (Jabal Marah) -- This splendid region of small mountains in Darfur Province (western Sudan) is popular with trekkers. In the center of Jebel Marra is an extinct volcanic crater with a lake called the "Eye of Jebel Marra." Most visitors pay for a truck ride to the area from Nyala (see separate paragraph). 60 mi/120 km northwest of Nyala.

JUBA -- Capital of Equatoria Province and terminus for Nile steamers, Juba (pop. 116,000) is a place to visit just to say you've been there. Although the government has control of the city, we would be wary of flights into the airport since rebels control the surrounding countryside (an Air Sudan jetliner was shot down in Juba a few years ago). 745 mi/ 1,200 km south of Khartoum.

KARIMA (Kuraymah) -- This small market town on the Nile north of Khartoum is near the ruins (small pyramids and a temple) of Jebel Bakal. Farther south in Kurru are other interesting antiquities (underground tombs with paintings). And just across the Nile by ferry are the ruins of Merowe (not to be confused with Meroe -- see separate paragraph), the site of the ancient capital of Napata. Karima cannot be reached by road, but it is on the railway. 210 mi/338 km north-northeast of Khartoum.

KASSALA -- Surrounded by strange jebels (rounded hills), Kassala (pop. 149,000) has an active suq (market) selling locally made handicrafts (jewelry, knives, swords). Women of the Rashida tribe (descendants of 19th-century immigrants from Saudi Arabia) make the silver jewelry. Kassala can be reached by bus from Khartoum or Port Sudan. 252 mi/405 km east of Khartoum.

KHARTOUM -- The arid capital city (pop. 800,000) of Sudan, at the junction of the White Nile and Blue Nile, merits a stay of at least two nights. It's an interesting place to walk around, snoop in shops and people-watch. Also take a ride on the Nile (in Khartoum or in nearby Omdurman -- see separate paragraph), then visit the National Museum (antiquities from around the country), ethnological museum (tribal artifacts), natural-history museum (local bird and wild-game displays) and Sunt Forest (near the Hilton -- a favorite spot for picnics). The most fascinating sight is the juncture of the White and Blue Niles. Al Mogran Family Park, an amusement park, is located at the point where the rivers flow together. After spending time at the confluence, take a ferry to Tuti Island for a look at a typical rural village. Consider excursions to Jebel Aulia Dam (great spot for bird-watching, fishing, picnics and people-watching) and the Sabaloka Gorge (the Nile's Sixth Cataract -- it's a three- or four-hour drive each way). Other trips -- by four-wheel-drive vehicles or local buses -- can be made to the ruins at Meroe and Shendi; they can be seen on a day trip, but we really recommend taking them in during a three-day trip.

KOSTI (Kusti) -- South of Khartoum on a new road, Kosti sits in an area that's usually considered safe. Visit the Kenana Sugar Project, as well as the Mahdi's Mosque on nearby Gezira Aba Island. Try the local fish from the Nile at one of the restaurants. The Nile steamer that used to travel from Kosti to Juba is not currently in service. 193 mi/310 km by road south of Khartoum.

MEROE -- On the east bank of the Nile northeast of Shendi, these ruins of pyramids, temples and palaces are remnants of the Meroitic era (350 BC to AD 350). The kingdom was influenced by Egyptian art and religion, but it became isolated, developing its own script and art. After weathering attacks by several tribes, the city was destroyed by the Christian kingdom of Axum (Ethiopia). Between the railway and the Nile, you'll see ruins of the Amon Temple, and 1 mi/2 km east of Meroe is the Temple of the Sun. The pyramids lie 3 mi/5 km from town. The nearest train station is in Kabushiya. 44 mi/70 km north of Shendi.

NUBA MOUNTAINS -- This region southwest of Khartoum is in an area that may be even more dangerous to visit, so check locally before venturing in. It's a beautiful region, and the resident Nuba tribe has managed to maintain many of its traditional ways (although the government has a campaign under way to clothe them). If the opportunity arises, see one of the local dances (and, if you have the stomach, one of their rather violent wrestling matches). Among the more interesting towns in the region are Rashad, Heiban, Kadugli and El Odaiya. Anyone visiting this area must have a lot of time; the roads are rough and transportation is unreliable. Take supplies, as food is scarce at some times of the year. 75 mi/120 km southeast of El Obeid.

YALA -- At the end of the western railway from Khartoum, Nyala is the nearest rail station to Jebel Marra (see separate paragraph). Pack animals may be purchased there for treks through Jebel Marra. There's also a government rest house. 569 mi/915 km west-southwest of Khartoum.

OMDURMAN -- The holiest site in Sudan is located across the Nile from Khartoum. Omdurman (pop. 526,000) makes a nice day trip to see the site of the Mahdi's Tomb (nonbelievers aren't permitted to enter), as well as Khalifa's House (relics of the Mahdi and British Sudan). The Old Dervishes Fort Museum (exhibits from colonial times) and a huge, fascinating market (excellent silver jewelry) are worth seeing. Don't miss the Hamed al Niel Mosque (Sufi "whirling" dervishes dance there an hour before sunset on Fridays). Omdurman presents quite a contrast to modern Khartoum. At the base of the Nile bridge, boat builders can be seen plying their trade. We consider Omdurman a must-see. 6 mi/10 km northwest of Khartoum.

PORT SUDAN -- The nation's principal port (pop. 207,000) on the Red Sea, Port Sudan doesn't have many attractions, though there are some good beaches. The ancient port of Suakin (see separate paragraph) lies 35 mi/58 km south, and the nearby resort of Arusa is a good place to snorkel. 411 mi/661 km northeast of Khartoum.

SHENDI (Shandi) -- On the Nile northeast of Khartoum, Shendi was a large 18th-century market town. Now it's mainly visited on the way to the Meroitic ruins of the Naqa and Musawwarat temples. Frequent bus service departs Khartoum. 109 mi/175 km by road northeast of Khartoum.

SHOWAK -- In eastern Sudan, Showak is the Sudanese headquarters of the United Nations High Commission for Refugees. Many refugee settlements may be found in this area. 85 mi/137 km southwest of Kassala.

SUAKIN -- This ancient Red Sea port is now inhabited mostly by cats. The town, best visited as a trip from Port Sudan, is on an island connected to the mainland by a causeway. Of interest are the ruined buildings, made of coral. 40 mi/64 km south of Port Sudan.

WADI HALFA -- The transit point of Wadi Halfa is to be endured, rather than enjoyed, while entering or leaving Egypt. There's really not much to see; the "highlight" of the area is a Chinese fish-processing plant. 578 mi/930 km by road north of Khartoum.

WAU -- Founded at its present site by the French in the 1890s, this capital of Bhar El-Ghazal Province (pop. 116,000) sits at the end of the southwest branch of the railway. Wau is in a largely Dinka tribal area that's been the longtime center of famine and war. There's a Catholic mission in Wau. 310 mi/500 km northwest of Juba.

IMPORTANT INFORMATION FOR UNDERSTANDING SUDAN

PROFILE

Geography

Area: 1.8 million sq. km. (695,000 sq. mi.); the third-largest country in Africa (after having been the largest until the July 2011 secession of South Sudan) and slightly less than a quarter the size of the continental U.S.
Cities: *Capital*--Khartoum (pop. 1.4 million). *Other cities*--Omdurman (2.1 million), Port Sudan (pop. 450,000), Kassala, Kosti.
Land boundaries: Central African Republic, Chad, Egypt, Eritrea, Ethiopia, Libya, and South Sudan.
Terrain: Generally flat with mountains in east and west. Khartoum is situated at the confluence of

the Blue and White Nile Rivers. The southernmost region is inundated during the annual floods of the Nile River system.
Climate: Desert and savanna in the north and central regions and tropical in the south.

People
Nationality: *Noun and adjective* (sing. and pl.)--Sudanese.
Population (July 2011 est.): 33,419,625; 49% urban.
Annual population growth rate (2011 est.): 2.8%.
Ethnic groups: Sudanese Arab (approximately 70%, including Shaigiyya, Ja'alin, Misseriya, Kababish and Rizegat), Fur, Zaghawa, Massalit, Beja, Nuba, and Dinka Ngok.
Religions: Islam (official), indigenous beliefs, Christianity.
Languages: Arabic (official), English (official), tribal languages (Nubian, Ta Bedawie, Fur, Zaghawa, Masalit).
Education: *Years compulsory*--8. *Attendance*--35%-40%. *Literacy*--69%.
Health: *Infant mortality rate*--71/1,000. *Life expectancy*--55.42 years.
Work force: *Agriculture*--80%; *industry and commerce*--7%; *government*--13%.

Government
Independence: January 1, 1956.
Type: Constitutional democracy in form. The last national elections took place from April 11-15, 2010. The next national elections are scheduled for 2014.
Constitution: The Interim National Constitution was adopted on July 6, 2005. It was drafted by the National Constitutional Review Commission, as mandated by the January 2005 Comprehensive Peace Agreement (CPA). The government is establishing a process to write a new constitution following the end of the CPA period.
Branches: *Executive*--Executive authority is held by the president, who also is the prime minister, head of state, head of government, and commander in chief of the armed forces. The executive branch also includes a first vice president and a vice president. As stipulated by the Doha Document for Peace in Darfur, the second vice president position is held by a person of Darfuri origin. *Legislative*--National Legislature. The National Assembly, the lower house, has 354 elected members. There is also an upper house, the Council of States, which is composed of two representatives from each of the nation's 15 states, and two observers from the Abyei Area. *Judicial*--High Court, Minister of Justice, Attorney General, civil and special tribunals.
Administrative subdivisions: Fifteen states, most with an elected governor, along with a state cabinet and elected state legislative assembly. States are divided into districts, with 133 districts comprising the 15 states.
Political parties: Seventy-two parties registered to take part in the April 2010 elections. Following the secession, there are many political parties, 70 of which are registered. All political parties were banned following the June 30, 1989 military coup. Political associations, taking the place of parties, were authorized in 2000. Some parties are in self-imposed exile. The principal national parties are the National Congress Party (NCP) and the Sudan People's Liberation Movement-North (SPLM-N), which is an offshoot of the South Sudan-based party and is currently banned by the Sudanese Government.
Central government budget (2010 est.): $13.35 billion.
Defense (2005 est.): 3% of GDP.

Economy
Natural resources: Modest reserves of oil, natural gas, gold, iron ore, copper, and other industrial metals.
Agriculture: *Products*--cotton, peanuts, sorghum, sesame seeds, gum arabic, sugarcane, millet, livestock.
Industry: *Types*--motor vehicle assembly, cement, cotton, edible oils and sugar refining.
Trade: *Exports* (2009 est.)--$10.29 billion f.o.b.: crude oil and petroleum products, cotton, gold, sorghum, peanuts, gum arabic, sugar, meat, hides, live animals, and sesame seeds. *Major*

markets--China, Japan, Indonesia, Egypt, United Arab Emirates, Saudi Arabia, Malaysia, and South Korea. Imports (2010 est.)--$9.176 billion f.o.b.: oil and petroleum products, oil pipeline, pumping and refining equipment, chemical products and equipment, wheat and wheat flour, transport equipment, foodstuffs, tea, agricultural inputs and machinery, industrial inputs and manufactured goods. *Major suppliers*--European Union, China, Malaysia, Saudi Arabia, Egypt, United Arab Emirates, and India.
Fiscal year: January 1-December 31.

PEOPLE

Sudan's population is one of the most diverse on the African continent. Within two distinct major cultures--Arab and sub-Saharan African--there are hundreds of ethnic and tribal subdivisions and language groups, which make effective collaboration among them a major political challenge.

The Sudanese are predominantly Arabic-speaking Muslims, though many also use a non-Arabic mother tongue--e.g., Nubian, Beja, Fur, Nuban, Ingessana, etc. Among these are several distinct tribal groups: the Kababish of northern Kordofan, a camel-raising people; the Ja'alin and Shaigiyya groups of settled tribes along the rivers; the semi-nomadic Baggara of Kordofan and Darfur; the Hamitic Beja in the Red Sea area and Nubians of the northern Nile areas, some of whom have been resettled on the Atbara River; and the Nuba of southern Kordofan and Fur in the western reaches of the country. Following the secession of South Sudan, there remain some small factions of Dinka (particularly the Dinka Ngok in Abyei), Shilluk, and the Nuer from the Nilotic tribes.

According to post-secession figures based on census results released in early 2009, Sudan's population has reached an estimated 33.4 million.

HISTORY

Sudan was a collection of small, independent kingdoms and principalities from the beginning of the Christian era until 1820-21, when Egypt conquered and unified the northern portion of the country. However, neither the Egyptian nor the Mahdist state (1883-1898) had any effective control of the southern region outside of a few garrisons.

In 1881, a religious leader named Muhammad ibn Abdalla proclaimed himself the Mahdi, or the "expected one," and began a religious crusade to unify the tribes in western and central Sudan. His followers took on the name "Ansars" (the followers) which they continue to use today and are associated with the single largest political grouping, the Umma Party, led by a descendant of the Mahdi, Sadiq al Mahdi.

Taking advantage of dissatisfaction resulting from Ottoman-Egyptian exploitation and maladministration, the Mahdi led a nationalist revolt culminating in the fall of Khartoum in 1885. The Mahdi died shortly thereafter, but his state survived until overwhelmed by an invading Anglo-Egyptian force under Lord Kitchener in 1898. While nominally administered jointly by Egypt and Britain, Britain exercised control, formulated policies, and supplied most of the top administrators.

Independence

In February 1953, the United Kingdom and Egypt concluded an agreement providing for Sudanese self-government and self-determination. The transitional period toward independence began with the inauguration of the first parliament in 1954. With the consent of the British and Egyptian Governments, Sudan achieved independence on January 1, 1956, under a provisional constitution. This constitution was silent on two crucial issues for southern leaders--the secular or Islamic character of the state and its federal or unitary structure. However, the Arab-led Khartoum government reneged on promises to southerners to create a federal system, which led to a mutiny by southern army officers that launched 17 years of civil war (1955-72).

Post-Independence

Sudan has been at war with itself for more than three-quarters of its existence. Since independence, protracted conflict rooted in deep cultural and religious differences have slowed Sudan's economic and political development and forced massive internal displacement of its people. Northerners, who have traditionally controlled the country, have sought to unify it along the lines of Arabism and Islam despite the opposition of non-Muslims, southerners, and marginalized peoples in the west and east. The resultant civil strife affected Sudan's neighbors, as they alternately sheltered fleeing refugees or served as operating bases for rebel movements.

In 1958, General Ibrahim Abboud seized power and pursued a policy of Arabization and Islamicization for both North and South Sudan that strengthened Southern opposition. General Abboud was overthrown in 1964 and a civilian caretaker government assumed control. Southern leaders eventually divided into two factions, those who advocated a federal solution and those who argued for self-determination, a euphemism for secession since it was assumed the south would vote for independence if given the choice.

Until 1969, there was a succession of governments that proved unable either to agree on a permanent constitution or to cope with problems of factionalism, economic stagnation, and ethnic dissidence. These regimes were dominated by "Arab" Muslims who asserted their Arab-Islamic agenda and refused any kind of self-determination for southern Sudan.

In May 1969, a group of communist and socialist officers led by Colonel Gaafar Muhammad Nimeiri, seized power. A month after coming to power, Nimeiri proclaimed socialism (instead of Islamism) for the country and outlined a policy of granting autonomy to the South. Nimeiri in turn was the target of a coup attempt by communist members of the government. It failed and Nimeiri ordered a massive purge of communists. This alienated the Soviet Union, which withdrew its support.

Already lacking support from the Muslim parties he had chased from power, Nimeiri could no longer count on the communist faction. Having alienated the right and the left, Nimeiri turned to the south as a way of expanding his limited powerbase. He pursued peace initiatives with Sudan's hostile neighbors, Ethiopia and Uganda, signing agreements that committed each signatory to withdraw support for the other's rebel movements. He then initiated negotiations with the southern rebels and signed an agreement in Addis Ababa in 1972 that granted a measure of autonomy to the South. Southern support helped him put down two coup attempts, one initiated by officers from the western regions of Darfur and Kordofan who wanted for their region the same privileges granted to the south.

However, the Addis Ababa Agreement had no support from either the secularist or Islamic Northern parties. Nimeiri concluded that their lack of support was more threatening to his regime than lack of support from the south so he announced a policy of national reconciliation with all the religious opposition forces. These parties did not feel bound to observe an agreement they perceived as an obstacle to furthering an Islamist state. The scales against the peace agreement were tipped in 1979 when Chevron discovered oil in the south. Northern pressure built to abrogate those provisions of the peace treaty granting financial autonomy to the south. In 1983, Nimeiri abolished the Southern region, declared Arabic the official language of the South (instead of English) and transferred control of Southern armed forces to the central government. This was effectively a unilateral abrogation of the 1972 peace treaty. The second Sudan civil war began in January 1983 when southern soldiers mutinied rather than follow orders transferring them to the North.

In September 1983, as part of an Islamicization campaign, President Nimeiri announced that traditional Islamic punishments drawn from Shari'a (Islamic law) would be incorporated into the penal code. This was controversial even among Muslim groups. Amputations for theft and public lashings for alcohol possession became common. Southerners and other non-Muslims living in the north were also subjected to these punishments.

In April 1985, while out of the country, Nimeiri was overthrown by a popular uprising in Khartoum provoked by a collapsing economy, the war in the south, and political repression. General Suwar al-Dahab headed the transitional government. One of its first acts was to suspend the 1983 constitution and disband Nimeiri's Sudan Socialist Union.

Elections were held in April 1986, and a civilian government took power. There were tentative moves towards negotiating peace with the south. However, any proposal to exempt the south from Islamic law was unacceptable to those who supported Arabic supremacy. In 1989, an Islamic army faction led by General Umar al-Bashir mounted a coup and installed the National Islamic Front. The new government's commitment to an Islamic state intensified the North-South conflict.

The Bashir government combined internal political repression with international Islamist activism. It supported radical Islamist groups in Algeria and supported Iraq's invasion of Kuwait. Khartoum was established as a base for militant Islamist groups: radical movements and terrorist organizations like Osama Bin Laden's al Qaida were provided a safe haven and logistical aid in return for financial support. In 1996, the UN imposed sanctions on Sudan for alleged connections to the assassination attempt on Egyptian President Hosni Mubarak.

Meanwhile, the 1990s saw a growing sense of alienation in the western and eastern regions of Sudan from the Arab center. The rulers in Khartoum were seen as less and less responsive to the concerns and grievances of both Muslim and non-Muslim populations across the country. Alienation from the "Arab" center caused various groups to grow sympathetic to the southern rebels led by the Sudan People's Liberation Movement/Army (SPLM/A), and in some cases, prompted them to flight alongside it.

The policy of the ruling regime toward the South was to pursue the war against the rebels while manipulating tribal divisions. Ultimately, this policy resulted in the rebels' uniting under the leadership of John Garang. During this period, the SPLM/A rebels also enjoyed support from Ethiopia, Eritrea, and Uganda. The Bashir government's "Pan-Islamic" foreign policy, which provided support for neighboring radical Islamist groups, was partly responsible for this support for the rebels.

The 1990s saw a succession of regional efforts to broker an end to the Sudanese civil war. Beginning in 1993, the leaders of Eritrea, Ethiopia, Uganda, and Kenya pursued a peace initiative for Sudan under the auspices of the Intergovernmental Authority for Development (IGAD), but results were mixed. Despite that record, the IGAD initiative promulgated the 1994 Declaration of Principles (DOP) that aimed to identify the essential elements necessary to a just and comprehensive peace settlement; *i.e.*, the relationship between religion and the state, power sharing, wealth sharing, and the right of self-determination for the south. The Sudanese Government did not sign the DOP until 1997 after major battlefield losses to the SPLA. That year, the Khartoum government signed a series of agreements with rebel factions under the banner of "Peace from Within." These included the Khartoum, Nuba Mountains, and Fashoda Agreements that ended military conflict between the government and significant rebel factions. Many of those leaders then moved to Khartoum where they assumed marginal roles in the central government or collaborated with the government in military engagements against the SPLA. These three agreements paralleled the terms and conditions of the IGAD agreement, calling for a degree of autonomy for the south and the right of self-determination.

End to the Civil War

In July 2002, the Government of Sudan and the SPLM/A reached a historic agreement on the role of state and religion and the right of southern Sudan to self-determination. This agreement, known as the Machakos Protocol, named after the Kenyan town where the peace talks were held, concluded the first round of talks sponsored by IGAD. The effort was mediated by retired Kenyan General Lazaro Sumbeiywo. Peace talks resumed and continued during 2003, with discussions focusing on wealth sharing and three contested areas.

On November 19, 2004, the Government of Sudan and the SPLM/A signed a declaration committing themselves to conclude a final comprehensive peace agreement by December 31, 2004. The declaration came in the context of an extraordinary session of the United Nations Security Council (UNSC) in Nairobi, Kenya--only the fifth time the Council had met outside of New York since its founding. At this session, the UNSC unanimously adopted Resolution 1574, which welcomed the commitment of the government and the SPLM/A to achieve agreement by the end of 2004, and underscored the international community's intention to assist the Sudanese people and support implementation of the comprehensive peace agreement. In keeping with their commitment to the UNSC, the Government of Sudan and the SPLM/A initialed the final elements of the comprehensive agreement on December 31, 2004. The two parties formally signed the Comprehensive Peace Agreement (CPA) on January 9, 2005. The U.S. and the international community welcomed this decisive step forward for peace in Sudan.

In January 2011, the South voted in a referendum to secede from Sudan. Ninety-eight percent of voters cast ballots for secession in mostly orderly and peaceful balloting. International and national observers hailed the referendum process as consistent with international standards and representing the free expression of voters. On July 9, 2011, the Republic of South Sudan officially declared independence, seceding from Sudan. Several violent conflicts flared up in 2011, including continued conflict in Darfur and in the three border states of Abyei, Southern Kordofan, and Blue Nile (the "Three Areas").

GOVERNMENT AND POLITICAL CONDITIONS

Officially, the politics of Sudan takes place in the framework of a federal presidential representative democratic republic, where the President of Sudan is head of state, head of government and commander-in-chief of the Sudan People's Armed Forces in a multi-party system. Legislative power is vested in both the government and the bicameral parliament—the National Legislature, with its National Assembly (lower chamber) and the Council of States (upper chamber). The judiciary is independent and obtained by the Constitutional Court. It is part of the Northern Africa grouping of the UN geoscheme.

However, following the Second Sudanese Civil War (1983–2005) and the now-low-scale war in Darfur, Sudan is widely recognized as an authoritarian state where all effective political power is obtained by President Omar al-Bashir and the ruling National Congress Party (NCP).

In 1993, Sudan was transformed into an Islamic authoritarian one-party state as al-Bashir abolished the Revolutionary Command Council and created the National Islamic Front (NIF) with a new parliament and government obtained solely by members of the NIF. At the same time, the structure of regional administration was replaced by the creation of twenty-six states, each headed by a governor, thus making Sudan a federal republic.

Executive posts are divided between the NCP, the SPLA, the Sudanese Eastern Front and factions of the Umma Party and Democratic Unionist Party (DUP).

According to the new 2005 constitution, the bicameral National Legislature is the official Sudanese parliament and is divided between two chambers—the National Assembly, a lower house with 450 seats, and the Council of States, an upper house with 50 seats. Thus the parliament consists of 500 appointed members altogether, where all are indirectly elected by state legislatures to serve six-year terms.

Despite his international arrest warrant, al-Bashir was a candidate in the 2010 Sudanese presidential election, the first democratic election with multiple political parties participating in twenty-four years. In the build-up to the vote, Sudanese pro-democracy activists say they faced intimidation by the government and the International Crisis Group reported that the ruling party had gerrymandered electoral districts. A few days before the vote, the main opposition candidate, Yasir Arman from the SPLM, withdrew from the race. The U.S.-based Carter Center, which helped monitor the elections, described the vote tabulation process as "highly chaotic, non-transparent and vulnerable to electoral manipulation." Al-Bashir was declared the winner of the election with sixty-eight percent of the vote.

SHARIA LAW

The legal system in Sudan is based on Islamic Sharia law. The 2005 Naivasha Agreement, ending the civil war between north and south Sudan, established some protections for non-Muslims in Khartoum. Sudan's application of Sharia law is geographically inconsistent.

Stoning remains a judicial punishment in Sudan. Between 2009 and 2012, several women were sentenced to death by stoning. Flogging is a legal punishment. Between 2009 and 2014, many people were sentenced to 40–100 lashes. In August 2014, several Sudanese men died in custody after being flogged. 53 Christians were flogged in 2001. Sudan's public order law allows police officers to publicly whip women who are accused of public indecency.

Crucifixion is a legal punishment. In 2002, 88 people were sentenced to death for crimes relating to murder, armed robbery, and participating in ethnic clashes, Amnesty International wrote that they could be executed by either hanging or crucifixion.

International Court of Justice jurisdiction is accepted, though with reservations. Under the terms of the Naivasha Agreement, Islamic law did not apply in South Sudan. Since the secession of South Sudan there is some uncertainty as to whether Sharia law will now apply to the non-Muslim minorities present in Sudan, especially because of contradictory statements by al-Bashir on the matter.

The judicial branch of the Sudanese government consists of a Constitutional Court of nine justices, the National Supreme Court, the Court of Cassation, and other national courts; the National Judicial Service Commission provides overall management for the judiciary.

FOREIGN RELATIONS

Sudan has had a troubled relationship with many of its neighbours and much of the international community, owing to what is viewed as its radical Islamic stance. For much of the 1990s, Uganda, Kenya and Ethiopia formed an ad-hoc alliance called the "Front Line States" with support from the United States to check the influence of the National Islamic Front government. The Sudanese Government supported anti-Ugandan rebel groups such as the Lord's Resistance Army (LRA).

As the National Islamic Front regime in Khartoum gradually emerged as a real threat to the region and the world, the U.S. began to list Sudan on its list of State Sponsors of Terrorism. After the US listed Sudan as a state sponsor of terrorism, the NIF decided to develop relations with Iraq, and later Iran, the two most controversial countries in the region.

From the mid-1990s, Sudan gradually began to moderate its positions as a result of increased U.S. pressure following the 1998 U.S. embassy bombings, in Tanzania and Kenya, and the new development of oil fields previously in rebel hands. Sudan also has a territorial dispute with Egypt over the Hala'ib Triangle. Since 2003, the foreign relations of Sudan had centered on the support for ending the Second Sudanese Civil War and condemnation of government support for militias in the war in Darfur.

Sudan has extensive economic relations with China. China obtains ten percent of its oil from Sudan. According to a former Sudanese government minister, China is Sudan's largest supplier of arms.

In December 2005, Sudan became one of the few states to recognize Moroccan sovereignty over Western Sahara.

In 2015, Sudan participated in the Saudi Arabian-led intervention in Yemen against the Shia Houthis and forces loyal to former President Ali Abdullah Saleh, who was deposed in the 2011 uprising.

ARMED FORCES

The Sudan People's Armed Forces is the regular forces of Sudan and is divided into five branches: the Sudanese Army, Sudanese Navy (including the Marine Corps), Sudanese Air Force, Border Patrol and the Internal Affairs Defense Force, totalling about 200,000 troops. The military of Sudan has become a well-equipped fighting force, thanks to increasing local production of heavy and advanced arms. These forces are under the command of the National Assembly and its strategic principles include defending Sudan's external borders and preserving internal security.

Since the Darfur crisis in 2004, safe-keeping the central government from the armed resistance and rebellion of paramilitary rebel groups such as the Sudan People's Liberation Army (SPLA), the Sudanese Liberation Army (SLA) and the Justice and Equality Movement (JEM) have been important priorities. While not official, the Sudanese military also uses nomad militias, the most prominent being the Janjaweed, in executing a counter-insurgency war. Somewhere between 200,000 and 400,000 people have died in the violent struggles.

INTERNATIONAL ORGANIZATIONS IN SUDAN

Several UN agents are operating in Sudan such as the World Food Program (WFP); the Food and Agriculture Organization of the United Nation (FAO); the United Nations Development Program (UNDP); the United Nations Industrial Development Organizations (UNIDO); the United Nations Children Fund (UNICEF); the United Nations High Commissioner for Refugees (UNHCR); the United Nations Mine Service (UNMAS), the United Nations Office for the Coordination of Humanitarian Affairs (OCHA) and the World Bank. Also present is the International Organization for Migration (IOM).

Since Sudan has experienced civil war for many years, many Non-Governmental Organisations (NGOs) are also involved in humanitarian efforts to help internally displaced people. The NGOs are working in every corner of Sudan, especially in the southern part and western parts. During the civil war, international nongovernmental organizations such as the Red Cross were operating mostly in the south but based in the capital Khartoum. The attention of NGOs shifted shortly after the war broke out in the western part of Sudan known as Darfur. The most visible organization in South Sudan is the Operation Lifeline Sudan (OLS) consortium.

Even though most of the international organizations are substantially concentrated in both South Sudan and Darfur region, some of them are working in the northern part as well. For example, the United Nations Industrial Development Organization is successfully operating in Khartoum, the capital. It is mainly funded by the European Union and recently opened more vocational training. The Canadian International Development Agency is operating largely in northern Sudan.

HUMAN RIGHTS

Since 1983, a combination of civil war and famine has taken the lives of nearly 2 million people in Sudan. It is estimated that as many as 200,000 people had been taken into slavery during the Second Sudanese Civil War.

Sudan ranks 172 of 180 countries in terms of freedom of the press according to Reporters Without Borders, yet more curbs of press freedom to report official corruption are planned.

Muslims who convert to Christianity can face the death penalty for apostasy, see Persecution of Christians in Sudan and the death sentence against Mariam Yahia Ibrahim Ishag (who actually was raised as Christian). According to a 2013 UNICEF report, 88% of women in Sudan had undergone female genital mutilation. Sudan's Personal Status law on marriage has been criticized for restricting women's rights and allowing child marriage. Evidence suggests that support for female genital mutilation remains high, especially among rural and less well educated groups, although it has been declining in recent years. Homosexuality is illegal and is a capital offense in Sudan.

DARFUR

A letter dated 14 August 2006, from the executive director of Human Rights Watch found that the Sudanese government is both incapable of protecting its own citizens in Darfur and unwilling to do so, and that its militias are guilty of crimes against humanity. The letter added that these human-rights abuses have existed since 2004. Some reports attribute part of the violations to the rebels as well as the government and the Janjaweed. The U.S. State Department's human-rights report issued in March 2007 claims that "*[a]*ll parties to the conflagration committed serious abuses, including widespread killing of civilians, rape as a tool of war, systematic torture, robbery and recruitment of child soldiers."

Over 2.8 million civilians have been displaced and the death toll is estimated at 300,000 killed. Both government forces and militias allied with the government are known to attack not only civilians in Darfur, but also humanitarian workers. Sympathizers of rebel groups are arbitrarily detained, as are foreign journalists, human-rights defenders, student activists and displaced people in and around Khartoum, some of whom face torture. The rebel groups have also been accused in a report issued by the U.S. government of attacking humanitarian workers and of killing innocent civilians. According to UNICEF, in 2008, there were as many as 6,000 child soldiers in Darfur.

DISPUTED AREAS AND ZONES OF CONFLICT

- In mid-April 2012, the South Sudanese army captured the Heglig oil field from Sudan.
- In mid-April 2012 the Sudanese army recaptured Heglig.
- Kafia Kingi and Radom National Park was a part of Bahr el Ghazal in 1956. Sudan has recognized South Sudan independence according to the borders for 1 January 1956.
- The Abyei Area is disputed region between Sudan and South Sudan. It is currently under Sudan rule.
- The states of South Kurdufan and Blue Nile are to hold "popular consultations" to determine their constitutional future within the Sudan.
- The Hala'ib triangle is disputed region between Sudan and Egypt. It is currently under Egyptian administration.
- Bir Tawil is a terra nullius occurring on the border between Egypt and Sudan, claimed by neither state.

REGIONAL BODIES AND AREAS OF CONFLICT

In addition to the states, there also exist regional administrative bodies established by peace agreements between the central government and rebel groups.

- The Darfur Regional Authority was established by the Darfur Peace Agreement to act as a co-ordinating body for the states that make up the region of Darfur.
- The Eastern Sudan States Coordinating Council was established by the Eastern Sudan Peace Agreement between the Sudanese Government and the rebel Eastern Front to act as a coordinating body for the three eastern states.
- The Abyei Area, located on the border between South Sudan and the Republic of the Sudan, currently has a special administrative status and is governed by an Abyei Area Administration. It was due to hold a referendum in 2011 on whether to join an independent South Sudan or remain part of the Republic of the Sudan.

PRINCIPAL GOVERNMENT OFFICIALS - CURRENT NATIONAL MINISTERS

Office	Incumbent	Website
Prime Minister		
First Lieu. General S.G Bakri Hassan Saleh	Minister of the Presidency Affairs	http://www.presidency.gov.sd/
Dr. Luka Biong	Minister of the Council of Ministers	http://www.sudan.gov.sd/
Lieu. General. Ahmed Awad Ibn Auf	Minister of National Defense	http://www.mod.gov.sd
Mr. Ibrahim Mahmoud Hamad	Minister of Interior	http://moi.gov.sd/
Mr. Ibrahim Ghandour	Minister of Foreign Affairs	http://www.mfa.gov.sd/
Mr. Mohammed Bushara Dousa	Minister of Justice	http://www.moj.gov.sd/
Mr. Ali Mahmoud Abdul-Rasool	Minister of Finance & National Economy	http://www.mof.gov.sd/
	Minister of Science and Communication	http://msc.gov.sd/ (down)

Mr. Kamal Abdul-Latif Abdul-Rahim	Minister of Human Resources Development	
Dr. Abdul-Halim Ismail Al- Mutaafi	Minister of Agriculture	http://agri-khs.gov.sd/indexen.php
Dr. Awad Ahmed Al- Jaz	Minister of Industry	
Dr. Azhari Al-Tigani Awad Al-Sayid	Minister of Guidance and Endowments	
Mr. Kamal Mohamed Obeid	Minister of Information	http://mininfo.gov.sd/en
Kamaladdin Hassan Ali	Minister of International Cooperation	
Mr. Lual Achuil Deng	Minister of Petroleum	
Dr. Peter Adok Nyaba	Minister of High Education & Scientific Research	
Mr. Farah Mustafa Abdalla	Minister of Public Education	http://moekh.gov.sd/en/
Mr. Kamal Ali Mohammad Ahmed	Minister of Irrigation & Water Resources	http://wre.gov.sd/en/
Eng Mr. Osama Abdalla Mohamed Al - Hassan	Minister of Electricity	http://wre.gov.sd/en/
	Minister of Dams	http://diu.gov.sd/en/
Mr. Eissa Bashari Mohamed	Minister of Science & Technology	
Mr. Al - Samawa'al Khalafalla Al-Quraish	Minister of Culture	
Dr. Abdalla Tiya Juma	Minister of Health	http://www.fmoh.gov.sd/ (down)
Ustaza\ Amira Al-Fadil Mohamed Ahmed	Minister of Welfare & Social Security	
Mr. Haj Magid Siwar	Minister of Youth And Sports	
Mr. Chol Ram Pang	Minister of Transportation	
Dr. Mostafa Osman Ismail	Minister of Investment	http://minv.gov.sd/en
Professor / Elias Nyamlel Wakoson	Minister of Foreign Trade	http://www.tpsudan.gov.sd/index.php/en/
Dr. Abdul-Bagi Al-Jailani	Minister of Minerals	http://minerals.gov.sd/en

Dr. Ahmed Babekir Nahar	Minister of Antiquities, Tourism & Wildlife	
Eng. Joseph Malwal Dong	Minister of Environment, Forestry & Physical Development	
Mr. Abdul - Wahab Mohamed Osman	Minister of Roads & Bridges	
Ustaza / Halima Hassaballah Al-Naeem	Minister of Parliamentary Affairs	
Mr. Dak Dob Bishok	Minister of Labor	
Dr. Faisal Hassan Ibrahim	Minister of Animal Resources & Fisheries	http://agri-khs.gov.sd/indexen.php
Mr. Joseph Lual Achuil	Minister of Humanitarian Affairs	
Dr. Yahiya Abdallah Mohamed Hamad	Minister of Communications & Information Technology	

Sudan maintains an **embassy** in the United States at 2210 Massachusetts Ave. NW, Washington, DC 20008 (tel: (202) 338-8565; fax: (202) 667-2406); and a Consular Office at 2612 Woodley Place, NW, Washington, DC 20008 (tel: (202) 232-1492; fax: (202) 232-1494).

ECONOMY

Overview

In 2004, the cessation of major north-south hostilities in Sudan and expanding crude oil exports resulted in 6.4% GDP growth and a near doubling of GDP per capita since 2003. The aftereffects of the 21-year civil war and very limited infrastructure, however, presented obstacles to stronger growth and a broader distribution of income. The country continued taking some steps toward transitioning from a socialist to a market-based economy, although the government and governing party supporters remained heavily involved in the economy.

The July 2011 secession of South Sudan had an immediate and profound impact on Sudan's economy, and the reverberations from the split will continue to resound in the coming years. While the composition of what the "new" Sudanese economy will be is unclear, the country will not be able to rely on the oil production and export that had served as the principal driver of growth since 2000. With much of its oil production having come from what is now South Sudan, Sudan has suffered a dramatic decline in its oil revenues. The government has targeted agriculture, mining, and enhanced oil production as sectors for development. With conflicts continuing on its southern borders, a virtual cessation in cross-border trade with the new South Sudan, and unresolved issues with both oil revenue sharing and an arrangement for transporting South Sudan oil to Port Sudan, Sudan and its people are not able in the near future to reap the benefits from its natural resources, rebuild its infrastructure, increase oil production and exports, and be able to attain its export and development potential.

Background

Sudan's oil production began in the late 1990s and grew rapidly starting in July 1999 with completion of an export pipeline that runs from South Sudan through the North to the Port of Sudan. Sudan produced an estimated 401,000 barrels per day (b/d) in 2005, which brought in about $1.9 billion and provided 70% of the country's total export earnings. As of 2007, oil production in Sudan was at 466,100 barrels per day. In 2010, oil accounted for over 90% of Sudan's foreign exchange earnings. Prior to South Sudan's July 2011 secession, roughly 75% of Sudan's oil production, representing almost 36% of government revenues, came from fields located in the South. Remaining production in Sudan barely covers domestic use.

Agriculture, which was the economy's mainstay prior to oil, accounted for about a third of GDP prior to secession. It represented 90% of Sudan's 2009 non-oil exports, and the sector employed about 80% of the labor force. Sudan's authorities are looking at increasing agricultural production in an effort to diversify growth; only an estimated 15%-20% of Sudan's arable land is cultivated. The authorities have launched an Agricultural Revitalization Plan to invest some $5 billion in the sector through 2012, and hope to attract strategic foreign investors. Cotton and gum arabic remain its major agricultural exports. Grain sorghum (dura) is the principal food crop, and millet and wheat are grown for domestic consumption. Sesame seeds and peanuts are cultivated for domestic consumption and increasingly for export. Livestock production has vast potential, and many animals, particularly camels and sheep, are exported to Egypt, Saudi Arabia, and other Arab countries. However, Sudan remains a net importer of food. Problems of irrigation and transportation remain the greatest constraints to a more dynamic agricultural economy.

Sudan's non-oil private sector remains nascent. Sudan ranked 154 in the Doing Business survey in 2010. Firms identify the top three constraints holding back growth and investment as political instability, corruption, and economic uncertainty. Transparency International ranked Sudan as 172 out of 180 countries in its 2010 corruption perception index. Competitiveness remains low due to high transaction costs, poor market institutions, lack of infrastructure, and high administrative barriers.

Sudan's growth has historically been unbalanced, with the majority of its manufacturing firms and irrigated land concentrated in the northern states of Khartoum and Gezira. The World Bank reports that there is a large disparity in development indicators between the best- and worst-performing states. Sudan's capital city Khartoum consumes nearly a third of Sudan's total electricity production, while less than 7% of households in the country have access to the national grid. Sudan's limited industrial development consists of agricultural processing and various light industries located in Khartoum North. In recent years, the GIAD industrial complex introduced the assembly of small autos and trucks, and some heavy military equipment such as armored personnel carriers and the proposed "Bashir" main battle tank. Although Sudan is reputed to have great mineral resources, exploration has been quite limited, and the country's real potential is relatively unknown. Small quantities of asbestos, chromium, and mica are also exploited commercially.

Since the global financial crisis of 2008 and the collapse of crude oil prices, Sudan has faced a severe foreign exchange reserves shortfall. While data is not made public on a regular basis, the International Monetary Fund reported that reserves at the Central Bank of Sudan fell below 2 weeks of import coverage at one point. As a result of the shortage of foreign currency, the Government of Sudan has significantly tightened conversion and transfer policies. Domestic businesses have no assurance of obtaining needed levels of foreign currency for international transactions. Foreign companies operating in Sudan must have the permission of the Central Bank of Sudan to repatriate profits and foreign currency. Changes to policies are introduced without warning and generally become effective immediately upon announcement.

Debt and Aid

Sudan has a severe external debt burden, with large and protracted arrears that limit both its relations with the international financial institutions (IFIs) and integration into the world economy. The country has not serviced the majority of its external debt since the early 1990s, although some creditors, including some offering more recent financing, are receiving repayments. The

United States accounts for $2.2 billion, of which $2.0 billion is in arrears. Sudan is subject to a variety of legal sanctions and legislative mandates that would complicate U.S. Government participation in IFI normalization and debt relief. Reducing U.S. claims would also require significant appropriations. Sudan's ruling NCP party views the provision of debt relief as critical for the North's economic prospects in view of Southern secession and closely links debt relief to the division of the country's oil revenues.

Historically, the U.S., the Netherlands, Italy, Germany, Saudi Arabia, Kuwait, and other Organization of Petroleum Exporting Countries (OPEC) have supplied most of Sudan's economic assistance. Sudan's role as an economic link between Arab and African countries is reflected by the presence in Khartoum of the Arab Bank for African Development. The World Bank had been the largest source of development loans but is currently unable to lend.

During the late 1970s and 1980s, the International Monetary Fund (IMF), World Bank, and key donors worked closely to promote reforms to counter the effect of inefficient economic policies and practices. By 1984, a combination of factors--including drought, inflation, and confused application of Islamic law--reduced donor disbursements, and capital flight led to a serious foreign-exchange crisis and increased shortages of imported inputs and commodities. More significantly, the 1989 revolution caused many donors in Europe, the U.S., and Canada to suspend official development assistance, although not humanitarian aid.

As Sudan became the world's largest debtor to the World Bank and IMF by 1993, its relationship with the international financial institutions soured in the mid-1990s and has yet to be fully rehabilitated. The government fell out of compliance with an IMF standby program and accumulated substantial arrearages on repurchase obligations. A 4-year economic reform plan was announced in 1988 but was not pursued. An economic reform plan was announced in 1989 and implementation began on a 3-year economic restructuring program designed to reduce the public sector deficit, end subsidies, privatize state enterprises, and encourage new foreign and domestic investment. In 1993, the IMF suspended Sudan's voting rights and the World Bank suspended Sudan's right to make withdrawals under effective and fully disbursed loans and credits. Lome Funds and European Union agricultural credits, totaling more than 1 billion euros, also were suspended.

DEFENSE

The Sudan People's Armed Forces is a 100,000-member army supported by a small air force and navy. Irregular tribal and former rebel militias and Popular Defense Forces supplement the army's strength in the field. This is a mixed force, having the additional duty of maintaining internal security. During the 1990s, periodic purges of the professional officer corps by the ruling Islamist regime eroded command authority as well as war-fighting capabilities. Indeed, the Sudanese Government admitted it was incapable of carrying out its war aims against the SPLA without employing former rebel and Arab militias to fight in support of regular troops. During the CPA period, Joint Integrated Units were formed to unite Sudanese Armed Forces and former SPLM rebels. After the secession of South Sudan, people of Southern descent were let go from the army and the Joint Integrated Units were dissolved.

Sudan's military forces historically have been hampered by limited and outdated equipment. In the 1980s, the U.S. worked with the Sudanese Government to upgrade equipment with special emphasis on airlift capacity and logistics. All U.S. military assistance was terminated following the military coup of 1989. Oil revenues have allowed the government to purchase modern weapons systems, including Hind helicopter gunships, MiG 23 fighter aircraft, mobile artillery pieces, and light assault weapons. Some military techniques are improvised, such as using Antonov transport aircraft as crude and inaccurate bombers. Sudan now receives most of its military equipment from China, Russia, and (until 2011) Libya.

FOREIGN RELATIONS

Solidarity with other Arab countries has been a feature of Sudan's foreign policy. When the Arab-Israeli war began in June 1967, Sudan declared war on Israel. However, in the early 1970s, Sudan gradually shifted its stance and was supportive of the Camp David Accords.

Relations between Sudan and Libya deteriorated in the early 1970s and reached a low in October 1981, when Libya began a policy of cross-border raids into western Sudan. After the 1985 coup in Sudan, the military government resumed diplomatic relations with Libya, as part of a policy of improving relations with neighboring and Arab states. In early 1990, Libya and the Sudan announced that they would seek "unity," but this unity was not implemented.

During the 1990s, as Sudan sought to steer a nonaligned course, courting Western aid and seeking rapprochement with Arab states, its relations with the U.S. grew increasingly strained. Sudan's ties with countries like North Korea and Libya and its support for regional insurgencies such as Egyptian Islamic Jihad, Eritrean Islamic Jihad, Ethiopian Islamic Jihad, Palestinian Islamic Jihad, Hamas, Hezbollah, and the Lord's Resistance Army generated great concern about its contribution to regional instability. Allegations of the government's complicity in the assassination attempt against the Egyptian President in Ethiopia in 1995 led to UNSC sanctions against Sudan. By the late 1990s, Sudan experienced strained or broken diplomatic relations with most of its neighboring countries. However, since 2000, Sudan has actively sought regional rapprochement that has rehabilitated most of these relations.

U.S.-SUDANESE RELATIONS

Sudan broke diplomatic relations with the U.S. in June 1967, following the outbreak of the Arab-Israeli War. Relations improved after July 1971, when the Sudanese Communist Party attempted to overthrow President Nimeiri, and Nimeiri suspected Soviet involvement. U.S. assistance for resettlement of refugees following the 1972 peace settlement with the south added further improved relations.

On March 1, 1973, Palestinian terrorists of the "Black September" organization murdered U.S. Ambassador Cleo A. Noel and Deputy Chief of Mission Curtis G. Moore in Khartoum. Sudanese officials arrested the terrorists and tried them on murder charges. In June 1974, however, they were released to the custody of the Egyptian Government. The U.S. Ambassador to the Sudan was withdrawn in protest. Although the U.S. Ambassador returned to Khartoum in November, relations with the Sudan remained static until early 1976, when President Nimeiri mediated the release of 10 American hostages being held by Eritrean insurgents in rebel strongholds in northern Ethiopia. In 1976, the U.S. decided to resume economic assistance to Sudan.

In late 1985, there was a reduction in staff at the U.S. Embassy in Khartoum because of the presence in Khartoum of a large contingent of Libyan terrorists. In April 1986, relations with Sudan deteriorated when the U.S. bombed Tripoli, Libya. A U.S. Embassy employee was shot on April 16, 1986. Immediately following this incident, all non-essential personnel and all dependents left for 6 months. At this time, Sudan was the single largest recipient of U.S. development and military assistance in sub-Saharan Africa. However, official U.S. development assistance was suspended in 1989 in the wake of the military coup against the elected government, which brought to power the National Islamist Front led by General Bashir.

U.S. relations with Sudan were further strained in the 1990s. Sudan backed Iraq in its invasion of Kuwait and provided sanctuary and assistance to Islamic terrorist groups. In the early and mid-1990s, Carlos the Jackal, Osama bin Laden, Abu Nidal, and other terrorist leaders resided in Khartoum. Sudan's role in the radical Pan-Arab Islamic Conference represented a matter of great concern to the security of American officials and dependents in Khartoum, resulting in several draw downs and/or evacuations of U.S. personnel from Khartoum in the early-mid 1990s. Sudan's Islamist links with international terrorist organizations represented a special matter of concern for the U.S. Government, leading to Sudan's 1993 designation as a state sponsor of terrorism and a suspension of U.S. Embassy operations in Khartoum in 1996. In October 1997, the U.S. imposed comprehensive economic, trade, and financial sanctions against the Sudan. In August 1998, in the wake of the East Africa embassy bombings, the U.S. launched cruise missile strikes against Khartoum. The last U.S. Ambassador to the Sudan, Ambassador Tim Carney, departed post prior to this event and no new ambassador has been designated since. The U.S. Embassy is headed by a Charge d'Affaires. The Embassy continues to re-evaluate its posture in Sudan, particularly in the wake of the January 1, 2008, killings of a U.S. Agency for International Development (USAID) employee and his Sudanese driver in Khartoum.

The U.S. and Sudan entered into a bilateral dialogue on counterterrorism in May 2000. Sudan has provided concrete cooperation against international terrorism since the September 11, 2001, terrorist strikes on New York and Washington. However, although Sudan publicly supported the international coalition actions against the al Qaida network and the Taliban in Afghanistan, the government criticized the U.S. strikes in that country and opposed a widening of the effort against international terrorism to other countries. Sudan remains on the state sponsors of terrorism list.

In response to the Government of Sudan's continued complicity in unabated violence occurring in Darfur, President Bush imposed new economic sanctions on Sudan in May 2007. The sanctions blocked assets of Sudanese citizens implicated in Darfur violence, and also sanctioned additional companies owned or controlled by the Government of Sudan. Sanctions continue to underscore U.S. efforts to end the suffering of the millions of Sudanese affected by the crisis in Darfur.

Despite policy differences the U.S. has been a major donor of humanitarian aid to the Sudan throughout the last quarter-century. The U.S. was a major donor in the March 1989 "Operation Lifeline Sudan," which delivered 100,000 metric tons of food into both government and SPLA-held areas of the Sudan, thus averting widespread starvation. In 1991, the U.S. made major donations to alleviate food shortages caused by a 2-year drought. In a similar drought in 2000-2001, the U.S. and the international community responded to avert mass starvation in the Sudan. In 2001 the Bush administration named a presidential envoy for peace in the Sudan to explore what role the U.S. could play in ending Sudan's civil war and enhancing the delivery of humanitarian aid. Andrew Natsios and subsequently Ambassador Richard Williamson served as presidential envoys to Sudan during the Bush administration. On March 18, 2009 President Obama announced the appointment of J. Scott Gration as the U.S. Special Envoy to Sudan.

On October 19, 2009, Secretary Clinton, accompanied by Special Envoy Gration and U.S. Ambassador to the United Nations Susan Rice, announced the Obama administration's new Sudan strategy. U.S. strategy in Sudan is comprised of three core principles: 1) Achieving a definitive end to conflict, gross human rights abuses, and genocide in Darfur; 2) Implementation of the North-South Comprehensive Peace Agreement (CPA) that results in a peaceful post-2011 Sudan, or an orderly path toward two separate and viable states at peace with each other; and 3) Ensuring that Sudan does not provide a safe haven for international terrorists.

In January 2011, Dane Smith was appointed Senior Advisor for Darfur. In March 2011, Princeton N. Lyman was appointed U.S. Special Envoy for Sudan.

Principal U.S. Officials

Chargé d'Affaires Steven Koutsis
A career member of the Senior Foreign Service, Mr. Koutsis was most recently Director of the Special Envoy's Office for Sudan and South Sudan. Prior to that, he was Deputy Chief of Mission in Ouagadougou, Burkina Faso. He has also served as Deputy Director and interim Director in

the Office of Central African Affairs, and as Team Leader of the Provincial Reconstruction Team in Diyala Province, Iraq. Other tours include Political and Economic Counselor in Monrovia, Liberia, and Deputy Chief of Mission in Nouakchott, Mauritania. He was Consular Section Chief in Damascus, Syria and in Abidjan, Cote d'Ivoire. His other assignments include Washington, D.C., Marseille, France, and Port-au-Prince, Haiti.

Charge d'Affaires--Mary C. Yates
Deputy Chief of Mission--Dennis Hankins
USAID Director--Barry Primm
Political-Economic Chief--Howell Howard
Public Affairs Officer--William Bellis

The **U.S. Embassy** in Sudan is located at Embassy Road, Kilo 10, Soba, off Wad Medani Highway, Khartoum (tel. 249-187-022000). Hours are 8 a.m. to 4:30 p.m. Sunday through Thursday.

TRAVEL AND BUSINESS INFORMATION

Travel Alerts, Travel Warnings, Trip Registration
The U.S. Department of State's Consular Information Program advises Americans traveling and residing abroad through Country Specific Information, Travel Alerts, and Travel Warnings. **Country Specific Information** exists for all countries and includes information on entry and exit requirements, currency regulations, health conditions, safety and security, crime, political disturbances, and the addresses of the U.S. embassies and consulates abroad. **Travel Alerts** are issued to disseminate information quickly about terrorist threats and other relatively short-term conditions overseas that pose significant risks to the security of American travelers. **Travel Warnings** are issued when the State Department recommends that Americans avoid travel to a certain country because the situation is dangerous or unstable.

For the latest security information, Americans living and traveling abroad should regularly monitor the Department's Bureau of Consular Affairs Internet web site at http://travel.state.gov, where current Worldwide Caution, Travel Alerts, and Travel Warnings can be found. The travel.state.gov website also includes information about passports, tips for planning a safe trip abroad and more. More travel-related information also is available at http://www.usa.gov/Citizen/Topics/Travel/International.shtml.

The Department's Smart Traveler app for U.S. travelers going abroad provides easy access to the frequently updated official country information, travel alerts, travel warnings, maps, U.S. embassy locations, and more that appear on the travel.state.gov site. Travelers can also set up e-tineraries to keep track of arrival and departure dates and make notes about upcoming trips. The app is compatible with iPhone, iPod touch, and iPad (requires iOS 4.0 or later).

The Department of State encourages all U.S. citizens traveling or residing abroad to enroll in the State Department's Smart Traveler Enrollment Program (STEP). A link to the registration page is also available through the Department's Smart Traveler app. U.S. citizens without internet access can enroll directly at the nearest U.S. embassy or consulate. By enrolling, you make your presence and whereabouts known in case it is necessary to contact you in an emergency and so you can receive up-to-date information on security conditions.

Emergency information concerning Americans traveling abroad may be obtained by calling 1-888-407-4747 toll free in the U.S. and Canada or the regular toll line 1-202-501-4444 for callers outside the U.S. and Canada.

Passports

The National Passport Information Center (NPIC) is the U.S. Department of State's single, centralized public contact center for U.S. passport information. Telephone: 1-877-4-USA-PPT (1-877-487-2778); TDD/TTY: 1-888-874-7793. Passport information is available 24 hours, 7 days a week. You may speak with a representative Monday-Friday, 8 a.m. to 10 p.m., Eastern Time, excluding federal holidays.

SUDAN LEGAL SYSTEM BASICS

As Africa's largest country, Sudan includes many religious, ethnic and socio-economic groups. Prevailing issues of access to resources, economic opportunity and power against the background of such diversity has unfortunately resulted in some of Africa's longest-running conflicts since the country became independent in 1956. These conflicts have included those between Muslim-Christian, Arab-African and nomad-farmer groups, e.g. The rule of law is but one of many casualties resulting from the permanent presence of conflict (or threat thereof) in the South, West and Eastern regions. Not surprisingly, historical, social and political factors have largely shaped Sudanese laws in terms of substance and application, including colonial legacies, a historically Arab-dominated central government and the presence of an intricate network of informal laws that are based upon religious, ethnic and/or tribal communities. The complexity of these factors renders it extremely difficult to distil a comprehensive overview of formal and informal Sudanese laws that are currently in operation. Rather, this article will attempt to present an elementary overview of principle Sudanese laws, as well as some contextual background as to the nature of the informal justice mechanisms that operate outside the formal legal mechanisms.

The laws includes criminal (Criminal Act, 1991; Criminal Procedure Act, 1991); civil (Muslim Law Act 1991); commercial (Banking; Investment Encouragement; National Petroleum Commission, Telecommunications, Copyright); public laws (Khartoum Public Order Act; Labour Act, 1997); as well as gender issues, and child rights and duties (Child Act 2004). A final section is included that lists important domestic legislation; as well as primary treaty law to which Sudan is a signatory. A list of useful electronically available resources is also provided, in particular, links to extensive reporting on human rights practices in Sudan.

CURRENT POLITICAL LANDSCAPE

Prior to independence in 1956, Sudan was jointly administered by Anglo-Egyptian forces following their capture of Khartoum in 1898. The north and southern regions of Sudan were administered separately until 1947, after which political power was placed within the hands of a northern elite that was composed largely of Arab ethnicity. Following independence, the North and South have been in almost constant conflict; the first civil war lasting from 1956 - 1972 and the second from 1983 to 2005. At present, "Sudan has an authoritarian government in which all effective political power lies in the hands of President Omar Hassan al Bashir and the National Congress (NC) Party inner circle, who have been in power since a 1989 military coup (that was) instigated and supported by the fundamentalist National Islamic Front (NIF). . In 2000, Bashir was re-elected, and his NC/NIF political party won 340 out of 360 seats in the Parliament in deeply flawed elections boycotted by all major opposition parties. NC/NIF members and supporters continued to hold key positions in the Government, security forces, judiciary, academic institutions, trade unions, professional associations, and the media."[1]

According to International Crisis Group, Sudan is divided by religion (70 per cent Muslim, 25 per cent animist, 5 per cent Christian), ethnicity (between African and Arab origin Sudanese), tribe and economic activity (between nomadic and sedentary cultures).[2] The principal conflict between the northern and southern parts of Sudan was borne out during 1956 - 72 and 1983 - 2005 and has cost an estimated 2 million lives, while displacing over 4 million people. The origins of what developed into a national conflict between the North and South have been said to lie in Sudan's colonial past; however, economic and political disparities, the discovery of oil-rich areas in the South, as well as regional power politics have also fuelled the conflict.

Not surprisingly, the early mixture of British and Arab rule, combined with more recent assertions of Islamisation by political forces in Khartoum[3], have had significant implications upon the composition of Sudanese laws. Indeed, the religious composition of the warring groups has also influenced the nature of laws administered in areas controlled by the Muslim-dominated central government and the Christian rebel movement in the South.

THE COMPREHENSIVE PEACE AGREEMENT (CPA)

A cease-fire was eventually declared between the Sudanese government and the Sudan People's Liberation Movement / Army (SPLM/A) in July 2002. Peace talks were carried on through 2003, though fighting also continued on both sides; eventually in 2005, a peace agreement between the Government of Sudan and the SPLM/A was reached. Highlights of the Comprehensive Peace Agreement include a Power Sharing Agreement, a Wealth Sharing Agreement and Security Protocol; and special power and wealth sharing agreements for the areas of Abyei, Southern Kordorfon and Blue Nile (also referred to as the Three Areas), which individually possess specific factors that precipitated and prolonged the conflict - including and especially resource wealth).

Despite the death of SPLM leader and Vice-President elect John Garang in August 2005, the peace process continued with the ratification of a new constitution in October 2005, the swearing-in of a new government (that divided executive posts between the ruling parties of the North and South) and the functioning of an autonomous Southern legislature and government. Much of Sudan's laws will undergo amendment following the new Constitution, which seek to balance interests and power between the South Sudanese and Central Governments.

The UN has deployed a multilateral peacekeeping observer mission to the South that is mandated to monitor the implementation of the agreement and support the building of national capacity until a referendum on the sovereignty of the south can be held in 2011. Despite all of this progress, tensions between the Government of National Unity (GONU), i.e. the National Congress, and the Sudan People's Liberation Movement (SPLM) remain live. The SPLM has accused the GONU of slowing down implementation of the Comprehensive Peace Agreement (CPA). The issues in dispute included the designated commissions by agreement, Abyei borders, withdrawal of the government army beyond the Independence border of January 1956, the volume and revenue of oil production, and the democratic transition, which had been extremely sluggish.[4]

CURRENT CONFLICTS - DARFUR AND THE EAST

The peace between the North and the South remains fragile, while other conflicts or threats thereof loom elsewhere in Sudan, notably in Darfur and Eastern Sudan. The central government continues to wage war in Darfur, since the taking-up of arms by the Sudan Liberation Army/Movement (SLA) and Justice and Equality Movement (JEM) rebels (predominantly African sedentary tribes of the Fur, Zaghawa and Massaleit) in February 2003. The central government responded by arming Arab "Janjaweed" militia, in addition to deploying the Sudanese army. Some estimate that Darfur conflict has displaced almost 2 million and taken anywhere from 200,000 - 400,000 lives. With much of the civilian population permanently displaced, the rule of law appears virtually non-existent. Humanitarian agencies such as International Rescue Committee together with the United Nations Development Fund have undertaken efforts to build "Justice Confidence Centres" in displacement camps, which aim to create community spaces for resolving disputes as well as information on human rights and local laws. To the East, a third conflict may escalate between the Government and the opposing "Eastern Front", who are in negotiations towards a peace agreement. The Islamist Ruling Party (known as the NCP - National Congress Party) is alleged to maintain dominance over the region by measures not unknown in Darfur - undercutting support for the opposition through patronage, divide-and-rule policies, and the creation of tribal militias.[5] International Crisis Group reports that some fear that humanitarian levels in the East have dropped lower than those in Darfur. Both situations bode poorly for rule of law and access to justice for local populations.

THE JUDICIAL SYSTEM

Arbiters of disputes and administrators of formal and informal laws come in various forms throughout Sudan, depending on ethnic, religious and political factors. Judicial courts are provided for under both statute *and* customary law while informal community practices also rely upon local chiefs, known as Sultans, to resolve disputes between community members. Indeed, "(t)he judiciary relies greatly on popular justice for solving disputes through methods of conciliation and the application of tradition."[6] Customary laws generally consist of non-state dispute resolution systems that are usually based upon local customary, traditional or tribal systems of justice. Given Sudan's ethnic and religious plurality, customary laws and practice are diverse, differing from tribe-to-tribe and community-to-community. Case reporting of decisions by the formal courts is published in the *Sudan Law Journal and Reports*, whilst laws are published in the *Sudan Gazette*.

According to Y. Sherif, Northern "judiciary structures are more developed but the independence of the judiciary seems to have been compromised - as evidenced by the arbitrary dismissal of qualified judges, attorneys-general and law officers. Existing legislation fails to guarantee the full spectrum of human rights and fundamental freedoms, while military decrees and emergency laws undermine those rights currently protected by statutory law."[7] Indeed, thought the "Constitution provides for an independent judiciary; however, the judiciary (is) largely subservient to the President or the security forces, particularly in cases of crimes against the state."[8]

Questions of independence reach beyond the judiciary to practising lawyers. Lawyers throughout Sudan must belong to the National Bar Association, which is based in Khartoum. Outside of Khartoum, the Association is viewed as being overly urban in both composition and its substantive focus and therefore removed from the daily needs and challenges outside of the capital. However, it is unfair to characterize an entire bar; indeed, the Association has endured its own difficulties even within Khartoum. In 1992, "the government amended the Advocate Act of 1983 in such a drastic way as to totally abrogate the Association's independence. For the first time in its history, the SBA has been reduced to another trades union. the Association has now been registered with the Registrar of Trades Union."[9] According to the U.S. Department of State, members of the legal profession are harassed by the Government viewed as political opponents; some have been detained, including the Director of the Darfur Lawyers Association, Mohamed Adomo, who was later released.[10]

THE SUPREME COURT

The Supreme Court is composed of seventy judges and operates through panels that are composed of three judges, which are presided over by the most senior of the three. Decisions are reached by a majority of opinion and are subject to revision only if and when the chief justice deems that an infringement of (*shari'a* laws) has taken place. In this case the Chief Justice convenes a five member panel, the majority of whom must not have participated in reaching the disputed decision in order to receive the matter. The court disposes of appeals against the judgments of the courts of appeal in civil, criminal and personal matter cases."[11] The Court also has "preliminary jurisdiction of a single judge to consider appeals against the administrative decision of the president of the republic of the governors and of the federal and state ministers. Appeals from the decision of this single judge's court are dealt with by panel of three Supreme Court judges."[12] Four circuits of the Supreme Court operate outside the capital in the western, central and eastern states.[13]

THE CONSTITUTIONAL COURT

In addition to the Supreme Court, the Sudanese judicial system includes four types of courts: regular courts, which primarily consider criminal and civil matters; special mixed security courts, military courts and tribal courts, which apply customary law to resolve disputes over land and water rights and family matters. The regular courts include Court of Appeal, the Public Courts[14] and District Courts[15] (courts of first instance).[16] The Constitutional Court considers:

a. Interpretation of the constitution when requested to do so by the President of the Republic, the National Assembly, half of the Governors of the states or half of the State Assemblies.

b. Suits from any aggrieved person to protect the freedoms and rights guaranteed by the Constitution after exhausting the executive and administrative remedies available.
c. Suits concerning jurisdictional conflicts between national and federal bodies.
d. Criminal procedures against the President of the Republic and the Governors under the Constitution or the laws.
e. Objections concerning the acts of the President of the Republic, the Council of Ministers or a National or Federal Minister if the objection concerns any infringement of the national constitutional system or the constitutional inviolable freedoms or rights.
f. Any other matters determined to be within the competence of the Constitutional Court.[17]

During a campaign of Islamisation in 1983, the central government reunified the civil and *shari'a* courts, which had earlier been made separate during colonialism. Subsequent constitutional reform did not alter the ability of formal courts to consider *shari'a* law.

MILITARY INTELLIGENCE/SECURITY CASES

"In addition to the regular police and the Sudan People's Armed Forces, the Government maintain(s) an external security force, an internal security force, a militia known as the Popular Defense Forces (PDF), and a number of police forces. The security forces (are) under the effective control of the Government. Members of the security forces (commit) numerous, serious human rights abuses."[18] Arrests and detention can occur extra-legally or under emergency powers. For example, individuals associated with armed forces rebelling against the government can be accused of crimes against the state (Chapter 5, Criminal Act 1991). Created under the Special Courts Act, **security courts** constituted of three civilian judges convene to hear such cases. Those in military intelligence custody who later find their case before such courts are not permitted representation by a lawyer, though they may be accompanied by a 'friend.' Accordingly, lawyers have attended security cases as such, though are not permitted to address the court. Overall, due process is not ensured in military or civilian courts.[19] Sentences are usually severe and implemented immediately; death sentences are referred to the Chief Justice and the Head of State.[20] It has been reported that children used by armed groups as spies have later been tortured to death in Military Intelligence custody.

ISLAMIC *HADD* CASES

Individuals may also be convicted of crimes defined in Islamic *shari'a* law, which can include Islamic *hadd* punishments of amputation and death. It has been noted that girls alleging rape can in turn be themselves accused of adultery in such courts. Charging women with adultery is not unique to North Sudan. Indeed, in a prison in the town of Wau, South Sudan, many women were in detention under the charge of adultery - either for having relations with a man before marriage and/or refusing marriage arranged by her family.[21]

POPULAR OR TRIBAL COURTS

Popular courts are staffed by respected community elders and enforce customary law that is not considered to be inconsistent with the law or public policy. Generally, judges are citizens of good conduct who are "well known, well reputed and reasonably well off in rural areas"; membership includes tribal chiefs, Omdas, sheikhs, and Nazirs.[22] Due process in customary courts does not appear to be clearly defined, rendering them vulnerable to arbitrary application of the laws. Cases in customary courts can be referred to statutory courts; such courts also have powers of detention.

SOUTHERN SUDAN

The parallel operation of formal laws with informal laws is particularly strong in Southern Sudan. During the civil war, "units of the armed forces and militias ruled by force of arms, and in many cases the accused were summarily tried and punished, especially for offences against public order."[23] Within the former SPLM controlled areas, SPLM de facto laws and decrees were undermined by a severe lack of judicial facilities and lack of trained personnel in the judiciary and law enforcement. These institutional short-comings remain today and pose serious challenges to justice reform and access. For example, in the Southern Kordofan state, there are less than 30 well-qualified judges and about 50 lawyers. Here, *shari'a*- based laws remained applicable during the war in those areas formerly-held by the Government of Sudan, while a common law system was administered in former SPLM/A rebel-controlled areas. Indeed, under the terms of the recent peace agreement for Sudan, customary law will dominate in the South Sudan. It is presently unclear how the customary law system will in the future formally interact with the development of a formal legal system in the South, as well as with the justice system in the north of the country. Recent outcry over the continued application of strict Islamic *shari'a* Law in Southern Courts that remain adjudicated by Northern judges suggests that law reforms required under the CPA are not being to the liking of Southerners.[24]

"The SPLM has a judicial system of county magistrates, county judges, regional judges, and a court of appeals."[25] A High Court is located in each Southern State whilst the Supreme Court is situated in Rumbek. Southern States will generally continue to have the two systems of formal and customary law operating until the new Government undertakes to merge them. The formal courts are located mainly in towns; their role is not well understood by the public. Public access to the courts has been criticized by outside observers as practically non-existent due to high user charges, cumbersome formal procedures and their distance from the people, especially poor rural communities. Limited operational budgets prevent courts to hear cases in rural areas or for judges/legal administration officers to monitor and guide traditional courts on points of law and procedures.

CUSTOMARY LAW

Justice John Wuol Makec writes in "*Legal Aid and its Problems in Sudan: Proposed Supplementary Mechanisms*":

> One of the main objectives of customary law is the establishment of peace and harmony between the parties and society as a whole through compromise, conciliation, and compensation or restoration of social imbalance created by the commission of wrong or criminal acts.[26]

The largely dualistic legal structure in Sudan results in several stages being passed before a matter reaches any formal justice institution (such as the police or statutory Courts) - if at all.

Indeed, there exists a strong customary law network through which personal problems are dealt with.

THE OPERATION OF CUSTOMARY LAW

Personal matters are generally governed by the religious laws of the particular individuals concerned: Muslims are usually governed by local interpretations of *shari'a* law, whilst Christians are governed by local understandings of sectarian laws. If an individual is of no formal religion, then personal issues are governed by the customary laws of his/her particular tribe. For example, the tribal laws of the Dinkas in the South are in fact codified and held by the local Mullah. Other local tribes rely upon an oral tradition that is according to custom.

For family disputes, often the father or the head of the extended family will resolve matters within the family unit. Beyond the family, people who are party to disputes, whether they are husband and wife or neighbours, will go to the local Sultan to resolve the issue. The Sultan applies local customary laws and tribal practices in reaching a resolution of the issues presented before him. In cases of dissatisfaction with his decision, either party will apply to the District Court Judge and appeal. However, the decision of the Sultan is usually respected by the District Court Judge in deference to his sound knowledge and practice of local customary law.

Mediating disputes is generally the means by which conflicts are handled within the community. Fully outlining the myriad of local practices requires deep knowledge and access to individual communities, which is beyond the scope of this introduction. Given the dire need for capacity-building of local police, the office of the attorney general and judiciary throughout Sudan - especially in post-conflict areas (and outside the capital), the dominance of the community/customary network holds much potential for justice advocacy. Naturally, customary law is weak in terms of human rights protections for women and children; nonetheless, individual interventions by local justice actors can serve to slowly improve and strengthen customary laws.

FORMAL LAWS

Sudan's formal legal system is grounded in British common law and Islamic law.[27] Sources of law are Islamic law, constitutional law, legislation, judicial precedent, and custom. In family law, judicial circulars (*manshurat*) issued by the Qadi al-Quda (first issued in 1916) served to institute reforms or instruct the application of particular interpretations.

CRIMINAL LAW

Sudanese criminal law includes elements from British colonial penal law, Egyptian civil code and more recently, what are known as the "September Laws," otherwise referred to as *hudud* (sing., *hadd*) or penalty prescribed by Islamic law.[28] The applicable criminal laws include: Criminal Act, 1991 and Criminal Procedure Act, 1991 (CPA); as well as *shari'a* and local custom. The following is an overview of general due process provisions[29]:

- Arrests under the CPA: An arrest may be undertaken in two modes: arrest by prosecution attorney or magistrate's warrant (s. 67) or arrest by a policeman or "People's administrator" (that is, chairman of a state-sponsored local committee for order) (s. 68). In Darfur, a "People's administrator" is usually a tribal leader, appointed by the Government under the 1991 Native Administration Act. People can be arrested without warrant if found in suspicious circumstances, or if found with property suspected as stolen, or for not giving their name and address.

- Recording arrest: Police must record arrests made without a warrant in a register of arrests (s. 75.2, s. 82), and inform the prosecution attorney or magistrate (s. 77).
- Interrogation: Investigations are carried out by the General Crimes Police (s. 39) and should be recorded in writing (s. 41) and include statements of the accused and decisions taken regarding charges (s. 42). Suspects may undergo medical examination for purposes of gaining evidence, not for protection (s. 49). If an accused confesses, a magistrate should immediately assess the voluntariness of confession and record his judgement (s. 60). Lawyers are not present at interrogation.
- Powers of detention: The CPA allows police to detain people for no more than 24 hours for inquiry; the prosecution attorney can renew detention for no more than 3 days for inquiry; the magistrate can renew detention weekly, for up to two weeks; the superior magistrate can renew detention weekly, for up to six months (s. 79). CPA allows for police supervision or restriction of movement of accused persons (ss. 84, 85).
- Records of detention: Magistrates need to record reasons for arrests in the Case Diary (*mahdar al-taharri*) (s. 79), and detainees can appeal detention (s. 179). Prosecution attorneys are required to inspect all people in custody daily (s. 81).
- Powers of detention in the CPA: Only a court can order detention for trial (s. 80). Courts can order detention for up to one month, renewable weekly, and superior magistrates can order detention for up to six months, renewable monthly.
- Bail: The CPA allows for bail against different guarantees (s. 105) for offences not involving compensation (*diyya*) or Islamic *hadd*punishments (ss. 107, 108). Any reasons for not releasing persons accused of bailable offences must be recorded (s. 108).
- Free legal representation: The CPA allows for free legal representation only for people facing the gravest charges (s. 135).
- Language: The CPA gives a right to translation of trial proceedings, but not other proceedings (s. 137).
- Sentencing: Sentencing may consist of physical punishment (such as lashings), compensation (for homicide or injury) and death. It is the trial judge's responsibility to explain the sentence and any appeal rights that are available to the convicted person and to other interested parties (CPA 171).

The amended Law of Criminal Procedure 1991 added additional powers to law-enforcement to investigate, arrest, interrogate or detain irrespective of magisterial investigation, as was lawfully required to guarantee the rights of persons in contact with the law.[30] Notwithstanding both of these acts, the National Security Act includes a provision authorizing solitary detention from nine months to a year, which has been alleged to be largely used to harass political opponents.[31] Against this legal backdrop, human rights organizations allege routine arbitrary detentions, extrajudicial killings and torture by central government agents.[32] Despite a Constitutional guarantee of fair and prompt trials, trials in "regular courts nominally (meet) international standards of legal protections. The accused normally have the right to an attorney, and the courts are required to provide free legal counsel for indigent defendants accused of crimes punishable by death or life imprisonment; however, there (are) reports that defendants frequently did not receive legal counsel and that counsel in some cases could only advise the defendant and not address the court."[33]

CIVIL MATTERS

Civil matters are formally governed by statute, but outside the capital are in practice resolved at through informal laws and long-standing community justice mechanisms. Disagreement over the outcome of such will lead the parties to then appeal to the formal justice system, though much discretion is generally accorded to the decision rendered by a local Sultan or popular court. Relevant formal laws include the Civil Transactions Act, the Family Code, 1991. Passed in 1991, the Family Code includes *shari'a* principles as well as interpretations of some*manshurat*, though the Supreme Court (*Shari'a* Circuit) is vested with the power to issue interpretations of Code. Hanafi *fiqh* is also established as a residual source of law.[34]

MUSLIM PERSONAL LAW ACT

The Muslim Personal Law Act 1991 requires that both parties to a marriage be past the age of puberty and consent to the marriage. A male guardian marries adult women with their consent, although the qadi is empowered to act in this capacity if her guardian refuses his consent without justification. The guardian retains entitlement to seek dissolution on the grounds of lack of kifa'a of the husband, where kifa'a is defined in religion and morals. The wife is entitled to maintenance, assessed according to the circumstances of the husband; however, the wife loses the right to maintenance if she refuses to move to the marital home or leaves it without a shari'a justification. Right to maintenance may be lost if the wife works outside the house without the husband's consent, provided he is not being arbitrary in such.

Reforms standard to the region to the rules on talaq have been introduced. These reforms include the validity of talaq in terms of its number in word or sign; talaq in the form of an oath; and talaq intended to induce someone to do something. As a further reform to what is known as classical law, the wife must be informed of her husband's revocation of a revocable talaq during her 'idda period in order for the revocation to be valid. A judicial divorce may be sought by the wife on the following grounds: a husband's incurable physical or mental illness rendering it impossible for the wife to continue to live with him without harm; a husband's impotence not curable within one year; a husband's cruelty, or discord between the spouses; a husband's inability to pay maintenance. Finally, a divorce by 'ransom' may be instigated where a wife who is held disobedient by the court may waive her rights in return for a divorce; arbitrators must be appointed if the husband refuses to agree to such, and if the wife establishes that she suffers from remaining with him, a talaq will be ordered by the court.

After divorce, the wife is entitled to maintenance for the `idda period and to mut`a, which is assessed according to the means of her ex-husband - but only to a maximum of six months of maintenance. Maintenance will not be accorded in such a manner if the divorce was a judicial divorce by reason of the man's poverty and inability to pay maintenance, or for some physical reason arising in the wife, or unless the divorce was by khul.' A divorced mother is entitled to custody of her male children till they are 7 years old and females till they are 9. This period may be extended by the court if it can be proven to be in the interests of the wards, in which case, custody will extend until the sons reach puberty and the daughters consummate marriage. The father or other male guardian is to maintain scrutiny of all matters related to the raising of the children in the custody of their mother. Child support is the responsibility of the father until the daughter is married and the son is of an age when he is able to earn his own living.

GENDER ISSUES

Women's community-based groups voice serious concerns with the prevalence of gender-based violence, which is considered to include: Early (forced) marriage of girls; Domestic violence; Rape; Female circumcision; Forced marriages of widows.[36] Additional prevailing gender issues include the right to own property; freedom of choice to enter into marriage; payment of dowry - bride wealth; wife inheritance; ghost marriages. Of note, the Convention on the Elimination of All Forms of Discrimination Against Women has not been signed and ratified by Sudan.[37]

CHILD RIGHTS AND DUTIES

While Sudan ratified the Convention on the Rights of the Child (CRC) without reservation, the prevalence of key child rights issues remain of concern, including child labour; choice of education; rights to own property; right to care and protection; and juvenile justice concerns. The Child Act 2004 prescribes laws for child welfare, juvenile justice issues (including children's rights during arrest and imprisonment), health, education, 'working child', and the broader subject of 'satisfying child cultural needs.' The legislation is due to be revised after the signing of the Interim Constitution and consequently, it is in force but not being implemented. As such, the act is seen more to serve as an advocacy tool.

JUVENILE JUSTICE

All children under seven are below the age of criminal responsibility. All those above 15 have reached the age of criminal responsibility. Children between seven and 15 are criminally responsible if they have reached puberty.[38] The Criminal Procedure Act 1991 (CPA) - which has few special protections for children in arrest and detention - is the law under which children are arrested and tried, and together with other legislation such as the Child Act provides the following:

- Children's arrest in the Child Act: The Child Act states that where a warrant is issued for children's arrest, they should be arrested by Children's Police (s. 51.1)
- Special provisions for children: The Juvenile Care Act 1983 says that parents/guardians or lawyers should be informed of any procedures involving children, as far as possible (s. 17b). Child Act: a parent/guardian and social welfare officer must be present (s. 50).
- Confidentiality: Children's trials are supposed to be in private Child Act (s. 64).
- Sentencing: Section 58 prescribes broad measures of 'corrective arrangements', which range from placing in the custody of family member or other adult, to being prevented from frequenting certain places or practicing certain jobs; the Act confers broad powers on the courts to prescribe measures it considers necessary for delinquent children or those 'susceptible to delinquency'; Article 85 stipulates that if a child between 15 and 18 years of age is found guilty of an offence punishable by death sentence, that child shall be sentenced to no less than 6 years, and no more than 10 years.
- Alternatives to imprisonment: The Criminal Act (s. 33.3) states that children should not be sentenced to jail except for the Islamic-defined crime of *haraba* (waging war against society). Child Act (ss. 60, 62) allow for a wide variety of non-custodial dispositions. The Criminal Procedure Act allows for suspension of sentence (s. 170). The Criminal Act alternatives to imprisonment include reprimand; awarding custody to the parent or other adult; or sending to a reform institution for a period between 2-5 years (s. 47).

THE CHILD ACT 2004

The Child Act 2004 repealed Juvenile Welfare Act 1983. Here, a child is defined as any individual below the age of 18, unless the more applicable law stipulates that the child has reached age of maturity. The Act establishes that the protection and best interests of the child will have priority in all decisions or measures concerning "childhood, family or environment' (Chapter Two, s. 5(b)).

In terms of education, 'free education in the basic stage' is affirmed as a fundamental right for child upon age 6, for which 'the state shall create a conducive atmosphere' (s. 27). Section 32 provides for a school record that contains a birth certificate as well as notation as to 'health condition, type of disability and social status' and level of education. Corporal punishment is prohibited (section 30(a)); however, amongst objectives of education of Sudanese child is the building of character in the child that shall 'worship Allah in Freedom.' This objective is clearly problematic in light of Sudan's ethnic and religious pluralism.

In relation to what is termed as 'child culture' and 'satisfying child cultural needs', the act maintains a broad prohibition of any publications and literary works that "appeal to child's instincts or urging (sic) him to indulge in behaviours contrary to society's values and traditions or encouraging delinquency" (s. 36). The state is obliged to establish bookshops for children, which are to be associated with children's clubs mandated under the Act.

With respect to child labour, children under age 15 are prohibited from employment in industrial work; however, children between the ages of 14 and 18 may participate in agricultural work that is not harmful to health, as well as apprenticeships - both of which are subject to Ministerial regulations (s. 39(2)(a)). Notably, section 41 prohibits the use of children in armed conflict, forced labour, illicit trade and sexual exploitation; and section 84(1)(d) establishes penal consequences for employers or manages for violations of such with max imprisonment of one year, or fine, or both. The Act also establishes labour requirements for the employment of children between 14 and 18 under the legislated exceptions. These include: medical checks by employers (s. 42), working hours not exceeding 6 hours daily with one hour break (s. 43(1)), prohibition of working between 8pm and 7 am (s. 43(3)).

The Act also prescribes government obligations in relation to child welfare. These include the establishment of "alternative welfare families" and institutions (s. 22 and 23 respectively); as well as correction houses for delinquent children (s. 24), and the employment of disabled children in state organs and public utilities (s. 55).

KHARTOUM PUBLIC ORDER ACT 1998

This Act governs certain activities within the Khartoum State. First, private or public parties are subject certain permissions (s. 5) and prohibitions, including "no dancing between men and women and women shall not dance in front of men" (s. 7(1)(b)). Other areas subjected to restrictions under the act include the use of public transportation (s. 9); a prohibition of begging and vagrancy (s. 10); license requirements for places of women's hairdressers (Ch. 5); and a prohibition of using loud speakers (Ch. 6). Penalties for infractions include fines, whipping and imprisonment (Ch. 7).

LABOUR ACT 1997

This Act applies to all workers except civil servants, members of the armed forces, domestic servants, agricultural workers, family members of an employer, and casual workers.

The Act establishes a Manpower Committee (Ch. II), which is responsible for *inter alia,* coordinating manpower-related issues within executive organs and the collection of related data.

The Act also addresses the Organization of Employment (Ch. III) through provisions governing employment agencies, private employment agencies, recruitment, apprenticeships, and registration of workers. Chapter Three includes a requirement that all Sudanese seeking employment outside of Sudan seek permission of the Federal Minister of Labour. (s. 14) Chapter Four's "Employment of Women and Young Persons" includes a prohibition of the employment of women in hazardous or arduous working conditions and during the night - save foradministrative or health-care jobs. In relation to children, Chapter IV forbids the employment of children (defined as persons under 12 years of age) and the employment of young persons (persons under 16 years of age) in specified tasks that are listed under section 21.

Chapter Five's "Contracts of Employment" regulates the types and contents of employment contracts and permitted modes of renewal. The sixth chapter, "Wages, advances and other allocations" governs the payment of wages while the seventh chapter, "Hours of work and leave" regulates the calculation of official hours of work, overtime work, types of leave (annual, maternity - four weeks prior to and following birth, sick, religious - namely, Hadj and Idda). The remaining chapters address "Termination of contract or employment" (Ch. VIII); "Severance pay" (Ch. IX); "Industrial Safety" - i.e. occupational health and safety (Ch. XI); "Labour disputes and stages of their settlements" (Ch. XII); and the "Stages of settling labour disputes" - i.e. negotiation and arbitration (Ch. XIII) and other general provisions concerning penalties, validity of contracts with successor employers, and labour inspection. (Ch. X). Despite the laws concerning workplace health and safety,working conditions are generally poor, and enforcement by the Ministry of Labour minimal.[39]

Additional legislation relating to labour issues include the Public Service Act (No. 5 of 1991) and its accompanying Public Service Regulations, 1995; as well as the Peasants' Organizations Act of 1976, which includes the treatment of agricultural workers. Relevant to broader public welfare are the Health Insurance Act, 2000, which addresses medical care and sickness benefit; and the Social Security Act of 1990, which addresses old age security, and survivor's benefits.

COMMERCIAL LAWS

BANKING LAW

Banking is governed by the Law on the Regulation of Banking and the Money Laundry Combating Act. The Bank of Sudan Act 2000 establishes the Bank of Sudan and provides for its objectives in relation to setting monetary and credit policy, currency and exchange rates as well as economic and social development (s. 6). The functions and powers of the Bank are executed through the Bank's Board (Ch. III) and the Governor (s. 10). The Act governs "Capital, Reserves and Profits" (Chapter IV); "Currency" (Ch. V); "Foreign Exchange - Operations" (Ch. VI); "Relations with other Banks" (Ch. VII)'; "Relations with the Government" (Ch. VIII); "Other Operations of the Bank" (Ch. IX); and "Accounts" (Ch. XI).

INVESTMENT ENCOURAGEMENT ACT, 1999 AMENDED (2003)

Laws such as the Investment Encouragement Act have likely much facilitated the ability of the ruling Islamists "to privatize most of the State's infrastructural establishments and key production units, including tanneries, textile factories, and railways."[40] This Act in particular aspires to "encourage investment in projects in the fields of agricultural, animal and industrial activities, energy and mining, transport, communication, tourism and environment, storage, housing, contracting, infrastructure, economic, administrative and consultative services, information technology, education, health, water and culture and information services and any such other field, as the Council of Ministers may specify." It consists of five parts, which include: "Encouragement of Investment"; "Privileges and Guarantees"; "Safeguard of Investment"; "Investment Organs"; and "Final Provisions." An anti-discrimination clause is provided for at the outset, which states that "no discrimination shall be made between invested money, by reason of its being local, Arab or alien, or by reason of its being public, private, co-operative or mixed sector" (s. 8(1)).

Certain fields are deemed strategic investment, namely those relating to infrastructure, roads, ports, electricity, dams, communications, energy, transport, contracting business, education, health and tourist and information technology services and water projects; relating to extraction of subterranean and deep seas wealth; agricultural, animal and industrial production; crossing more than one state; and any such other fields, as the Council of Ministers may prescribe (s. 9(1)). Those considered strategic projects are exempted from taxes from the business profits tax for a period of ten years (s. 10(1)(a)); as well as exempted from customs duties, or "customs privileges", as prescribed by the Minister (s.11(1)). State projects may also be exempted from taxes and fees (s. 13); likewise, federal projects also enjoy certain privileges, including exemption from local state taxes and fees (s. 14, 15).

Most notably, the Act provides for an explicit rule concerning expropriation. Specifically, the Act provides for the "non-nationalization, or non-confiscation of his project, non-acquisition of all, or part of the estates of the project thereof, or his investments, for public interest", with the exception that any such expropriation would have to be committed under the law and with "just compensation. (Emphasis added)" (s. 17(1)(a) - Investment Guarantees). Also noteworthy is a provision requiring that all investment projects require a licence (s. 19); the process for the granting of such licenses is governed under Chapter 4 - Safeguard of Investment, which includes a provision concerning "duties of the investor" (s. 25). The fifth and final chapter explains the relevant government bodies overseeing the Act, including the formation of a "Committee of Commissioners" (s. 27 - 30). The Act is unclear as to accountability for the granting of such licenses, which is problematic given the breathtaking breadth of investment activity that the Act potentially encapsulates.

NATIONAL PETROLEUM COMMISSION (NPC)

Since the discovery of oil in the South of Sudan, development and control over such has remained a difficult issue for some time, especially in relation to the conflict in South Sudan. Following the Sudan Interim National Constitution[41], Presidential Decree No. 37 (2005) was formulated concerning the establishment of the National Petroleum Commission (NPC). The Commission is primarily responsible for formulating policies and guidelines in relation to the development and management of the petroleum sector and to monitor the implementation of these policies to ensure that they "serve the best interest of the people of Sudan".

THE TELECOMMUNICATION ACT 2001

The Telecommunication Act establishes the National Telecommunication Corporation, which regulates and licenses the provision of telecommunications services. The National Telecommunication Corporation has suspended on-line publications, including internet site "Sudanonline" in March 2006. The Act ought to be considered against the broader efforts to curtail freedom of expression and freedom of the press by Sudanese authorities. Examples of such include: journalists being routinely subject to interrogation by the security prosecutor of crimes against the state; foreign journalists generally being denied access to the region of Darfur; and members of the media are usually urged on by government security officials to support foreign policy decisions by the President.[42]

The Act is applicable to those "licensed hereto, to install and operate a broadcast station, a public or private telecommunication network, or use frequencies or import or trade in telecommunication equipment, shall adapt their positions according to the provisions of this Act in a period not exceeding three months from the date of signature of this Act." (s. 3) The Act addresses issues such as the National Telecommunications Corporation's Establishment, the Headquarters and Supervision of the Corporation (Ch. II); the Management of the Corporation Establishment And Constitution of the Board (Ch. III); the establishment of Telecommunications, Equipment and Radio Stations, Possession and Use Of Telecommunication Network (Ch. IV); Licensing and Fees Licensing (Ch. V); Public Telecommunication Services Submission of Reports (Ch. VI); Inspection and Supervision Adherence to the License Conditions (Ch. VII); and General Provisions Connectivity of Licensed Telecommunications Networks (Ch. VIII).

COPYRIGHT AND NEIGHBOURING RIGHTS PROTECTION ACT 1996

This Act establishes intellectual property standards in relation to works, performances, etc. in Sudan. The Act establishes the "Scope of Copyright Protection," including Works Covered by the Protection (s.5), Works Not Covered by the Protection (ss.6 - 7), Copyright (s.8); "Ownership of Copyright" (Part III), including Author's Name (s.10), Joint Works (s.11). Cinematograhic and Analogous Work (s.12), Duration of Author's Protection (s.13), Restrictions on Copyright (s.14); the Transfer of Ownership of Copyright (Part IV), including Transfer of Moral and Financial Rights (s.15), Use of Copyright (s.16), Publishing Contract (s.17), Public Performance Contract (s.18), Vesting of Ownership of Copyright on Author's Death (s.19), Order of Publication and Falling of Works into the Public Domain (s.20), Invalidity of Acts of Third Party for Lack of Consent (s.21). Finally, the "Registration of Works and Contracts" (Part V) is provided for, as is Protection of Neighbouring Rights of Performers (Part VI); and the Infringement of Copyright and Legal Consequences Thereof (Part VII).

Treaties

Sudan is signatory to the following treaties:

- ICCPR & ICESCR (Accession 1986, without reservations)
- CRC (Signature & ratification 1990, without reservations)

SUDAN ENERGY SECOR - STRATEGIC INFORMATION AND DEVELOPMENTS

BASIC INFORMATION

Total installed electricity capacity: **2,542.6 MW**
Hydroelectric: **56.8%**
Steam Turbine: **17.5%**
Combined Cycle: **16.1%**
Diesel: **7.2%**
Gas Turbine: **2.3%**

Total primary energy supply: **15,815 ktoe**
Biomass: **67.9%**
Crude Oil: **33.5%**
Hydro: **1.8%**
Oil Product Exports: **-3.2%**

Distribution Lines Length Of 33,11,.415 Kv Lines			
Town	0.415kv (km)	11 kv (km)	33 kv (km)
khartoum	18875	1526.546	522.363
central Areas	10648	1641	21866
Eastern Area	1258	633	_
karema	445	25	209
Dongla	200	150	200
Wadi Halfa	183	23	_
Shendi	804.9	322.98	13
Attbra	685	265	84
Portsudan	450	140	10.50
Elobeid	1063	141.30	60
UmRwaba	133	12.32	_

Elfashir	216	55	_
Niyala	472.81	56	_
ElGinana	52.6	13.6	_
Juba	62	22	_
Wau	95.6	18.4	_
Malakal	50	15	_
Total	35693.91	5060.146	22964.863

The high proportion of biomass is due to a large population, located in rural areas with little or no access to the electricity grid, which relies heavily on biomass to meet heating and cooking needs.

Oil plays a major role in the Sudanese economy. In 2008, according to the IMF, oil represented 95% of export revenues and 60% of government revenues. After the declaration of independence of South Sudan in 2011, significant proportions of the country's oil reserves have been transferred out of the control of the Khartoum government. In 2009, there were announcements of natural gas discoveries in Sudan, but these have yet to be determined commercially viable.

Total electricity generation in 2009 was 6,800 GWh, of which renewable resources accounted for 3,288 GWh (47.8%).

Sudan is an oil producing country, largely self sufficient and able to export refined as well as crude petroleum products. Total petroleum exports in 2009 were 19,507 ktoe. However, Sudan still needs to import jet fuel. The country's proven oil reserves are 6.614 billion barrels (2008).

Oil exports were estimated at 383,900 bbl/day in 2009, while imports amounted to 11,820 bbl/day in the same year.

Sudan's national electric agency is now able to buy power from Ethiopia, after grid installations were completed in July 2009.

The national electrification rate in 2009 stood at 35.9%. Approximately 27.1 million people lack access to electricity in the country. Urban electrification in 2009 stood at roughly 52%, with rural electrification at 28%.

The National Electricity Corporation, the national electricity utility, transmits electricity through two interconnected electrical grids, the Blue Nile Grid and the Western Grid, which cover only a small portion of the country. Regions not covered by the grid often rely on small diesel-fired generators

for power. Transmission in the country operates at 300 kV, 220 kV and 110 kV, and distribution networks operate at 33 kV, 11 kV and 415 V.
The power sector in the country is subject to poor infrastructure and frequent outages. More than 70 % of the population live in rural and isolated communities with limited economic activities.

The current electricity distribution reflects that most of the Sudanese rural communities are not connected to the national grid system, and are also by-passed by the petroleum supply pipelines, and thus rely mainly on biomass. Many villages connect small generators to the ubiquitous diesel-powered irrigation pumps. This way of generating electricity is inefficient and expensive, and causes environmental problems. Domestic power consumption dominates the market, with approximately 65% of electricity consumption being attributable to the sector. Erratic power supplies (outages stood at 19 days per year on average in 2009) have contributed to a high level of private generator ownership, particularly in the commercial and industrial sectors. Approximately 41% owned and used private generators in 2009. Transmission and distribution losses in the same year stood at 22%, an average figure for the region, but still high enough to cause constraints on economic efficiency for the national utility.

Special measures are being taken to ensure that existing hydro facilities are protected from the extreme climate which results in silt build up, reducing their generation capacities. 70% of electricity generated in the country is consumed in the Khartoum area. Total primary energy supply per capita in 2009 stood at 0.37 toe. As is the case in many developing nations with a large rural population, the residential sector contributes most to final energy demand, due to the large amounts of fuel-wood used for basic energy needs. Given the high level of biomass use, there is a significant potential for the introduction of energy-efficient cooking stoves, as has been identified by some donor organisations.

ELECTRICITY MARKET

The Electricity Law 2000 offered the possibility of private sector investment in electricity generation, transportation or distribution. Through the Investment Law of 2001, private and foreign investments have been encouraged, resulting in the construction of new thermal plants with Chinese and Malaysian financing. However, there is little competition in the electricity sector. Each of the five state-owned entities in the electricity sector has a practical monopoly on its sector. There are a few privately owned diesel-powered generators that provide electricity in regions outside the coverage of the national grid.

The liquid fuels market is vertically integrated. Exploration and production are regulated by the Sudan National Petroleum Corporation with involvement from foreign companies. There are various companies involved in distribution and marketing of petroleum products in the country including Agip, Exxonmobil, Shell and Nile Petroleum, the South Sudanese national company.

The former national power utility, the National Electricity Corporation of Sudan (NEC, www.members.multimania.co.uk/necsudan), was unbundled in 2010 into five separate companies:

- The Merowe Dam Electricity Company Ltd.,
- The Sudanese Hydropower Generation Company Ltd. (http://shgc-sd.com/),
- The Sudanese Thermal Power Generation Company Ltd. (http://stpgc.com/en),
- The Sudanese Transmission Lines Company Ltd., and
- The Sudanese Electricity Distribution Company Ltd.

These five utilities are responsible for their titular sectors. The government wholly owns the utilities. Regions not covered by the national grid rely on privately owned small diesel-fired generators.

LIQUID FUELS MARKET

Foreign investors dominate Sudan's oil industry. They are led by the China National Petroleum Corporation (CNPC), India's Oil and Natural Gas Corporation (ONGC) and Malaysia's Petronas. These companies hold the largest stakes in the leading consortia operating in both countries: the Greater Nile Petroleum Operating Company (GNPOC), Petrodar, and the White Nile Petroleum Operating Company (WNPOC). The Sudanese National Petroleum Corporation (Sudapet, www.spc.sd), remains a minority shareholder in joint ventures with foreign oil companies because of its limited technical expertise and financial resources. The Corporation also acts as a regulator for the industry.

NATIONAL STRATEGIC PLAN FOR SUDAN

The National Strategic Plan for Sudan – the first since the signing of the Comprehensive Peace Agreement (CPA) – provides a framework for the country's peace and development efforts between 2007 and 2011. It gives priority to the construction of electricity distribution networks and rural electrification projects to promote sustainable economic development, as well as capacity building within institutions.

The government in Khartoum has announced plans to raise the country's electrification level from an estimated 30% to about 90% in the mid-term. Large investments into the medium and low voltage distribution grids will be necessary, but not sufficient to reach this ambitious goal within the government's allocated time limit. For example, the foreseeable increase in power consumption would require new generating capacity. Significant capacity additions have been made in recent years (1,980 MW from 2003-2011), however, the government's current target of 3,383 MW of total capacity by 2016 is still appearing overly ambitious.

The country has recently put into place a comprehensive policy on sustainable charcoal production, enabling exports of charcoal made from an invasive tree species.

Considerable diplomatic conflict has arisen since the declaration of independence of South Sudan in 2011 over the continued interdependence of the two countries' oil infrastructures. The CPA did not set guidelines on post-independence oil sharing mechanisms or transit fees, and South Sudan suspended oil production in January 2012, following disagreements over the exceptionally high transit fees imposed by the Khartoum government (US$ 32-36 per barrel, compared to the international average of US$ 1), and the non-release of considerable Southern crude, held in the North for transfer to the international market. Southern officials say that the North has misappropriated approximately US$ 815 million of oil revenues since independence. The diplomatic disagreement is ongoing.

The government formulated a 10-year strategic plan for the period 1992-2003, which set overall goals for economic development. This plan included the supportive role of the power sector in achieving these goals.

Sudan is a member of the Common Market for Eastern and Southern Africa (COMESA), and is also a member of the East African Power Pool (http://www.eappool.org/), a regional organisation created to promote integration of electricity networks, to improve energy security and increase energy access in all member states.

The Ministry of Energy and Mining (MEM) has the responsibility for formulating and implementing the energy policies in the country, as well as promoting and disseminating renewable energy technologies, and conducting energy and environmental studies.

GOVERNMETN AGENCIES

Sudan's energy sector has three main regulatory bodies dealing with electricity, petroleum and mining:

All of the regulatory bodies in the country are wholly owned by the state.

Sustainable energy falls under the purview of the Ministry of Energy and Mining, which regulates the Sudanese energy sector. The Renewable Energy Master Plan does not detail specific regulatory mechanisms for the promotion of sustainable energy.

The Ministry of Energy is composed of several institutions which are responsible for formulating and reviewing processes and plans to incorporate views of energy suppliers, i.e. market actors and representatives of consumers, in addressing the complex nature of the sector.

The current lack of any form of framework or regulation pertaining to sustainable energy in the country is a barrier to increased uptake. For example, the formation of a clear framework for private-sector actor participation in the energy sector, using renewable energy sources, for example under an IPP structure, would create a more favourable environment for investment in the sector.

Electricity: Electricity Regulatory Authority (ERA)

Petroleum: Sudanese Petroleum Cooperation (SPC, www.spc.sd)

Mining: Public Geological Research Authority (PRA)

The Ministry of Electricity and Dams (MED) within the MEM is responsible for the management of the electricity sector. The state-owned companies within the electricity sector report directly to the MED.

The Ministry of Science and Technology is involved in scientific research to promote sustainable economic development in the country.

Within the MED, the Dams Implementation Unit (DIU, http://www.diu.gov.sd) acts as the governmental body in project management for the country's hydropower projects.

The Energy Research Institute (ERI) undertakes renewable energy research and development programs as well as pilot project implementation.

The Forestry Research Institute is involved in biomass energy technologies.

Khartoum University and the University of Science and Technology have both undertaken research on renewables.

IMPORTANT DEVELOPMENTS

Final commissioning of the 1,250 MW Merowe Dam project was achieved in 2009. Agreements were signed in 2008 to expand capacity in the Elroseris Dam. These dams will increase the generation of electricity; and will also expand irrigated agriculture in the Gezira and Rahad Schemes and in the River Nile State in the North. An additional 905 MW of conventional thermal capacity is also under construction, consisting of the steam plants at Alfula and Kosti, expected to be commissioned in 2013 and 2012 respectively. A further 600 MW of coal-fired capacity is awaiting contract signatures, for construction near the Red Sea. Finally, work is underway to raise the 280 MW Roseires Dam, with completion of the project slated for 2013. The modifications will double the generating capacity of the dam, increasing its reservoir size to 7.3 billion cubic metres from 3 billion, and also double the capacity of the 15 MW Sennar Dam on the Blue Nile as a result.

In 2009, authorities secured a US$ 93 million loan from the Saudi Development Fund for the White Nile sugar project and for the heightening of the Roseires Dam, aiming to double its electricity generating capacity. Also, the Kuwait Fund For Arab Economic Development agreed to lend USD$ 52 million for the same dam project, while earlier the Saudi Development Fund contributed loans and grants amounting to USD$ 150 million to the Merowe Dam project.

Developments are currently under-way to inter-connect the power grids of Sudan, Egypt and Ethiopia, in an effort to promote cooperation and trade in the region. Arrangements for Sudan to import power from Ethiopia were fully completed in February 2012, and the country is set to import 100 MW from Ethiopia via two transmission lines (of 230 and 296 km) running from Bahir-Da and Metema in Ethiopia to Gedaref near the border in Sudan. The project is also set to reduce the country's carbon emissions, allowing it to replace thermal generation with Ethiopian hydropower.

RENEWABLE ENERGY

The **Sudan Renewable Energy Master Plan** was drafted in 2005 in an effort to promote the use of renewable energy sources, including priority projects such as PV installations and biomass co-generation, so as to avoid technological dependence on an oil-based market in energy sector development. Funding allocations for the program total approximately US$ 9.1 million, half-funded by bilateral/multilateral donors through grants or soft loans. Of this, US$ 4.25 million is allocated for the promotion of solar PV and SWH in the short term, with a further US$ 1.05 million for wind pumping. The medium-term plan to 2015 is estimated to require US$ 15 million of funding and targets a wide range of renewable options, including small-hydro power for rural mini-grids, development of the country's geothermal resources, and modern and improved bio-energy options.

Government priorities in the renewables sector include:

- Reducing unsustainable biomass use,
- Increasing wind energy use for rural on- and off-grid electrification, as well as in water pumping and agriculture,
- Increasing the dissemination of community-scale PV projects,
- Assessment of the geothermal and small-hydro potentials of the country, and the identification of priority projects.

SOLAR ENERGY

Average solar insolation in the country is roughly 6.1 kWh/m2/day, indicating a high potential for solar energy use. Total potentials over the course of a year have been estimated at 10.1 GJ/m2. A recent Global Environmental Facility (GEF), UNDP-funded project, utilised PV to electrify 13 rural and peri-urban communities, with some 45,000 households in the country now using PV systems.

WIND ENERGY

Average Wind speeds are estimated at 3-6 m/s; higher speeds have been recorded along the Red Sea coast. Average wind density in Sudan is estimated at 400 W/m2. Wind energy in Sudan is currently used for pumping water from both deep and shallow wells to provide drinking water and irrigation through the use of wind pumps. A Memorandum of Understanding (MOU) was signed in 2010 with the Dubai-based Omene Energy for the construction of 500 MW of wind power capacity along the Red Sea coast in Sudan, in blocks of 100 MW, to be operated under an IPP structure.

BIOMASS ENERGY

There is a vibrant co-generation industry in Sudan, with installed capacity estimated at 55.5 MW in sugar factories, mainly for own use. There are plans to further expand co-generation in sugar production with more advanced plant equipment. In addition, plans are currently being developed to use an agricultural pest, the Mesquite shrub, for household energy production. An estimated 41.4 million hectares of forest resources are present in Sudan, with an allowable cut of approximately 15.1 million cubic metres. In addition, significant potential exists for the utilisation of agricultural residues, particularly crop residues and animal waste. Also, the government plans to add significant bioethanol and biodiesel production capacity in the coming years, in the region of 60 million litres/year and 50 million litres/year respectively.

GEOTHERMAL ENERGY

Geothermal potential is estimated at 400 MW of power generation capacity. Potential geothermal fields have been identified near the Jabel Marra volcano, the Tagbo and Meidob hills, the Bayud volcanic field and the Red Sea coast. Hot spring temperatures in the Red Sea region range from 56ºC to 85 ºC. Two sites of particular interest in the region are the Suakin-1 and Bashayer-1A wells, which both have temperature gradients of over 70ºC. The country is currently collaborating with KenGen, the Kenyan national utility, to further build capacity and assess potentials in the region.

Hydropower

Total potential for hydropower in the country is estimated at 4,860 MW, with an annual production of 24,132 GWh. Small-hydro also offers a significant potential, with more than 200 suitable sites for in-stream turbines existing. Potential small-hydro capacity in 2009 was estimated at 58.68 MW. Recent capacity additions have included the 1,250 MW Merowe dam, commissioned in 2009.

PROSPECTS OF A NUCLEAR POWER PROGRAMME IN SUDAN

The need for electricity in Sudan is increasing rapidly for both industrial and domestic sectors. A previous study, conducted with IAEA support assess the demand for energy and electricity in Sudan and concluded that considering the first nuclear power plant in Sudan is justifiable. So, IAEA and the Government of Sudan have jointly started Project SUD/0/011 to support Sudan to determine the optimal energy generation mix, including the nuclear power for electricity generation.

Feasibility Study for the nuclear program has been carried out by overseas consultancy firm incorporation with national team.

The main outcome of the Feasibility Study is that introduction of nuclear power plant in Sudan electricity production and respectively construction of the first NPP in the country is *feasible and possible*. However it should be noted that introduction of nuclear power within Sudan energy production sector will require substantial efforts to address key issues relevant to the implementation of nuclear program in a country.

Site Survey/selection was Carried out by a Consultant firm and MED team.

*Nine potential sites were identified based on the IAEA Standards.

* MED is now preparing for the third phase: site characterizations to be carried out by an overseas contractor .

A national committee including members from relevant stakeholders participated in drafting the nuclear act (DNA) and complying with international instruments.

Existing enacted legislations pertaining to NPP has been reviewed by the national committee to identify and harmonize possible areas of intersections with the DNA.

existing enacted legislations studied so far were found to be in harmony with the DNA.

Nuclear related International instruments in which Sudan is Party/Signatory or considering to accede have been reviewed and reflected in the DNA.

The DNA and the final report recommending the consideration of instruments in which Sudan is non-party , have been prepared and it will be channelled through the national legislative system very soon.

The first regulatory body was established in 1996 under SAEC's Act (SAEC Board).

Regulations and codes of practices issued pursuant to the provisions of 1996 Act dealt with radiological safety.

*In 2010, the Minister of Science and Technology issued a decree that provided for the separation of the regulatory body (SNRRA) from the organizational structure of the SAEC i.e. the RB becomes semi autonomous.

The DNA called for the establishment of National Nuclear and Radiological Regulator (NNRR), it will be legally capacitated to issue all the necessary regulations and codes consistent with international standards for the management of nuclear and radiological activities.

The existing regulatory authority (SNRRA) is working closely with other stakeholders such as SAEC & MED to develop nuclear regulatory infrastructure.

Human Resource Development Master Plan under progress ,it will be completed in September this year and then will be implemented.

DRIVING FORCES

Lack of oil resources due to separation of Southern Sudan after referendum in 2011 (70% of Oil Production forgone).

Rapid increase in the demand in the last three decades.

Nuclear power represent a cheap energy generation resource.

deficiency of other resources such as hydro and renewable to cover the electricity demand expansion

Necessity of diversification of energy supply options

*Reduction of CO2 gases emissions

*Large territories of Sudan (low population density),

*Availability of cooling water .

SUDAN LOAD FORECAST

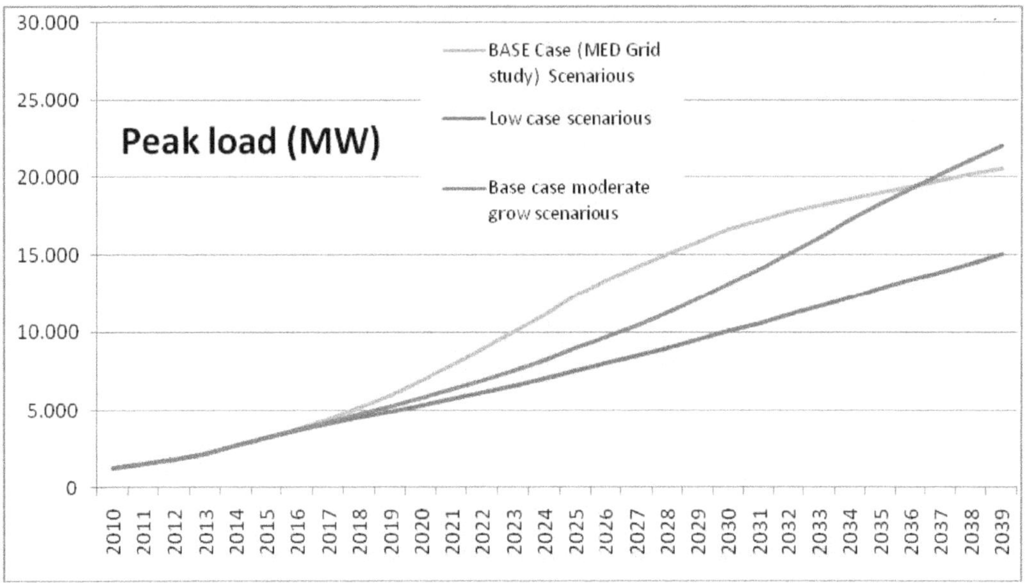

IMPEDIMENTS

*Public acceptance (Awareness)

*

Long construction time and high construction costs due to additional safety requirements after Fukushima.

*Financing

*Lack of human resources in nuclear field

*Enhancement of Infrastructure especially electric grid and roads.

PLAN FOR NPP IN SUDAN

between 2010 and 2039

Year	Loss Of Load Probability %	TOTAL CAPACITY ADDED BY YEAR [MW]	Coal Fired Steam 400 MW	Coal Fired Steam 600 MW	NPP 1000 MW	NPP 600 MW	Gas Oil CCGT 500 MW	Gas Oil CCGT 200 MW	Natural Gas CCGT	Hydro candidate	NPP Total In year [MW]	NPP Additions by year [MW]
2010	0.00	0	0	0	0	0	0	0	0	0	**0**	0
2011	0.01	0	0	0	0	0	0	0	0	0	**0**	0
2012	0.66	0	0	0	0	0	0	0	0	0	**0**	0
2013	2.15	0	0	0	0	0	0	0	0	0	**0**	0
2014	0.51	666	0	0	0	0	1	1	0	0	**0**	0
2015	0.00	458	0	0	0	0	1	0	0	0	**0**	0
2016	0.00	648	0	0	0	0	0	0	0	1	**0**	0
2017	0.00	312	0	0	0	0	0	0	0	1	**0**	0
2018	0.00	760	2	0	0	0	0	0	0	0	**0**	0
2019	**0.00**	**1,170**	**0**	**1**	**0**	**1**	**0**	**0**	**0**	**0**	**600**	**600**
2020	0.00	897	1	0	0	0	0	0	0	2	600	0
2021	0.00	950	1	1	0	0	0	0	0	0	600	0
2022	0.00	570	0	1	0	0	0	0	0	0	600	0
2023	**0.00**	**1,380**	**1**	**0**	**1**	**0**	**0**	**0**	**0**	**0**	**1,600**	**1000**
2024	**0.00**	**1,600**	**0**	**0**	**1**	**1**	**0**	**0**	**0**	**0**	**3,200**	**1600**
2025	0.00	1,245	2	0	0	0	0	0	1	1	3,200	0
2026	0.00	950	1	1	0	0	0	0	0	0	3,200	0
2027	0.00	950	1	1	0	0	0	0	0	0	3,200	0
2028	0.00	918	0	0	0	0	1	0	1	0	3,200	0
2029	**0.00**	**1,600**	**0**	**0**	**1**	**1**	**0**	**0**	**0**	**0**	**4,800**	**1600**
2030	0.00	918	0	0	0	0	1	0	1	0	4,800	0
2031	0.00	570	0	1	0	0	0	0	0	0	4,800	0
2032	0.00	666	0	0	0	0	1	1	0	0	4,800	0
2033	**0.00**	**1,600**	**0**	**0**	**1**	**1**	**0**	**0**	**0**	**0**	**6,400**	**1600**
2034	0.00	0	0	0	0	0	0	0	0	0	6,400	0
2035	0.00	0	0	0	0	0	0	0	0	0	6,400	0
2036	**0.00**	**1,000**	**0**	**0**	**1**	**0**	**0**	**0**	**0**	**0**	**7,400**	**1000**
2037	0.00	0	0	0	0	0	0	0	0	0	7,400	0
2038	**0.00**	**600**	**0**	**0**	**0**	**1**	**0**	**0**	**0**	**0**	**8,000**	**600**
2039	0.00	0	0	0	0	0	0	0	0	0	8,000	0
Total		20,428	9	6	5	5	5	2	3	5	8,000	8000

8/3/2012 Sudan Presentation

REACTORS TYPE , TYPE OF A FUEL CYCLE

Sudan shall use PWR reactors.

The open fuel cycle is going to be adopted, at least for the first NPP.

*Sudan strategy for ***back-end fuel cycle is sending*** the spent fuel to the supplier country.

*Sudan has no legal provisions governing transit or return of spent nuclear fuel and high level radioactive waste to other countries

The Criteria for selecting the reactor :

*Safety Considerations

*Proven technology

*

High Reliability

SUDAN ROLE IN DEPLOYMENT OF NUCLEAR POWER PLANTS BY FOREIGN SUPPLIERS

*While it is still subject to negotiations with vendor, the most suitable procurements strategy for the first NPP in Sudan will be super-turnkey contract. Hence the national participation will be quite limited.

Example:

i.Construction materials supply e.g. cement.

ii.Skilled personnel from conventional power plant , hydro plants and oil industry

III.LIMITED PARTICIPATION OF NATIONAL INDUSTRY

The priorities for Sudan regarding nuclear energy system sustainability are:

***Economics**

***Waste management**

***Proliferation resistance**

***Physical protection**

***Environment**

***Safety**

***Infrastructure**

Sudan existing and future cooperation with other countries in energy projects, nuclear and non-nuclear includes:

*Transmission line interconnection between Sudan and Egypt , feasibility study has been carried out.

*Transmission line interconnection between Sudan and Ethiopia , the line is already energized.

*Chinese and Indian contractors are working in construction of thermal power plants (3x135 mw and 4x125 mw resp.)

*German and British consultancy firms supervise the construction of the above mentioned projects. .

The positive aspect of cooperation in nuclear and non-nuclear fields foreseen by Sudan are:

*Capacity building

*Technology and know-how transfer

*Economical growth

*Reducing the cost of investment in human resources development

*Enhancement of national infrastructure e.g. national grid.

*Sharing of the experts in the nuclear field.

*Sharing of radioactive waste facilities.

The indicators to measure benefits and disadvantages of cooperation with other countries in nuclear energy projects:

*Technology transfer.

*Sustainable Technical support.

*Sustainable Solution for Waste storage .

*Solution for the gab in human resources.

*Minimizing electricity generation cost .

SUDAN MINERAL AND MINING SECTOR: STRATEGIC INFORMATION

MINERAL RESOURCES

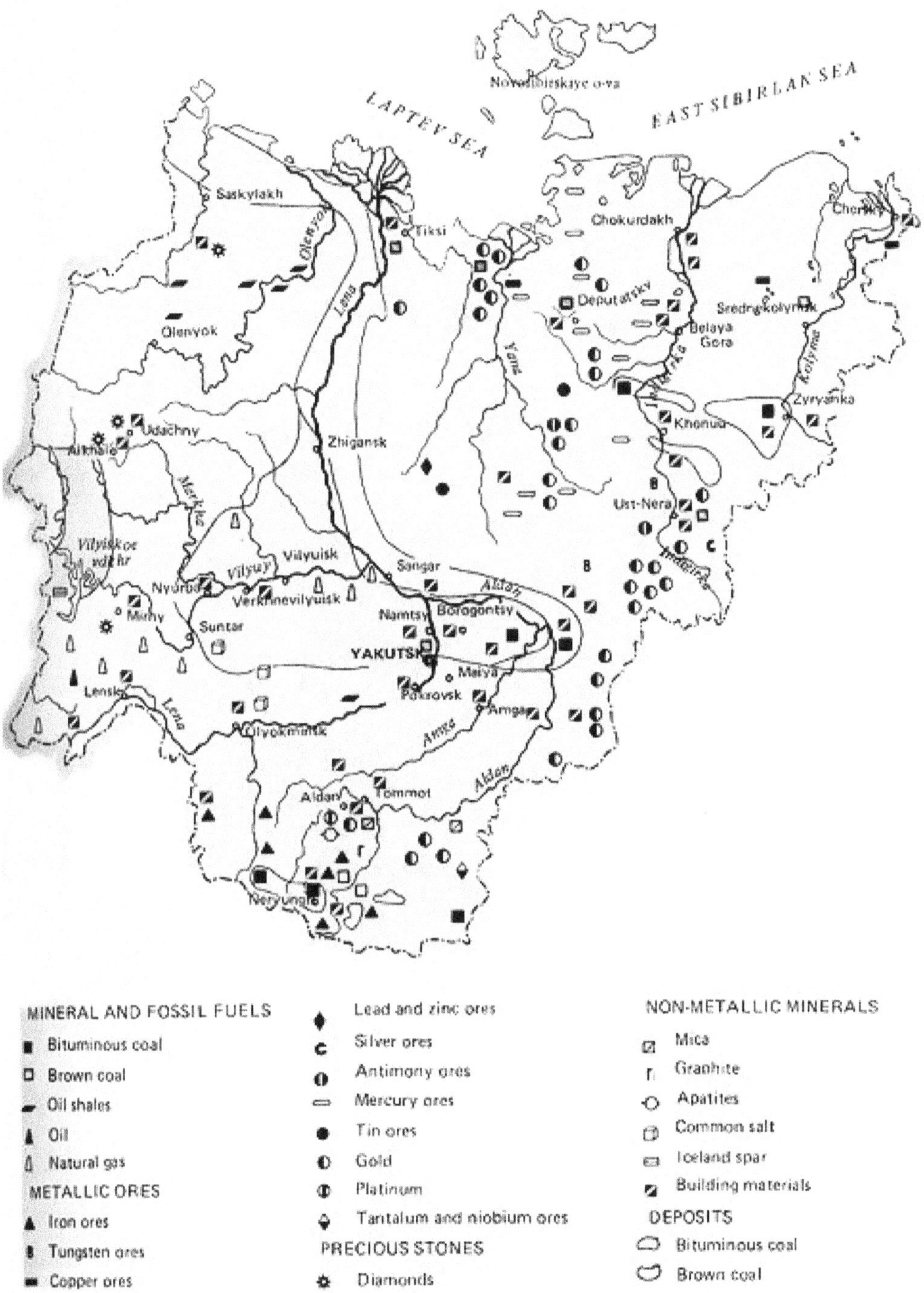

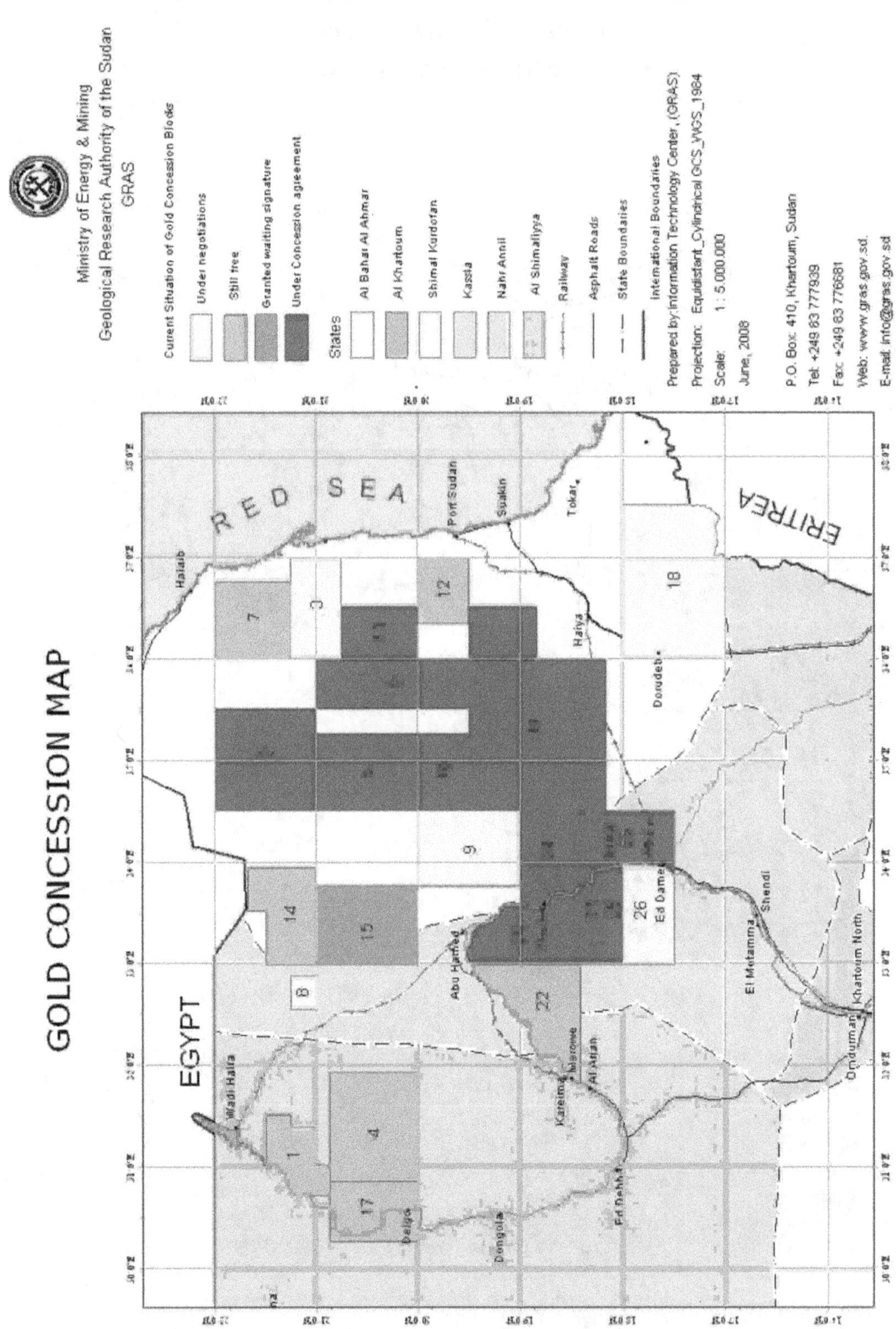
GOLD CONCESSION MAP
Ministry of Energy & Mining
Geological Research Authority of the Sudan
GRAS
Current Situation of Gold Concession Blocks
Under negotiations
Still free
Granted waiting signature
Under Concession agreement
States
Al Bahar Al Ahmar
Al Khartoum
Shimal Kurdofan
Kassla
Nahr Anil
Al Shimaliyya
Railway
Asphalt Roads
State Boundaries
International Boundaries
Prepared by: Information Technology Center, (GRAS)
Projection: Equidistant_Cylindrical GCS_WGS_1984
Scale: 1 : 5,000,000
June, 2008
P.O. Box 410, Khartoum, Sudan
Tel: +249 83 777939
Fax: +249 83 776681
Web: www.gras.gov.sd
E-mail: info@gras.gov.sd
EGYPT
RED SEA
ERITREA
Halaib
Port Sudan
Suakin
Tokar
Haiya
Derudeb
Wadi Halfa
Abu Hamad
Karima
Merowe
Al Artan
Dongola
Delgo
Ed Debba
Ed Damer
Shendi
El Metamma
Omdurman
Khartoum North

OIL AND GAS SECTOR

Sudan's oil exports represent over 90 percent of the country's total export revenues, but further development is hindered by conflicts and sanctions.

Oil plays a major role in the Sudanese economy. In 2009, according to the International Monetary Fund, oil represented over 90 percent of export earnings. For South Sudan (Juba), oil represented 98 percent of total revenues for the year compared to Khartoum at 65 percent. In 2009, there were announcements of natural gas discoveries in Sudan but these have yet to be determined commercially viable.

According to the International Energy Agency (IEA), combustible renewables and waste accounted for 68 percent of Sudan's total primary energy consumption in 2008, followed by petroleum (32 percent) with hydroelectric power accounting a small share. The large share of biomass in the energy mix represents a large population, located in rural areas with little or no access to the electricity grid, that rely heavily on biomass to meet heating and cooking needs. According to the IEA, approximately 27 million people in Sudan lack access to electricity, the country as a whole has a 31percent electrification rate with urban areas reaching 48 percent electrification and rural only 19 percent.

Sudan has been involved in two major civil wars since 1955 that have impacted the country's economic development, particularly its natural resources. The first and longest of the two wars was between the northern Sudanese government in Khartoum and the Sudan People's Liberation Army (SPLA) in the South that ended with the signing of the Comprehensive Peace Agreement (CPA) in 2005.

The CPA provides for some degree of autonomy for the South with equal sharing of oil revenues from oil produced in the South between both sides. Abyei, a significant oil producing region sits on the North/South Border. Under the CPA, Abyei was given special administrative status and has since suffered some clashes. In 2009, the Permanent Court of Arbitration in the Hague ruled on an ongoing border dispute that put two of Sudan's oilfields (Heglig and Bamboo) in the North rather than as part of the Abyei region, this decision, however, is still being disputed by the South and Abyei.

As part of the CPA, a referendum is scheduled for January 2011 at which time the South will decide whether or not to secede, and the Abyei region will decide on which side to join. The uncertainty regarding these referenda and concerns that delayed or disputed voting and/or further conflict could lead to additional sanctions have kept the oil industry from fully developing. While most of Sudan's oil is produced in the South, the export and refining infrastructure is entirely in the North.

The second conflict in Darfur brought with it international condemnation, internally displaced populations and sanctions affecting the country as a whole. The conflict has prevented oil exploration in the Darfur region, and the sanctions have prevented some international investment. The fighting itself has led to considerable infrastructure damage further limiting development.

OIL

Most of Sudan 's oil is produced in the South, but the pipeline, refining and export infrastructure is in the North of the country.

Sudan is developing its significant hydrocarbon resources. The country's oil exports, which have increased sharply since the completion of a major oil-export pipeline in 1999, account for 70 percent of total export revenues. Additional growth in Sudan's hydrocarbon sector will likely occur with a refurbished infrastructure, which has seen little improvement since the beginning of the country's civil conflicts in 1955. As of January 2007, according to the Sudanese Minister of State for Energy and Mines, Sudan is considering joining theOrganization of Petroleum Exporting Countries (OPEC) at some point in the future.
In January 2005, the Sudanese government in Khartoum and the Sudan People's Liberation Army (SPLA) in the south signed the Comprehensive Peace Agreement (CPA), which ended 21-years of civil war. Prior to the signing, several important issues were agreed upon by the two parties including the sharing of oil revenues (50:50). Also in 2005, President Bashir formed a border commission tasked with defining the border between northern and southern Sudan, in accordance to the CPA. Much of Sudan's oil producing region lies in the disputed border area.

Energy consumption in Sudan, by type, 2004. (Source: EIA, *International Energy Annual 2004*)
In 2004, Sudan's energy consumption mix was dominated by oil (93 percent), with the remainder coming from hydroelectricity (7 percent). Natural gas, coal, nuclear and otherrenewables are currently not part of the country's energy consumption mix. Between 1984-2004, the share of oil in Sudan's energy mix increased from 86 percent to 93 percent. Hydroelectricity consumption experienced a decrease, during the same time period, from 14 percent to 7 percent.

SECTOR ORGANIZATION

The Sudan National Petroleum Corporation (Sudapet) is active in Sudan's oil exploration and production. However, due to its limited technical and financial resources, Sudapet often develops joint ventures with foreign companies in oil projects. Foreign companies involved in Sudan's oil sector are primarily from Asia. They are led by the China National Petroleum Corporation (CNPC), India's Oil and Natural Gas Corporation (ONGC) andMalaysia's Petronas.

In October 2005, Sudan established the National Petroleum Commission (NPC) to bolster the development of the country's oil resources. To accomplish its mission, NPC allocates new oil contracts, and it ensures an equal sharing of oil revenues between the national government in Khartoum and the Government of South Sudan (GoSS). In addition, NPC is responsible for resolving duplicate oil contract issues in which the GoSS has allocated contracts overlapping contracts previously granted by Khartoum. NPC is currently scrutinizing duplicate contracts given to Total and White Nile Ltd. over Block B and the White Nile Petroleum Operation Company (WNPOC) and Ascom Group ofMoldavia over Block 5b. President Bashir is believed to co-chair the NPC with Vice-President Salva Kiir, who also heads the GoSS.

According to *Oil and Gas Journal* (*OGJ*), Sudan had five billion barrels of proved oil reserves in January 2010 up from an estimated 563 million barrels in 2006. Some analysts and government reports put the volume of Sudan's reserves above 6 billion. The majority of reserves are located in the South in the Muglad and Melut basins. Due to civil conflict, oil exploration has mostly been limited to the central and south-central regions of the country. Natural gas associated with oil production is mostly flared or re-injected. In 2009, there were announcements of natural gas discoveries in Sudan but these have yet to be determined commercially viable.

Exploration and development of Sudan's oil resources has been controversial. International human rights organizations have accused the Sudanese government of financing human rights abuses with oil revenues, including the mass displacement of civilians near the oil fields. Factional fighting in the South and rebel attacks on oil infrastructure have kept oil production and exploration from reaching full potential. China, the largest investor in Sudan, has had facilities attacked while at the same time, the country has faced international condemnation for its investments in Sudan.

Sanctions

The United States prohibits U.S. nationals from engaging in any transactions or activities related to the petroleum or petrochemical industries in the entire territory of Sudan (including Southern Sudan) as a result of the conflict in Darfur. For information on full U.S. sanctions, please see the U.S. Treasury Department's Office of Foreign Assets Control. Sudan also faces sanctions from the United Nations and the European Union which include arms embargos, travel bans and restrictions on financial activities that may impede the peace process – without specifically addressing the petroleum sector

Sector Organization

The Sudan National Petroleum Corporation (Sudapet) is active in Sudan's oil exploration and production. However, due to its limited technical and financial resources, Sudapet often develops joint ventures with foreign companies in oil projects but remains a minority shareholder. Foreign companies involved in Sudan's oil sector are primarily from Asia. They are led by the China National Petroleum Corporation (CNPC), India's Oil and Natural Gas Corporation (ONGC) and Malaysia's Petronas. Nilepet, South Sudan's national oil company, has also been involved in allocating licenses which has led to some conflict, specifically in Southern blocks that were licensed by the Northern government.

In October 2005, Sudan established the National Petroleum Commission (NPC) to bolster the development of the country's oil resources. To accomplish its mission, NPC allocates new oil contracts, and it ensures an equal sharing of oil revenues between the national government in Khartoum and the Government of South Sudan (GoSS). In addition, NPC is responsible for resolving duplicate oil contract issues in which the GoSS has allocated blocks overlapping contracts previously granted by Khartoum.

African Proven Oil Reserve Holders, 2010

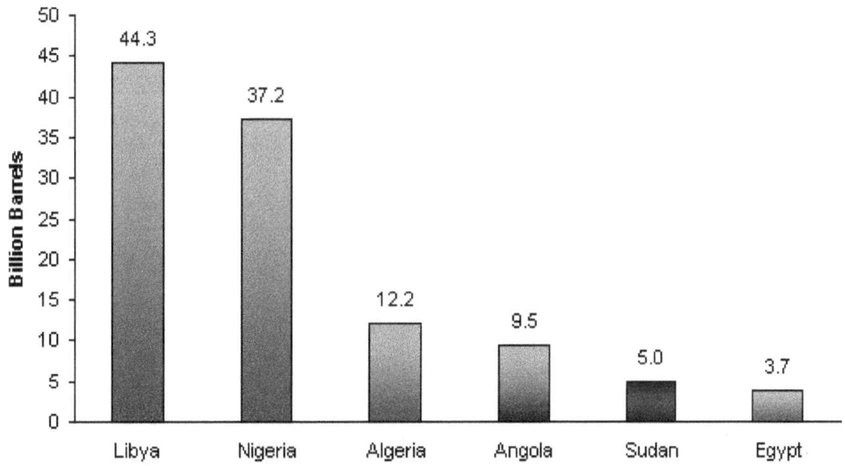

Source: *Oil and Gas Journal*

Exploration and Production

Oil production began in the late 1990s and grew rapidly starting in July 1999 with completion of an export pipeline that runs from central Sudan to the Port of Sudan. In 2009, EIA estimates that crude oil production averaged around 485,000 barrels per day (bbl/d). Recent production estimates reflect an increase in Dar Blend production that has offset declining production of Nile Blend crude.

Production is sourced from two groups of blocks plus output from smaller areas that have recently come on-stream (detailed descriptions are listed below). The first and oldest development is the Greater Nile Oil Project covering Blocks 1,2, and 4 that in 2009 was the source of an estimated 180,000 bbl/d of Nile Blend. The second major field encompasses Blocks 3 and 7, operated by the Petrodar consortium, which produced around 240,000 bbl/d of Dar Blend. Other smaller sources Include Block 6 which produced between 30,000 and 40,000 bbl/d of Fula Blend, and Block 5a, another source of Nile blend, which produced between 20,000 and 30,000 bbl/d in 2009.

Blocks 1, 2, and 4 (Nile Blend)

Blocks 1, 2, and 4 cover an area that straddles the North, South, and Abyei region. Production began in 1996 with the development of the Heglig and Unity Fields. Because the fields lacked access to markets, a consortium was developed to raise investment for a 1,000-mile pipeline from the fields to the Suakim oil terminal near Port Sudan. In September 1999, the first cargo of crude departed the export terminal. The blocks are now operated by the Greater Nile Petroleum Operating Company (GNPOC), a consortium of CNPC (40 percent), with partners Petronas (30 percent), ONGC (25 percent) and Sudapet (5 percent).

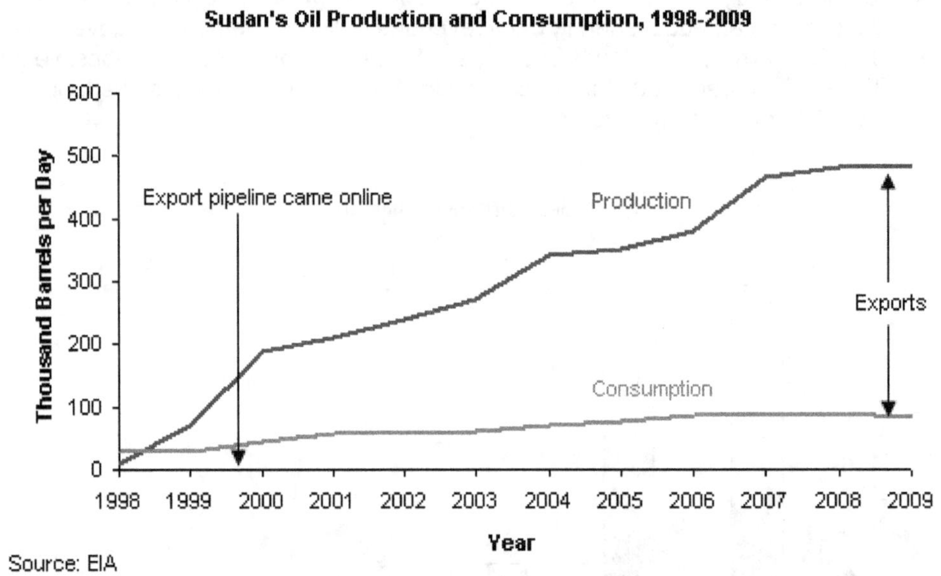

In 2009, combined production from Blocks 1, 2, and 4, including Abyei, was estimated to be around 180,000 bbl/d of Nile blend, reflecting a decline from a 2006 peak of over 270,000 bbl/d and is expected to continue to decline in the short-term, mainly from declines in the Heglig and Unity fields. The negotiations over the future of these fields and the Abyei region have delayed investments to offset declines.

Blocks 3 and 7 (Dar Blend)

Blocks 3 and 7 in the Melut Basin, South Sudan, are operated by Petrodar, a consortium of CNPC (41 percent), Petronas (40 percent), Sudapet (10 percent), Sinopec (3 percent), and Tri-Ocean Energy of Kuwait (3 percent). Located in the Melut Basin, the blocks contain the Adar Yale and Palogue oil fields, with estimated recoverable reserves of 460 million barrels. In November 2005, CNPC brought online the Petrodar pipeline linking the two blocks to Port Sudan. The pipeline has current throughput of 150,000 bbl/d and maximum capacity of 500,000 bbl/d.

In 2009, production from these two blocks was close to 240,000 bbl/d of Dar blend. Output rose from the startup of the Qamari field which came online in 2009. However, some analysts stated that full production increases might have been delayed due to the lack of export infrastructure. The heavy and highly acidic quality of this crude makes it less marketable and it trades at a discount to other benchmark crudes such as Brent and Minas.

Block 5a (Nile Blend)

In April 2005, the Sudanese government signed an agreement with White Nile Petroleum Operating Company (WNPOC) for the development of the Thar Jath and Mala fields on Block 5a. First oil from the block came online in June 2006 at an initial rate of 38,000 bbl/d. In 2009, the field was still producing between 20,000 and 30,000 bbl/d, full capacity was initially estimated at 60,000 bbl/d. Oil from the field flows through a 110-mile pipeline to Port Sudan. WNPOC is a consortium of companies, which include Petronas (69 percent and operator), ONGC (24 percent) and Sudapet (7 percent).

Block 6 (Fula)

In November 2004, CNPC brought online its Fula field on Block 6 at a rate of 10,000 bbl/d. Current output on the block is 45,000 bbl/d of highly acidic crude, and is expected to increase from the start up of the Jiake field announced in August of 2010. CNPC has constructed a pipeline that links the Fula field to the Khartoum refinery where it is processed largely for domestic use.

Other Blocks

Block B: Block B is located in southeastern Sudan and is licensed to Total. The company has faced several problems resulting from conflict in the area, licensing problems, and, more significantly, the existing consortium continues to seek a third partner to replace Marathon Oil, a U.S. company that was forced to pull out of its 32.5 percent interest as a result of U.S. sanctions.

Block 5B: Block 5B is located in the southern Muglad Basin and was initially under exploration by ONGC Videsh (23.5 percent stake) and Lundin (Sweden 24.5 percent) in partnership with Sudapet (13 percent), and Petronas (39 percent). In early 2009, two major stakeholders, ONGC and Lundin pulled out after negative drilling results. In August 2009, the National Petroleum Commission approved the participation of Ascom, a Moldovan firm in block 5B.

Block EA: The EA block is a relatively new block, marked out along a long narrow strip that runs along existing fields in the Muglad Basin. In August 2010 Star Petroleum (Luxembourg) announced the company was awarded an exploration and production–sharing agreement (EPSA) for Block E. Star Petroleum holds a 75 percent stake while Sudapet holds 20 percent, the remaining 5 percent is held by Hamla (Norway).

Sudan's Crude Oil Exports by Destination, 2009

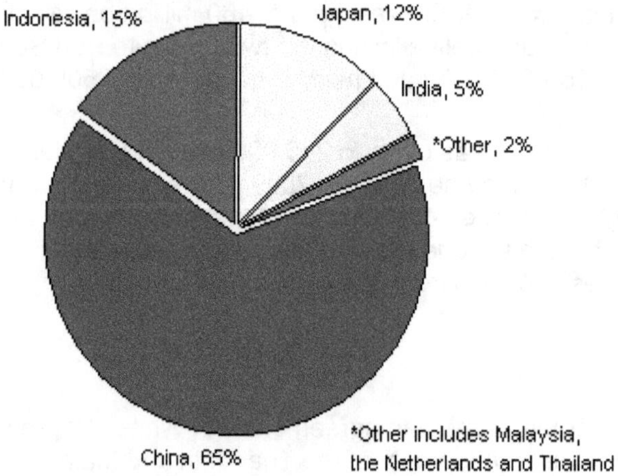

Source: EIA, FACTS Global Energy, Global Trade Atlas

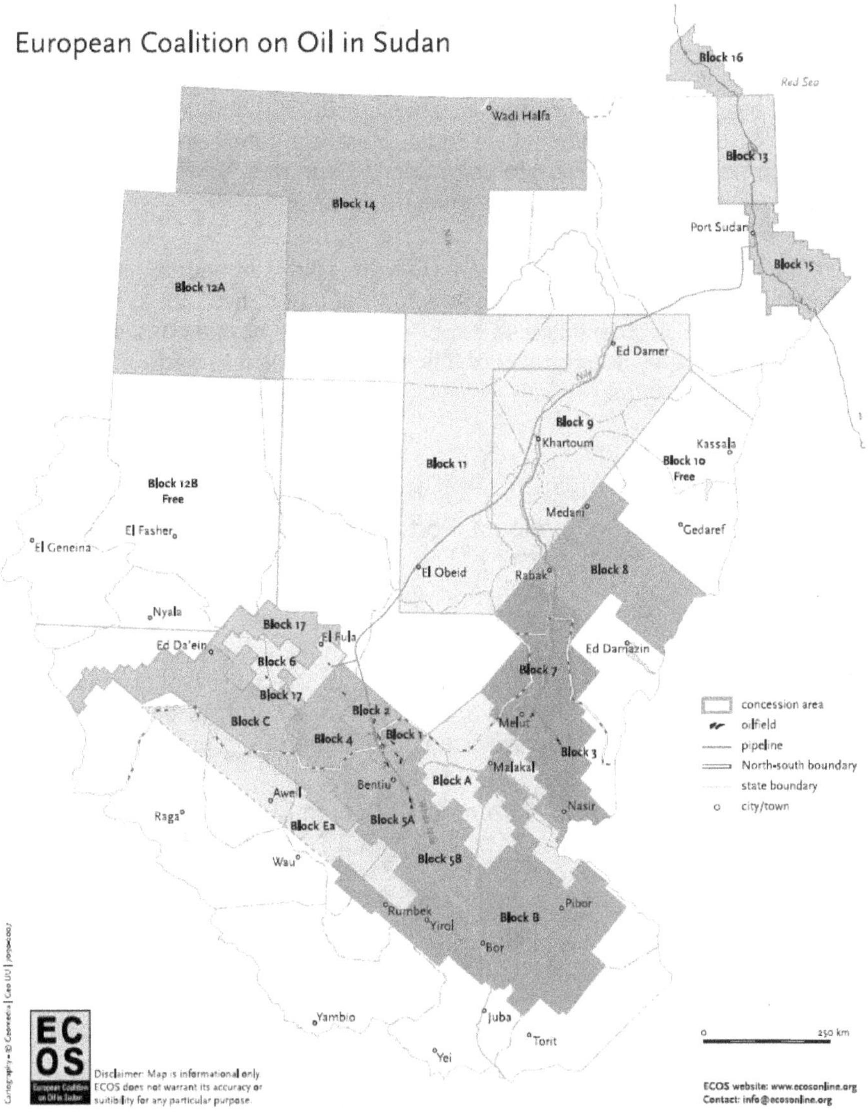

Block 1,2,4, GNPOC
- 40% CNPC
- 30% Petronas
- 25% ONGC Videsh
- 5% Sudapet

Block 3,7, PDOC
- 41% CNPC
- 40% Petronas
- 8% Sudapet
- 6% Sinopec
- 5% Al Thani

Block 5A, WNPOC-1
- 68,875 Petronas
- 24,125 ONGC Videsh
- 7% Sudapet

Block 5B, WNPOC-2
10% awarded to GOSS; composition to be renegotiated
- 39% Petronas
- 24,5% Lundin
- 23,5% ONGC Videsh
- 13% Sudapet

Block 6, CNPCIS
- 95% CNPC
- 5% Sudapet

Block 8, WNPOC-3
- 77% Petronas
- 15% Sudapet
- 8% Hi Tech

Block 9,11, Sudapak I
- 85% Zafir
- 15% Sudapet

Block 10, Free

Block 12A, Qahtani & Others
- 33% Qahtani
- 20% Ansan
- 20% Sudapet
- 15% Dindir Petroleum
- 7% Hi Tech
- 5% A.A. In.

Block 12B, Free

Block 13, CNPC, Pertamina & Sudapet
- 40% CNPC
- 15% Pertamina
- 15% Sudapet
- 10% Dindir Petroleum
- 10% Express Petroleum & Gas
- 10% Africa Energy

Block 14, Petro SA
- 80% Petro SA
- 20% Sudapet

Block 15, RSPOC
- 35% Petronas
- 35% CNPC
- 15% Sudapet
- 10% Express Petroleum & Gas
- 5% Hi Tech

Block 16, Lundin

Block 17, Ansan
- 66% Ansan
- 34% Sudapet

Block A, Sudapak II
- 83% Zafir
- 17% Sudapet

Block B, Total
- 32,5% Total
- 27,5% Kufpec
- 10% Sudapet
- 10% GOSS
- 20% open

Block C, APCO
- 65% Hi Tech
- 17% Sudapet
- 10% Khartoum State
- 8% Hegleig

Block Ea, Free

Exports

In 2009, Sudan produced close to 485,000 bbl/d and consumed around 90,000 bbl/d. The remaining crude was exported almost exclusively to Asian markets. According to international trade data, in 2009 China imported close to 250,000 bbl/d (65 percent of total Sudanese exports and 6 percent of Chinese imports) followed by Indonesia (60,000 bbl/d) and Japan (50,000 bbl/d). Additional importers of Sudanese crude include India, Malaysia, the Netherlands and Thailand. Sudan also exports some processed fuels to neighboring countries. Ethiopia imports most of its fuel from Sudan but official data on trade volumes is not available.

Sudan has two major oil streams, the Nile and Dar Blends. Nile is a medium, sweet crude with an API of 34. Nile blend is exported to Asian markets and trades at a discount to Indonesian Minas, the Asian benchmark crude. Dar blend is also exported to Asian markets and while production of this stream is growing, the heavy sour quality of this crude causes it to trade at a discount to Minas and other benchmark crudes.

Refining

Sudan has three refineries located in Khartoum, Port Sudan, and El-Obeid. The Khartoum refinery was expanded in 2006 from a capacity of 50,000 bbl/d to 100,000 bbl/d. The expansion allowed for the processing of both Nile and Fula blends of crude for domestic consumption as well as product exports. The Port Sudan facility is located near the Red Sea and has a refining capacity of 21,700 bbl/d. In September 2005, a contract was awarded to Petronas to build a new refinery at Port Sudan. The refinery was to be designed to process the highly acidic Dar blend but this project has been postponed several times and the status is currently unknown. The El-Obeid refinery is the smallest with an estimated capacity of 10,000 bbl/d.

In the event of a Southern secession the government of South Sudan has announced plans to build additional refining capacity in the South as well as a 2,200-mile (3,600 km) pipeline from the South to Kenya's port in Lamu.

FULA CRUDE

Test	Method	Unit	Results
Density 15°C	ASTM D4052	kg/l	0.9353
API Gravity			19.7
Sp.Gravity 60/60° F			0.9358
Bottom Sediment & Water	ASTM D4007	vol.%	2.4
Water	ASTM D4006	vol.%	2.3
Reid Vapoure Pressure	ASTM D323	kpa	3.45
Total Acid Number	IP177	mgkoh/g	8.82
Flash point	IP170	° C	48
Pour point	ASTM D5853*	°C	12
Total Sulphur	IP 336	wt%	0.10
Total Nitrogen	ASTM D4629+	wt%	0.2609
Salt Content	IP 265	mg/1	35
Ash Content	ASTM D482	%mm	0.254
Wax Content	UOP 46	wt%	9.3
Kin. Viscosity @50°C	ASTM D445	mm2/kg	707.4
Kin. Viscostiy@100°C	ASTM D446	wt%	111.8
Characterization factor	UOP 375	mm^2 /s	12.3
Gross Calorific Value	ASTM D240	mm^2/s	43.96

Asphaltenes	IP 143		0.15
Sodium (Na)	CBA 21	mg/kg	15.4
Potassium (K)		wt%	9.3
Copper (Cu)		mg/kg	0.6
Lead (Pb)		mg/kg	0.4
Iron (Fe)		mg/kg	30.6
Nickel(Ni)		mg/kg	16.5
Vanadium (V)		mg/kg	0.6
Calcium (ca)		mg/kg	1427
Magnesium (mg)		mg/kg	5.2
Conrnadson Carbon Residue	IP 13	%wt	7.3

PDOC CRUDE OIL BLEND

Test	Method	Unit	Results
Density at 15°C	D 5002	kg/L	0.8955
Specific Gravity at 60/60° F	Conversion		0.8960
API Gravity at 60° F	Calculated		26.42
Sulphur	IP 336	% Wt.	0.116
Mercaptan Sulphur	UOP 163	mg/kg	1
Hydrogen Sulphide	UOP 163	mg/kg	< 1
Total Nitrogen	ASTM D 3228	% Wt	0.449
Basic Nitrogen	UOP 269	% Wt	0.1
Reid Vapour Pressure at 100° F	IP 69	psi	#
Pour Point	IP 15	° C	+ 42
Kinematic Viscosity @ 15° C	IP 71	cSt	#
Kinematic Viscosity @ 25° C			#
Kinematic Viscosity @ 35° C			#
Kinematic Viscosity @ 40° C			#
Kinematic Viscosity @ 55° C			108.7
Kinematic Viscosity @ 100° C			22.61
Total Chloride	UOP 779	mg/kg	11
Conradson carbon residue	IP 13	% Wt.	7.49
Total Acid Number	IP 177	mgKOH/g	2.8
Wax Content	UOP 46	% Wt.	19.8
Metals			
Nickel	ASTMD 5863	ppm Wt	57.8
Vandium			0.8
Iron	IP 470 (Mod.)		7
Asphaltene	IP 143	% Wt.	0.06
Ash Content	IP 4	% Wt.	0.036
Salt Content	IP 265	PTB	51
B.S. & Water	ASTM D 4007	% Vol.	1.80
Water Content	IP 74	% Vol.	1.70
Flash Point	IP 34 (Mod.)	° C	Below 36
Mercury	Cold Vapour	ppb	< 1
Composition (C1-C5)	IP 344		
Methane		% Wt.	0.00

Ethane	% Wt.	0.00
Propane	% Wt.	0.20
I-butane	% Wt.	0.35
n-butane	% Wt.	1.22

CRUDE OIL GENERAL TESTS FOR 90/10 NILE/THAR JATH BLEND

Test	Method	Unit	Results
Density at 15°C	ASTM D4052	kg/m^3	864.8
API Gravity	IP Table 51	Degree	32.04
Bottom Sediment & Water	ASTM D4007	vol. %	0.8
Water	ASTM D4006	vol. %	0.75
Reid Vapour Pressure	ASTM D5191	kPa	<0.5
Total Acid Number	IP 213	mgKOH/g	0.36
Total Acid Number	ASTM D664	mgKOH/g	0.396
Conradson Carbon Residue	ASTM D189	%wt	4.8
Micro Carbon Residue (MCRT)	ASTM D4530.	%wt	4.7
Flash Point	IP 170	°C	<30
Pour Point	ASTM D97	°C	+ 33
ASTM Colour	ASTM D1500	-	>8
Total Sulphur	ASTM D4294	wt %	0.073
Salt Content	IP 265	mg/l	174
Nitrogen Content	ASTM D4629	mg/kg	1060
Ash Content	ASTM D482	% m/m	0.020
Wax Content	BP 237	wt %	32.4
Kinematic Viscosity @ 40°C	ASTM D445	mm^2/s	No Flow
Kinematic Viscosity @ 50°C	ASTM D445	mm^2/s	32.91
Kinematic Viscosity @ 70°C	ASTM D341	mm^2/s	15.8
Kinematic Viscosity @ 80°C	ASTM D445	mm^2/s	11.31
Characterisation Factor	UOP 375-59	-	12.5
Gross Calorific Value	ASTM D240	MJ/kg	45.477
Mercury	ICP	ppm	<1
Asphaltenes	IP 143	wt %	0.05
Distillation	ASTM D86		
IBP		°C	120
5% recovery		°C	164
10% recovery		°C	211
20% recovery		°C	290
30% recovery		°C	335
40% recovery		°C	348
50% recovery		°C	358
60% recovery		°C	364
70% recovery		°C	Onset of cracking
80% recovery		°C	
90% recovery		°C	
95% recovery		°C	
FBP		°C	

Cracking Point		°C	364
Recovery/Residue/Loss		% vol	84/16/0
Metals			
Sodium (Na)	Ash & ICP	mg/kg	16
Potassium (K)	Ash & ICP	mg/kg	76
Copper (Cu)	Ash & ICP	mg/kg	<1
Lead (Pb)	Ash & ICP	mg/kg	<1
Iron (Fe)	Ash & ICP	mg/kg	1.8
Nickel (Ni)	Ash & ICP	mg/kg	7.4
Vanadium (V)	Ash & ICP	mg/kg	1.7
Arsenic (As)	Ash & ICP	mg/kg	<1

EXPLORATION AND PRODUCTION

Oil production has risen steadily since the July 1999 completion of an export pipeline that runs from central Sudan to the Port of Sudan. In 2006, crude oil production averaged 414,000 barrels per day (bbl/d), up from 363,000 bbl/d in 2005. According to Angelina Tany, Minister of State for Mines and Energy, Sudan plans to be producing one million bbl/d ofcrude oil by the end of 2008.

GREATER NILE OIL PROJECT

In 1996, Canadian independent Arakis Energy (Arakis) began development of the Heglig and Unity fields (Blocks 1, 2, and 4), which contain estimated recoverable reserves of 600 million - 1.2 billion barrels of oil. Because the fields are not located near the Red Sea coast, Arakis entered into a consortium with the Greater Nile Petroleum Operating Company (GNPOC) to raise investment for a 994-mile pipeline from the fields to the Suakim oil terminal near Port Sudan. In September 1999, the first cargo of crude departed the export terminal. Although GNPOC originally constructed the pipeline with throughput of 150,000 bbl/d, its has since been increased to 300,000 bbl/d, while maximum capacity is estimated at 450,000 bbl/d. As of January 2007, combined production from Blocks 1, 2, and 4 was estimated at 260,000 bbl/d. The GNPOC joint venture is operated by CNPC (40 percent), with partners Petronas (30 percent), ONGC (25 percent) and Sudapet (5 percent).

BLOCKS 3 AND 7

Recent activity in the Sudanese oil sector. (Source:IHS Energy GEPS Reports, March 2007)
In June 2004, Petrodar, a consortium of CNPC (41 percent), Petronas (40 percent), Sudapet (8 percent), Gulf Oil Petroleum (6 percent), and the Al-Thani Corporation (5 percent) awarded a $239 million contract to Malaysia's Ranhill International and Sudan's Petroneeds Services International for development work on Blocks 3 and 7. The blocks contain the Adar Yale and Palogue oil fields, with estimated recoverable reserves of 460 million barrels. As of January 2007, Blocks 3 and 7 combined produced an estimated 165,000 bbl/d of oil. The fields could reach peak production of 200,000 bbl/d by late 2007. In November 2005, CNPC brought online the Petrodar pipeline linking the two blocks to Port Sudan. The pipeline has current throughput of 150,000 bbl/d and maximum capacity of 500,000 bbl/d. The project also includes a 300,000 bbl/d central processing facility at Al-Jabalayan and production facilities at Palogue.

BLOCK 5A

In April 2005, the Sudanese government signed an agreement with WNPOC for the development of the Thar Jath and Mala fields on Block 5A. First oil from the block came online in June 2006 at an initial rate of 38,000 bbl/d. As of March 2007, the field was still producing at 38,000 bbl/d, while full capacity is estimated at 60,000 bbl/d. Oil from the field flows through a 110-mile pipeline to

Port Sudan. WNPOC is a consortium of companies, which include Petronas (68.875 percent and operator), ONGC (23.125 percent) and Sudapet (8 percent).

BLOCK 6

In November 2004, CNPC brought online its Fula field on Block 6 at a rate of 10,000 bbl/d. Current output on the block is 40,000 bbl/d, but is expected to eventually reach 80,000 bbl/d. CNPC has constructed a pipeline that links the Fula field to the Khartoum refinery.

Exploration and development of Sudan's oil resources has been controversial. International human rights organizations have accused the Sudanese government of financing human rights abuses with oil revenues, including the mass displacement of civilians near the oil fields. Factional fighting in the South and rebel attacks on oil infrastructure have kept oil production and exploration from reaching full potential to date. In October 2004, for example, the Sudanese government prevented a militia attempt to sabotage the country's main oil export pipeline. However, the 2005 Comprehensive Peace Agreement (CPA) between the northern government in Khartoum and the GoSS could facilitate additional investment in both production facilities and new exploration initiatives in Sudan. In January 2005, after the official signing of the CPA, IOCs including Total, Marathon Oil Corporation, and the Kuwait Foreign Petroleum Exploration Company (KFPEC) renewed their exploration rights in southern Sudan.

EXPORTS

In 2006, Sudan consumed 94,000 bbl/d and exported approximately 320,000 bbl/d of crude oil, with the majority of crude destined for Asian markets. According official trade statistics as reported to the Global Trade, Sudan shipped 124,000 bbl/d of its crude exports to Japan in 2006. China also imported a significant portion of Sudanese crude exports in 2006 averaging 99,000 bbl/d. Additional importers of Sudanese crude include South Korea, Indonesia, and India. According to the *International Crude Oil Market Handbook*, Sudan's "Nile" export crude blend is considered sweet and light, having a gravity of 33 degrees API and a low sulfur content of 0.045 percent.

REFINING AND DOWNSTREAM

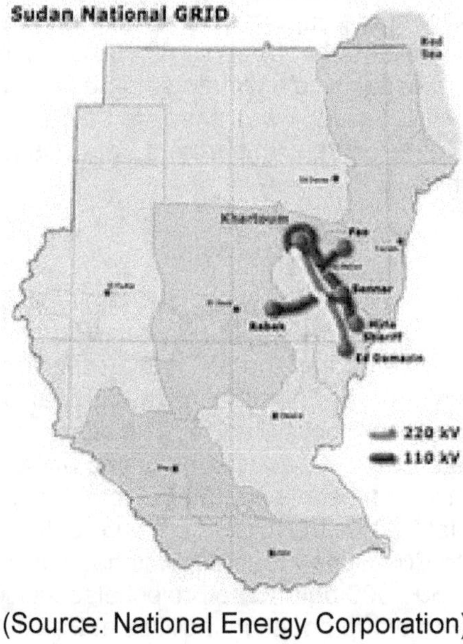

Sudan's national power grid. (Source: National Energy Corporation)

According to *OGJ*, Sudan's refineries in Khartoum and Port Sudan had total combined refining capacity of 121,700 bbl/d as of January 2007. In July 2006, CNPC announced the completion of the Khartoum refinery expansion project, which doubled the refinery's capacity from 50,000 bb/d to 100,000 bbl/d. The Khartoum refinery processes Nile blend crude, which has a low sulfur content and high fuel-yield. The additional refinery capacity from the expansion should help alleviate the short supply of refined products available in Sudan, while giving the country some additional export capacity.

The Port Sudan facility is located near the Red Sea and is Sudan's smallest refinery, with capacity of 21,700 bbl/d. In September 2005, a contract was awarded to Petronas to build a new refinery at Port Sudan. The refinery will be designed to process Dar blend crude, which has high-acid content and is found in Sudan's Melut basin. The refinery will have capacity of 100,000 bbl/d and could be operational in 2009. Petronas is joined with the Sudanese Ministry of Energy and Mining in a 50:50 partnership in the project.

IMPORTANT INFORMATION AND DEVELOPMENTS

Sudan is one of the rich countries in natural resources, oil, minerals, and hydro-electric generation resources. But attention to utilization of natural resources came late when the first Energy and Mining Ministry was established in the country in 1976, which included the Department of Geology, Rural Water Supply Corporation, the Petroleum General Corporation, the Pipelines General Corporation, Petroleum Products, The Geological Researches General Corporation, The Electricity and Water General Corporation which was later divided into two by the establishment of the Ministry of Electricity.

EXPLORATION OF OIL RESOURCES:

The exploration of the oil resources is one of the most significant achievements in the Sudan in the last decade, when the country's imports of petroleum products amounted to $400 million per anmum, consuming a great portion of the hard currency revenues. Early attempts of exploration of oil began since 1959, then the American Chevron Company came in mid seventies to confirm the existence of large oil reserves in the country, but the Company suspended its work and finally withdrew from the country in 1990.

However Sudan was determined to utilize its oil and was endeavouring to diversify sources of dealings and adopted an open door policy with different states in the world. The outcome of this policy was the establishment of a national consortium to implement the policy of utilization of oil; by the end of 1996 the following bodies were established:

1) The Chinese National Petroleum Company (CNPC), 40%
2) The Malaysian National Petroleum Company, 30%.
3) The Canadian State Co. (replaced by an Indian Co.), 25%
4) The Sudanese Sudapet Co., 5% and that was the greatest breakthrough in Sudan oil production.

Drilling:

Drilling exploration began in the two areas of Heglieg and Al-Wihda in 1996 while the commercial production of the ore started in 1999 with 20.7 million barrels increased to more than 150 million barrels in 2004.

Construction of the pipeline:

Within the plan to develop the oil resources in the country, the construction of a 1610 km long pipeline from the production areas to the port of exportation at the Red Sea and with it began exportation and international marketing of oil. Another pipeline was constructed from Fula oil field up to Khartoum Refinery.

Oil Refineries:

There are five oil refineries in the country; Port Sudan, Concorp, El-Obied, Abu-Gabra, and Khartoum Oil Refinery. Abu-Gabra refinery was constructed in 1992 with a capacity of 2000 bpd, El-Obied in 1996 with 10,000 barrels/day capacity, and the Concorp Refinery in Al-Shajara, Khartoum in 1999. The Khartoum Refinery at El-Giely was established and operated in 2000 with a capacity of 50,000 bpd, the first phase of expansion completed in 2004 when its capacity raised to 62,000 bpd while the capacity shall rise to 100,000 bpd by the completion of the second stage of expansion. This refinery has had the decisive role in the realization of a self-sufficiency in petroleum products. Sudan production has increased to 200,000 bpd by the end of 2005 and the government share would rise to 80%.

The establishment of Khartoum oil refinery has paved the way for Sudan to enter the world of petro-chemical industry, when Khartoum Petro-chemical Factory was established at El-Giely for the production of plastics in a partnership between the Ministry of Energy and Mining and the Chinese National Petroleum Company (CNPC).

IMPORTANT DEVELOPMENTS

UNITISATION AGREEMENT

Is the legal formula used in the petroleum industry did not find his version of Arabization in legal books, which carried them, so I saw the contribution that I know call it "unified contract" for the purposes of this paper, because it calls for consolidation of oil operations of the geological survey and research, drilling and extraction, production and transfer, refining and sale between the two working in different fields within the borders of one country or even among the fields that cross the borders of two, which could be termed a "unified contract transboundary"

INTER-STATE UNITISATION AGREEMENT

This formula was used in America to exploit the common fields spanning the borders between two companies or two or even two terms have appeared ad-hoc basis for the use of this contract in America because the owners of the fields adjacent each was digging several wells in a competitive manner on the outskirts of the border with the other field, but not prove the usefulness of this drilling random economic has been replaced by the use of this type of contract. In this regard, U.S. law has used the theory or doctrine

RULE OF CAPTURE DOCTRINE

For the Exploitation of joint fields are what might be called the theory of "capture", which says that the person who took advantage of the extracted oil has the right to exploit what Astkrjh, this theory did not find acceptance in international law, as it practically led to the drilling competitive terms that each party will try to dig the largest number from wells on the border of the field with the other party which would lead to exchange a lot of money may not be enough, oil coverage and lead to loss of high economic and environmental damage, and that if the field is stretched across an international border, it could lead to the violation of the sovereignty of the neighboring country (Smith and others) and so it was agreed that contracts consolidated or bilateral agreements for the exploitation of common fields is the way that replaced the theory of "baiting" as a fair process and justified in the eyes of international law and common legal sense, but that the world is legal Onorato believes that countries that have oil fields shared by the "legal obligation" to cooperate in the mutual independence of the field.

Above it is clear that the unified contract is a type of collaborative contracts, we urge and work for the joint exploitation of common fields. This type of contract would be beneficial to Sudan in the event of separation or in the case that the extraction of oil affects two or even two. Sudan theoretically knew this type of contract, as the Convention on the Sudanese government and Petronas signed in 2003 to exploit oil field No. 8 had demanded that in case of discovery of oil extended outside the borders of Sudan, the Minister of Energy and Mining is obliged to coordinate and agree with the neighboring country on the development, exploitation and production common field (Article 3), here we see that looks to the legislature as if it were such a situation and do better because the field No. 8 nearby not only for the South but has an extended border with Ethiopia. Each case in this regard, we find that Sudan had developed primary bases for this type of contract that can be built upon, developed and because Sudan lacks comprehensive legislation so when you put any legislation New Oil must ensure this type of contract details more precise, and in any case, we see that must now embark on a model contract contains details and conditions of such type of contract also did a lot of countries such as Ecuador.

The second type of cooperation would be to hold a kind of bilateral agreements, known as contracts for the development of common areas

THE JOINT DEVELOPMENT AREA

A kind of bilateral agreement between the two companies not to develop a common area, whether it is the discovery of oil resources by the mother that it is possible that there are natural resources there are strong indications of this. This contract differs from the type that the previous bilateral agreement for cooperation between the two states for the development of a common area rather than an oil contract, as it is not the oil companies may also be in the unified contract. This type of contract has been tried since the sixties of the last century has proved successful in many countries in terms of the telly and sharing costs of research and extraction of oil as he helped solve problems contentious as between Australia and East Timor, as well as between Saudi Arabia and Bahrain, Saudi Arabia and Kuwait in the neutral zone.

Sudan has his own experience in this area, where a disagreement arose with Saudi Arabia, with respect to exploration in Abajr red when Saudi Arabia announced at the beginning of the seventies that the limits of its territorial waters extend to 200 km to the sea and when the object Sudan has been formed a joint committee agreement was signed between the two countries to take advantage of common wealth of the Red Sea in the shared area, which starts from the point reaches the depth of the sea to 1000 meters from both sides (Article 5 of the Sudan and Saudi Arabia in 1974.) agreement was signed by the Sudanese foreign minister, then-Mansour Khalid, despite the fact that this Convention has not been brought to fruition was not serious and productive because the burden of the costs of the Joint Committee was to be borne by Saudi Arabia alone, making the initiative dies in the cradle, but the experience in itself worthy of contemplation and study of the people matter, especially that Sudan has signed an agreement with Saudi Arabia for exploitation of minerals in the same region in the 19/05/2010, although the Convention recent "secret" which does not allow comments, and related metals is only oil, but it is important to establish conditions which guarantee the interests of the nation. This type of agreement is important because it helps in resolving the dispute over the region and Hlaib Qasdha of sea area is still occupied by Egypt since 1992 and without signs of a solution despite reports that mention that Egypt continues to exploit the riches of the disputed area.

This kind of bilateral agreements can also be used in cooperation with the South in the event of separation for which he is to ensure the peaceful exploitation of the resources of the shared area and gives signals reassuring for oil companies to invest in a quiet area not in dispute because the capital is a coward and run away from areas of conflict and wars, especially the oil investment because it is the most dangerous and Mjazvp. For what have mentioned about the examples above for the common areas are all coastal areas and far from populated areas, which makes cooperation in the border areas between north and south is different and faces a lot of different challenges, as the border areas of common to be developed areas are landlocked, but are areas of either agricultural or pastoral and populated (Madjak Doqot) and the presence of this population brings with it many of the problems relating to the law of land and environmental laws and human rights.

Also, the cooperation of this kind needs a degree of transparency and clarity in the accounts and the terms of contracts and away from the bribery and corruption, financial and administrative management of the two countries, it also requires a degree of mutual trust between the parties so as to avoid what happened in the experience of the states of "Sao Tome Principe and Nigeria," which did not achieve results desired rate of corruption and lack of transparency. In all cases, the development of legislation and development of models for such contracts and agreements and to benefit from the mistakes of others are effective ways to develop legislation and productive decades incomplete, especially that of those contracts and agreements have been used as a means to resolve or prevent conflict and they may also help in extinguishing any future conflict potential with the South (Aoukongioov)

THE INFRASTRUCTURE OF THE OIL:

It should be noted that most of the infrastructure related to oil exist in the north, although the southern view of the skepticism, since the eighties when he was replaced Nimeiri the basic proposal to build a refinery Bentiu to turn the proposed Kosti before settling on a pipeline to Port Sudan alternative to the refineries, and Southerners consider a policy of "deliberate" and followed by Governments of the North, but the government in the north are attributable to lack of security in the south during the war that spilled over into 2005. In any case, the presence of these structures increases the importance of what we went to him the importance of cooperation between North and South. North of the South needs to continue to derive income from the oil south to maintain economic stability and thereby political by what has been achieved after the signing of the Comprehensive Peace Agreement.

On the other hand, the South, as a locked without a maritime performing, you must cooperate with the North as all the infrastructure for marketing of oil present in the north, or at least more advanced in the north lines pipes carrying oil - refineries - export ports - roads, airports - services firms, as well as the trained manpower in the field of oil by the entire North. At the same time, the decades of war has made the south lacks all types of infrastructure, in this framework and as long as oil is the only source of income for the South, it is difficult to imagine the survival of the South without incomes of oil in the south can get on the incomes of oil from non-cooperation with the North at least in the foreseeable future. Cooperation North - South is not impossible as evidenced in the present moment, in practice, the cooperation North - South began in 2009 when the Commission declared the National Petroleum that they had established the required map for decades oil to Block IE and covering the South - west and passes through the wing of the blocks 5A and 5B in use. Also, the National Committee have formed a joint committee of representatives of the Governments of the North and the South to negotiate with the company (Supere Htc Resources and Oil) and the Spanish (Business Monitor). In this regard, in my view, the same oil which is used by America to the temptation of movement of the signing of Naivasha, I see no objection to also be used as a catalyst of political and economic for the motivation of cooperation - North and South can experience the National Committee to continue if further oil for use as a political pressure on the other side.

In line with what the organization have mentioned high Gulwbal tennis has developed a proposed five-point agreement calls for development of new "alternative" to the sharing of oil wealth after 2011. Proposal Gulwbal tennis is based on the current agreement will expire in 2011 if there must be an "alternative agreement" for the continuation of the parties in obtaining revenues similar to the pre-2011, a proposal is simple based and predicated on the basis can be tested and make sure it is based on the compensation the northern government financially in return for allowing to the southern government to use oil pipelines, ie, that the Government of South rental oil pipeline to displace oil to the world market in exchange for between $ 3-8 dollars a barrel has been confirmed Gulwbal and forget that the sum of this proposal will not be less than its revenues for the North on the incomes of the wealth sharing agreement signed by the Naivasha agreement. Gulwbal and suggests that this system must be subject to the control system and transparency reveals the terms of the contract and is subject to scrutiny and independent monitoring, and should adopt a mechanism for settling disputes between the parties, and begin to review and set up an account of the existing agreements. The method of calculation phase should not depend on the numbers given by companies, the ratio of charge to give the final numbers less than it produces and the two parties on both sides of the tube should maintain accurate records of oil carry-over through a pipe. Some are betting that the South can build a line of pipelines and private, but all signs indicate that it needs at least three years and he needs to $ 1.5 billion for construction of the pipeline proposed to build from the south to "Lamu" in Kenya and many experts believe that this line will not be economically viable for the south compared with the north line of the high cost burdens to the infant state, and to intercept the mountains of Kilimanjaro route pipe, which requires the building of ten stations to "strengthen" It is certain that the South can not survive without oil revenues or stop production until completion of the construction of the line.

From my point of view, the proposal Gulwbal tennis represents a fair and pragmatic and Oakie of petroleum expected conflict can occur between the parties. This agreement makes the parties Ihsan important not to go to war because they will feel the benefit, which Jnyaha of oil, which Sevqdanh reference to the war, where it is worst-case scenario for both parties because the war will affect the oil industry as the manufacturers will be forced to stop operations, partly because the war this time will not be like previous ones, where it will reach the fields, companies and their workers may be used by the Air Force to bomb production platforms, storage tanks, pipelines, refineries, fields, and their consequences on both sides to prevent the other party to benefit from the revenues of oil, so the companies will be reluctant to invest more money in a war zone, which affect the industry oil in the short and long run and to stop their incomes and their evolution. At the same time, military expenditure will take the largest share of the revenues that should have been directed to the development. In this direction, the World Bank predicted that Khartoum would resort to war if I expected that it will provide them access to the rate of oil fields, either the Government of South Van Jwha of the war will be in the case of defending the right to self-determination "referendum" ... Do you endorse the prophecy of the World Bank that the it will reveal the coming days.

IMPORTANT LAWS AND REGULATIONS

OWNERSHIP OF OIL

Under Sudanese law, all petroleum found in its natural state in the strata of the earth or in the continental shelf is deemed to be the property of the state.

The exploration and exploitation of oil resources in the Sudan is regulated by the Petroleum Resources Act, 1972 and the Petroleum Resources Regulations, 1973. These two pieces of legislation regulate the petroleum activities onshore and offshore.

The 1972 Act provided for the grant of an exclusive exploration license followed, in the case of oil discovery, by a lease which gives the exploiter an exclusive right to exploit the discovered oil.

In order to render the legal framework for the exploration and exploitation of oil more flexible, the Petroleum Resources Act 1972 was amended in 1975 by the adoption of Section 25. This introduced a sweeping change. This new section in its latest version gives the Minister of Energy and Mining, with the approval of the Board of Petroleum Affairs and the consent of the Council of Ministers, the right to make any agreement for the exploration and exploitation of oil in the Sudan. These agreements may be in the form of production sharing agreements.

Since 1975 all such agreements have been of the Production Sharing Agreements (PSA) form.

The PSA embodies all the rights and obligations of the Government and the Oil Company. The Oil Company, under these agreements, recovers its exploration cost from an agreed percentage of the production. The remaining part of production, the Profit Oil, is distributed between the Oil Company and the Government according to the percentages agreed upon between the two parties. Section 25 of the Petroleum Resources Act states clearly that in case of contradiction between the provisions of the PSA and the Act, the provisions of the PSA shall prevail over the Act.

The procedure for obtaining a concession in the Sudan starts by submitting an application by the interested oil company to the Director of the Geological Research Authority Survey (GRAS). The application to be made on the form and contain the particulars are set out in Schedule 1 of the Petroleum Resources Regulations 1973.

The Oil Company shall provide particulars as to its financial and technical abilities in compliance with Section 7 of the Petroleum Act. Eligibility of applicants shall be based on their technical and financial capabilities.

In the Sudan two petroleum departments are involved in petroleum activities, namely: the Geological Research Authority (GRAS) established by the Geological Research Authority Act 1986, and the General Petroleum Corporation (GPC) established under the Public Petroleum Corporation Act 1976. GRAS is the regulatory arm of the Government and GPC is the commercial arm of the Government. The capital of GPC is 100% contributed by the Government.

GPC takes a minority participation in the PSA with the Prospective Oil Company as a non-paying partner till a commercial discovery is made. In determining the shares of the profit oil, the above is taken into consideration along with the tax laws. Equipment of the Oil Company used in petroleum operations Is exempt from customs duties. The oil discovered and exported is exempted from any export tax or any formalities hindering such exportation.

Exchange rights are provided for in the PSA and the company is given the right to sell its share of the oil outside the Sudan and to keep the proceeds outside the Sudan. The company have the right to import foreign currency to finance its local operations. any surplus local currency is authorized to be repatriated. The PSA gives the Minister of Energy and Mining the right to supervise the activities of the Oil Company. This supervision is implemented by the GRAS.

Finally, the legal framework for exploration and exploitation of oil in the Sudan is flexible and gives the Minister of Energy the right to reach any type of agreement with the oil companies provided that such agreement suits the needs of both parties. The agreement adopted by the parties need not be a PSA type, but could be any other legally acceptable form.

BASIC LAWS

The export of the first shipment of Sudanese oil on August 30, 1999 came almost two decades since Chevron Oil Company made its major discoveries of oil in the Southern Sudan. The discovery of oil came at a time when economic development in Sudan was at its peak. The economic potential of Sudan was highlighted by a report of the Food and Agriculture Organisation (FAO), depicting Sudan as the potential "Breadbasket of the World". Sudan will have to achieve this by cultivating 60 million feddans of unexploited arable lands to produce sugar, wheat and textiles. Investors from Arab oil- producing countries were invited to invest their accumulating oil revenues. That trend was triggered by the 1973 Israeli-Arab war, and gained such momentum after the FAO's anticipatory report that Arab investors realised the necessity to do so in an Arab country. Large-scale development activities were underway when Chevron announced its discovery of oil in the south of Sudan. This gave new impetus to the developments' programmes, and raised the hopes of Nimeri's Government for a better economy.

Such hopes, however, were soon fell on the stony reality of economic crisis. There were several reasons for Sudan's economic setback. Most prominent among these was the rise of oil prices in the 1970s. This had the direct effect of substantially increasing Sudan's fuel bill to meet energy demands in industrial and agricultural projects, and an indirect one reflected in the drain of Sudan's most qualified professionals, skilled workers and manual labourers who were too frustrated by the deterioration of the economy to resist the temptation of incomes in the Gulf states. The fuel bill, as table 1 below shows, constituted a systematic source of drain on Sudan's foreign exchange earned from exports. This situation became worse when Sudan was unable to raise new loans to pay its foreign debts; this had a direct impact on the industrial and agricultural production and consequently reduced the amount of foreign exchange. In its turn, this resulted in a severe balance of payment deficit which is still plaguing the Sudanese economy.

Hence, the Government realised that development of Sudan's oil discoveries was the only recourse left to pay back its foreign debts and improve its economy. The Government and Chevron Oil Company started, therefore, to consider their plans of how best to utilize Sudan's oil, once production started. The two parties realised that the original Production Sharing Agreement, concluded in 1975, was not satisfactory and could not fulfil their aspirations. The Government and Chevron agreed in 1983 to amend the original agreement to meet the objectives of their new plans. The amendments provided, inter alia, for the construction of a pipeline to export oil to Port Sudan. This plan replaced the original proposal for construction of a refinery in the south. The idea of exporting crude oil via Port Sudan, however, has not been tolerated by the people from the south who suffered most from the economic crisis; and in a counter measure to the central government's plans, the rebels attacked a Chevron camp in the south and killed three of Chevron's staff in February 1984.

Thus, oil discovery in Sudan became a political issue and was one of the factors behind the on-going civil war in the south. The failure of Nimeri's Government, as well as all the Governments which succeeded it, to end hostilities in the south has had a very negative effect on the oil activities in Sudan. The fuel bill was a major problem despite the considerable efforts by successive governments to impose various policies of rationing fuel. Some of these policies, however, have aggravated and led to increasing shortages in fuel rations.

The current Government, which came to power in 1989, has thus experienced a severe energy crisis and shortages of fuel and electricity. Considerable domestic unrest was built up as a result of these problems. The Government became aware that the only way to extricate itself from shackles of this crisis was by improving the conditions of investment in order to attract foreign investors to search for more oil in Sudan, and also to develop the oil fields discovered in the west and the offshore gas reserves discovered in the Red Sea in the east of the country. Although initially there have been considerable efforts to promote the oil industry, these efforts seem to have suffered from several shortcomings.

The first shortcoming relates to the fact that many of these efforts were undertaken as part of a programme to improve the investment conditions in general. Oil industry is a high risk sector, it poses new problems and authorities lack expertise. It thus requires a separate consideration. Secondly, there has been no comprehensive legal analysis or assessment of the regime, whether by reference to contracts or to the petroleum law, which regulates oil exploration in Sudan. Thirdly, although there has been some academic discussion along these lines by scholars, this discussion was unfocussed and heavily influenced by the optimistic conditions and concepts of international oil industry in the early seventies. Now the industry is undergoing enormous changes, mostly because of the low prices of oil in the 1990s which forced oil companies to focus on cost-cutting and mergers rather than production growth. This has a direct effect on reducing the availability of funds for exploration, which in turn influenced the investment decision-making. After two years of strong prices, oil companies, without jeopardizing these cost-cutting efforts, are increasing their budgets for exploration and production. The present-day exploration and development terms have to reflect the market realities.

In this paper an attempt is made to explore avenues relating to overcoming these, and many other shortcomings. It endeavours to ascertain, inter alia, the actual role and impact of the terms which define the legal and commercial relationship for exploration, development and production of oil, between an investor and the Government of Sudan. This will be done by surveying the contractual provisions of previous contracts and those of the main law, and considering their legal implications.

In conclusion, the importance and vital significance of oil to the Sudanese economy attracted the writer to this subject in the first place. Tempted by the fact that the oil industry in Sudan is in its infancy, and feeling that this subject has not received sufficient attention, it was deemed useful to examine and re-evaluate the legal relationship between Sudan and the oil companies. It is hoped that this paper will be able to identify the problems of oil investment in Sudan, to analyse these problems and help to anticipate the future.

SUDAN LAW ON PRODUCTION OF OIL:-

In outlining the historical development of the laws on production of oil in Sudan, three distinct phases can be observed. Each period is characterised by certain trends which shape the course of petroleum industry in this country. The first phase traces the history of basic petroleum legislation in Sudan and the oil activities undertaken under these legislation. The second phase reviews the contractual setting emerges as confidence in oil potential rises. And the final period examines the taxation terms and the implications which they may have on the exploration operations.

By understanding how laws on production of oil have been developed, this will, necessarily, serve as background to understand some of the specific legal problems dealt with in detail.

2.1. Enactment of Basic Petroleum Legislation:-

The Sudan history of enactment of a separate petroleum legislation is a comparatively recent one. However, the first attempt to pass a legislative framework to regulate searching for all minerals, including oil, was instigated by a concern over the question of the proprietary rights to minerals in the ground. It was decreed by the British during the colonial period when Sudan was governed by both Britain and Egypt in 1899. By vesting the ownership of all minerals, including oil, in Sudan in the condominium government, it was suggested that the two states where trying to "avoid conflicting claims as to which of the two ruling states owned the minerals in the colony, and at the same time to prevent settlement by Egyptian and British subjects attracted by the possibility of acquiring freehold title to in situ resources".

Thus, in Sudan the history of a separate legislation regulating the petroleum activities began after independence in 1956. That was in the form of the Petroleum Resources Development Act 1958,and its regulations which were promulgated in 1959. From 1959 to 1972, several licences were granted by the Government to oil companies including Agip, General Exploration Company of California, Digna, Continental Oil Company, Shell and BP. The work carried out under these licences was, however, unsuccessful. These licences were terminated either upon expiration or by being surrendered to the Government.

In 1972, the Petroleum Resources Development Act 1958 was repealed by the Petroleum Resources Act which has been the basic petroleum legislation since then. The 1972 Act, like its predecessor, starts by vesting in the state all proprietary interests in petroleum, together with the exclusive right of exploration and production.

Interests in petroleum resources in Sudan are granted, therefore, under statutory authority. The authority empowers the appropriate bodies to grant such interests in two forms of contractual arrangements; licences and leases, in accordance with the relevant legislation and any regulations promulgated thereunder, and separate forms of petroleum agreements, such as the production sharing agreements.

Thus, the Petroleum Resources Act 1972 vests the power to grant licences and leases, subject to the approval of the Council of Ministers, in the Board of Petroleum and Mining Affairs (BPMA). Before granting licences or leases the Minister of Energy and Mining is required by s.24(1) to make regulations prescribing certain licensing procedures. In considering the application for licences and leases the BPMA must take into consideration, in addition to the terms of the relevant regulations, the statutory guidelines set out in detail to help determine the eligibility of applicants.

Apart from the licence and lease forms, the Sudan Government has statutory authority to enter into different kinds of petroleum agreements. Special reference is given to such kind of agreements which provide for the sharing of production between the Government and the other contracting party. Thus s.25 provides:-

> "...the Minister may, on the recommendation of the Board and after obtaining the consent of the Council of Ministers, enter into any agreement for the exploration, development and utilization of petroleum. Such agreements shall provide for the sharing of production between the Government and the other contracting party in accordance with the terms, covenants and conditions embodied in such agreements or shall provide for the exploration, development and utilization of petroleum in any other manner agreed upon..."

According to this Act, the Minister's power to enter into different forms of oil agreement is conditional upon obtaining the recommendation of the Board, and the consent of the Council of

Ministers. The Act makes no reference to the procedure or the criteria necessary for the grant of these agreements.

After enacting its main petroleum legislation, the Government in Sudan granted licenses to search for petroleum both onshore and offshore. In Sudan, no separate system of licensing for offshore areas exists despite the fact that most of the Sudanese licenses granted under the first petroleum legislation, the 1958 Act, were offshore licences.

2.2. The Contractual Setting:-

In Sudan, as mentioned above, this right to conduct petroleum operations can be granted by virtue of a production-sharing agreement, or a two-stage system of a licence and a lease. The Energy Minister is to prescribe the licensing procedures by issuing regulations which are expected to regulate the licences and leases forms and not, as we shall see, the production-sharing agreements.

The holders of these forms are entitled to different rights. For example, a licence under the two-stage system, confers on the licensee the following rights:-

> "(a) the exclusive right of exploration,
>
> (b) the right, upon discovery within the licence area, to the grant of one or more leases within such area in accordance with the conditions prescribed in this Act and the regulations made therein."

Thus, a licence in Sudan does not authorize its holder to recover petroleum. The licensee has only a statutory right in case of discovery, to apply for and obtain a lease. The licence work obligations are specified in detail in the standard form of the licence which is set out in schedule 2 of the Petroleum Resources Regulations of 1973. The licensee has to carry out these obligations with due diligence, failure to fulfil them entitles the Government to terminate the licence.

The lease in Sudan, furthermore, is to be negotiated on individual basis, and its terms are specified at the time of the agreement. The important terms, however, are specifically mentioned in the 1972 Act, such as the maximum duration of the lease; the size of the lease area; the rent and tax rates. The Petroleum Resources Act of 1972 is, unfortunately, silent about the actual rights conferred by the lease. However, in light of the fact that it is an offence under the Act to undertake or attempt to undertake petroleum production without a lease, one may suggest that the lessee is eventually given the exclusive right of exploration and production. Also, in Sudan a mining lease and a petroleum lease are rather indistinguishable. A mining lease confers on the lessee the right to dig for minerals, coupled with a grant to carry them away. It is exclusive in the sense that no other person is entitled to conduct such activities in the lease area. It does not, therefore, concern with the legal right to exclusive possession of the land itself.

In Sudan, these elements make the mining and petroleum lease, similar to the English licenses, akin to the profit a prendre. Under a profit a prendre concept, minerals becomes the property of the licensee upon recovery. The licensee does not own minerals in situ, which in this case is owned by the state. The title, as stated before, passes upon reduction into possession. The point of this reduction in petroleum is said to be at "wellhead", or sometimes earlier than that point. Concentration, therefore, will be on the lease, rather than the licence, in Sudan being the form which entitles its holder to recover petroleum.

The agreements which can be concluded by the Sudan Government by virtue of s.25 of the 1972 Act do, however, specify the rights and obligations of the two parties in considerable detail. All production- sharing agreements which have been concluded by the Government were, similar to the leases, negotiated on individual basis. They were similar in format with variations regarding duration, royalties, taxes, work programmes and expenditure. The most distinguished feature of these agreements is the fact that the rights and obligations of the parties may prevail even over the provisions of the Act in the event of inconsistency between the provisions of the agreements and those of the Act. Thus each production-sharing agreement in Sudan stands on its own.

In its effort to develop the oil industry that has long been hampered by the civil war, lack of finance, and United States hostility which blocks badly needed debt relief and rescheduling, the current Government of Sudan has managed to conclude several exploration and Production Sharing Agreements with oil companies of diverse nationalities. The results of the new exploration were very promising and confirm the high prospectivity of the areas. The outcome of the development of the old fields made Sudan oil production run at about 200,000 bpd and account for 16 to 17 percent of GDP. Oil exports represents now more than 70% of total exports. This helped Sudan to achieve in 2000 its first trade balance surplus in its modern history, when exports exceeded import by $200 million.

TAXATION OF PETROLEUM AGREEMENTS

The taxation system plays the key role in the profitability of oil investment. It is usually drawn up with the primary objective of allocating economic benefits to the host country and the oil company. If not appropriate, it is likely to have a distorting influence to decision-making process relating to investment and production of oil resources. In particular, it could contribute negatively to slowing down the pace of development, inhibit exploitation of new areas, or development of marginal or frontier areas. It may also cause a premature abandonment or shutdown of fields.

Designing an optimal taxation system is consequently an important and difficult task, because it has to accommodate the host government's interest in collecting early immediate revenues, as well as future revenues in the case of commercial discovery on the one hand, and the oil companies' interests in securing a rate of return on their investment on the other hand. An optimal system also has to be flexible in adjusting itself to the highly uncertain elements involved in calculating the economic rent, such as fluctuations of output, prices and costs. This is essentially why oil companies favour devices which target profits rather than gross revenues.

In structuring their tax systems, host governments have employed different devices in order to capture a "reasonable" share of the expected "economic rent" of petroleum exploitation. These devices have been incorporated in three stages namely; pre-production, production, and payments based on net income. The devices used in the pre-production include surface rental fees and various kinds of bonuses. Although the amounts of rental fees are generally small, bonuses tend to be large and are considered by some oil companies as one of the factors which inhibit investment. The negative effect of bonuses comes from the fact that they are not related to profits and are paid long before production commences. Thus it has been stated that:

> "Oil companies are looking for oil and profits, consequently, they prefer to put their money into research and exploration, not governments coffers to ease the balance of payments problem requirement to bring funds into the country"

Thus, pre-production payments, though they are likely to add in a small way towards companies' interest in rapid recovery, they do not have such a significant effect on the exploration and development decisions as payments during production, and those based on net income.

In Sudan, various conventional devices for taxation have been employed by the Government. These devices depend on whether the right for exploitation is given under the licensing system of the Petroleum Resources Act 1972, or under a Production- Sharing system. The taxation package under the former consists of surface rental fees, royalty and a state-participation or Income Tax option. Under the latter it is various kinds of bonuses, a production-sharing and income tax.

Under Sudan petroleum laws the licence's and lease's surface rents have been fixed, surprisingly, since 1958. They were stipulated for originally in the Petroleum Resources Development Act 1958 before being included in the present Act of 1972. They are very low. The Sudanese licensee is required to pay LS 500 upon the grant. Also required is a payment of a surface rent of LS 10 in respect of each 100 sq. km. or part thereof, for each of the first 4 years of the term of the licence, and of LS 200 for each year during which the term is extended. Under a lease, however, the payment takes the form of an annual rent payable in advance. It is of LS 60 in respect of each sq. km. or part thereof.

The small amount of fees has highlighted another major problem associated with the use of local currency in developing countries. Macro mismanagement policies of distorted exchange rates and un-controllable inflation are likely, furthermore, to diminish any value arising from these fees. Thus, instead of being fixed, the rate of the fees would generate a reasonable income to the government if negotiated on a case-by-case basis, and were increased each time a licence or lease is renewed.

As far as royalty is concerned, it is fixed at a rate of 12½% of the well-head value of all crude oil and gas produced from the leased area. The main risk of a flat royalty like this, is the possibility of invoking a situation where it exceeds the profits, hence making the cost exceed the revenues. This could result in rendering oil fields non-profitable, and therefore leading to a premature abandonment of the field. Marginal fields and less profitable fields are at risk of paying royalties. That is why the UK abolished royalties so as to encourage more exploration and development of smaller and marginal fields.

A solution which could be offered to make the Sudanese royalty rate less regressive and hence a more efficient instrument, is the sliding scale system according to which the rate of royalty increases in accordance with output. Critics of this solution regard it as being an improper measure because it is still linked to production rather than to value. In other words, if oil prices fall, or costs increase, high production will not necessarily mean that the field is profitable. Another problem associated with the sliding scale measure, is the difficulty in designing a proper chart for the rates of production and royalty, which would help avoid the situations of what is known as the "notch" problem.

In order to avoid the shortcomings of the sliding scale formula, oil companies in some countries like Canada, are given an opportunity to recoup a certain rate of return on their investment, before a progressive incremental scale of royalty is paid. The weakness of this solution is that it is most unlikely to be accepted by a developing country (Sudan for example), which is all the more keen to acquire early revenue from its oil resources.

A further intricacy regarding royalty, especially under the Sudanese Act, is that no allusion has been made to the process or procedure by which royalty oil at the well-head would be evaluated. This would bring with it a major problem of taxation, i.e. determining the real value of oil production, costs and many other issues arising out of the internationally integrated operations of oil companies.

In addition to royalty, a lessee company in Sudan is required by the Petroleum Resources Act 1972to pay a corporate tax at the rate of 50% of net profits. This requirement will take place only if the Government decides not to undertake its option of participation in the share-capital of the company. Thus, under s.11 of the 1972 Act, the Government reserves for itself the right to participate in the share-capital of the lessee company in case of a commercial discovery of up to 50%.

Under the production-sharing system, on the other hand, the taxation devices are various kinds of bonuses, a production-sharing, and income tax. As pointed out earlier, various kinds of bonuses must have been introduced to offset the small amount of fees paid under the main Petroleum Act.

Thus, once production starts, the Government and contractors are entitled to take and dispose separately of their shares of oil production. This right, which gives the contractor a direct ownership of its share, was very important for the US companies, such as Chevron and Sun Oil, because it enabled them to avoid first anti-trust issues which militate against joint marketing, and secondly the US tax regime which will treat a joint venture as an "association taxable as a corporation."

However, before distribution of oil, the contractor recovers all his costs and expenses relating to the petroleum operations, out of an amount of petroleum equal in value to maximum of 30% (under the Chevron, Sun Oil and Panoco agreements) or 35% (as in the Total agreement) annually of all crude oil production in the contract area. This amount of oil is referred to as "cost oil". The costs and expenses include all operating expenses, exploration expenditure which is recoverable at the rate of 20% (under the Chevron, Sun Oil and Panoco agreements) or 25% as in the Total agreement.

In order to protect the Sudan Government in pricing, the cost oil is valued at the weighted f.o.b. price, realised on sales to non- affiliated companies. If the costs and expenses in any year exceed the value of all petroleum produced in that year, the excess may be carried forward until fully recovered.

After deducting the cost oil, the balance of crude oil, generally known as "profit oil", is taken and disposed of separately by the Government and the Contractor in certain proportions, when a certain level of production is attained.

A corporate tax is, furthermore, payable under the Production- Sharing Contracts. The contractors were required to pay to the Government income taxes out of their share of oil production. The payment of this tax is of vital importance for companies from the USA, the UK, France and Japan for tax purposes. These countries impose income tax upon the world-wide trading profits of their contractors, and in order to prevent a double taxation on income earned outside their countries, allows tax paid to host governments, in which such income is earned, to be credited against their tax.

In Sudan the income tax law had been one of the laws which were changed by the Government in 1984 in order to bring them into conformity with Islamic Law. A new law, entitled the Zakat and Taxation Act 1984, was enacted and came into force as of the 26th of September 1984. The implementation of that Act was made subject to regulations passed thereafter, and contained significant amendments to the Act. Had it not been for these amendments, the Act would have had a damaging effect on oil operations in Sudan. Special attention has been given to the effect of two sections under the Act. Under the first section a new tax called the Development and Investment Tax (introduced under s.59) may be imposed at the discretion of the President at the rate of 10% on Sudanese, foreign or joint capital invested in Sudan. Under the second section (s. 63(c)) no exemption from the payment of Zakat or tax should be given to any person. The subsequent amendments, however, stated that these sections had been inconsistent with the state policy of encouragement of investment, and they were consequently abolished. The Government subjected oil operations to the provisions of the Encouragement of Investment Act.

This change has resulted in a significant reduction in the rate of corporation tax, otherwise imposed on companies. Furthermore, under all Production-Sharing Contracts a safeguard against higher taxes was included. It ensured that if, at any time in the future, the government changes the tax rate, and that change results in a rate greater than 60% of the net profits, then the parties shall agree to adjust their share of oil profits to ensure that the net income is the same, prior to the imposition of the new tax rate. The most important result of the Sudanese Government's prompt response to need for change, has been its ability to reflect the true spirit of partnership. Irrespective of whether or not the response has been for its own benefit, it is an indication of the Sudanese Government's flexibility in adjusting itself to the highly uncertain elements involved in calculating tax.

RECENT INCENTIVES FOR PETROLEUM EXPLORATION

In its efforts to attract capital and technology, Sudan has passed recently its latest Encouragement of Investment Act 1999. The aim of this Act, like its predecessors, is to assist in encouraging investment in projects which contribute to the plans of the development, and national and foreign projects, whether initiated by the public sector, private sector, cooperative sector or mixed sector. The 1999 Act expressly guarantees non-discrimination by prohibiting distinctions between these projects in granting privileges and guarantees.

The Act provides for a wide range of privileges and facilities which can be granted to investors. They differ according to the nature of the project, strategic or non strategic or, federal or state. They include a total or partial exemption from business profits tax or custom duties, allotment of land necessary for the project, grant of credit ceilings and special rates of depreciation of assets.

To serve these ends, s.17 of the 1999 Act provides for the guarantee against nationalisation, confiscation, expropriation or sequestration of investors' projects and capitals. Different rules apply for each case. Thus, while the guarantees against nationalisation and confiscation of investors' projects are made in absolute terms, sequestration of capital requires an order of a competent court. Also no expropriation of an investor's property is guaranteed except for the public good, by virtue of a law and upon payment of just compensation.

Furthermore, s.17(c) & (d) guarantee for foreigners repatriation of capital in case of non execution of the project, liquidation, disposal of the project, partially or wholly in any form, in the currency in which the capital was imported, provided that all obligations due to the Government are paid.

In case of disputes relating to investment, the 1999 Act requires disputes to be submitted to arbitration. The provisions of the Unified Convention of Investment of Arab Capitals in Arab Countries 1980, Convention on the Settlement of Investment Disputes between Arab Countries 1974, Convention on the Settlement of Investment Disputes between States and Nationals of Other States 1965, Convention for Economic, Technical, and Commercial Cooperation between Countries of the Islamic Conference Organisation 1977, and any other Convention to which Sudan is a party, are to apply to the legal dispute.

Sudan will be confronted in the future with problems similar to those faced by other producing countries. The ability to overcome these problems will depend very much on having a clear legislative and foreign investment policies which create a climate of investor confidence, and lay the foundations for trust and equitable distribution of benefits. The Government must make sure that the regulatory regime is simple, clear, and, most important of all, contain the main general principles in the legislation itself, and make them subject to regulation. This will ensure flexibility and enable the government to be adjustable and respond quickly enough to market conditions. Simplification of licensing procedures, and introduction of competition and transparency is bound to bring immediate benefits. The strategy of Sudan to adopt a new investment law with lucrative incentives is a step in the right direction. But the main immediate challenge for Sudan is political stability which is closely linked to economic prosperity and development of the country.

OIL WEALTH LAW

Law of oil wealth for the year 1998 (1)

CHAPTER I PRELIMINARY PROVISIONS

Title of the law.

This is called a law, "the law of oil wealth for the year 1998."

Repeal and saving.

2 (1) shall be repealed:

(A) the Petroleum Act of 1931,

(B) The law of oil wealth for the year 1972,

(2) in the law of the General Authority for Geological Research for the year 1986:

(A) in Article 7:

(I) repealed, paragraphs (b) and (c) and (h),

(Ii) in paragraphs (g) and (I) and (f) Delete the words "oil" and "oil" wherever it appears.

(B) in Article 21 (a).

(3) Despite the cancellation contained in items (1) and (2) remain with all regulations, orders and procedures and permits issued under those laws in effect, taking into account the point of jurisdiction and the licensing authority to be repealed or amended.

Interpretation.

3 in this Act, unless the context otherwise requires:

"Reserve" means the reserve can be calculated after the drilling, development or production of oil fields and has that part can be extracted from the hydrocarbons under the conditions prevailing economic and techniques when calculated,

"Land" means:

(A) any land within the borders of Sudan, including the regional land submerged permanently or intermittently,

(B) the continental shelf of the Sudan or the region adjacent to the sea area within the deep sea and space to be determined by law,

"Secretary-General" means the Secretary-General of the institution designated in accordance with the provisions of Article 21.

"Exploration" means all of the search for oil for the purposes of detection, including surveys and geological studies, geophysical and geochemical surveys and air tests as well as drilling and exploration and to identify the fields and that of oil,

"Production" means the extraction of oil from any field and eat the oil extracted and processed and transferred to Venatis or refinery or pipeline in the field or close to it,

"The oil" means an agreement between the institutions and companies in accordance with the provisions of Article 6,

"Development" means all operations and activities of oil and in accordance with the work programs and budgets approved in both the Convention and include the following: (a) drilling of wells, installation of plugs, drilling oblique and complete and processed for the purpose of production, (b) the design and construction, installation, operation, service and maintenance of equipment, pipelines and networks roads and other infrastructure, water, electricity and other networks, facilities and installations needed for production from these wells and extracting oil and keep it, processing, preparation and storage, gas flaring is learned from it and transfer and export of crude.

"Drilling" means the Earth's surface hole drilling, whether vertically or diagonally or horizontally and include processes that will prevent the hole from collapsing,

"Oil field" means an area of land was proved that the oil in a single layer or multiple layers and in economic quantities,

"Pipeline" means a pipeline used to transport hydrocarbons through pipes is designed according to the specifications set by the institution or agree with them and include the identification of the track line,

"Means the consolidated account closing account of the Foundation and its subsidiaries and shares in companies and institutions that contribute to the other and that for each

Of profits and losses, "financial year,

"Petroleum operations" means operations and exploration drilling, exploitation and development, production and select the fields and refining, manufacturing, storage, transport and distribution, import and export, for the oil,

"Council" means the Board of Oil origin according to the provisions of Article 14 (1),

"Warehouse" means any place licensed to oil storage or handling it, and includes in addition to the reservoirs and umbrellas for storage and contents of all means of transportation of oil and distribution stations,

"Establishment" means the Sudanese Petroleum Corporation established under the provisions of Article 18,

"The oil area" means the area which gives them the rights of oil exploration and production under the Convention on oil, clarified lines of latitude and longitude,

"Exploration area" means the area covered by the exploration license, which specifies an area to the Convention on the apportionment of the production,

"Exploration permit" means the license is awarded by the Foundation to explore for oil in accordance with the provisions of this law,

"Oil" means:

(A) All hydrocarbon natural condition, whether all the liquid densities or natural gas or gaseous material associated with the oils and products that can be produced from the earth,

(B) asphalt materials and solid hydrocarbons that can be produced directly or Bazaptha in oil or gas, (c), all material derived from hydrocarbon materials referred to in (a) and (b),

"Minister" means the Minister of Energy and Mining.

CHAPTER II OWNERSHIP OF THE OIL EXPLORATION AND LICENSING CONTROLS

State ownership of oil. (2)

4 (1) oil is located in the consignment of natural layers of the earth or the continental shelf of the Republic of Sudan's national wealth owned by the state-run national government brokered by the institution.

(2) sets out the institution of the national government share of net oil product as determined by production sharing agreements as a share of the State after deducting all expenses and commissions and assigned by the Board of the Foundation according to the provisions of Article 24 (f) of this law.

(3) No person shall explore or research or exploration or extraction of oil or any oil operations in any other place in the Republic of Sudan unless authorized to do so in accordance with the provisions of this law.

Into force of the oil and exploration license.

5 Do not be to the oil exploration license or entered into by the minister with the companies in accordance with the provisions of this Act take effect only after it agreed by the Council.

Conditions to be met by the companies.

6 should be at the conclusion of any agreement or the granting of oil exploration license to its subsidiary companies or group of oil companies or a holding, that the following conditions are met in those companies which are:

(A) technical competence and sufficient experience of the previous activity in the oil industry,

(B) the financial ability to implement its contractual obligations,

(C) its commitment to the policy of the state assessments in the field of oil,

(D) registration of a branch in Sudan,

(E) to accept and comply with any other conditions determined by the Board from time to time.

Permit for exploration.

7 (1) submit to the Secretary-General's request to obtain a license for exploration on the form established in accordance with the provisions of this Act and the regulations issued thereunder.

(2) exploration license entitles the holder to the right of entry into force and during the exploration for oil and execution of the works necessary for the purposes of license in the exploration area.

(3) Notwithstanding the provisions of clause (2) exploration license does not entitle the holder to any right to:

(A) the exploitation of oil or work on the production in the exploration area unless authorized to do so,

(B) any well drilled for the purpose of production in the exploration area unless authorized to do so under the oil deal.

Commitment of companies to continue operations exploratory

8 is not permissible for any company contracted under the agreement or granted the license to explore the retention areas license without you the work of the expedition on an ongoing basis unless granted by the Minister exception temporarily on reasonable grounds, in all cases must include any oil deal or exploration license system and the formulas to give up, so do not keep However, those companies producing fields or areas of those regions in which the exploration or those areas that companies are obliged to implement an exploration program or a developing them.

The duration of the agreement of oil.

9 (1) does not exceed the duration of the agreement, inter alia, oil in the twenty-five years in its limit for the purposes of development and production to include such periods of time to explore the stages do not exceed in the whole six years.

(2) does not exceed the duration of the exploration license for three years in maximum and shall be renewable only once for the same period.

(3) Notwithstanding the provisions of clause (2) If the licensee to fulfill all its obligations in accordance with the license conditions the Minister may at the request of the licensee has the recommendation of the Secretary-General to extend the period of validity of license for a period not exceeding two years to complete any operations Additional exploratory.

The pipeline.

10 (1) Any company contracting with the institution that establishes or manages a pipeline or shipping facilities and oil storage and export only after obtaining the approval of the minister in accordance with the requirements prescribed.

(2) to all contracting companies, which have a surplus of energy needs in the transport of oil pipelines or any other way to put at the disposal of excess capacity and the establishment of the institution may dispose of them in the manner it deems appropriate.

(3) to all contracting companies that have an oil pipe can not be transferred or any other means to place at the disposal of the enterprise that oil and institution shall be entitled to transfer or dispose of it in the manner it deems appropriate.

Exchange controls. (3)

11 companies are contracting with the Foundation for the Law of the organization dealing in foreign exchange for the year 1981 and the regulations, orders and publications issued by the Central Bank of Sudan to manage foreign exchange resources, taking into account the following:

(A) that the company is contracting right to retain abroad the amounts they receive from their share of the proceeds of oil exports, according to the oil agreement concluded with them to provide information related to the Central Bank of Sudan through the Foundation,

(B) be to the contractor the freedom to bring in free currency to do its work and the implementation of their obligations under the agreement concluded with the oil,

(C) may be to the contractor to obtain the currency of Sudan and keep it for the implementation of its contractual obligations through the sale of foreign exchange according to prevailing prices and through official channels,

(D) the Company may return to the outside Sudan amounts in excess of its requirements in accordance with the agreement concluded with the oil that is in the same currency conversion which Astjlapt by those amounts or any other currency that is convertible, after the review procedure mediated by the institution,

(E) contracting companies must be registered with the Central Bank of Sudan capital in kind and in cash as well as loans obtained for the implementation of its contractual obligations.

Data and technical information.

12 should the contractor to keep the inside Sudan, the origin of all data, information and analysis and samples resulting from petroleum operations carried out by the in Sudan and may

not be exported abroad or disposed of in any other way only after obtaining prior permission in writing from the Secretary-General to be returned their original state to Sudan again in the case of export.

Obligations of the contracting companies.

13 (1) company is committed to contracting operations in the oil to follow all the technical assets prevailing in the oil industry and in accordance with the provisions of this Act and the regulations issued thereunder.

(2) Any contractor that you work in any land utilized Kamravq public or privately owned, but after obtaining the prior permission of the Secretary-General, in coordination with the competent authorities.

(3) No Contracting Ijoslcharkp direct exploration or drilling or any other work affecting public utilities, buildings, fixed or any existing facilities only after obtaining the approval of the Secretary-General.

(4) contracting companies take into account environmental health and safety procedures and take necessary measures to prevent pollution of the environment as a result of any of the oil operations in implementation of the agreements concluded with them.

(5) subject to the contracting companies to state-imposed restrictions on production, export and domestic discharge of oil.

CHAPTER III MOBILE OIL

Section I Council of Oil

The establishment of the Council and its composition.

14 (1) Council shall be called the "Council of Oil" in charge of oil and all oil operations and the development of policy and guidelines relating to oil and the organization and supervision.

(2) The council is as follows: (4)

(A) President of the Republic Chairman

(B) and Minister of Energy and Mining Member and Vice-Chairman

(C) and Minister of Finance and National Economy Member

(D) a member of the Minister of Investment

(E) a member of the Minister of Justice

(F) Six members with competence, experience and interest in oil affairs appointed by the President of the Republic.

(3) The Secretary-General Rapporteur of the Council.

Terms of reference of the Council and its powers.

15 The Council's functions and powers, the following:

(A) goal-setting, policy development and vacation plans and programs of the oil,

(B) approve the budget of the institution and the consolidated account of profit and loss account and closing of each fiscal year, vacation profits transferred to the government and determine the reserve funds,

(C) approval of contracts with oil companies and the granting of exploration licenses,

(D) approve the plans developed by the Foundation to improve and develop ways of working methods,

(E) The granting of customs exemptions for inputs to the oil industry by the provisions of the agreements concluded,

(F) The granting of tax exemptions according to the provisions of the agreements concluded,

(G) to obtain periodic reports on the progress of the institution and may request any other reports,

(H) approve the by-laws regulating its proceedings and its meetings.

Council meetings.

16 (1) The Council shall meet periodically once every three months at least and may hold an emergency meeting at the invitation of the President.

(2) The quorum for any meeting attended by six members to be provided, including the president and his deputy.

(3) shall take decisions by majority vote of members present in the case of an equality of votes the Chairman shall have a casting vote.

Interest disclosure.

17 should each member of the Council have an interest, directly or indirectly in any matter before the Board for consideration that is conducive to the Council the nature of the interest with which it is not permissible for him to participate in any deliberation or any decision issued by the Council for that matter.

Section II Foundation

Establishment of the institution-based supervision.

18 (1) Notwithstanding the provisions of the law of public institutions for the year 1996 created a public institution called "the institution of the Sudanese oil" and have an independent legal personality.

(2) be the headquarters of the institution in Khartoum and may with the consent of the Minister, may establish branches or offices inside and outside the Sudan.

(3) organization under the supervision of the minister.

Purposes of the institution and its authorities.

19 (1) in the framework of the objectives, plans and policies are determined by the Council of the institution and the authorities the following purposes:

(A) the development of the oil wealth and proper exploitation,

(B) the management of all oil operations in the country, control and supervise the operations and be the sole concessionaire in all oil operations,

(C) the responsibility to provide the needs of the country's various oil products,

(D) within and outside the Sudan operations of exploration and the search for and producing oil and so on its own or through companies owned or jointly with others,

(E) refining the oil and filter,

(F) marketing of oil and its products and distribution,

(G) D pipelines and the establishment of storage depots and other oil installations, operation and maintenance,

(H) The transfer of oil and its derivatives, marketed inside and outside the Sudan and carry out all operations necessary to achieve this purpose,

(I) the development of specifications of oil products, review and approval, quality control,

(J) the adoption of the best ways to maintain the oil wealth,

(K) oversight of all oil operations and persons engaged in such operations in order to achieve the purposes of this law,

(L) the development of programs for the training of cadres and qualify them for the implementation of the work in the oil industry and oil operations alone or in conjunction with any other relevant jurisdiction,

(M) the establishment and ownership of oil ports, operation and maintenance to be used for the purposes of oil products in coordination and agreement with the competent authorities,

(N) conduct research and studies of all oil operations,

(O) the construction of property, plant and facilities necessary to carry out its functions and is owned and invested,

(A) borrow money from any point inside and outside the Sudan, or lent to carry out their work and the financing of projects in accordance with the conditions established by the Minister in consultation with the Central Bank of Sudan and approved by the Board, (5)

(Q) the establishment of subsidiary companies and owns stock in any corporation,

(R) enter into contracts or entering into any commitments inside and outside the Sudan in order to carry out their work,

(S) to conclude oil deals and the recommendation of the Council the granting of exploration licenses in accordance with the policies passed by the Council and be responsible for following up their implementation,

(T) any other functions that may be necessary to carry out their work.

(2) The Corporation may authorize any one to technically and financially capable to practice any of the purposes set out in clause (1) Madet when necessary.

Terms of reference of the Minister.

20 (1) The Minister shall be responsible for monitoring the implementation of policies set by the Council and respect to oversee the management of the institution and take the necessary measures to enable it to achieve its objectives on the basis of technical and commercial sound.

(2) Without prejudice to the generality of the provisions of subsection (1) regard the minister as follows:

(A) monitor the implementation of the institution of policies determined by the Council and make sure it is carrying out its terms of reference and powers on the basis of technical, commercial and sound economic,

(B) to oversee the procedures and conditions for the invitation of national oil companies and foreign participation in the negotiations with the institution regarding production sharing agreements or to obtain licenses for exploration,

(C) determine the total area that can be customized for each company or group of companies,

(D) determine the limits of oil production and export policies,

(E) leave the institution plans to develop the oil industry in various fields,

(F) determine the policies of pricing oil exporter, importer and its derivatives in consultation with the Minister of Finance and National Economy,

(G) To sign agreements on oil exploration licenses on behalf of the Foundation after the Board approval,

(H) To represent the organization in international organizations,

(I) the signing of international conventions in the field of oil after the approval of the Council,

(J) To raise the proposal of the organizational structure and conditions of service of staff of the Council of Ministers for approval by him after the recommendation of the Minister of Finance and National Economy and Minister of Labour and Public Service and Human Resources Development and the Supreme Council of wages, (6)

(K) Raise the projects administrative and financial regulations of the Council for approval,

(L) supervision of state-owned companies operating in the oil sector and the issuance of general directives concerning the policies and action plans and the companies to abide by such directives,

(M) agree to open bank accounts in local currency and foreign inside and outside the Sudan in consultation with the Central Bank of Sudan, (7)

(N) the appointment of employees of the institution on the recommendation of the Secretary-General and in accordance with regulations of the institution,

(3) The Minister may delegate any of its powers contained in clause (2) The Secretary-General or any other person in accordance with the conditions and controls which it deems appropriate.

Appointment of the Secretary-General and the terms of reference.

21 (1) The institution of a year of people with appropriate qualifications and experience appointed by the President of the Republic by decree on the recommendation of the minister that the resolution establishes the allocations and conditions of service after the recommendation of the Minister of Finance and National Economy and Minister of Labour and Public Service and Human Resources Development and the Supreme Council of the wage. (8)

(2) The Secretary General is the Chief Executive Officer is responsible to the Minister for the management of the institution and in accordance with the Council's policy and guidance, policies and decisions issued by the Minister and in particular be responsible for the proper management of funds, property and strengthen the organs, and without prejudice to the generality of the foregoing to be the Secretary-General the following powers:

(A) program development and detailed plans for the development of the institution and submitted to the Minister for approval and supervision of the implementation,

(B) take any action deemed necessary for the management of the institution, organization and conduct daily,

(C) supervision of all departments of the institution and to ensure the accuracy of performance, improvement and coordination between different departments in order to achieve harmony in the performance,

(D) the preparation of estimates of the annual budget and development budget and submit to the minister,

(E) Disbursement of funds for operating expenses in accordance with the budget of the Authority,

(F) the construction work by the Authority,

(G) represent the institution and speak on their behalf before the competent legal and other relevant bodies within the Sudan and the signing of contracts, except agreements and oil exploration licenses,

(H) preparation of recommendations relating to conditions of service of employees of the institution and presented to the Minister,

(I) to propose the organizational structure of the institution and submitted to the Minister,

(J) Any other actions are necessary to direct its terms of reference,

(3) is not permissible for the Secretary-General to conduct any substantive changes in the organs of the institution without the consent of the Minister,

(4) Secretary-General may delegate any of his powers or terms of reference for any of his aides, according to the conditions and controls which it deems appropriate.

To observe confidentiality.

22 Members of the Council and all employees of the institution into account the Secretariat in all matters related to the institution in accordance with confidentiality regulations, decisions and systems.

CHAPTER IV FINANCIAL PROVISIONS

Devolution of property.

23 (1) goes to an institution assigned by the Council of Ministers of the fixed and movable assets for oil and without prejudice to the generality of the foregoing goes to the Foundation the following:

(A) All equipment and laboratories and any other items owned by the state, relevant to oil and that as decided by the Council of Ministers,

(B) All projects of exploitation and extraction of oil Sudanese state-owned,

(C) the government's shares in existing companies, which the Council of Ministers Oiloltha of the institution.

(2) An estimate of property, rights, debts and obligations that accrue to the Corporation under the provisions of subsection (1) and include Bdvatrha amount equal to the value of the net for it.

Financial resources of the institution.

24 The financial resources of the institution:

(A) include in their books in accordance with the provisions of Article 23,

(B) stocks and shares, which contribute to the institution in companies owned wholly or in part,

(C) upon return of the net profits and net profits of its subsidiaries or contribute to,

(D) returns from the investment of its funds,

(E) borrow money,

(F) of funds allocated to them by the Council,

(G) fees and land rental, gifts and rewards (bonus) that accrue to it by the conventions of exploration and oil production.

Use the resources of the financial institution.

25 (1) use of financial resources for the Foundation to achieve its purposes only.

(2) Without prejudice to the generality of the provisions of subsection (1) use the resources of the institution in the following:

(A) management of the institution and its performance,

(B) payment of the obligations of a financial institution,

(C) to exchange all the operating expenses of the institution, including the appropriate allocation of credit for consumption and replacement.

(D) payment of corporate capital, which contributes to the establishment or contribute to the companies that subscribe to,

(E) the payment of salaries, allowances, bonuses and benefits of after-service for staff organization and remuneration of members of the Council. (9)

CHAPTER V PROVISIONS OF THE VARIETY

Customs and tax exemption.

26 (1) companies, which may be a party to the Convention on oil or those employed by contractors and engineers to import consent of the Council and in accordance with the provisions of the oil deals signed exemption from customs duties and tax in whole or in part:

(A) equipment and machinery and equipment and other resources allocated for use in petroleum operations and the recommendation of the institution,

(B) of goods and commodities, which was passed from the time of the last decisions of the Minister on a recommendation from the institution, according to the provisions of Article 15 (1) (e) of this law.

(2) The provisions of subsection (1) on goods and things that can be purchased from national products.

(3) are devices, machines and equipment for the operations of oil and goods and other articles of the customs duties in accordance with the provisions of the Customs Act 1986, when sold in the Sudan, with the consent of the institution, and everyone agreed that the association on the sale or transfer of ownership of any of the things mentioned in clause (1) to provide to the customs authorities prior to the sale or ownership statement confirming that after obtaining the approval of the Agency and pay on demand as assessed by the customs authorities of import duties only if the sale or transfer of ownership to other companies contracting with the institution, which enjoys the same exemptions.

(4) The export of oil output in Sudan and its derivatives and all kinds of goods and imported items, specified in item (1) to the outside of the duty-free.

(5) the institution shall be exempt from taxes and customs duties for machinery and equipment, materials and vehicles and machinery imported for the projects in the area of oil and with the consent of the Council.

Foundation-owned companies.

27 companies are wholly-owned institution or assisting or participating in and working in the field of oil in the governance of companies contracted to implement the provisions of this Act with respect to similar activities.

Contracting corporate accounts, books and review.

28 (1) should the contractor to retain all books and records of the business and accounting within the Sudan, taking into account the preservation of the accounting system, which consistent with the general principles of accounting known worldwide in the oil industry.

(2) The auditing of accounts and records of contractors mediated institution for the purposes of the apportionment provisions of the conventions of production.

Foundation's accounts, books and review.

29 (1) The Corporation shall notify the Council by the Minister when you open bank accounts in accordance with the provisions of the law.

(2) The Foundation reserves the calculations are correct and comprehensive income and expenses in accordance with the principles of sound accounting.

(3) organization is budget on the basis of sound accounting and balancing development with the adjournment of the Council for approval.

(4) The Foundation reserves the money to the general reserve fed from time to time from the surplus resources of the institution with the consent of the Council.

(5) The Foundation reserves the regular record of fixed assets and movable and review this record year.

Review.

30 The National Audit Office or any other auditor approved by the Auditor General and under his supervision audit of the Foundation annually. (10)

The continuity of employees of the institution.

31 oil workers continue to Ministry of Energy and Mining in the service and be absorbed into the institution as it provides the structure and functions according to the new job description.

The rule of the provisions of this law.

32 provisions of this Act prevails in case of conflict with the provisions of any other law to the extent that removes the conflict.

Crimes and punishments.

33 (1) commits an offense if that person:

(A) The exploration or search for oil without having the license for exploration or oil deal valid and issued under the provisions of this law, is punishable by imprisonment for a term not exceeding five years or fine or both, in the case of continuing to commit crime punishable by an additional fine for each day continues to commit the crime,

(B) The production of oil or attempts to do so without having the oil deal issued under the provisions of this law is punishable with imprisonment for a term not exceeding seven years or fine or both, in the case of continuing to commit crime punishable by an additional fine for each day of continuing to commit crime,

(C) The initiation of any work of the oil out of the license contrary to the provisions of the Convention or a license, punishable by a fine, in the case of the violation may continue to license revocation or to the oil exploration.

(2) any items obtained as a result of a person for committing an offense under the provisions of paragraphs (a) and (b) of item (1) shall be the property of the state is entitled to reimbursement of those things or their value and profits derived from them.

(3) Without prejudice to the provisions of clauses (1) and (2) or any other more severe penalties provided for in any other law, any person who violates the provisions contained in chapter II of this Act and the regulations issued thereunder fine.

Authority of the institution to issue directives to correct the situation.

34 If found the institution that there is a waste of materials, oil or there pursuant to endanger the lives of people or property in danger as a result of Petroleum Operations under way, notify the institution based so to correct the situation and repair the damage within a reasonable period determined by it, if not find the direction of any response from those who do so, right have to take legal action on those violations before the competent courts.

The authority to issue regulations.

35 (1) The Council shall leave the regulations necessary to implement the provisions of this law.

(2) Without prejudice to the generality of the provisions of subsection (1) may be provided in these regulations on the following issues:

(A) administrative and financial systems and technical operations related to oil,

(B) regulations on the exercise of rights granted under exploration licenses and leases,

(C) the method of collection of fees, royalties, taxes and descent of the Foundation paid by the contractor,

(D) the foundations of the Organization for the transfer of oil and gas pipelines and the uses and the rules and procedures for licensing the establishment of these lines and export facilities, storage and uses,

(E) the rules and specifications of organizing, storing and distributing petroleum products and gas,

(F) financial and administrative systems and technical issues related to the oil and financial control systems and administrative and technical contracting companies,

(G) the establishment of specialized departments of the institution and organization within the organizational structure,

(H) regulate the relationship with the companies owned by the institution and those that contribute to the taking into account the laws that govern this area,

(I) To organize technical information, records and how to prepare, preservation and storage,

(J) The composition of the specialized technical committees and terms of reference,

(K) form and manner, which is the Foundation's accounts and its budget, and organization of warehouse and rules of procurement and contracting,

(L) guarantees the security and safety and the preservation of the institution and petroleum operations,

(M) conditions of service of employees of the institution.

MINERAL RESOURCES DEVELOPMENT ACT AND MINING FOR THE YEAR 2007

CHAPTER I PRELIMINARY PROVISIONS

Name of the law.

This is called the law a "law of development of mineral resources and mining for the year 2007."

Repeal and saving.

2 The Law of Mines and quarries for the year 1972, to continue to work cheap mineral exploration and certificates of registration lookup zones absolute and mining contracts and contracts for the extraction of salt, gypsum, procedures, measures and rules, orders and regulations issued thereunder in force until repealed or amended in accordance with the provisions of this law.

Interpretation.

3 in this Act, unless the context otherwise requires:

"Exploration" means the investigation intensified and expanded in the examination of the land and the interior, by all means, geological or geophysical or geochemical or remote sensing, and all the surveys of other necessary and drilling of all types, methods and all activities that apply in the examination of the earth and its interior extensively, which lead to know the extent of material mineral ores and other mining and determine the location and the degrees and forms of their concentrations and stocks and their habitats host area search or license also includes all the necessary studies and other detailed laboratory tests for evaluation to determine the feasibility and economic exploitation,

"Research" means the total Initial investigations for minerals and mining other test surface or the interior, by all means and in particular means geological or geochemical or geophysical performed to identify the nature of mining materials from their physical properties, chemical or other or the work of drilling a test or holes to verify of the presence or possible presence,

"License" means the license granted to any natural person, legal person or to search for exploration or mining materials,

"Mining" means all operations and activities of geological and engineering types that are in the mines to track down the minerals and mining materials other collected and processed using the technologies of engineering and the physical, chemical, metallurgical, biological and otherwise the purpose of separation of the components of the elements, minerals, or concentrates or to convert it directly through any type of processors for the component metal Oosnai for commercial purposes,

"Government" means the national government,

"Rocks and industrial minerals" means all rock, metal, or a solid natural origin are above or below the earth's surface, can be converted to treatment methods of mining or various industrial product industrial or commercial. With the exception of these metals and raw materials of organic materials,

"Contract mining" means the lease granted to any natural person or legal entity of production and commercial exploitation of mineral materials,

"Committee" means the committee established under the mining provisions of Article 19,

"Director" means the Director General of Geological Research,

"Minerals" means all mineral substances of natural origin, consisting of the elements and inorganic chemical compounds and has a chemical structure and physical properties and specific situations and include precious metals,

"Precious metals" means gold and platinum group metals, silver,

"Mine" means land that contain materials mining, and it is based or underneath any operations in order to obtain materials, mining, other than materials quarries, including the land upon which the necessary facilities and assistance for the work of mining, such as roads and airports and other means of transport, offices, laboratories, workshops and warehouses used for the purposes of mining the various denominations,

"Mining materials" means the natural minerals and ores, rocks and industrial minerals and chemical elements, and rock layers and mineral deposits and precious metals , precious stones and semi-precious stones and the like, salt, gypsum, or any other material the government decides it is material mining, as well as mineral water, which are above the earth's surface or in the interior that are usable and preparation for commercial purposes and are excluded from these materials materials quarries, coal and petroleum as defined by the law of oil wealth for the year 1998 or any law that amends or replaces it,

"Quarries materials" means the rocks and stones and a concrete , sand and clay are used directly for the purposes of construction and paving of roads without the need for any processing manufacturing, which does not contain any mineral or metal can be extracted through mining and treatment recognized in the field of mining,

"Authority" means the General Authority for Geological Research,

"Ministry" means the Ministry of Energy and Mining,

"Minister" means the Minister determined by the President of the Republic.

CHAPTER II OWNERSHIP OF RAW MATERIALS AND THE ORGANIZATION OF MINING EXPLOITATION

Ownership of the materials mining.

4 are the property of the State represented in the national government all mining materials located above or below its territory or under its territorial waters or on the continental shelf and have the absolute right in the search and exploration for each mining materials and dispose of it.

Regulate the exploitation of mining materials.

5 (1) The Commission shall, in accordance with the provisions of this law by organizing the exploitation of materials and supervision of mining operations and exploration and production,

mineral exploitation and control of everything related to it from the manufacture, transfer or storage.

(2) The Commission may, that the realization of research and exploration for mining materials and related and use either stand-alone directly in this case have a right to the conservation area that perform the research work of geological or mining the length of research, exploitation, production, or to entrust it to others or in partnership with others to the conditions prescribed in this Act and the regulations issued thereunder.

Research and exploration for minerals and materials mining.

6 (1) Any person may search for minerals and mining materials to the conditions and provisions prescribed in this Act and the regulations issued thereunder.

(2) The exploration for minerals and materials mining and exploitation in the territory of Sudan, including the territorial waters of any landowner license issued in accordance with the terms and provisions prescribed in this Law.

(3) Notwithstanding the provisions of items (1) and (2) Any of the Council of Ministers upon the recommendation of the Minister, to issue a ban on exploration or mining and exploitation of any mineral or material mining are of particular importance to national economy, and in this case, cancel all exploration licenses and mining contracts previously awarded or exploitation.

(4) the Council of Ministers assigned the work of self-exploration or mining or any other means in accordance with the conditions and controls assessments.

(5) The Authority shall compensate the licensee that his license was canceled just compensation.

(6) If the licensee did not accept the compensation offered by the Commission shall constitute a tripartite arbitration in which the license is revoked and the two chosen president of the arbitral tribunal whose decision shall be bindingon the parties.

Preparation of records and to limit requests.

7 The Commission shall prepare records of the names of applicants for permission to search for different kinds of mineral substances as specified in regulations, which restrict other applications that are sent to the license in the exploration for mining materials and records of the names of owners of mining contracts.

Types of licenses and mining contracts.

8 (1) The Commission may with the consent of the Minister and to conclude licensing contracts for mining in the following manner:

(A) a general license to search for minerals and mining materials, and ensure that this license is issued has the right to enter the area covered by the license and surface sampling for the purposes of the study with the exception of those areas licensed for non-absolute as areas of exploration or mining contract which was concluded,

(B) exploration license absolute guarantee is issued has the right to prospect for minerals or mining materials in the region covered by the license, including the research of geological, geochemical, and drilling exploratory and sampling for analysis and technical studies and technological that are required by the inside or outside the Sudan,

(C) The mining, to ensure the contractor the right to obtain mining materials covered by the contract in the area authorized by all means scientific, technical and technological available to him, and marketing of such production or dispose of it by any other means in accordance with the provisions of this Act and the regulations issued thereunder,

(D) the mining small, to ensure the contractor the right to extract mineral substances covered by the contract in the region licensed by traditional means or scientific, technical and technological simple at his disposal, and marketing of such production or dispose of it by any other means in accordance with the provisions of this Act and the regulations issued thereunder,

(E) The extraction of minerals and industrial rocks, and the contractor to ensure the extraction and processing of materials from the region to be determined by the contract and marketed in accordance with the provisions of this Act and the regulations issued thereunder,

(F) A director of the licensing and exploitation contracts after the approval of the Minister on behalf of the Committee.

(2) Notwithstanding the provisions of subsection (1) The Minister may on the recommendation of the Committee to conclude special agreements with any company granting a concession to explore for any of the metals including precious metals or mining materials and exploitation on the basis of participation or the apportionment of production or any other form of conditions it deems appropriate, may also be granted under those agreements on preferential features in accordance with the Investment Promotion Law of 1999 or any other law to replace it.

(3) The Minister may cancel the licenses, contracts and agreements set forth in this Act if the licensee violates any provision of this License or the contract or the terms of the agreement or violation of this Act or any of the terms of the regulations made thereunder.

Terms of the license or contract.

9 without prejudice to any requirement of the General Conditions, shall include the license or contract the following data:

(A) metal or mineral materials, which issued the license or contract for,

(B) Area covered by the license or contract and map showing the boundaries and geographic location,

(C) The period of the license or contract and the extent to which the period of renewal,

(D) the financial capability and technical expertise,

(E) any other conditions with a special dye as determined by the regulations.

CHAPTER III MINING

Report detect when mining materials.

10 (1) Any person reveals a metal or ore from ore mining materials to inform him of the Committee in writing.

(2) The Commission shall register the right of disclosure to that person, and have a detector right of priority in obtaining a license for exploration for the metal or material mining are required to apply for the license within four months from the date of notification of the Committee on this disclosure with the completion of the terms set forth in Article 11.

(3) If the period referred to in item (2) did not make the request detector to obtain a license research priority will be given in accordance with the provisions of precedence set forth in Article 7.

Conditions to be provided in the student license.

11 required to give the student a license search or disclosure or mining contracts to:

(A) possess the technical competence and sufficient experience in the field of mining,

(B) Have the financial ability to implement its contractual obligations to the face which is approved by the Commission,

(C) is committed to the policy of the State in the field of mining and environmental protection,

(D) accompanied by the registration certificate if the student's name or work in Sudan, a branch of the company if a company from outside the Sudan,

(E) accept and fulfill any other conditions determined by the Commission from time to time,

(F) shall pay rental fees or requirements or financial contributions.

Issuance of the license and renewal.

12 (1) exploration license issued by a decision of the Minister on the recommendation of the Committee and the regulations shall specify the terms of the license and renewal.

(2) Notwithstanding the provisions of subsection (1) The Minister may not comply with the renewal of the license if it determines that the site or in part may become ready for production based on the recommendation of the Commission and the licensee to apply for contract mining in accordance with the license terms for exploration after that the Commission shall notify in writing so , as the Minister may not renew a license if it determines that the licensee has breached its obligations.

The right to license.

13 Do not permissible for the licensee in exploration that searching for ore or ores Ooumouad mining other than the raw material of mineral licensee to disclose unless crude this article or material mixed with the raw material of the licensee to disclose and can not be mining one without the other, may in this case, to obtain the approval of the Committee to add the name of this article or other mineral substances mixed Kamaadn to accompany the exploration license issued to him.

Fees and rent.

14 In addition to the fees established in accordance with the schedule attached to this law, gets all the license for exploration, research or contract for mining annual rent as determined by the regulations for each square kilometer, or any unit of measurement other by the regulations of the area of the exploration area, contract mining, and regards any part of these units standard and the whole unit.

The right to obtain a contract or mining exploitation.

15 Internally the licensee in exploration during the period of validity of the license the right to obtain a contract for the exploitation of mining, all the space exploration by the licensee or in some of the conditions and regulations stipulated in this Law and regulations issued thereunder.

Compensation.

16 (1) must be the work of the search or licensee exploration in the land of Agheiron refrain from any action that would damage the surface of the land or to deprive the owner of his property, usufruct, if the result of the currency of any damage to the surface of the land or to deprive the owner of the use of his property, is committed to fair compensation .

(2) is the valuation of compensation, by a committee formed by the minister's decision of the relevant and competent.

(3) If the refusal of the licensee or owner compensation ability of the Committee, a panel of judges representing the three parties to the conflict and chaired by the Ministry and shall specify the parties the decision of the jury.

Report in the case found traces.

17 (1) The licensee shall notify the Ministry with all losralih effects and old buildings or Crafts, whether antique or antique within the limits of the license contract as soon as find them and to cease all operations research or exploration or mining, which may cause damage to her .

(2) the ministry to address the General Assembly to consider the effects of the notification and report thereon.

(3) No licensee may continue in operations research or exploration or exploitation in the archaeological site without the approval of the General Authority for Antiquities and under control, if not approved immediately stop operations at the archaeological site or revoked license or contract.

The responsibility of the licensee.

18 Licensee shall be solely responsible to third parties for all damage resulting from its work, and upon payment of all damages that may result from lawsuits or claims, or actions taken by others in this regard.

CHAPTER IV COMMITTEE

Establishment of the Commission.

19 commission shall be created under the provisions of this law is called the "Committee for mining," be responsible to the Minister on the implementation of the provisions of this Act and the regulations issued pursuant thereto within the limits of established policy, and the Committee to submit its recommendations to the Minister to decide where.

Formation of the committee and supervision.

20 (1), constitute a Committee of the decision of the Minister, the President is a full-time and the number of members representing the ministries and relevant bodies and competent and experienced and know-how and interest in the affairs of Mineral Resources and Mining and the Commission shall have a full-time secretary for the implementation of its decisions.

(2) The Committee shall be subject to the supervision of the minister.

Committee terms of reference and powers.

21 (1) The Commission shall have the following functions and powers:

(A) policy development and vacation plans and public programs for research and exploration and production of metals and mining materials and submit them to the Minister for approval,

(B) recommend to the Minister for the granting of licenses for exploration and mining contracts to individuals, corporations and other legal entities,

(C) recommend to the Minister for the granting of customs exemptions for equipment and exploration equipment and inputs to the mining industry by licensing agreements or contracts or agreements to be submitted to the Minister of Finance and National Economy,

(D) to recommend to the Minister for the granting of tax exemptions in accordance with the provisions of the agreements concluded,

(E) enter into contracts and issue licenses after approval of the Minister on such contracts, licenses,

(F) monitoring and follow-up to the technical aspects of mining operations,

(G) follow-up to restrict the holders of licenses and contracts regulations banning the use of and follow-up training and compliance to ensure the equipment and machinery, workers and the introduction of safety measures in mines against various risks such as is usual in the mining and the preservation of the environment in accordance with the standards and provisions set forth in the legislation on this,

(H) Develop a list of internal organization of work and procedures of its meetings,

(I) any other functions or powers are necessary to perform its functions approved by the minister.

(2) The Committee may delegate any of its powers contained in this Act to the Chairman or by the Director or any of the members or any committee formed for this purpose and that the conditions and regulations as it deems appropriate.

Responsibilities of the President of the Commission.

22 (1) The Chairman of the Committee responsible for monitoring the implementation of policies established by the Commission and the respect of overseeing the work of the Committee and take necessary action to enable it to achieve its objectives on a sound footing.

(2) Without prejudice to the generality of the foregoing to be Chairman of the Committee the following powers:

(A) monitor the implementation of decisions of the Commission,

(B) to oversee the procedures and conditions for inviting individuals and national mining companies, foreign and other legal entities and to participate in the negotiations on the conclusion of the research and mining agreements or contracts or to obtain licenses and exploration of mineral materials,

(C) To raise the draft conventions of research and mining to the minister for signature after they satisfy the aspects of negotiation, legal and other necessary

(D) any other powers delegated to him by the Commission.

CHAPTER V GENERAL PROVISIONS

Appeal against decisions of the Commission.

23 Any applicant or holder of a license or contract may appeal to the Minister against any decision taken by the Commission and, within fifteen days from the date of issuance of that resolution, in the case of non-issuance of the Minister its decision in a period of thirty days from the date of filing the appeal to consider this as a rejection of the request.

Offences and penalties.

24 (1) shall be guilty of a crime if that person:

(A) The search for exploration or mining materials, but materials quarries, without having to have a valid license, shall be punished upon conviction to imprisonment not exceeding one year or a fine determined by a court, or both,

(B) The mining operations or attempts to extract the mineral substances without having the search valid license or contract mining, punishable by imprisonment for a term not exceeding two years or a fine determined by the court or both.

(2) in all the cases provided for in paragraph (b) should govern the court to confiscate metals and mining materials that were committed upon the violation and forfeiture of any profit the result of them, and any machinery and equipment used in the collection, extraction, processing and migrated crude or products inside and outside the region for the benefit of the state.

The competent court.

25 be the First Criminal Court is the court competent to hear violations of the provisions of this Law and regulations issued thereunder.

The authority to issue regulations.

26 (1) The Minister may issue regulations to implement the provisions of this law and to achieve its objectives.

(2) Without prejudice to the foregoing may provide such regulations as follows:

(A) persons or bodies that can apply for the licenses, contracts, and how to make such requests under the provisions of this law,

(B) the financial terms of rent and how to pay the fees prescribed in the schedule attached to this law,

(C) the preparation of records and to limit requests.

Table
(14 Article)

Amount of the fee in pounds	Service provided	Thread
1500 5000	(A) the application fee and to consider(B) issuance fee	1. License public research
1500 5000	(A) the application fee and to consider(B) issuance fee	2. Absolute exploration license (private)
1500 5000 10000	(A) the application fee and to consider(B) issuance fee(C) A waiver or transfer	3. Mining license
1500 4000 7000	(A) the application fee and to consider(B) issuance fee(C) A waiver or transfer	4. Small mining license
1500 4000 10000	(A) the application fee and to consider(B) issuance fee(C) A waiver or transfer	5. A license to Salinas and Aljbasat
1500 5000 10000	(A) the application fee and to consider(B) issuance fee(C) A waiver or transfer	6. License, industrial minerals and rocks
Amount of the fee in pounds	(A) of the samples even weighing 50 kg	7. Licence fees

THE MINES AND QUARRIES ACT (I972)

In accordance with the provisions of article 14 of the republican order No. 5 the president hereby makes the following act: ,

1. TITLE AND COMMENCEMENT

This Act may be cited as "The Mines and Quarries Act, 1972" and shall come into force on the date specified by the Minister by an order to be published in the Gazette.

2. REPEAL

The Mines & Quarries Ordinance 1950 is hereby repealed. All licenses and leases granted under the Mines and Quarries Ordinance 1950 and remaining in force at the date of the coming into force of this Act shall be deemed as if granted under this Act.

3. DEFINITIONS

In this Act, unless the context otherwise requires, the following expressions shall have the meanings hereby respectively assigned to them:

'The Government': means the Government of the Republic of Sudan;

'The Minister': means the Minister of Energy and Mining;

'The Board': means the Mines and Quarries Board set up under section 6 of this Act;

'Mine': means any land in, upon or under which operations are undertaken for the getting of any mineral other than Quarried Material;

'Mineral': includes all natural mineral substances (other than the agricultural surface of the land) including mineral waters lying in, upon or under land which are capable of use for manufacturing or mercantile purposes, but excludes petroleum as defined in the Petroleum Resources Development Act, 1958 or any other law which replaces it;

'Quarried Material': means rock, stone (including limestone), gravel, sand and clay;

'Quarry': means any land, in, upon or under which operations are undertaken (whether by

surface or opencast working or otherwise) for the getting of quarried material.

4. OWNERSHIP OF MINERAL RESOURCES AND QUARRIED MATERIAL Save as hereinafter mentioned, the property in all minerals and quarried materials lying in, upon or under land or under territorial waters or upon the continental shelf of the Republic of Sudan, is vested in the Government which shall have the exclusive right of prospecting for and getting such minerals.

5. PLAN FOR PROSPECTING AND DEVELOPING MINERALS The council of Ministers shall prepare the plan for the prospecting and development of Mineral resources and quarried materials of the Republic of Sudan, and the Council may delegate its powers to a special committee of ministers.

6 THE MINES AND QUARRIES BOARD

6.1 There shall be constituted a Mines & Quarries Board which shall be responsible to the Minister for carrying out the provisions of this Act in accordance with the policy laid down by the Government. The Board shall submit its recommendations to the Minister who shall take decisions upon them.

6.2 The Board shall consist of the following: The Under Secretary of the Ministry of Energy and Mining Chairman (The Director of the Geological Research Authority of Sudan shall act as chairman during his absence).

Director of the Geological Research Authority of Sudan Member

Director of the Industrial Development Department Member

Director of the Survey Department Member

Commissioner of Lands Member

Representative of Ministry of Planning Member

Representative of Ministry of Treasury Member

Representative of Ministry of Economics and Trade Member

Representative of Ministry of Interior Member

Representative of Ministry of Justice Member

Representative of Ministry of Local Government Member

Three further members among whom one member shall be from the Union of Industries to be appointed by the Minister for a term of two years, which may be renewed. The Board shall have a permanent secretary for executing its decisions.

7. LICENCES AND MINING LEASES

7.1 The board may issue, subject to the approval of the Minister, the following licences a leases:
a) A general prospecting licence, authorising the holder to enter upon and prospect for minerals in the licensed areas.

b) An exclusive prospecting licence, authorising the holder to enter upon the licensed area for the purpose of undertaking geological, geophysical, and test drilling and the getting of samples for testing their quality and feasibility.

c) A Mining Lease authorising the Lessee to get minerals from the area comprised in the lease by means of all available scientific methods, and to sell or dispose of the produced by any method not inconsistent with the provisions of this Act or any other Act.

d) A Quarrying licence authorising the holder to get quarried materials from a quarry as provided for in the licence and to sell them in accordance with the provisions of this Act or any other Act.

e) A mining lease for salt or gypsum authorising the, holder to get salt and gypsum from the area comprised in the lease and to market them in accordance with the provisions of this Act or any other laws.

1. The Board may delegate its powers to the Chairman or any regional authority in connection with kiln and quarrying licences for the getting of sand and gravel.
2. **TERMS OF LICENCES AND MINING LEASES**

Every licence or lease issued hereunder shall include the following particulars: a) The mineral or minerals or in the case of a quarrying licence the quarried materials in

respect of which it is issued; b) The area or areas comprised therein; c) The period for which it is granted including any periods for which it may be renewed; d) The conditions subject to which it is granted; e) The consideration payable therefore.

9. COMPLAINT AGAINST DECISIONS OF THE BOARD

An applicant for or a holder of a licence or lease may submit a complaint to the Minister against the decision of the board and the decision of the Minister in this respect shall be final and shall not be liabe to appeal before the courts.

10. SPECIAL LEASES AND CONCESSIONS

10.1 The Minister may after consultation with the Board enter into agreements for the getting of mineral deposits under special circumstances.

10.2 The Minister may grant special concessions under the Development and Promotion of Industrial Investment Act, 1972 to the Lessee in the areas where mining conditions and transportation are difficult or for any other considerations.

11. PENALTIES

II.la Whoever prospects for minerals (other than quarried materials) without being in possession of a valid prospecting licence issued hereunder shall be liable to a fine which may amount to £S. 500 or to imprisonment for a term which may extend to one year, or to both.

II.lb Whoever mines or attempts to mine any mineral (other than quarried material) without being in possession of a valid exclusive prospecting licence or a mining lease issued hereunder in respect of that mineral and covering the area mined or attempted to be mined shall be liable to a fine, which may amount to £S. 500 or to imprisonment for a term, which may extend to one year, or to both.

II.lc Whoever quarries materials without being in possession of a valid quarrying License-issued hereunder shall be liable to imprisonment for a term which may extend to three months or to a fine which may amount to £S. 100. Provided that it shall not be an offence for a natural person to quarry quarried materials without being in possession of such licence, if the quarried materials are required solely for his own personal use and not for gain or for use in or for the purpose of any business of his, and in such case person shall not require a quarrying licence hereunder.

II.ld Whoever being in possession of a valid licence or lease issued hereunder, commits any breach of the terms or conditions of such licence or lease shall be liable to a fine which may amount to £S. 100 and in addition the licence or lease shall be liable to cancellation.

11.2 The property in any mineral got by any person otherwise than in accordance with the provisions of this Act shall, as between such person and the Government, remain vested in the Government and such mineral or its value (including any profit made on its realisation) shall be recoverable by the Government accordingly.

12. SAVINGS

Nothing in this Act contained shall prejudice or affect:-

a) The existing and recognised customary rights of the native inhabitants of any part of the Sudan to get certain minerals in certain areas for their own benefit without grant or licence from the Government;

b) The rights and liabilities under the existing law of private owners or occupiers of the surface of any land affected by the provisions of this Act in respect of such surface.

13. POWER TO MAKE REGULATIONS

13.1 The Minister may make regulations for carrying out the Provisions of this Act and for, the fulfilment of its aims.

13.2 Without prejudice to the generality of the aforesaid, the regulations may provide for:

a) the persons or organisations by whom and the manner in which applications for, licences and leases under this Act may be made.

b) the fees to be paid on any such application and the amount, which shall be allotted to training, research and development in mining activities.

c) the financial obligations (by Royalties or otherwise) subject to which licences and leases shall be granted.

THE MINES AND QUARRIES REGULATIONS (1973)

In exercise of the powers conferred on him by Section 13 of the Mines and Quarries Act, 1972 the Minister of Energy and Mining hereby makes the following Regulations:

1. TITLE

These regulations may be cited as “the Mines and Quarries Regulations, 1973”.

2. REPEAL

The Mines and Quarries Regulations, 1959 are hereby repealed; but notwithstanding that all the rights granted or decisions made under those regulations shall remain in force and be deemed as if granted or made under these regulations.

3. DEFINITIONS

In these Regulations, unless the context otherwise requires, the words and expressions appearing herein shall have the same meaning as set out in section 3 of the Mines & Quarries Act 1972.

4. APPLICATIONS FOR LICENCES

4.1 Applications for general prospecting licences, exclusive areas registration certificates, mining leases, salt and gypsum leases and quarrying licences shall be made and contain the particulars provided for in the forms set out in the First Schedule attached to these regulations.

4.2A fee of £S. 5 shall be payable by the applicant on each such application.

4.3 Where the applicant is a company or a partnership, evidence of registration in accordance with the laws of the Sudan shall accompany the application.

1. Where the applicant is an alien, or a company incorporated Outside the Sudan, no mining lease shall be granted to the applicant until he forms and registers a company in the Sudan in accordance with the Sudanese Companies Law.
2. **LICENCES AND LEASES FORMS:**

Minerals Prospecting Licences, Mining leases, Salt and Gypsum lease, Exclusive Areas Registration Certificates and Quarrying Licences shall be granted on the prescribed forms shown in Sections I, II, III, IV, V of the Third Schedule attached to these Regulations.

6. DEMARCATION OF AREAS

Lease areas, quarrying licence areas and exclusive prospecting areas shall be demarcated in accordance with the provisions contained in the Second Schedule attached to these Regulations.

1

7. SPECIAL PROVISIONS AS TO PROSPECTING LICENCES

7.1 Where in any case, two or more holders of prospecting Licences issued in accordance with the Mines and Quarries Act, 1972 apply for registration of an exclusive prospecting area thereunder, the whole or part of which is included in more than one of those applications, the Board shall, unless in its opinion there are adequate reasons to the contrary, prefer the applicant whose application was first received.

7.2 The Board may at any time, without giving reasons, exclude from a prospecting licence any part of the area comprised therein and the licensee shall, on receipt of notification of such exclusion, cease to prospect in the excluded area, but in the case of an exclusive prospecting area he shall be entitled, as from that date, to a proportionate reduction of the annual rent payable under the licence.

7.3 Any mineral obtained by a licensee in the course of prospecting under a prospecting licence or the course of proving an exclusive prospecting area thereunder, shall be the property of the Government.The licensee shall hold the mineral to the disposal of the Government and shall not remove it or dispose of it, without the written consent of the Government, save only the amounts taken for the purpose of examination and analyses.

7.4 The fee for a licence shall he £S. 50 and £S. 25 for its renewal.

1. The annual rent in respect of an exclusive prospecting area shall be £S. 15 per square. kilometre or any part thereof, and shall be payable in addition to the licence fee.
2. **SPECIAL PROVISIONS AS TO MINING LEASES**

8.1 A mining lease shall only be granted to a holder of a prospecting licence covering the area in question. Nevertheless, the Minister, on reasonable grounds, may invite tenders for mining leases or grant a mining lease, by a special agreement to a person not holding such prospecting licence.

8.2 The area of a mining lease shall not exceed 476 feddans, provided that the Board may, taking into consideration the nature of the mineral or minerals to be mined and the experience and compectence of the applicant, authorize an increase of that area.

8.3 The lease area shall be rectangular in shape and its width shall not be less than one fifth of its length.

8.4 The annual rent shall be £S. 2 per feddan, provided that the minimum rent payable for any mining lease area shall be £S. 20.

1. The rate of royalty shall not exceed 7% of the value of the metals or minerals produced at the average world market price.
2. **SPECIAL PROVISIONS AS TO QUARRYING LICENCES**

9.1 The area of a quarrying licence shall not exceed 100 feddans and it shall be of square or rectangular shape and in the latter case its width shall not be less than one fifth of its length.

9.2 The annual rent shall be £S 8 per feddan or any part thereof provided that the minimum rent for any quarrying area shall not be less than £S. 20.

2

1. The annual rent for brick kilns shall be £S. 10 for any area not exceeding two feddans and five pounds for any additional feddans or any part thereof.
2. Any licensee for the production of cement shall pay annually on first day of July, a royally at the rate of Pt. 1 per ton of clinker produced during the previous twelve months.

1. The government may, if it is proved that this royalty is less than any other royalty payable on each, cubic metre of limestone, sand or gravel or clay, collect the higher rate.
2. **POWERS OF THE DIRECTOR OF THE GEOLOGICAL RESEARCH AUTHORITY OF SUDAN**

11.1 The Director of GRAS shall have the power to verify all applications submitted to the Board and to ensure their compliance with the conditions and particulars required and to take any action he considers necessary before submitting such applications to the Board.

11.2 The Director of GRAS shall sign on behalf of the government all licences and Leases approved by the Board.

11.3 The Board may delegate to the Director of GRAS its powers at any time as it sees fit.

11.4 The Director of GRAS or his authorised agents shall have the power to inspect all mines and quarries for the purpose of following the progress of work and production, and to ensure the compliance with these Regulations or the Mines and Quarries Act, 1972 by license and lease holders.

Made under my hand. This Tenth day of January 1973. Minister of Energy and Mining.

HIGHLIGHT OF THE FINAL CONCESSION AGREEMENT

DEFINITIONS:

Final Agreement: is the agreement to be negotiated and concluded between the Government of Sudan as First Party [FP] and any potential competent investor as Second Party [SP] based on the General [Highlight] given below. Effective Date: means the date of signature of this Agreement GRAS: means the Geological Research Authority of the Sudan, the authorized governmental institution under the Ministry of Energy and Mining.

Grant of Exploration Rights and Terms: § The [SP] shall be granted an exclusive prospecting licence to prospecting for.........and associated metals and minerals in .... Block. There shall be an initial exploration period of three (3) years with two (2) extensions of one (1) year each.. § At any time during the exploration period the [SP] may voluntarily relinquish all or any part of the concession area or withdraw from its commitments under this agreement by providing the [FP] with at least sixty (60) days' written notice of its intention to do so, provided that all the [SP]'s obligations incurred in terms of this agreement up to the date of such withdrawal have been met. § At the end of the initial exploration period the [SP] shall relinquish [50%] of the original concession area and [50%] of the remaining area at the end of each one [1] year extension thereof. At the end of the entire exploration period the [SP] shall relinquish the remainder of the concession area not then converted into a Mining Lease [s] or Mineral Discovery Area [s].

Work Programme and Budget during the exploration period: § The [SP] shall commence exploration not later than six [6] months after the effective date. GRAS shall make available to the [SP] all pre-existing information with respect to the concession area. § The [SP] shall spend a minimum sum of US Dollars ....on exploration operations during the first exploration year. For the subsequent explorations years expenditure shall be agreed upon between the two parties according to the progress of work.. § In the event that no mineral discovery is made by the end of the exploration period or in the event that the [SP] surrenders its exploration rights under this agreement prior to such time, the [FP] shall not bear any of the aforesaid costs and expenses incurred by the [SP]. § The [SP] shall advance all the necessary funds for the execution of the agreed upon exploration work programme. § The [SP] shall have the right to keep foreign currency transferred from outside the Sudan in special foreign currency accounts opened for the purpose of financing its activities

contemplated in this Agreement with commercial banks of its choice in the Sudan, and to convert foreign currency to Sudanese currency, at rates determined by the Bank of Sudan, as and when required.

§ The [SP] shall supply GRAS with periodic statements of exploration activities showing costs incurred.

Operation After Commercial Discovery: § Once a feasibility study has been completed and a decision is taken to develop and exploit the discovered ore bodies, the [FP] and the [SP] shall jointly incorporate a mining company [MC] in terms of the Sudanese Companies Act of 1925 and subject to the laws and regulations in force in the Republic of the Sudan within [90] days after the aforesaid decision. The Memorandum of Association of the [MC] shall be annexed to the Final Agreement. § The [MC] shall be the holder of the Mining Lease[s] then issued to cover the whole area[s] capable of commercial Production. Issuance of the Mining Lease[s] by the [FP] shall be within thirty [30] days after incorporation. § The term of the Mining Lease[s] shall be twenty-one [21] years renewable based on convincing evidences. § Each Mining Lease is two [2] square kilometers in addition to any land and surface right needed for infrastructures required by the [MC] to maintain its operations. § The [MC] shall entrust its mining operation to its General Manager who shall be nominated by the [SP]. § The (MC] shall at all times and without any limitation, tax or duty be free to transfer, in any freely convertible currency to any of its shareholders any funds representing its share of the profits or repayment of loans. § The [MC] shall have the right to export and sell metals and minerals produced from its mines overseas and locally. A necessary percentage of the export returns may be kept abroad in hard currency accounts in banks of international repute and of the company's choosing for the purposes of maintaining productive mine outputs by the direct payment to overseas suppliers of goods and services, repayment of loans, interest, financial charges royalties & dividends. § The [SP] and/or the [MC] may bring into the Sudan non-Sudanese expatriate personnel as in the judgment of the

[SP] and/or the [MC] is required to carry out operations efficiently and successfully and where Sudanese personnel with the appropriate qualifications skills and experience are not available.

POLLUTION AND CONSERVATION OF ENVIRONMENT:

The [SP] and/ or the [MC] shall conduct its operations with due regard to the environment and immediately surrounding communities. The [SP] and/or the [MC] shall procure the drawing up of an environmental Protection and Management Programme, which shall accord with standards acceptable to Third Party financiers and approved by the [FP] and /or the [MC] shall abide by the provisions thereof.

TAX, DIVIDENDS, ROYALTIES, GOVERNMENT PARTICIPATION:

§ The [SP] and/or the [MC] shall be subject to the taxation regime [including law, rate and practice] in force in the Sudan as at the Effective Date. § The [MC] shall for accounting purposes be entitled to amortize all capitalized

pre-productions costs over an agreed upon period. § All Royalties payable to the [FP] shall be tax-deductible § It shall be the sole prerogative of the [MC], through its Board of Directors to determine

the timing and extent of the issue of any dividends by the [MC]. The Bank of Sudan shall be notified of all foreign currency transfers relating to dividends.

§ With effect from-the commencement of commercial production , the [FP] shall be entitled to a royalty equals to ....% of the total sale revenue of ....and associated metals and minerals.

§ The [FP] shall be entitled to a.........% interest in the [MC] which shall consist of: i- a ....% free carried interest, and ii-a........% repayable carried interest.

§ The [FP] shall be entitled, free of any payment obligation, to have discharged on its behalf by the [SP] the subscription price of ......% of all shares issued by the [MC], and extended on its behalf by the [SP] 10% a of all shareholder loan funding raised by the [MC].

§ The . ...% repayable carried interest shall be treated as a loan from the [SP] to the [FP] repayable in the manner described below: i-Shall be deemed advanced on the dates on which the [SP] subscribes for shares

in, or advances shareholder loans to, the [MC]. ii-Shall bear interest at a rate of LIBOR Plus 2% per annum. iii-Shall be repayable , until fully paid up, only from:

-.........% of the dividends or other distributions received on shares the

subject of the repayable carried interest. -.........% of interest received in respect of any shareholder loan the subject of the repayable carried interest. -........% of any principal repayments received in respect of any shareholder

loan the subject of the repayable carried interest -100% of proceeds on disposal of the repayable carried interest; or -100% of any Liquidation proceeds in respect of the repayable carried interest; or

TAXES AND CUSTOM EXEMPTIONS:

1-During the exploration period the [SP] shall be exempt from any defense or like tax, sales or service tax, regional or local taxes, capital gains tax, Depreciation tax and import /export duties of all equipment or materials required by the [SP] for the conduct if its activities in terms of the final Agreement. 2- The [MC] shall be exempt from the following taxes and duties.

i-Tax on turnover, defense tax, regional or local taxes . ii- Business profit tax from incorporation until the termination of [10] years period. iii-Any withholding profit tax. iv- Reduction of other taxes. v-Exemption of custom duties in regard to the import/export of all equipment and materials required by the [MC] for the conduct of its activities in terms of this agreement.

DISPUTES AND ARBITRATION:

Any dispute, controversy or claim arising out of or relating to this Agreement between the [FP] and the [SP] and /or the [MC] which can not be settled amicably shall be settled by arbitration rules in accordance with the rules of conciliation and arbitration of the International chamber of Commerce. The award of the arbitrators shall be final and binding on the parties and subject to no appeal.

LAWS AND GOVERNING LAW:

§ The [SP] and/or the [MC], its agents and subcontractors shall observe, comply with and abide by Sudanese Laws and regulations for the safe and efficient performance of operations carried out for the execution of this Agreement, including but not limited to sanitary regulations, for the conservation of the environment and natural resources of Sudan, security and employment Laws and regulations.

§ This Agreement shall be governed and construed in accordance with the Laws and regulations of the Republic of the Sudan. However, in the event of any contradiction between the Laws and regulations aforesaid and the provisions of this Agreement, the provisions of this Agreement shall rule.

Additional Provisions to be addressed and included in the Final Agreement:

1-Definitions

2- Annexes: -Description of the concession area. -Draft of Memorandum of Association of the [MC] -Accounting Procedure. -Framework of Environmental Protection and -Management Programme.

3- Relinquishments of Concession Area. 4- Local Contractors and Locally manufactured Materials. 5- Books of Account.

6- Records, Reports and inspection. 7-Force Majeure. 8- Breach of Agreement and right to terminate. 9- Indemnity.

10- Confidentiality. 11-Assignment. 12-Office and Service of Notice.

THE GEOLOGICAL RESEARCH AUTHORITY OF THE SUDAN(GRAS)

MEMORANDUM OF UNDERSTANDING(MEMO)

This Memorandum of Understanding (MEMO) is made and entered into this day the ……...............................between the Director General of the Geological Research Authority of the Sudan (GRAS) as the First Party and ………………………………………………………………..as the Second Party for the reservation of concessionary rights for the exploration, development, exploitation and disposal of…………………and associated metals and minerals within the area given the name…………………………….and referred to as block number……..(Area).

WITNESSETH

Whereas, All minerals in their natural state in the Repbulic of the Sudan are the property of the State; and

Whereas, The Government the Repbulic of the Sudan wishes to promote the exploration for, development and exploitation of those minerals; and

Whereas, the First Party and the Second Party are desireous to enter int a contract to provide for the exploration, development, exploitation and disposal of ....and associated metals and minerals within the abovementioned Area in the the Repbulic of the Sudan; and

Whereas, The Minister of Energy & Mining, on behalf of the Government of the Republic of the Sudan is, in terms of the Mines & Quarries Act, 1972, entitled to grant the the exploration and mining concessions aforesaid and is, in terms of the Encouragement of Investment Act, 2000, entitled to grant the privileges thereof.

Now, therefore, the Geological Research Authority of the Sudan (GRAS) and the Second Party agreed upon the following, as basis for the proposed final agreement for the exploration, development, exploitation and disposal of ....and associated metals and minerals, within the abovementioned Area:

1-The Government of the Repbulic of the Sudan will grant the

Second Party subject to the terms, covenants and conditions that shall be agreed upon by the Parties in the final Agreement, an exclusive authorization to prospect for.....................and

associated metals and minerals in the Area where no such concession already exists.

2-Starting from the commencement of the production of

.....................and associated metals and minerals, the

Government shall be entitled to a royalty of 7% of the total gross production of ....and associated metals and minerals.

3-There shall be an Initial Exploration Period of …………….. years starting from the Effective Date of the Agreement (the date of signature of the Final Agreement). Two successive extensions of one(1) year each to the initial exploration period each shall be granted to the Second Party at its option upon a written application to GRAS prior to the expiration of the initial period . The

Agreement shall be terminated If no Commercial Mineral Discovery is notified to the First Party by the end of the Exploration Period.

4-The Exploitation Period shall be twenty-one(21) years from the date of the first Commercial Production. This period may further be renewed for an agreed upon period of time on the same terms if needed and provided that the Company is not in breach of its obligations in terms of the Agreement.

5-The Second Party shall bear and pay all Exploration, Development and Exploitation Costs and expenses, required for carrying out all such activities and operations under the Agreement. In the event of Commercial Production, the Second Party shall be entitled to recover all costs and expences in the following manner:-

a] Operating Expenditure, is to be recovered in full (after deduction of royalty).

b] ....% of the remaining revenue shall go to the recovery of exploration and exploitation (including development) expenditure and any other expenditure.

c] ....% of the remaining revenue shall be divided by the Government of the Repbulic of the Sudan and the Second Party according to their respective shares in the Company.

6-If no Commercial Discovery is established by the end of the Exploration Period, the Government of the Repbulic of the Sudan shall not bear any of the aforesaid costs and expenses incurred by the Second Party.

7-The Second Party shall prepare an annual exploration work programme and Budget for excuting the activities it proposes to carry out in the Area. The Exploration work programme and Budget shall be subject to revision and acceptance by the First Party. The work programme and Budget shall at least be sufficient to satisfy the Second Party's minimum expenditure obligations for the period it covers.

a) The Second Party shall spend a minimum sum of...U S Dollars(US$..............) on Exploration operations and activities related thereto during the first Exploration Year.

b) Thereafter, the Second Party, in each subsequent Exploration Year, shall be obliged to prepare an annual exploration work programme and Budget for excuting the activities it proposes to carry out in the Area. The Budget shall at least be sufficient to satisfy the Second Party's minimum expenditure obligations for the period it covers.

8-On Commercial Discovery, the Second party and the Government of the Repbulic of the Sudan shall enter into a partnership agreement and such agreement shall be subject to the laws and regulations in force in the the Republic of the Sudan. a) A joint Mining Company will be incorporated in terms of the laws and regulations in force in the Sudan. b) The First Party shall be entitled to a ....% interest in the Company which shall consist of a ....% "free carried interest" and a ....% repayable carried interest. c) The Second Party shall be entitled to ....% interest in the Company.

9-Sudanese nationals should be employed and trained to participate in all operations in the Sudan and abroad for higher qualification.

10-The Government of the Repbulic of the Sudan agrees to provide the necessary required land in the mining area for the installation of machinery, plant, offices, and other buildings at nominal charges according to the Mines & Quarries Act, 1972.

11-Tax holiday shall be granted according to the Ecouragement of Investment Act, 2000 and any other provisions granted by it.

12-The Second Party shall be entrusted with the management of the project through an Exploration Management Committee, composed of two members from each party.

13-The project shall be exempt from custom duties on all equipment, materials, vehicles...etc and together shall enjoy all other incentives included in the Ecouragement of Investment Act, 2000.

14-The Second Party shall be free to employ competent foreign experts not available in the Sudan, subject to the approval of the Exploration Management Committee.

15-The Company shall, after consultation with the Government of the Repbulic of the Sudan, prepare to carry out specialized training programmes for all of its Sudanese employees engaged in the operations with respect to applicable aspects of the mining industry. The Company undertakes to replace gradually its expatriate staff by qualified Sudanese nationals as they are available.

16-The Second Party shall pay to GRAS during the Exploration Period US$...................... for training and US$...................... for technical assistance and a lesser amount to be agreed upon during the mining period to be paid annually by the Company.

17-Within the lifetime of this MEMO, the Government of the Repbulic of the Sudan and the Second Party shall sit together to begin serious negotiations to reach and sign a Final Agreement detailing the above provisions.

18-Following the signature of the Final Agreement the Second Party shall start shipping equipment and machinery for the commencement of work within.......................months from the Effective Date.

19-This Memorandum is valid for a period of................months from the date of its signature.

FOR THE GEOLOGICAL RESERCH FOR THE SECOND PARTY
AUTHORITY OF THE SUDAN (GRAS)

....
DR. OMER MOHAMED KHEIR ....
DIRECTOR GENERAL ....
DATE .... DATE ....

PROCEDURES FOR THE ACQUISITION OF AN EXPLORATION AND MINING RIGHTS IN AN AREA

Normally, the procedure for acquisition of an exploration and mining concession area starts by a visit of an expert(s) representing the intending party to the Geological Research Authority of the Sudan (GRAS). Whereupon, information concerning the various areas of interest is made available to the expert(s). Such verbal and written information, may enable a preliminary selection of a block, or an area composed of more than one block, that suites the investor or company needs. The selection process could further be enhanced by permitting a short field visit to the area(s) if so required by the expert.

Immediately after the field visit to the chosen area and where a positive opinion is formulated about any of the blocks by the expert, a memorandum of understanding **(MEMO)** may be signed between GRAS and the Investor. The **MEMO** is normally valid for a period of two to three month and deals with some major issues of importance if any future Concession Agreement is to be concluded between the parties in relation thereto.

It is recommended that before the expiry date of the **MEMO,** the Investor and GRAS, start negotiating with each other, so as to frame and build a detailed working agreement that determines the rights and obligations of each party, all through from exploration to exploitation and up to mine closure. When such an agreement is finalized, it is then goining to be signed, on behalf of the Government of the Sudan, by the Minister of Energy & Mining (as the First Party) and the Investor (as the Second Party). From the signature date, the Investor will be granted the block or area selected under the terms, covenants and conditions set out in the Agreement.

The Agreement grants the Investor the privileges contemplated in The Encouragement of Investment Act, 2000. It also gives the Investor the right to explore the Concession Area(s) for an Exploration Period of two to three years extendable for two more years.

> If on the bases on the Exploration activities during the Exploration Period, an economically viable ore deposit was discovered, a Mining Company between the Parties, has to be incorporated in terms of the Companies Act, 1925 of the Republic of the Sudan. The Company will be granted Mining Lease(s), each of two square
>
> kilometres, as may be required for covering the whole area capable of Commercial Production.

The Investor should provide enough guarantee for financing all phases of Exploration and Exploitation activities.

If the Investor feels confident about the potentialities of the area he selects, negotiations for concluding a final Concession Agreement could start right from the beginning and, thus, no need for a **MEMO** in this case.

THE INVESTMENT (ENCOURAGEMENT) ACT, 1999

Be it hereby passed, by the National Assembly, and assented to, by the President of the Republic, in accordance with the provisions of the Constitution of the Republic of Sudan 1998, the following Act.

CHAPTER 1: PRELIMINARY PROVISIONS TITLE AND COMMENCEMENT

1. This Act may be cited as the, "Investment (Encouragement) Act, 1999," and shall come into force as from the date of signature.

Repeal and saving

2. The investment (Encouragement) Act 1996, shall be repealed, provided that all the regulations and orders made and measures taken, thereunder, shall remain in force as if they were made or

taken under the provisions of this Act, until repealed or amended.

Provisions of the Act to prevail

3. The provisions of this Act shall, in case of inconsistency with the provisions of any other law, prevail to the extent of removing the inconsistency between them.

Application

4. The provisions of this Act shall apply, as to such extent as may achieve its objects thereof; provided that the Provisions of the same shall not prejudice such privileges, exemptions and otherwise of guarantees, prescribed to the projects existing at the time of coming into force of this Act .

Not-with-standing the provisions of sub- section (1) , all exemptions given to the imports of projects according to the previous investment laws shall be revoked, and the provisions of section 11 here-to shall apply there-to provided that the existing projects at the coming into force of this Act which are regulated by special Agreements concluded with the government of the Sudan, shall be exempted.

Interpretation

5. In this Act, unless the context otherwise requires, : "Competent Minister", means any of the Federal ministers, " Invested Money", means: The local currency paid by the Investor to be used in the establishment, operation, modernization, rehabilitation or expansions of the project,

The foreign convertible currency transferred through one of the banks registered with the Bank of Sudan, to be used in the establishment, operation, modernization, rehabilitation or expansion of the project,

The local currency, by which satisfaction, upon the approval of the competent bodies, is made to meet obligations due for payment to the Investor, in foreign currency, where the same is used in the establishment , operation, modernization, rehabilitation or expansion of the project,

The Corporeal capital and any other rights, such as mortgages, debt securities and all the similar rights, dividends, shares and debentures pertaining to companies, and any form of participation therein, the machinery, equipment, apparatuses, materials and other requisites and the means of conveyance imported, from abroad, or the local ones , for the establishment, operation, modernization, rehabilitation or expansion of the project,

The incorporeal rights and intellectual property rights, trade marks, patents, industrial designs, which are used in the project; provided that such rights are registered, in accordance with the provisions of the law pertaining to each, and owned by the investor, or licensed to use the same, on the part of the proprietor thereof, profits as may be achieved by the project, where the capital of the project is completed therewith, or invested into any other project,

"Investor " means the person who invests his money, in accordance with the provisions of this act, in any project whether he is a Sudanese or non-Sudanese,

"Project", means any economic activity, whatever its legal form may be, which is included in to any of the investment fields, set out in this Act, and such project which may be prescribed by the Council of Ministers in accordance with the objects of encouragement of investment provided for by virtue of section 6, and the approval of such project shall take place in accordance with the provisions of this Act.

"The Ministry " means the Ministry of National Industry and investment,

"The Minister " means the Minister of National Industry and Investment.

"The Minister Concerned " means any of the Federal Ministers.

"The State Minister " means the state minister to be determined by the Council of Ministers of the state to be concerned with the investment.

CHAPTER 2: ENCOURAGEMENT OF INVESTMENT

Objects of Encouragement of Investment

6. This Act aims at encouraging investment in such projects as may achieve the objects of the development plans policies and investment initiatives by the Sudanese and non-Sudanese private sector, co-operative, mixed and public sector: and without prejudice to the generality of the foregoing, it aims at the encouragement of investment in the projects of any of the fields set out in section 7, and the rehabilitation projects

Fields of Investment

7. This Act encourages, investment, in the fields of agricultural, animal and industrial activities, energy and mining , transport, communication, tourism and environment, storage, housing, contracting, infrastructure, economic, administrative and consultative services, information technology, education, health, water and culture and information services and any such other field , as the Council of Ministers may specify.

Prohibition of discrimination between projects

8. For the purposes of this Act, no discrimination shall be made between invested money, by reason of its being local, Arab or foreign or by reason of its being public, private, co-operative or mixed sector.
No Discrimination shall be made between such similar projects, as may be specified by the regulations, with respect to granting privileges or guarantees.

Chapter 3: Privileges and Guarantees

Branch1 Strategic Projects

9.
(a) Investment, in the following fields, shall be deemed strategic investment, namely those:

relating to infrastructure, roads , ports, electricity, dams communications, energy, transport, contracting business, education, health ,tourism and information technology services and water projects;
relating to extraction of subterranean and deep seas' wealth;
agricultural, animal and industrial production;
crossing more than one state;
Any other fields, as the Council of Ministers may prescribe.

(b) The regulations shall specify the strategic projects in the fields provided for in sub- section (1).

Branch2 Privileges Exemption from taxes

10. Subject to the provisions of section 19, such strategic project, as may be specified by the regulations , shall enjoy, after being registered in accordance with the provisions of the laws organizing the same the exemption, from the business profits tax for a period not less than ten years, which shall commence, as of the date of commencement of commercial production, or practice of the activity , and the Minister may increase the period, mentioned in this sub-section, as he may deem fit;
Subject to the provisions of section 19, the minister may grant the none strategic project as may be specified by the regulations, after being registered in accordance with the laws organizing the same, exemption from the business profits tax for a period not exceeding five years which shall commence as of the date of commencement of commercial production, or practice of the activity, and the minister may increase the period, mentioned in this sub-section for another period not exceeding five years.

Exemption from custom fees

11. Subject to the provisions of section 19, the strategic and none - strategic project specified by the regulations after being registered accordion to the laws organizing the same ; shall enjoy the customs privileges as may be decided by the Council of Ministers.
Notwithstanding the provisions of sub-section (1), the customs privileges, with regard to Vehicles, cars, Mini Buses and station cars, shall be granted as specified by the regulations.
The Council of Ministers on the recommendation of the minister may amend the specified customs privileges wherever he thinks fit.

Project granted the privileges of allocation of land and depreciation account

12. The Minister may grant the strategic and non-strategic project, in co-ordination with the bodies concerned, from such lands , as may have been planned by the competent bodies;
The privilege of depreciation account of the assets, as to such renewal value, as may be specified by the regulations and in accordance with the circuits of operational work;
Consider any such loss , as may have occurred, during the period of exemption, provided for in section 10 as if such loss have occurred during the last year of that period .

Grant of privileges to state projects

13. The state's minister may grant the state's project, as may be specified by the regulations, the following privileges:

total, or partial exemption, from taxes and fees, as may be levied by a state's, or local law, for a period not exceeding five years; provided that he may, upon the approval of the state's Council of Ministers, extend such exemption for anther similar period;
any other state's taxes, or fees, as may later be levied on the project;
allocation of the land necessary for the state's project, at the encouragement price, in co-ordination with the bodies concerned, from the lands allocated by the competent bodies.

Grant of federal privileges to state projects

14. The Minister, upon the recommendation of the state's minister, may grant a state's project the privileges provided for in section 10.
The state's minister , upon delegation by the minister, may grant a state's project the privileges, provided for in section 10, as to such condition and safeguards, as the minister may deem fit.

No taxes or fees to be levied on federal projects

15. No state, or locality shall levy any state's, or local taxes, fees or rates, on any investment project federally licensed, during the period of the tax exemption , provided for in sections 10 and 11, save in consideration of such services, as may be of public nature, performed by the state or the locality.

Preferential privileges

16. The Minister may grant preferential privileges to such projects, as may satisfy any of the following features:
direct investment towards the less developed areas;
assist in the development of export capabilities of the country;
contribute to achievement of integrated rural development;
create great chances of work;
strive to develop scientific and technological research;
re-invest the profits thereof.
For the purposes of sub-section (1), privileges mean any of the privileges provided for in sub-section (1), privileges mean any of the privileges provided for in section 10, or 11, with respect to the size, extent, or term thereof, as the regulations may specify.

Branch 111 Guarantees Investment guarantees

17. An Investor shall enjoy the following guarantees:
he non-nationalization, or non- confiscation of his project, non-acquisition, of all, or part of the estates of the project thereof, or his investments, for public interest, save by law and in consideration of just compensation;
the non- attachment, non-confiscation , non-custody or non-sequestration of the property of his project; save under a judicial order.
the remission of the invested money , in case of the non-execution of the project, at the outset , liquidation, or disposal of the same, in any of the ways of disposal totally or partially in the currency in which it has been imported; on condition of satisfying all the obligations legally due thereon, and in the case of non-execution of the project, at the outset, machinery, equipment, apparatuses, means of conveyance and other requisites, which have been imported for the project, may be re-exported, whenever all the obligations, mentioned in this paragraph have been satisfied;
the remission of the profits and the cost of financing for the foreign capital, or loans, in the currency in which such capital or loan has been imported, at the date of accrual, after payment of the obligations legally due on the project;
the import of such raw materials, as the project may need, and export of the products thereof, after the automatic registration, of the investment project, on to the Exporters and Importers Register.
For the purposes of paragraph (c) of sub-section (1), the money invested, in foreign currency, into the project, shall be specified, and the elements thereof shall be valued, upon the approval of the Minister, and shall be registered, with the Bank of Sudan.

Protection of the privileges and guarantees

18. Notwithstanding the provisions of any other law, no administrative body shall refrain from implementing the privileges and guarantees, granted under the provisions of this Act

Chapter 4: Requirements of Investment Issue of license to the Investor to establish a project

19. Subject to the provisions of section 4, no person shall establish any project in the Sudan save after obtaining a license therefore from the minister or the state minister as the case may be in

accordance with the provisions of this Act.
Subject to the provisions of subsection (1), no license shall be granted for foreign or mixed investments by the states save after approval of the Minister.

Presentation of Feasibility study of the project

20. No project shall be granted license, nor shall it be granted any such privileges and guarantees, as may be set out in this Act, save after presenting a technical and economic feasibility study of the project.

Request of grant of license and privileges

21. The application for the grant of license to any project , or of any of the privileges provided for in this Act, shall be presented, on the prescribed form as follows:

strategic and non-strategic federal projects, to the ministry;
strategic and non- strategic state's project, to the state minister.

Grant of license

22. The Ministry or the state ministry shall , upon receipt of a complete license application, for any project, transfer the application to the federal competent minister, or the state's minister, as the case may be, within one week, to obtain the preliminary approval of establishing the project.
The federal competent, or state minister, as the case may be, shall determine on the application for preliminary approval, and send the same , to the Ministry, or state ministry, as the case may be, within seven days of the date of receipt of such application.
In case of not sending the preliminary approval in the period provided for in sub-section (2), the minister, or the sate minister shall determine on the application after lapse of such period.
In all cases, the minister, or the state minister, as the case may be, shall determine on the license application within a period not exceeding thirty days, of the date of receipt of the complete application from the investor.
Every applicant, for license, shall be entitled to submit complaint to the Federal, or state Council of Ministers, as the case may be against the non-determination of his application in accordance with the provisions of sub-section(1) , to determine his grievance , within a period of one month, of the receipt of the complete complaint

Delivery of the land allocated to the project

23. The Federal or state competent authority shall deliver the land to the project within a maximum period of one month of the date of granting the license.

Conditions to continue enjoyment of the license and privileges

24. No investor shall take any of the following measures, during the period of validity of the license and privileges, granted under the provisions of this Act, without obtaining a written approval, from the minister , or the state minster, as the case may be, the measures being to:
conduct any amendment or alteration of the size of the project, or the object for which the license has been granted , or transfer the project from the place thereof as prescribed in the license;
use or sell any of the equipment, machinery, apparatuses, materials or spare parts, with respect to which privileges have been granted, for any other purpose other than the purpose for which the the license has been granted;
change the purpose of use of the land allotted to the project, sell, mortgage or hire the same totally or partially.
Not –with-standing the provisions of sub-section (1), an investor may dispose of the existing

project, without changing the purpose licensed thereto totally or partially, whether by sale, gift, mortagage, hire or partnership such disposal shall take place in accordance with the provisions of the laws in force.

Duties of the investor

25. The Investor shall:

commence executing the project within a maximum period of twelve months of the date of receipt of the land unless such period has been extended on the part of the minister or state minister for any such period as he may deem fit;
submit to the Minister , the competent minister and the state minister periodical reports every six moths during the period of validity of the privileges on the progress of the operation of executing the project up to the date of commencement of production, or practice of activity;
keep regular books, and maintain records, where in the assets of the project exempted from customs duties, and the exempted imported materials shall be recorded.
present to the minister , the competent minister and the state minister annually during the period of validity of the privileges a copy of the annual accounts of the project approved by a certified auditor.

Contravention of the provisions of this Act by the investor

26. The investor shall be deemed to have committed a contravention to the provisions of this act where he:
contravenes the provisions of section 19,24 and 25.
unlawful methods as may result in obtaining any benefit in accordance with the provisions of this Act, for himself or any other person; gives false or misleading information, or uses such suspends the project, without reasonable cause.
contravenes the laws of the country, in such manner as may endanger the security and safety thereof .
Without prejudice to any penalty provided for in any other law, the minister, or the state minister, as the case may be, may in case of commission by the investor of any of the contravention provided for in sub-section (1), impose any of the following sanctions in accordance with the size of the contravention, the circumstances of commission thereof, and the extent of such damages which affect the national economy namely:
warn him to remove the reasons of the contravention if the same is necessary within such period, as he may specify;.
decrease the period of any privileges granted to the project or the size thereof;
deprive him from any of the privileges and guarantees provided for in this Act;
revoke totally or partially the privileges and such revocation shall result in binding the investor to restitute the value of the material benefit gained in obtaining any previous privileges, where gaining such benefit results from occurrence of the reason which led to the issue of the decision of revocation;
cancel the license, and such conciliation shall result in acquisition of the land granted thereto under the provisions of this Act.
An Investor in respect of whom a decision under the provisions of subsection (2), has been passed , may complain ,to the Federal, or state council of ministers, as the case may be, within one month of the date of being notified of the decision, and the decision, there-after in this respect, shall be final; provided that this provision shall not prevent the Investor from access to courts.

Chapter 5: Investment Organs Constitution of the committee of commissioners

27. The Minister shall constitute the committee of commissioners from a chairman and number of

members representing the competent bodies having relation to investment form the ministries and Competent government units; provided that the post of any of them shall not be less than head of the unit, or whoever may deputize him and shall be fully and officially authorized by the body which he represents, and the committee shall include representative of the private sector.

Functions of the committee

28. The Committee of Commissioners shall have the following functions, to:
consider the extent of compatibility of the project with the priorities of investment in the strategic fields;
consider the needs of the strategic projects as regards infrastructure and basic services needed and the extent of availability or possibility of providing the same;
consider the needs of the project of manpower and the specialized one to be procured from abroad in accordance with the prevailing laws;
achieve the sector investment plans through the approved and proposed investment projects;
co-ordinate between the Ministry and the competent Ministries and the states in every thing, as may concern investment projects especially as regards the map of investment lands.
The committee may call any competent person or body upon discussing any matter as may fall within the competence of such committee , and he shall not have the right to vote.

Functions of the federal ministries

29. The federal ministries concerned with investment, shall have the following functions:

specify priorities and lay down investment policies, at their ministries;
prepare sector investment maps;
approve on principle the establishment of the project upon such preliminary feasibility study as may be transferred thereto, by the ministry ; provided that the final feasibility study of the project shall be presented to the Ministry.
follow up the execution of the projects concerning the Competent ministry and submit periodical reports, as the Minister may require.

The state investment

30. An investment Act shall be promulgated, by a state law in the states, as to the form of the Federal Investment (Encouragement) Act,1999.

Chapter 6: Final provisions Investment Maps

31. The Ministry shall lay down the national investment map in accordance with the policies and directives of the National Economic Planning Council; provided that the same shall include specified percentages for the federal projects in the states, and submit the same to the Council of Ministers for approval thereof provided further that the investment map shall include sector of investment maps as may be prepared by the federal ministries and ministries of investment in the states.

Settlement of investment disputes

32. Save settlement of such disputes, as may be governed by the provisions of agreement set in subsection (2), where a legal dispute relating to investment arises,the same shall be submitted to conciliation or arbitration.
The provisions of the Investment of Arabic Capitals in Arab States, Consolidated Agreement 1980, the Settlement of Investment Disputes, between Arab States Agreement 1974, The Settlement of Investment Disputes between States and citizens of other states Agreement 1965,

the Economic, Technical and Trade Co-operation between states parties to the Islamic conference organization general agreement 1977 and any such other agreement in this respect as the Sudan may be a party thereto, shall apply to every legal dispute as may directly arise out of any of such agreements.

Power To make regulations

33. The Council of Ministers, upon the recommendation of the Minister, may make the necessary regulations for the implementation of the provisions of this Act. Without prejudice to the generality of the foregoing, such regulations may include the following matters:

specification of the type and size of the projects, as may be granted preferential privileges.
Laying down requirements for the prevention of overlapping between federal, state and local investments.
Specification of the strategic and non- strategic; projects.
The procedure of applying for the grant of license and privileges and specifying the type and size thereof;
Specifying the service fees.
The requirements and bases pertaining to control and follow- up of the projects licensed, under the provisions of this Act.

INVESTING IN SUDAN: STRATEGIC AND PRACTICAL INFORMATION

STRATEGY OF MANUFACTURING INDUSTRIES SECTOR FOR THE PERIOD (2007-2030)

Industrial sector is considered as one of the important locomotives for economic and social development in any country. In that context its development requires strategy that takes into consideration coordination and linkages with other sectors of the economy such as agriculture, energy, technology, trade and human resources strategies...etc.

It is worth mentioning that the industrial sector represents cornerstone in any comprehensive development, because of the high value added for that it can realize in processing the raw materials that are produce by the other sectors. And moreover the employment opportunities that it can avail. It also contribute for the comprehensiveness of national production in local, regional and international markets in this upcoming globalization era and there is no doubt that industry has an important role in encouraging production and availing the opportunities for resettlement, security and for the any civilized community.

Industrialization always reflects signs of development , higher standards of living such as industrial strategy that takes into consideration all these points and concentrates on the necessity to realize comprehensive industrial development that helps to transform the agricultural economy into strong industrial economy that maximize the value added, , the agricultural and animal products of the country.

Provisional Programs for Implementing the 25 years Strategy for the Manufacturing Industries Sector:-

The First five years Program:-

Encouraging the existence of industries:-

1. Development of industries with relative benefits
2. Export oriented industries
3. Vertical development projects
4. Bye- products waste manufacturing products.
5. Rehabilitation and operation of idle capacities.
6. Information and electronic industries
7. Intermediate industries.

Program for the second five years:-

1. Encouraging the existence of specific industries such as:-

1. Manufacture of consumption goods and assembly (televisions, refrigerators, etc...)

2. Industrializing industries such as (machines and equipments, spare parts,...etc)

3. Feeding engineering and chemical industries which provide products that considered as principal base to the developed industries.

Program for the next ten years:-

The program is focusing on:-

1. High capacity industries that benefits on the economies of scale.

2. Manufacturing of machinery and equipments.

3. Bio technology projects

4. Giant and nuclear energies

Program for the Last five years:-

Encouragement of giant industries (ships, airplane, rockets, satellite,...etc)

Objectives of the five years strategy in the manufacturing sector:-

1. To raise the contribution of the manufacturing industries in GMD , export and in Government revenue and GNP

2. To raise productivity and competitiveness in the national industrial values in order to realize high capacity utilization and to operate idle capacities.

3. To target self sufficiency in consumption and food industries through exploiting domestic resources and efficiency linkages with agricultural sector and other sectors such as technology, energy, trade and services.

4. To follow market oriented policies in production being an important tool in industrial and economical development. And adopting policies and programs to encourage exports in order to incorporate in the international market.

5. To apply the requirements of total quality management and the standards specifications.

6. The application of environment friendly measures in the industrial sector and anti industrial pollution legislations:-

    - Issuance of laws and regulations governing industrial pollutants

    - Dissemination of information on industrial security and safety in the industrial enterprises.

- Transfer and resettle of technologies for the use of national industries.
- Utilization of appropriate technologies that suit Sudan conditions.
- Dissemination of environmental awareness.
- Planning and adoption of environmental regulations and projects that lead to obtain of the ISO 14000 .
- The introduction of technologies that assist in purchase products and recycling and the treatments of industrial waste.

7. Establishment and development of industrial zones and communities and the basic infrastructure and provide services.
8. Provision of facilities and incentives and patronage for national industrial development and its protection from unfair competition and preparation for the entrance to the international and regional markets.
9. To facilitate in obtainment of industrial financing for the different manufacturing sub-sectors through and regional institutions and creation of special organizations for financing industry.
10. Human resources development in all disciplines to meat the requirements of industry in the following measures:-
    - Continuation of capacity building to adapt the new economic changes in the world by strengthening administrative and technical means.
    - To cope with the changing working relations and procedures as a result of supply new technologies.
    - Set up mechanisms for completion and for coordination to strengthening capabilities in technology management
    - Upgrade performance and management procedures, production and productivity as the different levels of the manufacturing sub -sectors
    - Development of human resources through strengthening capabilities and skills to meat present and future requirement through the exchange of experience and technologies resettlement.
    - Exchange of experience in human resources development with friendly countries and international and regional organizations.
11. Creation of a media base of micro and artisan manufacturing activities in order to realize development in the States and the national level by exploring resources, creating employment opportunities and income generation activities.
    - Providing industrial climate for the development of micro and artisan manufacturing activities

- Encouragement of private sector investment and technical and technological education.

- Encourage transfer of modern technologies in the area of micro and artisan manufacturing activities.

- The development of micro enterprises and the technologies applied in order to strengthening their competencies at the regional and international levels.

- Upgrading technical designing capabilities and standards specifications in micro and artisan manufacturing activities.

- Linking micro and artisan manufacturing activities sector with universities and applied research institutions at the national levels and also with relevant regional and international organizations.

- Establishment of micro and artisan manufacturing clusters to encourage competency and marketing and to link them with SMEs which they feed.

12. Encourage establishment of heavy industries and industrialize industry to transfer and resettle this technologies in Sudan.

13. Introduction of brain power industries which are link to information technologies i.e. (software and hardware).

14. Adaptability to development of technology and informatics in the industrial sector and strengthening networking in the information services and link with regional and international networks.

15. Issuance of intellectual property regulations, patents and applied scientific research for the industrial sector.

16. Development of internal relations in the area of industry to transfer experience and technologies and to mobilize technical assistance through the consolidate development and support to regional alliances and initiatives such as the alliance for the industrialization in Africa, NEPAD, etc... and encouragement of bilateral and multilateral relations with friendly countries.

INDUSTRIAL INVESTMENT

Sudan has a very unique geographical location and an area of about one million square miles. Bordering nine African countries, and also distinguished by its fertile land, heavy rains and the availability of water resources River Nile, Blue Nile, White Nile, Bahr Al- Arab and underground water.

Sudanese land is rich in mineral resources and oil (metal, silver, petrol, natural gazes,. etc).

Sudan is a member of many international and regional agreements i.e. COMESA and Arab Trade Organization

There are many free zones areas at Port Sudan and Algeli towns.

The telecommunication network and the seaports Basheir, Osman Digna, Swakin at the Red Sea Bank.

INDUSTRIAL INVESTMENT IN SUDAN

Investment climate is defined as the total of political, economic, social, legal and administrative conditions that affects directly and indirectly the development of investment.

Salient factors that make Sudan attractive for investors:-

- Strategic location in the heart of Africa
- Natural resources
- Abundant human resources
- Positive economic transformation
- Political stability
- Membership of international and regional agreements
- Encouraging investment Legislations

STRATEGIC LOCATION

Sudan is a vast country with an area of about one million square miles and lies between 5-25 North of the Equator. The country is vested with abundant natural resources an excellent geographic location with variegated climates from South to the North. This resources form the basis for industrial development, over and above the Sudan enjoys the third largest industrial basis in Africa after South Africa and Egypt. Although the utilize capacities are low ranged between 20-25 %.

The installed capacities are higher than the national needs thereby considerable surplus for exports to neighboring countries if full capacities can be exploited example of existing manufacturing industries are , sugar, flourmill, edible oil, soaps, detergents, shoes industry and dry batteries…etc.

NATURAL RESOURCES

Sudan national resources are as follows:-

1. Agricultural resources.
2. Animal resources.
3. Fisheries resources.
4. Forests resources.

5. Mineral resources.

6. Human resources.

In addition to the widely extended land and water resources.

Agricultural Sector:-

Agricultural sector a leading sector that activate to the manufacturing industries in the country. Agricultural crops provide the industrial sector with a high ratio of its inputs.

In the year, 99/2000 the agricultural licenses is estimated at (404) thousand Fadden. Its production and produced about 147 metric tons.

The cultivated areas in cotton is amounted to 404 thousand

Sudan is distinguish by the highly production of oil seeds particularly vegetable oil.

Animal Resources:-

This sector contributes effectively to the GNP and GDP. Growth rate in the animal wealth is estimated at (103) million compared with 59 million heads in the year 90-91. Being the main of red meats and their products.

Also animal hides and skins are being used as inputs in the manufacturing of leather and leather products

Fishes resources:-

Sudan fish resources is estimated at 56 thousand tons per year, the main fishing areas are Malakal, Gabal Aawlia, Wadi Halfa in addition to the Sea products at the Sea Sea.

Forest Recourses:-

Forestry is one of the important natural resources. And its products form an important input for manufacturing import substitutes and export oriented products. Sudan has a rich forestry and the main include teek, mahogany, Seder, ebony and acacia syal, acacia Senegal, eucalyptus ...etc. Wood can be used in the following: building poles, and telephone poles ...etc.

MINERAL RESOURCES

The geology of Sudan indicates one of the richest countries in mineral resources. The following mineral ores have been discovered all over the country: iron, cooper, chrome, manganese, gold, silicon, in addition to lime stone, marble, gypsum, mica, talk, natural gas. Over and above, the country is endowed natural resources and a lot of training institutions which assist in developing these resources

Human Resources:-

Besides the natural resources , Sudan has a large number of human resources. And there are many achdemic establishments and centers to develop manpower.

LEGISLATIONS AND REGULATIONS

The investment encouragement law of 1999 amended 2000 is considered as one of the most comprehensive laws in the area. Because it has encompassed .. of the previous investment encouragement laws in the agricultural, animal, manufacturing, energy and mining, transport , communication, tourism , environment , storing, real states contracting , basic infrastructure , administrative services , education services health, water , culture and information.

The main privileges of the investment encouragement law:-

- These federal law that supersedes over all the other laws
- It has enough .. against unnatural risks ,Knowing that Sudan is a member in the Arab and international guarantee organizations
- The law trust the local and foreign investors equally in rights and duties and granting concessions and incentives.
- Article No. 1 of the law gives full custom exemption for capital goods and article No. 2/10 gives the strategic projects tax holidays for business profit and from 5-10 years and for non strategic projects 5 years renewable for another 5 years.
- The accession of Sudan to COMESA aimed at developing trade and remove custom berries. This gives investors the chance to promote their production and exchange rate with COMESA countries in accordance with the general regulation laws.

INVESTMENT OPPORTUNITIES IN SUDAN

All the above avail the following investment opportunities:

Food Industries:-

- Production processing of and preserving of meat and meat products
- Manufacture of dairy products
- Processing and preserving of fruits and vegetables
- Processing and preserving of fish and fish products
- Manufacturing of starches and starch products
- Manufacturing of bakery products
- Manufacturing of cocoa , chocolate and sugar confectionery

- Manufacturing of other food products
- Manufacturing of animal feeds.

Textile and leather Industry:-

- Preparation and spinning of textile fabrics , weaving of textile
- Finishing of textile
- Manufacturing of knitted and chocolate fabrics and articles
- Manufacturing carpets and rugs
- Manufacturing of cordage, rope, twine and netting

Manufacturing of Wood and wood products:-

- Manufacturing of wooden containers
- Manufacturing of furniture
- Manufacturing small products of wood
- Manufacturing of forced paper utensils and other house utensils

Manufacturing of paper, publishing and printing:-

- Manufacture of pulp and paper board.
- Manufacture of other article of paper and paper board
- Manufacture of containers of paper and paper board

Manufacture of Petrochemicals:-

- Manufacture of rubber tires and tubes
- Retreating and rebuilding of rubber tires
- other rubber products
- Cutting shaping and finishing of stones
- Manufacture of molasses
- Refining of petrol
- Manufacture of caustic soda

- Manufacture of pesticides
- Refractory clay products
- Manufacture of cement, lime and plaster

Manufacture of basic Metals:-

- Manufacture of basic iron and steel
- Casting of iron and steel

Manufacture of Fabricated Metal, Machinery and Equipments:-

- Manufacture of hand tools, Manufacture of agricultural and forestry machinery
- Manufacture of special purpose machinery
- Manufacture of containers
- Manufacturing of furniture
- Manufacturing of lamps and lightening equipments
- Manufacturing of medical and surgical equipments and other appliances
- Manufacturing of metallic products for construction
- Manufacturing of tanks, reservoirs and containers
- Building and repairing of ships and boats
- Manufacturing of office accounting and computing machinery
- Manufacturing
- Manufacturing of electric equipments and house ware
- Manufacturing of insulated wire and caplets
- Manufacturing of engines and turbines
- Manufacturing of motorcycles
- Manufacturing of bicycles
- Manufacturing of invalid carriages
- Manufacturing of sport goods

- Manufacturing of sewing machines needles
- Manufacturing of children carts
- Manufacturing of toys
- Manufacturing of pencils

Packing Industry:-

- Plastic Sacks
- Plastic containers
- Plastic barrels

- Manufacturing of paperboard

SUDAN INDUSTRY: STRATEGIC INFORMATION AND CONTACTS

STRATEGIC BUSINESS AND INDUSTRIAL CONTACTS

i) The Sudanese Businessmen & Employers Federation
Tel: 00-249-11-431279/431277/431278
Fax: 00-249-11-431281/431283
President: Mr. Izz Eldin Elsayed

ii) Sudanese Chambers of Industries Association
Tel: 00-249-11-471716/471717/471719
Fax: 00-249-11-471720
President: Mr. Saud El Berier

iii) Union Chambers of Commerce
Tel: 00-249-11-772346/776518/781886
Fax: 00-249-11-780748
e-mail: chamber@sudanchamber.org
Director General: Mr. Ibrahim Mohamed Osman Elnus

iv) Chambers of Small Industries Corporationbr> Tel: 00-249-11-331554
Fax: 00-249-11-331554

v) Businesswomen's Union
Tel: 00-249-11-797012
Fax: 00-249-11-797012

vi) Ministry of Industry & Investment Authority
P.O. Box 6286, Khartoum
Tel: 00-249-11-771063
Fax: 00-249-11-770156

DIRECTORY OF MEMBERS OF CHAMBER OF COMMERCE & INDUSTRY. LIST OF IMPORTANT BUSINESS HOUSES.

1. Hashimali Mohamed Kheir
General Manager
Wafi Foreign Trade & Investment
P.O.Box. 12136, Khartoum, Sudan
Tel: 00-249-11-787742/787750
Fax: 00-249-11-787749
2. Tariq Sir El Khatim
General Manager
Sidco Intl Co. For Import & Export
P.O. Box. 8142, Khartoum, Sudan
Tel: 00-249-11-477773
Fax: 00-249-11-464885
Mob: 00-24912304863
E-mail: sideoint@emirates.net.ae

3. Khalid Elhag Elhatir

Chairman
Mawafi Trading & Industrial co.
Al Barka tower, 3rd floor, office no. 609
P.O. Box: 13252, Khartoum, Sudan
Tel: 00-249-11-787384/789413
Fax: 00-249-11-787383
E-mail: nawafi@sudnet.net

4. Taha Elsayed Elroubi
President
Taha Elsayed Elroubu & Co
I.D.E. Place Ave P.O. Box: 467, Khartoum, Sudan
Tel: 00-249-13-334253
Fax: 00-249-13-334252
E-mail: TERCOSD@TERCOTEL.COM

5. Union Chambers of Commerce
P.O.Box: 81, Khartoum, Sudan
Tel: 00-249-11-772346/776518/781886
Fax: 00-249-11-780748
E-mail: chamber@sudanchamber.org
Web: http://www.sudanchamber.org

6. Sudanese Free Zones & Markets
Khartoum, Sudan
Tel: 00-249-11-272981
Fax: 00-249-11-272416/271485
E-mail: SFZ-FREEZONES@HOTMAIL.COM

7. Sudanese Businessmen & Employers Federation
Tel: 00-249-11-431276/431277/431278
Fax: 00-249-11-471220

8. Sudan Seaport Corporation
P.O.Box: 2534, Khartoum
Tel: 00-249-11-775859/779114

9. Sudan Shipping Line Corp.
P.O. Box: 1731, Khartoum, Sudan
Tel: 00-249-11-781675
Fax: 00-249-11-777902

10. the strategic Reserve Authority
P.O. Box 298, Khartoum
Tel: 00-249-11-779415/796227
Fax: 00-249-11-772595

11. Eng. Eltigani A. Farah
Giad For Automotive Industry Co. Ltd
P.O. Box: 444, Khartoum
Tel: 00-249-11-201290
Fax: 00-249-11-201373
E-mail: giadcars@suanmail.net
12. Khartoum Petrochemical Co. Ltd (KPC)

Gaili, Khartoum North, sudan
Tel: 00-249-13-350361
Fax: 00-249-13-350362

MINISTRIES COMMERCE, INDUSTRY, HEALTH, FOOD, OIL & GAS

i) Minsitry of Foreign Trade
Tel: 00-249-11-772793/772640
Fax: 00-249-11-773950/776359
Email: tic@sudanmail.net

ii) Ministry of Industry
P.O. Box: 6286, Khartoum
Tel: 00-249-11-771063
Fax: 00-249-11-770156

iii) Ministry of Health, Khartoum
Tel: 00-249-11-778704/772843/778704
Fax: 00-249-11-778704

iv) Ministry of Agriculture & Forestry
P.O. Box: 283, Khartoum
Tel: 00-249-11-770586

v) Ministry of Energy & Mining
Tel: 00-249-11-780478-77347-775428-773196
Fax: 00-249-11-777940-773663

4. Trade Point G. Director: AL-Fatih AL-Zein AL-Taib
For Trade Enquiries: trade@sudantradepoint.org
TPSudan@hotmail.com

For General Information: info@sudantradepoint.org
TPSudan@hotmail.com

Tel: 00249-11-762581, 00249-11-762583
Fax: 00249-11-788116
Mobile Phone: 00249-12141213. 00249-12140081

LEADING SUDAN COMPANIES

Company Name	PO Box	Phone 1	Fax	Mobile	Activity	Exp. Items	Imp. Items
Gedarif Oil Factory				+24912223886	Impex	Grains	Spare Parts
Niesser Pharmaceutical Co	44494	+24911787361	+24911787360	+24912305323	Importer		Medical Supplies
Ismaeil Opticals	6059	+24911788450	+24911788450		Importer		Glasses
Marawi Investment Co	2136	+24911779030			Serviceprovider		Toothpaste
Nur Al Huda Enterprises	2643	+24911785094	+24911775740		Impex	Meat	Chemicals

A\Moniem Industrial&Engineering Co.	2413	+24911777624	+24911773132	+24912304017	Impex	Meat	Chemicals
Trans Sudan Transportation Enterprise	720	+24911472210	+24911471636		Impex		Automobile
Elbarbary Motors Co. Ltd	760	+24911472209	+24911465625		Impex		Automobile
Hafez Elsayed Elbarbary Co. Ltd	760	+24911472208	+24911471636		Impex		Building Materials
Altawfig Warehousing Enterprise	27	+24931123859	+24931123895		Impex		Automobile
Almagboul Brothers Corporation Limited	1593	+24911776425	+24911770218		Impex		Agriculture Equip
Masa Contracting Co. Ltd		+24911226023	+24911225864	+24912349104	Importer		Automobile
Bashir Elnoor Elsafei		+24915590025		+24912368751	Importer		Food Stuff
Rikaz International Investment Co. Ltd		+24911785877	+24911785801	+24912307646	Importer		Cement
Modren Agriiculture Co.	825	+24911777166	+24911770139	+24912360995	Importer		Chemicals
Elrashideen For Investments Co. Ltd	11772	+25911779375	+24911779355	+24912391383	Importer		Medical Supplies
Chemimport Co. Ltd		+24911777166			Importer		Chemicals
Mina Talk Factory	1144	+24911776002	+24911782221		Importer		
Ayat For Trading&Investment Co. Ltd		+24911781998		+24912300571	Impex	Meat	Transport Products
Refrigeration House Ltd	2892	+24911771829	+24911772201		Importer		Spare Parts
Coldair Engineering Co. Ltd	804	+24913330482	+24913330975		Impex		Spare Parts
Golden Gate Co. Ltd	1111	+24911483865	+24911483865	+24912304824	Impex		Electrical Appliances
Kambal International Co.	10336	+24911779337	+24911775887	+2491235852	Impex		Medical Supplies
Almohandis Paint Factory	10008	+24915558317	+24915561255	+24912346612	Importer		Raw Material
Hagkol For Trading&Service Co.	5050	+24911472482	+24911467910	+24912358891	Importer		
Medco Co. Ltd		+24911798060	+24911798058	+24912394401	Impex		Cement
Aljadawel Althahabia For		+24911479982	+24911479983	+24912306477	Exporter	Dura	

Investment Co. Ltd							
M.M. Pharma&Chemical Co. Ltd	1449	+24911788833	+24911771393		Importer		Medical Supplies
M&S for Human Drugs&Veterinary Service Ltd	1449	+24911782640	+24911771398		Importer		Medical Supplies
Yarmouk United Co. Ltd	10665	+24911784881	+24911771405	+24912303120	Impex	Grains	Spare Parts
Emarets Metal Company		+24913325836		+24912391952	Importer		Raw Material
Al Turath Emarets Factory For Alluminum		+24913325836		+24912391952	Importer		
Elmozn Trading&Service Co. Ltd				+24912210669	Impex		Electrical Appliances
Mohamed Erbab Esmail		+24915591710			Impex	Grains	
Arcory International Eng Trade &Service Co	4291	+24911784383	+24911774337	+24912390932	Impex	Live Stock	Transport Products
Alpha Medical Ageneis Co. Ltd	3541	+24911797484	+24911782787		Importer		Medical Supplies
Alsabr For Import&Export Co. Ltd	5067	+24911473470	+24911475855	+24912301342	Importer		Building Materials
Ahbab Allah Foir Import&Export Co. Ltd	5067	+24911462497	+24911475855	+24912301342	Importer		Building Materials
Alnour Global Invest Co.	11715	+24911777334	+24911783635	+24912305560	Impex	Meat	Electrical Appliances
Saad Sweets Co. Ltd	603	+24911471583	+24911467179		Impex		Raw Material
Masang Kofa Co.	13186	+24913660980	+24911477642		Impex	Live Stock	
Seiseban Trading Co. Ltd	2276	+24911782652	+24911777245	+24912390164	Importer		
Fadoas Trading and Investment Co.		+24911792224	+24911792226	+24912300211	Impex	Live Stock	
Green Saloon	369	+24911772861		+24912344054	Importer		
Gebal Al sharag Investment		+24911797755	+24911797755	+24912309808	Impex	Grains	Food Stuff
Hadir International Co. Ltd	12637	+24911464328	+24911464328	+24912303858	Impex	Veg / Fruits	Medical Supplies
Avia Trans Air Transport Co. Ltd		+24911482786	+24911482787	+24912133472	Impex		Transport Products

Almahari International Co. Ltd		+24911792 490	+24911792 489		Impex	Meat	
Mahibbah Trans Contiinental J.V.Co.	11967	+24911794 266	+24911793 662		Impex		Electrical Appliances
The Misr Concretd Devolopment co.Sudan	290	+24911463 540	+24911473 025	+24912387924			Building Materials
Doctors Co. Ltd	6008		+24911797 817	+24912132728	Impex		Medical Supplies
Abu Nassier Trading&Service Co.	1470	+24911795 339	+24911788 854		Exporter	Live Stock	
Sky International Co. Ltd	2052	+24911777 694	+24911776 767	+24912229780	Impex	Grains	Electrical Appliances
Switch Co.for Trading&Egineering	6590	+24911489 166	+24911489 164	+24912208362	Impex	Grains	
Internet International Trade&Transport Co.	8185	+24911770 054	+24911778 753	+24912301851	Impex	Grains	Food Stuff
Azza for Food Processing&Packing	8185	+24911770 05	249117787 53	+2491230185	Impex	Grains	Food Stuff
Abdelmoneim Medical Industries Co. Ltd	355	+24911784 981	+24911779 578		Importer		Medical Supplies
African Poultry Co. Ltd	1913	+24911772 944	+24911772 944	+24912390437	Impex		
Engineering Automotive Co.	837	+24911460 892	+24915568 732	+24912304175	Importer		Automobile
Avico Drugs&Investment Co. Ltd	12015	+24911787 513	+24911773 571	+24912375744	Importer		Medical Supplies
Afrotan Co. Ltd	1103	+24911770 363	+24911772 673	+24912304643	Impex		Chemicals
El Nil Photo Studio	280	+24911770 363	+24911772 673	+24912304643	Impex		
Alomeria Trading & Investment co.	44914	+24911780 940	+24911776 262	+24912307220	Impex		Electrical Appliances
Kenana sugar Co. Ltd	3632	+24922470 3	+24911220 563	+24912357826	Impex	Sugar	
Therwat International Co. Ltd		+24911780 872	+24911773 094		Importer	Meat	
Ashraf Co. Ltd	3077			+24912380605	Impex	Grains	Food Stuff

Coral Co. Ltd	1899	+24911469 250	+24911469 248		Impex		Medical Supplies
Coral Hatcheries & feed Production Farms	1899	+24911469 250	+24911469 248				
Khartoum Spinning & Weaving Co. Ltd	193	+24913330 073	+24913340 726	+24912381332	Impex		
Integrated Solution Co. Ltd	912	+24911790 901	+24497907 03	+24912391045	Importer		
United Petroleum Co.	12964	+24911488 796	+24911488 797	+24912390152	Impex		
Cofftea Trading Co. Ltd	3561	+24911774 530	+24911770 687		Impex	Sessame	
Geogabe Trading Co. Ltd	1138	+24911770 939	+24911770 789	+24912346050	Exporter	Veg / Fruits	
Andrawos Commercial		+24911774 720	+24911772 584	+24912344803	Importer		
Abd Allah Elfadil Ebrahim		+24915590 642	+24911466 502	+24912300521	Impex	Veg / Fruits	
Sisoba for Exp & Imp. Co.		+24911777 980			Importer		Medical Supplies
House Blasit Inserback				+2491230465	Importer		Packing Materials
Omdurman Medical Trading Agencies	13419	+24911783 989	+24911785 256	+24912392835	Impex		Chemical s
Ulisse Adventres Co. Ltd			+24911798 887	+24915511371	Impex		
Tolia Industries Metal Equipment Co.		+24911486 863	+24911486 864	+24912364447	Importer		
El Hag Abbas El Hag Siddig	531	+24915552 791			Impex	Grains	Home Applienc es
Mohammed Abbas E l Hag Siddig	531	+24915554 311			Impex	Hide/Skins	Home Applienc es
Mirghni Abbas El Hag Siddig	531	+24915555 024			Impex	Hide/Skins	Home Applienc es
Salah El Gousi Co.	50	+24915555 191			Impex	Grains	Chemical s
Kamal Al Gousi Co.	2028	+24915556 044			Impex	Grains	Electrical Applianc es
Abu Haraz Co. Ltd		+24915556 062	+24915556 052		Importer		Building Materials
A Safwa for Development & Animal Production	12957			+24912133195	Impex	Meat	Building Materials
Al Edahim		+24911573	+24915573	+24912360272	Impex		Building

Investment Co. Ltd		226	226				Materials
Abu Assabei For Transport & Investment Co.				+24912390427	Importer		Clothes
Srindra for Export & Import		+24913340036			Importer		
Maysa For Trading & contracting		+24911424813		+24912305790	Impex	Grains	Electrical Appliances
White Nile Plastic Co.	459	+24913312225	+24911780249		Importer		Spare Parts
Dali Lemousine	459	+24911781506	+24911780246		Importer		Automobile
Elshatrab Decoricatoraoil Mill	459	+24915570400	+24915570400		Impex		Spare Parts
Eldali & Elmazmoum National Co.	459	+24911781506	+24911780246		Impex	Grains	Food Stuff
Omeir International Commercial Co.	568	+24915556186	+24911234213	+24912301625	Importer		Food Stuff
Styrex Co.		24913339171		+24912304667	Importer		Raw Material
Sinan Trading & Contracting Co. Ltd		+24911796097	+24911796096	+24912280225	Serviceprovider		
Snnen for Agriculture & Investment Co. Ltd	1679	+249777254			Impex	Veg / Fruits	
Emdad for Investment Co. Ltd		+24913343133		+24912236038	Impex		Food Stuff
Fasco Co. Ltd	6314	+24911779030			Importer		Spare Parts
El Ismaili for Trading/Transport/Investment Co	4291	+24911784963	+24911785757	+24912393816	Impex	Grains	
Chemicals & Plastics Co. Ltd	1905	+24911778044	+24911778045	+24912301657	Impex		Chemicals
Elmedani Brothers Co .Ltd	5193	+24911467930	+24911471403	+24912303098	Importer		Spare Parts
Abou Haraz Co. Ltd		+24915556052	+24915556052	+24912348253	Exporter	Meat	
Bittar Engineering Ltd	1011	+24911771045	+24911780102	+24912300513	Impex		Electrical Appliances
Mona Sultan International Co.	305	+24911436198		+24912226930	Exporter	Veg / Fruits	
Umeish for Export & Import		+24915592385			Importer		
Tarig Commercial Co.	459	+24911781506	+24911780249		Importer		Transport Products

Sennar Agricultural Service Center	459	+24951140 751	+24951140 751		Importer		Transport Products
Eldali & Elmazmoum For Earth Moving&	459	+24911781 506	+24911780 246		Importer		
Gezera Trade Services Co.	1321	+24911783 358	+24911779 060		Impex		Transport Products
Al Mukhtar Enterprises	3715	+24911778 346	+24911771 478	+24912300492	Impex	Hide/Skins	Spare Parts
Astral Trading Co.	44310	+24911773 171	+24911783 255		Importer		Chemical s
Elmehad International Co. Ltd	3124	+24911772 152	+24911773 979	+24912308999	Importer		
El Sari Co. Ltd	3179	+24911783 004			Impex		

SELECTED COMPANIES

Saria Complex

It is one of the largest industrial complexes in Sudan that produces more .industrial technology ts and household appliances Electronic Assembling different types of domestic produc 60than Factory Electric Equipment Factory Plastic Factory Automotive Battery Factory Readymade 11 470891 + :Sudan Tele -Khartoum North 5183 :Box.O.Clothes Packing Factory Shoe Factory P 249 11 477113 + :Fax 470895 /249
http://www.sariacomplex.com/
http://www.almasarra.htg-sdn.com/

Geological Research Authority of the Sudan GRAS

represents the State Geological Survey (GRAS)The Geological Research Authority of the Sudan rivers and the continental shelf of ,and is the guardian of all metals and minerals within the lands The 410Box .O .It comes under the umbrella of the Ministry of Energy and Mining P .the Sudan :Fax249 1 83777939 + :dan TelSu 11111Geological Research Authority of The Sudan Khartoum 249 1 83776681+
http://www.gras-sd.com/

Sigma-Tau SUDAN Ltd
- .the plant was equipped initially to produce the following pharmaceuticals :Production facilities DRAY POWDERED - ,TABLETS This was shortly followed by -LATIN CAPSULES HARD GE CREAMS AND OINTMENTS The plant ,PASTES -SYRUPS -FOR ORAL SUSPENSIONS Million per annum Tablets 100is Hard gelatin capsules (considering one shift per day)capacity Million per 3Million per annum suspension Syrups 4nnum Dry powder for oral Million per a 80 annum
http://www.betasudan.com/sigmatau.htm

Haggar Holding
a cigarette ,cultivation of Virginia tobacco in Southern Sudan (HHC)Limited .Haggar Holding Co &HAGGAR CIGARETTE)trict of Equatoria another factory in Khartoum factory in the Yei Dis was stalished for planting and (STCP)Coffee Plantations &Sudan Tea (TOBACCO FACTORY processing both crops Acquired shoe manufacturing company LARCO Acquired bottling factories Established a company for developing solar energy resources in (FORAT)and (PASGIANOS)

Established HAGGAR PETROLEUM SERVICES COMPANY (SUDAN TECHNO SOLAR)Sudan
,Khartoum North 236Box .O.P 249 13 335940 +Fax 249 13 335193 +249 13 335937 +Tel
Sudan

http://www.haggarholding.com/

Sudan Rotomouls Co
,flower pots RAD-traffic road barrier -traffic cone -crystal -cubic -vertical -horizontal -Water tanks
576560 / 15-249 + :Fax 577995, 576550 / 15-249 + :Dorman industrial area Tel -SQR Um
11111code/ 11639:Box .O.P
http://www.sudanrotomould.com/

The Sudan Cotton Company

-Barlaman Street Khartoum 249 183 770703+ :Fax 249 183 775755 771567 779573 +: :Tel
Sudan -Khartoum , 1672 :Box.O.Sudan P
http://www.sudancottonco.com/

Coldair Engineering Company CEC

CEC currently .is part of Haggar Holding Company (CEC) .Coldair Engineering Company Ltd
er coolers and wat ,evaporative air coolers ,chest freezers ,manufactures domestic refrigerators
door commercial refrigerators for supermarkets-glass

http://www.coldairengineering.com/

AHMED OSMAN ABDALSALAM GROUP
http://www.aoag.biz/

Alsalam Cement Production Company ACPC
Ahmed Osman Abdalsalam Group
http://www.alsalamcement.com/
موطرخلا : 00249183474685 ديربـ قودنص: 00249183473944 سكاف 00249183474681 00249183474683
44058

http://www.smfsteel.com/

Molutech Aluminium

,Molutech Aluminium that provides consulting and professional services to global customers
Sudan -aluminium and development of custom applications Khartoum ,offering domain expertise
245 923 00249 187 245 922 00249 187:Tel
http://www.molutech.com/

Banan Plastics Factory -مصنع بنان للحبال ومنتجات البلاستيك
0024915251110:Tel
http://www.bananfactry.com/

IMPORTANT BUSINESS CONTACTS

SUDAN BUSINESS SERVICES

- **Century GSE**

Qualtiy used ground support equipment and asset managment services.
Address: 5383 Hollister Ave. Suite 220
Phone: 805 637 9514
E-Mail: techinfo@centurygse.com

- **Salvo Grima (Freeport) Operations Ltd**

Salvo Grima Freeport Operations are fiscal representatives in Malta offering ...
Address: Ground Floor, Freeport Centre, Port of Kalafrana
Phone: +356 2220 7000 E-Mail: jperegin@salvogrima.com.mt

- **Web Desiging**

indiacraze Megrisoft Web Solution Provider offers Web Hosting, Web Promotion, ...
Address: #191713, Delhi
Phone: 011-2242413 E-Mail: nitinstar76@yahoo.com

- **spacemaker**

Spacemaker Self Storage provides business storage and domestic storage ...
E-Mail: space@cherryaid.co.uk

- **Kda Home Biz 4 U**

Learn how to build a home based business through network marketing to earn a ...
E-Mail: dion@kdahomebiz4u.com

- **Nationwide Self Storage**

Nationwide Self Storage provides business storage and domestic storage ...
E-Mail: nationwide@cherryaid.co.uk

- **Mosaic Services**

Offers Search engine optimization services, Latent Semantic Indexing (LSI) ...
Address: G-60, East of Kailash, New Delhi, India
E-Mail: sarika@ebrandz-online.com

- **Profit-Unlimited**

Work at Home Ideas and Opportunities, 5 Different Streams of Income All from ...
Address: 3842 W. Hatcher Rd.
Phone: 1-602-568-6456 E-Mail: mike@profit-unlimited.com

- **Reliant Marking Tools Manufacturer Birmingham UK**

Reliant Marking Tools UK: manufacturers of stencils, dies, marking tools, ...
Address: Unit 2 Benson Ind. EST. Benson Road Hockley

Phone: 0121 359-3366 E-Mail: webmaster@reliantmarkingtools.co.uk

- **Waterstore Trading Company**

Waterstore Trading Company is a phones superstore, we are the online electrical ...
Address: 19624 e montview dr
Phone: 13035749369 E-Mail: waterstore@usa.com

- **import/export**

Our company is called World Trade Hall. We are a private international services ...
Address: No#234,Pasdaran ave,11th floor
Phone: +98-21-22554000 E-Mail: marketing.division@gmail.com

- **RETAIL MANAGEMENT SOFTWARE**

WE ARE IN SOFTWARE DEVLOPEMENT & SALES. SOFTWARE LIKE PETROL PUMP MANAGEMENT ...
Address: B/215, Kailash Industrial Complex,Parksite, Vikhroli(West),Mumbai-400079.
Phone: +91(022)55551855 E-Mail: info@artrm.com

- **transaltionpro**

translation agency offers quality and efficiency french englsih spanish
Address: wolseley
Phone: 02078701068 E-Mail: info@translationpro.co.uk

- **curs valutar**

Provides currency exchange informations, currency statistics and related ...
Address: Lebedei no.5
E-Mail: mirceam321@yahoo.com

- **Sme telecom**

Sme Telecom - Providing UK Non Geographic Numbers and advanced call handling ...
Phone: 020 70 60 50 20 E-Mail: sudesh@smetelecom.com

- **GBS Freight Services**

We are a UK based freight forwarding & logistics organisation providing ...
Address: 25 Highfield Road
Phone: +44 (0) 1322-288061 E-Mail: steve@gbsfreight.co.uk

- **Business English UK c/o AREL**

Learn professional English in England. Business English UK offers links to high ...
Address: 56 Buckingham Gate
Phone: +44 207 802 9212 E-Mail: biseng@theenglishlanguage.org

- **DiscountSourcesDirect**

Discover Where To Get Top Brand Products At Knock-Down Clearance Prices.

Address: Arlington Road
Phone: $4 07768 018900 E-Mail: submission@sebiz.net

- **My Swag Bag Cashback and Rewards Service**

MySwagBag is a cashback and rewards website for members to get free cashback, ...
Address: 3rd Floor
Phone: 0035040335 E-Mail: submission@sebiz.net

- **Fabulous wooden doors**

Fabulous wood doors veneer, plywood, solid, molding doors.
Address: 12/234, ziang street 001#Linhu economic zone. Qidu town.wujiang.JS.
Phone: 008651263815408 E-Mail: cmanjunatha81@yahoo.com

- **Everest Metal Industries**

Manufactures and exports builders hardware, kitchen cabinet hardware, brass ...
Address: C-2/107, GIDC, Jamnagar - 361004
Phone: +91-288-2560827 E-Mail: sales@everestmetal.com

- **Venus Industries**

Manufacturer and exporter of brass hardware, door hardware, brass hinges, door ...
Address: 378/4, GIDC, Jamanagar - 361004
Phone: +91-288-2560596 E-Mail: mail@venus-ind.com

- **Welding machine**

Dear sir/madam, ...
Address: Room602,NO195,Fengxiyuan,Gangbei Street,Guangzhou,China
Phone: 86-020-36228308 E-Mail: dashengaw@gmail.com

- **Electrical Brass Components P Ltd**

makers of metal components of all types
Address: 14th Floor Nariman Point Bombay 400021
Phone: 91-9821074335 E-Mail: sales@electrical-brass-components.com

- **manufacturing**

I have a small company in Romania and I have a space good for manufacturing . I ...
Address: metalurgiei
Phone: 0040788411234 E-Mail: gabidanserv@rdslink.ro

- **Entreprendre en Roumanie / Invest in Romania**

I'm offering my help to people who want to come to Romania for business or just ...
E-Mail: alegria_peach@yahoo.com

- **Business English UK c/o AREL**

A free portal guide for English for business and professional language training ...

Address: 56 Buckingham Gate
Phone: +44 207 802 9212 E-Mail: biseng@theenglishlanguage.org

- **Printing,Packaging, Binding Machinery**

We are the largest manufacturer of Die Cutting Machine, Corrugated Box Plant, ...
Address: J-126B, Vishnu Garden ,
Phone: 011-25153953 E-Mail: friendsengg@friendsenggcorp.com

- **ukdir.biz**

Comprehensive UK business directory online for everything from small business ...
Phone: 234567 E-Mail: buylinks@gmail.com

- **Bracebridge Engineering Ltd UK**

Bracebridge an engineering company has been supplying quality presswork and ...

- **Graphcard Inc.**

Register with an online payment solution available to Internet shoppers ...
Address: 31 Olowu Street, Ikeja, Lagos, Nigeria
Phone: 234 803 326 8306 E-Mail: uofulue@yahoo.com

- **Mobile Phone Universe**

More Mobile Phone sites than you can find in a month of Sundays. Check them out ...
Address: 231 Rotherhithe Street
Phone: 020 7136 4963 E-Mail: mob-u@all-mobilephones-uk.com

- **Swedish Translator**

My name is Mattias Bergström and I translate all kinds of texts from English, ...
Address: Fredsgatan 11
Phone: § E-Mail: mattias@swedishtranslator.se

- **Emaze Holdings - Website Design**

Emaze Holdings creates professional websites, as well as logo creation, and ...
E-Mail: tsinfield@emazeholdings.com

- **Translation services lingo24**

Provides the translation services for most of the worlad languages.
Address: 18-20 Queen's Road
Phone: +44 (0) 870 765 4646 E-Mail: info@lingo24.com

- **Clear Answers Ltd.**

UK specialists in accident and personal injury claims, offering a unique ...
Address: Mallards House, Cottage Drive West
Phone: 0845 601 0303 E-Mail: claim@injury-compensation.org.uk

- **Premier ors**

Professional ing services providing high quality copywriting, copy ing ...
Phone: (905) 814 7928 E-Mail: president@premiertutoring.com

- **crgate.com**

Eliminate bad debt from your business forever! One Click to protect your ...

- **Dynamic Exim Corporation**

Indian merchant exporter of pharmaceutical machinery,mini tablet press machine, ...
Address: 242 Indraprasth, Near Nobat Press, Jamnagar Pin 361001
Phone: +91-288-2556844 E-Mail: mail@dynamiceximcorp.com

- **PRO CAR AUDIO INSTALLATIONS**

Installations services for your car audio systems, cd/mp3/dve players, ...
Address: 1 Ural Court, DANDENONG NORTH
Phone: 0422 227 110 E-Mail: imran.m@optusnet.com

- **Instant Publisher Platinum CDROM**

750 Books, Reports & Manuals You Can Reprint & Sell and Make a Fortune! How to ...
Address: 1200 Scotia Dr., #201
Phone: 561-582-1874 E-Mail: krismoor57@yahoo.co.in

- **Companiesmadesimple - Company Formation Services**

Same day company formations. Free online company name search. Start your ...
Address: 145-157 St John Street, London.
Phone: 02072537272 E-Mail: leonw@westbury.co.uk

- **Web Design and Software Programming**

Global Info Factory is a team of IT professionals providing IT services: Web ...
E-Mail: support@globalinfofactory.com

- **Jovial Enterprises**

We are importers, exporters and sourcing agents from india. Kindly contact us ...
Address: Pullichira Post, Kollam, Kerala, India. PIN-691304
Phone: + 91 9895254088 E-Mail: jovialent@rediffmail.com

- **DataWORKS Canada**

Canadian direct marketing company, specializing in business mailing lists, fax ...
Phone: 1-877-492-4200 E-Mail: sales@canadiandata.com

- **Tourism Milodon chile**

Milodon Tourism, a leading tour operator company in the Chilean Patagonia, ...
Address: urmeneta 729

Phone: 562-8562610 E-Mail: milodon.cl@gmail.com

- **Web Design and Software Programming**

Global Info Factory is a team of IT professionals providing IT services: Web ...

- **Electrical Brass Components P Ltd**

maker of Brass comonents and electrical fittings
Address: 1406 Dalamal towers Nariman Point Mumbai India
Phone: 91-22-56371096 E-Mail: sales@electrical-brass-components.com

- **Scientific & Audio Visual Instruments**

Manufacturers, & exporters of Scientific, medical and Audio visual products ...
Address: 171, Industrial Area, Ambala Cantt. India
Phone: 0171-2699712 E-Mail: jmt@sancharnet.in

- **Rajhans Impex Pvt Ltd**

Manufacturer of copper & brass ingots and billets, copper alloy extrusion, ...
Address: Plot No. 8, GIDC, Phase II, Dared, Jamnagar 361004. Gujarat. India
Phone: + 91 - 288 - 2730971 E-Mail: info@rajhansimpex.com

- **Best Plastic Processing Machinery**

High End Manufacturer & Exporter of plastic processing Machinery & spares
Address: kundanahalli
E-Mail: renukatan70@yahoo.com

- **Phoenix Telco**

UK based telephone call provider offers cheap international phone calls to the ...
Address: 5 Banbury Curt, Woodstock Avenue
Phone: 0208 5664826 E-Mail: phoenix@telecom-links.net

- **Document-Doctor**

Professional writing and ing service for all English language business ...
Phone: 44+ 7956874194 E-Mail: webmaster@document-doctor.co.uk

- **Scopulus Business Resources**

online Business resources, company formation, legal documents, accounting ...
Address: 39 Almer Road
E-Mail: craiy@scopulus.co.uk

- **Canada Pardons**

Canada Pardons is a leading Canadian firm specializing in helping people with ...
Address: 3442 Yonge Street.
Phone: 4164889000 E-Mail: submission@sebiz.net

PROFESSIONALS IN SUDAN

1. **Simulation Services**
   Provides custom simulation models that improve energy, logistics, healthcare ...
   Address: 0367 Oslo
   Phone: - E-Mail: temp1@simulationservices.com

2. **uttam consultants**
   we assist in getting you in india for higher studies we also provide you ...
   Address: flat 12 shantha paradise 121 wheeler road cox town
   Phone: 091 080 25485909 E-Mail: kiranku_2000@yahoo.com

3. **Online Divorce Directory**
   Online-Divorce-Help.org is a web directory of Divorce related legal and other ...
   Address: 231 Rotherhithe Street
   Phone: 020 7136 4963 E-Mail: wt@online-divorce-help.org

4. **Oxford College**
   $10 dental cleaning for children 5-16 years of age. $20 dental cleaning for ...
   Address: 670 Progress Avenue
   E-Mail: dentalhygiene@hotmail.com

5. **Search Recruitment**
   List of Uk Industrial Manufacturing jobs are updated daily at Search ...
   Address: 198 West George Street
   Phone: 0141 272 7777 E-Mail: search@hire-exchange.com

6. **Online Divorce Directory**
   Online-Divorce-Help.org is a web directory of Divorce related legal and other ...
   Address: 231 Rotherhithe Street
   Phone: 020 7136 4963 E-Mail: wt@divorce-uk.org

7. **UK Industrial & Manufacturing Jobs at Search Consultancy**
   List of Uk Industrial Manufacturing jobs are updated daily at Search ...
   Address: 198 West George Street
   Phone: 0141 272 7777 E-Mail: search@hire-exchange.com

8. **CARTER MORGAN**
   INTERNATIONAL MODELS REQUIRED. 18-26 ATTRACTIVE FEMALES REQUIRED FOR OVERSEAS ...
   Address: park st
   Phone: +44775 4126756 E-Mail: jameslouis1@yahoo.co.uk

9. **International Personnel Consultants., Inc**
   Professional, Skilled, Non-skilled, Health Care, Technical, Construction, ...
   Address: 1903 Jollibee Plaza Bldg., Emerald Ave., Ortigas Centre, Pasig City, Philippines

Phone: 0063-2-6872247 E-Mail: alex@ipc.com.ph

10. **An Online UK Divorce Resource Directory**
Find services and information related to divorces in the UK : Divorce-UK.org
Address: Flat 5, 1 Holmbush Rd
Phone: 0208 780 5493 E-Mail: info@divorce-uk.org

11. **Web Design and Software Programming**
Global Info Factory is a team of IT professionals providing IT services: Web ...

12. **Omaya China Business Consultant Company**
Business consulting, china consulting, China consultant, China Investigation, ...
Address: Fengtai District, Beijing, China
Phone: 86-10-83823755 E-Mail: 86-10-83822706

13. **Emigrateforgood**
EMIGRATE to NEW ZEALAND I'll deal with immigration papers, Expression of ...
E-Mail: draco2464@hotmail.com

SUDAN FINANCE COMPANIES

1. **Financial Freedom Made Simple**
Learn to take control of your financial distress with a free directory. The ...
Address: Nordjordkroken 8
Phone: +47.91-31-27-02 E-Mail: shiva2000@gmail.com

2. **pikecpa**
New Hampshire CPA Firm, located in the Seacoast NH and Portsmouth NH areas, ...
Phone: 12345678 E-Mail: devkumar123@gmail.com

3. **1 Personal Finances - Information On Home Finance, Corporate**
1 Personal Finances has information on Insurance, Loans, Cr Cards, ...
Address: 36 Walton St
Phone: 01226 231525 E-Mail: stefan@1-personal-finances.com

4. **DebtFreeToday**
Online debt consolidation services. Non profit debt consultations providing ...
Address: 4604 S Ironwood Ave
E-Mail: di_promote@yahoo.com

TRAVEL TO SUDAN

- **Cheap Airport Parking UK Gatwick, Heathrow, Stansted & Major**

Cheap Airport Parking - save up to 60% with cheap airport parking fees at major ...
Address: 15 Tunwell Greave, Sheffield S5 9GB

Phone: 0114 2467240 E-Mail: rpday@parkandsave.com

- **Cobico Travel & Tours Ltd**

Mauritius,a paradis island situated in the Indian Ocean. ...
Address: 89 Saint Jean Road Quatre Bornes
Phone: 4674084 E-Mail: kity@cobicogroup.com

- **Cobico Group**

Mauritius is a small paradis island situated in the Indian Ocean. ...
Address: 89 Saint Jean Rd Quatre Bornes Mauritius
Phone: 4674084 E-Mail: 4674052

- **Cruisestore**

Book cruise holidays to destinations across the world with TheCruiseStore.co.uk
Address: Holiday House, Sandbrook Park, Sandbrook Way
Phone: 01706 742 500 E-Mail: cruise@holiday-travel-flights.com

- **Travel agent**

My Qatar offers cheap flight from UK to Doha, Dubai, Muscat, Jeddah, Riyadh, ...
Address: 372-374
Phone: 2085181010 E-Mail: ajay@cityvacations.co.uk

- **Ibonia**

Votre billets d'avion charter avec Avion-charter.fr. Comparez votre billet ...
Address: 33 rue Ratsimilaho Antaninarenina
E-Mail: ibonia@avion.fr

- **PlaceClick Brisbane**

A general directory about Brisbane. Here you will find everything you need to ...

- **Map South Pacific**

South Pacific maps and travel guides to Tahiti, Fiji, Samoa, Vanuatu, Easter ...
Address: 1-5765 Turner Road
Phone: 1-250-756-0333 E-Mail: webmail@mapsouthpacific.com

- **Sofia Hotels on-line reservations**

On-line reservations at the best prices for all Sofia hotels

- **Expat Blog**

Expat-Blog.com is an open community dedicated to expatriates and their ...

- **DIY Travel Directory**

Accommodation and travel resources for independent travellers.

- **TRAVEL AGENCY**

Climbing,Horseriding,Roundtrips,Cruises,Ski,Rafting
Phone: 00359 32 653001 E-Mail: info@interjet-bg.com

- **Casas rurales, empresas de turismo activo y restaurantes**

Directorio de Casas rurales, hoteles con encanto, empresas de turismo activo y ...
Address: Julio A Roca 252 - Piso 1
Phone: 03546 461410 E-Mail: links@sleepinspain.com

- **discovering peru**

discover the unknown jungle and beautiful landscapes of the Andes in the ...
Address: lima
Phone: +5112427521 E-Mail: discoveringperuref@yahoo.com

- **Alessandro**

Low cost flight search engine and many tools that help you planning your ...

- **Thomas Cook**

Cheap holidays from Thomas Cook, book last minute deals online at ...
Address: Thomas Cook Business Park, Coningsby Road
Phone: 0870 750 5711 E-Mail: tc@holiday-travel-flights.com

- **Cheap Cruise**

Find more information out about cruises, mini cruises or chat in the forum and ...
E-Mail: forum@passionforcruising.com

- **111 Travel Directory**

Bed and breakfasts and lodging, including hostels and hotels. Searching for a ...

- **Athens Hotels**

Complete list of Athens hotels with detailed description photos and rates. ...
E-Mail: webmaster@travel-guide-greece.com

- **Globebookings**

Discount Hotel reservations with Globebookings in Cuba, Dubai, Singapore, Hong ...
Address: Vaclavske namesti 55
Phone: 420 245 005 631 E-Mail: info@globetravelgroup.com

- **Italy hotels reservations - Travel Mall**

Your personal online Mall for travel services reservation in Italy. Hotels and ...

E-Mail: info@travel-mall.net

- **Cheap City Breaks**

We offer bargain short breaks, cheap city breaks and cheap weekend getaways.

- **villasandbeds ltd**

providing a good range of vaction villas and apartments with private pools in ...
Address: 9 mill drive
Phone: 0044 1323491440 E-Mail: info@villasandbeds.com

- **UK Short Breaks**

Short weekend and midweek breaks in the UK, at luxurious hotels in beautiful ...
E-Mail: chris.hough@g-mapps.com

- **Lightfoot Travel**

Lightfoot Travel is your one stop shop for all your travel needs. Plus, click ...
E-Mail: BLitefoot@aol.com

- **City Portals**

City Portals - - accomodation, travel, tourism and business city information ...
E-Mail: ads@cityround.com

- **Discover China**

Information about independent travel in China, Hong Kong and Taiwan.

- **Electrobug Technologies**

Electrobug provides real-time, online pricing intelligence tools for making ...
Phone: +91-124-5034024/25 E-Mail: devrishi.arora@electrobug.com

- **1000 Tips 4 Trips: Travel Tips and Advice**

Over 1000 travel tips and hints submitted by users from around the world. ...

- **Sea& Desert Tours**

Incoming agent in Sudan , Libya and Egypt
Address: Khartum
Phone: 002 010 1380612

- **World-wide travel guide**

Travel guide to destinations, based on geographic region. ...

- **travel**

Travel portal offering flights, hotels, car hire, tailor-made and round the ...

E-Mail: neetu.chillar@tecnovate.co.in

- **Canuck Abroad**

A resource for expatriates and travellers backpacking in Europe or living ...

- **Thai-Experience.org**

Gain a deeper insight into Thai culture by volunteering in Thailand. Teach ...
Address: Km6 Udon-Nongkhai Highway
Phone: +66 42 411 079 E-Mail: sabine@thai-experience.org

- **tourism**

Welcome visitor's who'd like to visit Ukraine! (Kyiv). May 2005 year. ...
Phone: +380503213178 E-Mail: valera77@bigmir.net

- **1st Cruise Holidays**

Merranean Cruises, Caribbean Cruises, Mini Cruising Holidays with P&O, ...
Address: Flightline House, Westcliff, Essex, England.
Phone: 0800 316 5550 E-Mail: andy@flightline.co.uk

- **BestBuyAir**

Discount travel agent. Discount airfare, hotels, rental cars, cruises, vacation ...

- **TravelMake**

Travel for less. Save up to 65% on hotels, air tickets, cruises, rental cars ...

- **Xcape With us**

An online accommodation booking company.
Address: Gran via Asima
Phone: 0034 971 43 69 00 E-Mail: naomi.fryer@xcapewithus.com

- **Charmardon Consultants**

This one stop search shop offers search engines, news, travel, help & ...
E-Mail: info@trying2findu.com

- **Train Travel World**

TrainTravelWorld.com is a specialized directory of Train Travel web sites from ...
Address: Flat 5, 1 Holmbush Rd, Putney
Phone: 0208 780 5493

- **Secure Airport Parking at Birmingham**

Airport parking voucher available immediately online and via email wih full ...
Address:

Phone: E-Mail: submission@tridentindia.net

- **Car Parking at Manchester Airport**

Monitored car parking at Manchester airport. Easy online booking and instant ...
Address:
Phone: E-Mail: submission@tridentindia.net

- **Luton Airport Parking**

Luton airport parking in secure monitored parking compounds. We have car parks ...
Address:
Phone: E-Mail: submission@tridentindia.net

- **Airport Parking Heathrow**

Park your car safely at Heathrow airport whilst on holiday. Our online booking ...
Address:
Phone: E-Mail: submission@tridentindia.net

- **Compare hotel rates before you go!**

35.000 hotels at 5.300 cities of 110 different countries. HotelsFare.com is ...
E-Mail: cheap_flight@yahoo.com

- **Holiday Zone**

Holiday Accommodation directory australia wide.
E-Mail: info@holidayzone.com.au

- **Voyagenow**

Book a hotel for today or one year in advance. We cater for Business ...
Address: 1st floor 128 hindley street adelaide
Phone: 618 84155110 E-Mail: frank@e-channel.com.au

- **TravelRomp.com**

Hotels, Cars, Flights - We make the world your playground!

- **Golden Key**

Offering Vietnamese day courses (and longer) - learn essential words and ...
Address: 30 Hoa Ma
Phone: 04 9714880 E-Mail: info@goldenkey.edu.vn

- **Canuck Abroad**

A resource for expatriates and travellers backpacking in Europe or living ...

- **Trip-Savers.Com**

Discount Airfare, Hotel Reservations and Car Rentals worldwide. ...

Address: 9036 S. Knox Ave.
Phone: 7082299769 E-Mail: techsupport@trip-savers.com

SUDAN RECREATION AND LEISURE

-
- **Parish Chest**

The premier online family history and genealogy shop where you can buy just ...
Address: ancestors
Phone: 01872 - 864807 E-Mail: forefathers@btconnect.com

- **Beyond Retreats - Yoga and Sport Holidays**

Offers unique yoga breaks and yoga holidays at beautiful venues within the UK ...
Address: PO Box 46523
Phone: 0207 226 4044 E-Mail: br@holiday-travel-flights.com

- **Bedlam Weekends**

Online quotations, making it easier to plan your Stag, Hen or other event, with ...
Address: 28 Great King Street
Phone: 0131 558 19 19 E-Mail: info@bedlam.co.uk

- **Epeco Enterprises Ltd.**

Looking for a place to rest when you want to go for summer or winter. Our ...
Address: P.O. Box 68130-00200. Nairobi.Kenya
Phone: +254(0)722 255 311 E-Mail: epeco99@yahoo.com

- **Best Online Casino**

We review online casinos and help you find a honest online casino.

- **Langtry Manor Hotel**

The Langtry Manor offers some of the most stylish hotel accommodation in ...
Address: Derby Road
Phone: 01202 553 887 E-Mail: lillie@langtrymanor.com

- **A1 Online Slots**

Slot machine guide to online slots. How to play slots, tips, strategies, ...
Address: 55 Bluey Plaza
Phone: 012145 5 825 E-Mail: amuzemeats@hotmail.com

FOOD AND DRINK

1. **Maad Food Ind.Co,L.L.C**
   We, Maad Food Ind. Co, L.L.C are happy to inform you that we are one of the ...
   Address: 1km. up to police station of Tabriz - Mianeh road.
   Phone: +98-411-6300463 E-Mail: sale@chocomaad.com

2. **The Sweetmaster**
   Your favourite traditional old fashioned sweets, candy, and confectionery from ...
   E-Mail: desousacosta@hotmail.com

3. **CORNUCOPIA**
   Horn of Plenty provides a secure shopping experience that fulfills your needs, ...

4. **CakeChannel.com**
   Find 1.000+ wedding cake pictures, designs and ideas
   Address: 29 Carpenter St
   Phone: 732-936-9336 E-Mail: enezok@yahoo.com

5. **Wedding Cakes Channel**
   Wedding cakes: pictures, designs and ideas
   Address: 29 Carpenter St
   Phone: 732-936-9336 E-Mail: enezok@yahoo.com

6. **Candocandy online Sweets and Candy**
   Traditional British Sweets, Chocolate, Toffee, Fudge and Gift Hampers. Find ...
   Address:
   Phone: E-Mail: sales@candocandy.com

7. **Micro Diet**
   Micro diet
   Address: Phoenix Az
   E-Mail: info@classichits.com

AUTOMOTIVES IN SUDAN

- **ChipsAway Fareham**

Smart car repair in Fareham, Hampshire: Repair of alloy wheels, bumper scuffs, ...
Address: 20, Gudgeheath Lane
Phone: 01329 517576 E-Mail: webmaster_pioneer@yahoo.com

- **Firstcar**

Buy and sell new and used cars online specialising in young driver's ...E-Mail: firstcar@cherryaid.co.uk

- **Car Culture**

Car accessories for all motorists including lighting, gear knobs, alarms and ...

- **Electrical Brass Components**

makers of auto electrical components and cable lugs, battery terminals
Address: Alamal Towers Nariman POint Mumbai
Phone: 91-9821074335 E-Mail: sales@electrical-brass-components.com

- **Picknbuy24**

"Japan's No.1 used car dealer Network-Pick'nBuy24com.Car auction, car import, ...

- **M-BenzForum**

M-BenzForum is an online community for owners and enthusiasts of Mercedes Benz ...
E-Mail: andry_budiman2004@yahoo.com

- **Car Smart Online Automotive Auction**

Car Smart Online Automotive Auction - Buy and Sell everything and anything 100% ...
Address: 5 Linton Road
Phone: 01132664562 E-Mail: sales@car-smart.co.uk

- **Electrical Brass Components P Ltd**

makers of electrical parts and auto parts
Address: DalamAl Towers N. Point BOMBAY INDIA
Phone: 91-22-56371096 E-Mail: sales@electrical-brass-components.com

- **Goela engineers**

India tractor parts - producers and exporters of spare tractor part like ...
Phone: 0091-9810645100 E-Mail: agromachine@touchtelindia.net

- **Monu exports**

India's largest manufacturer, Exporter and Supplier, specialized in - ...
Phone: 91-11 -23913292 E-Mail: agromachine@touchtelindia.net

- **Pistonrings**

Piston rings by India piston-rings is one of the leading names in the industry ...
Phone: 91-11- 23966973 E-Mail: agromachine@touchtelindia.net

- **agromachine**

Used Tractors by AgroMachine. You've located the most powerful and complete ...
Phone: 32(0)52 55 31 28 E-Mail: agromachine@touchtelindia.net

- **Simeon George**

Seeking a joint venture cheap automobile manufacturer
Address: 9791 Westheimer road , Houston , Texas 77042
E-Mail: twinsint@yahoo.com

SUDAN INTERNET AND COMPUTERS

- **50000_CPUs_Harnessed**

Our group's goal is bring together 50000 CPUs for the purpose of forming a ...
Phone: 1-770-443-0115 E-Mail: sabarnett@yahoo.com

- **World Digital**

Offering digital media such as software, games, ebooks, audiobooks, mobile ...
E-Mail: inform@wdeonline.com

- **lizratechnologies**

Lizra Technologies is a specialist web, software development firm providing ...
E-Mail: jeena@lizratechnologies.com

- **LinkAssistant SEO Tool**

Increase your link popularity with LinkAssistant - powerful SEO software for ...
Address: Nezalezhnasti ave, 72a-86

- **Ambergreen Internet Marketing**

Search engine and internet marketing online traffic solutions through SEO, paid ...
Address: 111 George Street
Phone: 0131 225 7020 E-Mail: agim@all-web-design.com

- **esrmtech**

worldwide distribution of electronic components with emphasis on obsolete and ...
Address: D-325, Defence Colony 1st stage, Peenya Industrial estate
Phone: 91-11-24799792 E-Mail: hms_osa083@yahoo.com

- **GulfClick.NET Co**

GulfClick.Net is one of the leading web services provider located at KUWAIT ...
Address: hawally
Phone: 965-2650262 E-Mail: adib@newgulf.net

- **Adult Website Promotion Services**

Adult Website Promotion services sell porn - we offer free porn movies, free ...
Address: 101-New Street, New York, USa
Phone: 123-343-4545 E-Mail: harshseo@gmail.com

- **UK Webmaster World Link Exchange Directory exchange reciproc**

Add your website to uk webmaster world link exchange database free of charge ...
Address: Hereford
Phone: 8070 440 150 E-Mail: luqman@velnet-ngr.com

- **Wura - World - Internet Website Directory**

add your website to our internet website directory free of charge.
Address: Hereford
Phone: 80707 440 150 E-Mail: luqman@velnet-ngr.com

- **UK Web Directory**

UK Web Directory, Web Site Hosting Directory and web hosting resources UK
Address: Hereford
Phone: 08707 440 150 E-Mail: luqman@velnet-ngr.com

- **Cheap Web Hosting Directory, Web Design, Search Engine Promo**

Web Hosting Directory with cheap web hosting plans, domain registration, web ...
E-Mail: service@asterhost.com

- **Cut Price Ink 4U**

Cut Price Ink 4U offers inkjet cartridges, laser toners and printer accessories ...
Address: Victoria Market
Phone: 01453 543676 E-Mail: sales@cutpriceink4U.co.uk

- **Softafrik Arts Ltd**

Need a brilliant cost effective software solution for your enterprise? Big or ...
Address: Crescent Rd, Buruburu, Nairobi, Kenya
Phone: +254 (0)721991155 E-Mail: skmwenda@yahoo.com

- **SEO List Find search engine marketing companies**

SEOLIST.com is a List for SEOs Worldwide. You'll find everything you need for ...
Phone: 9815612193 E-Mail: seolist@gmail.com

- **Ambergreen Internet Marketing**

Boost your website traffic through SEO, paid listings and trusted feed.
Address: 111 George Street
Phone: 0131 225 7020 E-Mail: 0131 225 7030

- **UK Internet WebSites Directory**

UK Web Directory is collection of Internet web sites or web pages related to ...
Phone: 2627884 E-Mail: ukwebdirectory@gmail.com

- **iSys Group**

Worldwide manufacturer of high quality direct thermal printers, thermal inkjet ...
Address: 911 - 28 Street N.E., Calgary, AB, T2K0V6, Canada
Phone: 403.204.5200 E-Mail: customerservice@isys-media.com

- **Banner ad design**

Professional and affordable banner ad design including eye-catching flash ...
Phone: 07913520180

- **Net Explorers**

Net Explorers are providers of professional web hosting UK, web design and ...
Address: 22 Stainburn Crescent
Phone: +44 113 3683073 E-Mail: ne@cool-web-hosting.com

- **Webxperience! Directory**

Features a searchable, spam-free, human-ed directory of the Web. ...
Address: Bucharest
E-Mail: team@webxperience.org

- **HomeHighlight - Free for reprint home and family articles**

A virtual community offering free for reprint articles regarding home, family, ...
E-Mail: support@homehighlight.org

- **BusinessHighlight - Free for reprint business articles**

A virtual community offering free for reprint articles regarding ...
E-Mail: support@businesshighlight.org

- **Questlaunch - Web Search Portal**

Search the world wide web. Webmasters use the pay per click ...
Phone: 555-5555 E-Mail: admin@questlaunch.com

- **Bid Up**

Bid Up Online Auction - Buy and Sell everything and anything with no final ...
Address: 5 Linton Road
Phone: 01132664562 E-Mail: sales@bidup.org

- **Web Design and Software Programming**

Global Info Factory is a team of IT professionals providing IT services: Web ...
E-Mail: support@globalinfofactory.com

- **EmailAway.com**

Check any POP3 or IMAP4 email account from any computer, anytime, for free. ...

- **Sadikhov.com**

Free MCSE, CCNA, CCNP, A+, OCP and other certification resources for IT ...
Address: Bashir Safar Ogli
Phone: 994 50 2139190 E-Mail: admin@sadikhov.com

- **Web Design and Software Programming**

Global Info Factory is a team of IT professionals providing IT services: Web ...
E-Mail: support@globalinfofactory.com

- **Ink Cartridge Directory : TOPINK.com**

TOPINK is your online ink cartridge directory. Check out our top ink cartridge ...

- **Little Effort......More Earning**

Spare a few hours on your PC to earn more by posting Ads. Basic knowledge of ...
E-Mail: padma_sen@netambience.com

- **AssureYourPrivacy.com Privacy Protection Softwre**

Remove web tracks, computer tracks, sensitive information beyond recovery from ...

- **PromoteClick.Com**

Delivers targeted traffic at wholesale prices. Target your campaign by ...
E-Mail: vojin@net.yu

- **K Web Marketing**

K Web Marketing provides turnkey solutions for your web marketing needs. We do ...
E-Mail: jason@kwebmarketing.com

- **Stephen Hoods**

online resource directory
Address: d-47 new dekhi
Phone: 01825 723008 E-Mail: submit@online-global-directory.com

- **Ringtonescharts.com**

Style your Mobile with Ringtones Real Sounds and True Tones.
E-Mail: link@ringtonescharts.com

SUDAN BOOKS AND MEDIA

1. **Miranda Book PUblishers**
   A source of classic books about the Knights of Malta, Maltese history, ...
   E-Mail: gouldian@nextgen.net.mt

2. **Best-Compare Limited**
   Find the best price for Books, CD - DVD. We search all the retailers in seconds ...
   Address: 61 Victoria Road
   Phone: 7654321 E-Mail: response@best-compare.com

3. **Shriramsharma.com**
   Three free e-books on Indian Kundalini Yoga correlated to Neurosciences-ESP, ...
   Address: Visnagar Road
   E-Mail: ashokrawal@shriramsharma.com

4. **CORNUCOPIA**
   Horn of Plenty provides a secure shopping experience that fulfills your needs, ...
   E-Mail: llcrtr@yahoo.com

5. **Instant Publisher Platinum CDROM**
   750 Books, Reports & Manuals You Can Reprint & Sell and Make a Fortune! How to ...
   Address: 1200 Scotia Dr., #201
   Phone: 561-582-1874 E-Mail: rranwarhussain56@yahoo.com

6. **Magazine Subscriptions**
   MagazineSubscriptions.com is one of the larger magazine subscription sites. We ...
   E-Mail: links@magazinesubscriptions.com

7. **Police Test Prep**
   Police Test Prep essential study guide for all aptitude, pati, bpad, wct, ...
   Address: 2 Stockman Crescent
   Phone: 416 885 0258 E-Mail: cbedwell@policetestprep.com

8. **MJ**
   I have books of all kinds for sale, old, religious, many different subjects. My ...
   Address: 412 main street Salem WV
   Phone: 304-782-3191 E-Mail: FoxNwsFan@aol.com

9. **Mums Mag**
   Motherhood resources like articles, things to do, information about products & ...
   Address: 14 Myro Drive, Glenmore, Durban, South Africa
   Phone: +27 (0)31 261 6866 E-Mail: monique@mumsmag.co.za

SUDAN MERCHANDISE-STORES

- **Myjewelz Diamond Jewellery**

Online sellers of Diamond Jewellery
Address: 1406 Narman Point Mumbai India
Phone: 91-22-56371095 E-Mail: sales@myjewelz.com

- **Hand Tools & stationery**

We Are Exporting Brass Hand Tools, Stationery, Plastic Ware, Water Proofing ...
Address: Opp: Dreamland No.33Cinema ,Tribhuvan Road
Phone: 5182673 E-Mail: chandrashe81@yahoo.com

- **Custom Trading Cards | Schedule Cards**

Personalized, specialty trading and schedule cards for police and fire ...

- **Baby Boom 2000: Baby Nursery Store for Baby travel System, b**

BabyBoom 2000 specialize in Baby Travel Systems, Sleeping Bags, Rockers and ...
Address: 4 NEW POND PARADE,WEST END ROAD
Phone: 01895 675596 E-Mail: webmaster@babyboom2000.co.uk

- **Blue Nile TV**

Blue Nile TV Produces quality TV programmes and broadcast them to the Audiences ...
Address: Debreziet Road
Phone: +251 1 16 99 61 E-Mail: blueniletv@yahoo.com

- **Gift Baskets Shipped Worldwide**

Unique gift baskets for all occasions. Featured on the NBC Today Show, with ...
Phone: 888-291-4039 E-Mail: April@WyomingImpressions.com

- **szjingfeng**

Fabulous wood doors veneer, plywood, solid, molding doors ...
Address: 12/234, ziang street 001#Linhu economic zone. Qidu town.wujiang.JS. china
Phone: 008651263815408 E-Mail: sureshdasani56@yahoo.com

- **Knife Country, USA**

Offers hunting, fishing, camping, pocket and kitchen knives. Specializing in ...

Address: 7111 Dixie hwy., 109
Phone: 877-399-1564 E-Mail: jterryah@knifecountryusa.com

- **Diamond Pendants India P Ltd**

makers of Diamond pendants in various shapes
Address: 1406 Dalamal Towers
Phone: 91-22-53555344 E-Mail: sales@diamond-pendants-india.com

- **High end Hydraulic Hose.**

Low cost high quality Manufactures of Hydraulic and stainless steel hose ...
Phone: 51170190/51272190 E-Mail: shilparud74@yahoo.com

- **Swimming Pools World**

All kind of swimming pools. Best swimming pool supplies.

- **dental equipments**

Manfacturer & Exporter for all dental Equipments.
Address: 368/3, MES Road, Jalahalli Industrial Area.
Phone: 28381345/2838443 E-Mail: abbrenian@yahoo.com

- **eMarksoft Inc.**

Offering server side graphing & charting & drawing components software for data ...
Address: Fl.9 Bond Building

- **Best Buys Online**

Online Shopping Mall. We offer quality gifts, jewelry, brand name electronics ...

- **Best Buys Online**

Online Shopping Mall. We offer quality gifts, jewelry, brand name electronics ...

- **2Guitar.com**

Learn How to Play the Guitar. We offer 6 comprehensive ebooks on mastering the ...
Address: 207 728 country hills road nw
Phone: 4035030177 E-Mail: support@pixelzen.com

- **Engagement Rings India P Ltd**

makers of engagement rings in diamond
Address: 1406 DalamAl Towers MumBai 21
Phone: 56371095 E-Mail: sales@engagement-rings-india.com

- **moneyprogram**

make money do nothing...only send out customised mails through official built ...
Address: box 4907 s/l

Phone: +234-8037139723 E-Mail: elisfid@yahoo.com

- **luminous network**

A seller company in the market of oil production is offering a ...
Address: 7 enitan road,surulere
Phone: +234-8037139723 E-Mail: elisfid@yahoo.com

- **luminous network**

A seller company in the market of oil production is offering a ...
Address: 7 enitan road,surulere
Phone: +234-8037139723 E-Mail: elisfid@yahoo.com

- **Engagement Rings India Ltd**

makers of diamond engagement rings and wedding rings
Address: 1406 Dalamal Towers Bombay 400021
Phone: 91-22-56371095 E-Mail: sales@engagement-rings-india.com

- **Diamond Engagement Rings India**

Makers of engagement rings in Diamonds
Address: 41, Yusuf Building Pudhonie Bombay 3 INdia
Phone: 91-22-56371095 E-Mail: sales@engagement-rings-india.com

- **Wyoming Impressions**

Top quality gift baskets for all occasions shipped worldwide from the U.S.
Phone: 888-291-4039 E-Mail: April@WyomingImpressions.com

INVESTMENT AND BUSINESS OPPORTUNITIES AND CONTACTS IN INDUSTRY

INVESTMENT OPPORTUNITIES IN THE OIL INDUSTRY

The Untapped Potential

A Country of Potential
Sudan's vast and varied landscape has long been acknowledged as one of the potential and richest in Africa. It has only recently (around the mid-seventies) been discovered that the subterranean geological formations are also prospective of oil resources.

Exploration Potential
Across the interior of the Sudan there are three related major sedimentary basins running northwest to southeast, each of which is composed of a complex system of sub-basins. The largest and most important of these is Al-Muglad Basin which measures 1200km x 300km, with sediments reaching 16000 m. This basin comprises amongst many prospective oil fields, the well-known Unity and Heglig oil fields, now producing about 250000 BBL per day. Mulut basin ranks second, with an area amounting to 65000 Sq. km and a sedimentary thickness of up to 13700m. In this field there has been so far one noteable discovery of about 5000 BBL per day, while still grossly underexplored. The Blue Nile Basin is the third of these systems, having a total area of 66000 sq-km, and a sedimentary cover of up to 9144m.

Other prospective areas than these three basins lie in the north west of Sudan bordering Egypt and Libya as well as the Red Sea coast and littoral.

Concessioning Rights and Blocks
All these prospective basins are subdivided into blocks for concessioning to investors on basis of exploration and production agreements. So far a number of consortium of companies and individual companies have been granted rights and are active in exploration, development and production activities. These including, China National Petroleum Company, Petronas of Malaysia, Lundin of Canada, OMV of Austria and Total of France.

The Export Pipeline
Recently a crude oil pipeline for export (1610 km length, 28 inch dia.) has been commissioned. and export crude from Heglig and Unity is flowing to world markets via the newly constructed Bashayer Marine Terminal.

Crude Oil Quality
Crude oil from the Sudanese interior is a very sweet crude with sulphur content less than 0.4 percent. It is paraffinic, with API 34 gravity, and is on high demand in the Far East and the Pacific.

The Refining Industry
On refining industry, a new complex refinery has been constructed north of Khartoum. with a capacity of 50000 bbl per day. This refinery is sufficient for the country's demand, and has surplus gasoline for export (unleaded and high octane),

There are other simple refineries of low capacities namely Abu Gabra (2000 bbl per day), Alobeid (10 000 bbl per day), and Concorp Refinery (5000 bbl per day).

The existing refinery in Port Sudan, with a capacity of 250,000 bbl per day, will be rehabilitated, and horizontally and vertically expanded for export purposes. It is a promising area for incestors.

Other Opportunities
There will be further opportunities in other aspects of the oil industry, concurrent and following increased exploration, development and production activities in fields, such as petrochemicals, transport of oil products and distribution.

ENERGY SECTOR

Investment Opportunities in the energy sector
Energy is one of the most attractive areas of investment. Present and future prospects of energy sources include petroleum production and refining, thermal power generation, hydropower generation and renewable energies. One of the primary objectives of the National Electricity Corporation is to increase the current National Electric Grid by more than ten times by the year 2002. In addition to the cost-effective hydropower in the country, building thermal power generation plants near oil refineries seems attractive and economically sound. Sudan is rich in solar energy, with daily solar radiation and sunshine availability for more than ten hours throughout the whole year. Uses of biogas are also present with all the essential local requirements.

For the Generation and Transmission Development Programme the government is inviting investors in Independent Power Producing (IPP) arrangement.

An increase in the generating capacity should also have corresponding important investments for transmission and distribution lines, which could account for more than a third of capital expenditures in this sector in developing countries, Strategists in the energy sector are keen

□ to supply energy to all industrial sectors which are dependent on domestic energy surplus.
□ To draw a kind of co-ordination between the energy producing sector, and the consuming ones.
. to preserve the environment by organizing exploitation of the natural energy resources especially those connected to the forest, and to reforest new areas in order to create an ecological balance.
. to technologically promote the energy techniques especially in fields of new and renewable energy that depends on domestic sources.
. to establish energy preservation and conservation policies.
□ to train and develop the human manpower employed in the different fields of energy supply.
Due to the huge increase of new capacity requirements, the electricity sector can no longer depend on the government for new investment, especially, when the government has to cut public expenditure in order to balance the budget, control inflation and address various requirements in the social sectors, as well as to meet public debt reduction targets. The Government formulated the National Energy Plan with the following objectives:

to expand electric generation and services to regions and towns in order to promote economic and social development and improve the quality of life for the people.

. to eliminate power shortages and unreliability of supply, by effecting huge increase in the power generation capacity within the coming years.
. to encourage the private sector to invest in the power sector.
. to provide electricity at the lowest possible cost to meet the needs of the growing economy.
. rehabilitating and improving the system efficiency.

□ to encourage the interconnection with neighbouring countries.
. to manage the existing load and future growth in demand to ensure better utilization of power.

In 1999 a Genera] Secretariat was established to represent the National Electricity Corporation in dealing with independent power producers. Foreign and local investors are to be approached to play their role. Independent Power Producers (IPP) are to be welcomed in one of the following forms:

. Build, Own & Operate (BOO)
. Build, Own, Operate and Transfer (BOOT) Build, Operate and Transfer (BOT) Build, Own and Lease (BOL)
. Rehabilitate, Operate and Transfer (ROT) Rehabilitate, Own and Operate (ROO)
For further information on IPP and the new generation projects please contact the Secretariat General at the following address:

Independent Power Producer and New
Generation Projects General Secretariat,
99, Gama's Avenue,
Khartoum, Sudan
Tel: 00-249-11-785007 Ext.150
Tel/Fax: 00-249-11-782351
Email: aminl@mail.necsudan.com
Email: ippngp@niail.necsudan.com

NEW AND RENEWABLE ENERGY
There are new and renewable energy schemes in Sudan including improved charcoal stoves, solar energy and wind power. There are also various researches and activities on biogas technology and stowage of peanut shells, bagasse and cotton stalks and other agricultural remains into compressed cubes. Investment in these areas, including the provision of relevant technologies, is also in demand.

THE MINING SECTOR

Sudan is one of the few remaining countries in the world which possess a huge wealth of undiscovered natural minerals. The Arab Mineral Organization, in its geological study of Sudan, pinpointed 36 natural minerals scattered around 245 locations. 'These included gold, silver, chromite, iron, magnesium, copper, zinc, nickel, lead, tungsten, asbestos, talc, kaolinite, phosphate, quartz, uranium, granite, feldspar and sulphate minerals.

THE MINING SECTOR'S STRATEGIES, POTENTIALITIES AND INVESTMENT OPPORTUNITIES

The Sudan's strategies in this sector are summarized as follows:
. to intensify the exploration operations and rehabilitate the available quarries and mines by introducing advanced technology.
. to invest and utilize the undiscovered mineral deposits in some domestic industries.
. to increase production of chromium by threefold, mica by fivefold, gypsum by tenfold, and increase gold production by rehabilitating the present mines and striking some new sites.

In order to realize these objectives, new investment horizons will be created by enterprising in new exploration operations or establishing new quarries and export the surplus, or providing some aiding services, in addition to contributing to the rehabilitation works of the existing projects.

The large landmass of the Sudan involves a variety of rock formations that have developed over several geological eras. This has resulted in the occurrence of significant deposits of major minerals and hydrocarbon resources. The source of major minerals like gold, iron, copper, silver etc. are called basement complex rocks of the Precambrian age that extend over half the country, especially in the northern. eastern, and western parts. Sedimentary rocks considered to be the main source of oil and water resources also extend for about half the land mass of the Sudan.

Major deposits of minerals and oil have been identified in various parts of Sudan. Deposits of gold, chromitc, iron, copper, manganese and Tungsten have been identified in commercial quantities. There are also large deposits of copper, zinc, silver, uranium, lead and asbestos. At present only gold and chromite are mined and there are still further unexploited huge reserves of gold-Gold reserves occur in the eastern and northern parts of the country. It is estimated that there are more than 6 million tons of ore with a gold content varying from about 10 grams per ton depending on the location. The Ariab region in Hastern Sudan is a major area of gold deposits that is currently being mined. It is estimated that there are hundreds of tons of gold deposits in this region,

Large-scale exploration and mining of gold began about a decade ago although gold has been mined in Sudan through traditional methods for several centuries. The use of modern exploration techniques has rcsulrcd in a marked increase in the discovery of gold reserves. (In 1994, Sudan exported 2,883 kilograms of gold, an increase from the 1,521 kilograms exported in 1993).

Gold mining is undertaken by the Ariab Mining Company, a joint venture between the Government of Sudan and a French agency.

Chromite is mined in the Liaaicrn part of Sudan where there are reserves of over a million tons of very high-grade ore. Chromite is used . - in the metallurgical and chemical induslrics and in the production of refractory bricks. (Exports of chromium reached 55,000 tons in 1994). Solar salt from the Red Sea is also produced in commercial quantities of more than 200,000 tons per year. Sudan's reserves of iron ore are very extensive with an iron content of uplo Ci0 percent. Iron ore reserves are located in the western part of the country and in the east in the Red Sea Hills.

There are more than 250 million tons of gypsum located in the vicinity of Khartoum and the Red Sea coast and several million tons of marble also located in the eastern part of the country. Magnetite, used in the manufacture of heat resistant porcelain and magnesium salts have also been discovered in the central part of the country with reserves currently estimated at millions of tons. Around 6,000 tons of ore that contains deposits of uranium remain undeveloped in the western part of the country.

INVESTMENT OPPORTUNITIES IN THE KHARTOUM STATE

Khartoum State is one of Sudan's twenty-six states and is situated at the centre where, Khartoum, the federal capital, is located.

. The total area of the state is 22,000 square kilometers.
. Its population is about five million inhabitants.
. The annual average rainfall is 150mm from July 15th To October 15th.
. The White Nile, the Blue Nile and underground water constitutes the main water sources.
. The fertile cultivable land is extended along the White Nile, the Blue Nile and the River Nile banks.
. The Khartoum State is also home to huge animal wealth.
. Rich sites for mineral resources are on the northern and southern parts of the state.
. Services and infrastructure are also available-

. The Khartoum State is the main commercial centre in Sudan.
. Many specialized research centres are available in the state.

Investment in the Khartoum State is enhanced by the various steps taken, including:-
. Adherence to economic liberalization policy;
. Continuation of privatization policy;
. Sudan's participation in various international and regional investment guarantee institutions;
. Establishment of a stock market;
. Amendment of customs and taxation rates;
. The most flexible procedure for imports and exports;
. Stability of the Sudanese Dinar against other currencies;
. The considerable widening of the umbrella of investment activities all over the country in addition to the very stable and secure environment.

GENERAL ADMINISTRATION FOR INVESTMENT
General Guidelines:
To obtain a licence for a project covered by the Encouragement of Investment Act, investors are requested to note the following procedures:

. Submit a written application to the Director General, General Administration for Investment, with the feasibility study of the project and the certificate or contract establishing the company (in the case of companies).
. Fill in the "Project Form",
. Obtain the initial approval for the project.
. Register a Trade Name or Trade Mark for the project.
. Obtain a License for the project.

Procedures to Enjoy Customs Privileges:
To enjoy customs privileges outlined in the Encouragement of Investment Act, investors are requested to submit a full list of the imported component of the project (list of imported items must be included in the project license).

The list of imported items is to be submitted to ihe Director General, General Administration for investment, along with other necessary documents.

INVESTMENT IN THE FIELD OF ECONOMIC SERVICES:
Investment opportunities in the field of economic services in the Stale of Khartoum appears as a natural outcome of the progress achieved in areas of industry and agriculture. This was made possible in light of the increasing population in the state and the rising demand for necessary services.

Encouraging Factors:
. The ever increasing population of the capital and the resultant demand for more services.
. The current developments in industrial and agricultural projects in the capital gave way lo the growth of accompanying services.
. The substantial facilities accorded to investors in the fields of economic services vide the Encouragement of Investment Act of 1999.
. The availability of attractive tourist sites.

Investment Opportunities in Economic Services:
. Basic services (Education, Health etc);
. Agricultural and Veterinary fields;
. Infrastructure (construction of roads, bridges, communication etc);

. Tourism and Hotels;
. Transportation Services;
. Consultancy Services;
. Housing and Construction;
. Information Technology

Investment in the Agricultural Sector:
Khartoum State is characterized by its huge agricultural potentialities, where cultivable land extends along the White Nile, the Blue Nile and the River Nile.

As a result of these potentialities, many mixed farms have been established under the public sector and other regional institutions e.g. the Arab Company for Agricultural Development. In addition to that, other major projects have also been established which cover thousand feddans of irrigated lands including the proposed Sondos Agricultural Project.

Attractive Factors:
. Existence and availability of specialized consultative and agricultural centres.
. Availability and accessibility to various means of communication.
. Availability of different means of transportation.
. Availability of surface roads all over the state.
. Availability of tourist and hotel services.
. The country's target to double its agricultural exports capacity.

Agricultural Investment Opportunities:
. Production of field crops and green fodders.
. Production of vegetables, fruits and dates for export.
. Animal production in the field of poultry and cows fattening.
. Production of milk and its products, Breeding of domestic animals.
. Breeding of bees for honey production.
. Fish breeding and farming.

The vast areas for agricultural investment in Khartoum State reflects promising opportunities for investors as well as providing them with opportunities to start investment through rehabilitation of existing projects that may require the same.

Investment in the Industrial Sector:
Khartoum State has witnessed various patterns of industrial investment since independence with several multi-sector industrial areas.

Opportunities for further industrial investment with full guarantees capable of realizing comprehensive development in the industrial field are available.

Attractive Factors:
. The rapid improvement in living standards.
. o The large market, local and in the neighbourhood of Sudan.
. o The rapid increase in the Khartoum State population.
. o Availability of skilled manpower.
. The arrangements undertaken by the government that correspond to the international economic changes in the light ofglobalization.
. The endeavors shown by Sudan to establish industrial areas provided with the necessary infrastructure that could help the investor to immediately start his targeted activity.
. The commencement of exportation of oil is a major development with positive spillover effects on all economic activities.

Investment Opportunities in the Industrial Sector include:

The Food Industry:

Development and improvement of canning industry and vegetables and fruit concentrates; improvement of dry food industry; milk industry and its products;

water bottling; development of infant food; meat processing; cold stores and ice-making factories.

Engineering and Metallic Industry:

Manufacturing the spare parts for production sectors; manufacturing of machines and agricultural and irrigation tools, manufacturing of hand tools; manufacturing of hotel and kitchen appliances; manufacturing of foundries and lathes; manufacturing of oil pipes.

Chemical Industries:

Dry and liquid batteries: manufactured cleaners; production of concentrates of medicinal and aromatic plants.

Human and Veterinary Medicines:

Manufacturing of human and veterinary medicines (antibiotics, syrup etc.); intravenous solutions; medicated ointments; disposable syringes; medicated plastic bands; pressuring ribbons; medical muslins; handkerchiefs and flasks.

Assembly Industries:

Electronic Industries; bicycles and motor-bikes; trucks, trailers and cars; diesel motors; power generators; solar and wind power generators; water pumps.

Building and Construction Materials

Gypsum Products; bricks; ceramics; sanitation equipment; cement and sand-based paint; decoration stones; isolating materials; all types of wires for construction (grated wire, fencing wire etc); locks and door handles; electronic equipment (bulbs, lamps etc); electric wires, connections and connection pipes; roofing material (metal); glass; pre-fabricated buildings; paint components.

Stationery:

Printing plates; engineering sets; liquid glue; chalk

Textiles:

Colouring and painting of cloth; tapestry of fabrics for curtains and furniture; carpets; fishing nets; cotton spinning and knitwear; reprocessing of cotton yarn for the manufacture of spinning and knitwear; components of textile and spinning machines.

Packing Materials:

Paper, cartons; glass and plastic containers and covers; aluminum foil.

Hospital and Clinic Equipments:

Beds; operation tables; tools; laboratory equipments.

Sports Equipments:

Clothing, balls, net etc.

Ready-Made Clothes, Shoes and Leather:

Stuffing materials; buttons, flyers and coloured ribbons; shoe soles, heels, laces, buckles ad adhesive materials; jewellery and ornaments.

Re-Processing of Industrial Residues

Furniture and Decoration Materials
Fiberglass Products
Printing and Press Machinery
For please contact: Khartoum State
Telephone No:00-249-I 1-783332/778673
Fax No: 00-249-11-778673

INFRASTRUCTURE AND ECONOMIC SERVICES SECTOR

The economic services sector is central to the development of all other sectors. It contributed 44 percent of the National Domestic Product in the year 1999.

This sector includes various infrastructure and economic services. Great opportunities exist in both of them.

Potentialities and Opportunities in the Transport Sector
Sudan's development strategy aims at increasing the land transport capability by twenty times, paving more tarmac roads, connecting the whole country by proper means of air transport, and promoting the present airports and airstrips in order to make Sudan a real transport and communications centre at international and regional levels. The river transport sector is also being modernized and its capability increased twenty times. Some industries to manufacture means of transport such as vehicles, river vessels etc., locally in Sudan are given prominence in the investment strategies.

Realization of these objectives generates many investment opportunities, and the private sector is expected to contribute the greatest portion under the privatization policy.

Among the investment opportunities in the transport sector, the following opportunities can be cited: Transportation needs of all sectors using specialized haulage techniques and means; establishment of maintenance workshops and spare parts centres; investment in river transport; and investment in the air transport sector - both passenger and cargo services.

Rail Roads: The Railway Corporation is among the largest networks of transport on the African Continent extending about 4,750 km- The railway line covers the whole country from Port Sudan in the East to Nyala in the West, and Wadi Haifa in the North to Wau in the South.

The Corporation is engaged in transporting passengers, goods and livestock. Due to recent developments in the transport field, the Railways Corporation started rehabilitating and revitalizing itself by working on a sound commercial basis. Investment in the rehabilitation requirements of Sudan Railways is considered a priority.

Roads: In 1998 Sudan's road system totalled between 20,000 and 25,000 kilometres, comprising an extremely sparse network for the size of the country. Asphalted all-weather roads, excluding paved streets in cities and towns, amounted to roughly3,000 to 3,500 kilometers of which the Khartoum-Port Sudan road accounted for almost 1200 kilometers. There are between 3,000 and 4,000 kilometers of gravel roads located mostly in the southern region where lateritic road-building materials are abundant. In general, these roads are useable all year round, although travel might be interrupted at times during the rainy season.

Small private companies, chiefly owner-operated trucks, furnished most road transport. The government has encouraged private enterprise in this industry, especially in the central and eastern parts of the country, and the construction of all weather roads has led to rapid increases in the number of hauling businesses.

Inland Waterways: The Nile River provides an important inland transportation route. Its overall usefulness, however, has been limited by natural factors, including a number of cataracts in the main Nile between Khartoum and the Egyptian borders. The White Nile to the south of Khartoum has shallow stretches that restrict the carrying capacities of barges, especially during the period of low water, and the river has sharp bends. A major impediment to traffic has been the spread of the water hyacinth.

Civil Aviation: The creation of the Civil Aviation Authority dates back to 1936. The first airport was established east of Khartoum during World War II. Currently the Corporation has more than 17 airports in Sudan, the biggest being the Khartoum airport. Domestic and international air services are provided by Sudan Airways, a government-owned company. Many foreign carriers operate from Khartoum. The company has a fleet of Boeing and Airbus planes. Sudan Airways is also heading towards privatization to which strategic and credible partners are invited.

River Transport and Shipping: Presently Sudan has an operational deep harbour, Port Sudan, situated at the Red Sea. The Port, built to complement the railroad line from Khartoum to the Red Sea, serves as the entry and exit point for the country's trade. Another port, Osman Digna of Suakin, was opened in January 1991, and is capable of handling an estimated 1.5 million tons of cargo. It is also a passenger terminal. Interested investors in this field are invited.

Sudan Shipping Line: Established in 1959, Sudan Shipping Line (SSL) is the national sea carrier and ship owner. It is in fact one of the largest and oldest shipping companies in the Arab and Middle Eastern region.

Sudan Shipping Line expanded the volume of its operations and diversified its fleet units to 15 various multi-purpose vessels of total capacity TDW of 159,000 M.T.

SSL started with equal shared capital between the Central Bank of Sudan and the Yugoslav Foreign Trade Bank. However later on, the Government of Sudan bought the shares of Yugoslavia, and SSL capital has been fully owned by the Government of Sudan since January 1967. SSL is keen to secure eminence as well as to play a positive role in the country's socio-economic activities.

Warehousing and Storage: The warehousing sector is central in the economies of production especially in the agricultural sector. Despite the availability of many dry and cool warehousing containers in Sudan, storage capabilities do not meet the present demands and do not cope with the increasing storage requirements that have emerged lately.

Warehousing and storage demand is an essential investment area. Building dry or cool storage facilities, establishing mobile fridge container transport units, the rehabilitation of the present storage facilities, like raising the capacity of Port Sudan granary to 100,000 tons, arc attractive opportunities.

Housing and Construction: The housing and construction sector builds houses, hospitals, educational institutions, roads, bridges, airports etc. This sector faces great challenges in order to keep abreast with the development and the overall investment climate in Sudan. Great investment opportunities are available in this sector.

Communications: Telecommunications are being modernized. A satellite ground station near the capital working with the International Telecommunication Satellite Corporation (Intelsat) provides direct dialing between Sudan and Europe, North America, and other parts of Africa. In addition, a second satellite ground station is linked to the Arab Satellite (Arabsat)'s network serving members of the League of Arab States. Sudan is also member of the African RASCOM project.

The Telecommunications exchange was greatly improved with the establishment of Sudanese Telecommunication Company (Sudatel) a public share-holding company, with the aim of extending telecommunication services and modernizing equipment and networks.

The Educational and Medical Services: Educational and medical services are generally provided by the stale-owned educational institutions and the Ministry of Health's hospitals. Because of the high demand, investment opportunities are left open to the private sector to venture in establishing specialized private hospitals, importing of modern diagnostic centres; to establish educational institutes in the various fields of science and technology, vocational, medical, engineering, agricultural, veterinary and economic training fields.

FREE TRADE ZONES

The Sudanese Free Zones and Markets Co. (SFZ)

The Sudanese Free Zones (SFZ) is one of Pioneering Economic Institutions in the country. It is one of the companies which guarantees freedom of capital movement and provides suitable investment climate for both the local and foreign investors. It is one of basic pillars of Sudanese Liberalization Policy.

The Sudanese Free Zones & Markets Co. was established in 1993 to adopt, enhance and implement the Free Zones concept in Sudan in addition it its commitment to a wide range of Duty Free Business & Exhibition Industry.

THE RED SEA FREE ZONE:

Located at a focal point connecting the port of Sudan, Port Sudan international Airprt, Kharloum-Port Sudan Highway and Suakin Harbour, a 26 sq. km, coastal area at the Red Sea has been planned as the Red Sea Free Zone. The Master Planning of this area was earned out and concluded by the NCCC of Tian Jin Economic Development Area of China. The RSFZ is now prepared to host all kinds of investment activities. The inclusive planning of this area is very much qualified to host:

. Free Zone Port
. Infrastructure Investment Projects
. Multi-economic activities
. Exports Processing Industries
. Industries and Assembling investments
. Banking and Insurance activities
. A wide range of related services/investments

AL GAILI FREE ZONE

Located (60) km. north of Khartoum (Capital of Sudan). This area is allotted and is now being planned to cover (20) sq.km. This area is significant since it is:

. Located within a fast economic booming circle accessed to the country's main Oil Refinery Station.
. Linked with active business and industrial communities in Khartoum, the heart of the nation's economy.
. Well connected with traffic networks of air, highways and railways extending beyond Sudan's boundaries into the African markets.

INVESTMENT GUARANTEES
Sudan is a signatory to the conventions on Arbitration and Investment Guarantees and is a member of:
a) The Arab Agency for Investment Guarantees,
b) The International Agency for Investment Guarantees.

The Sudanese Free Zones Act of 1994 stipulates:
□ No property, assets, funds or other possessions are subject to nationalization or confiscation.
□ The right of IMPORT EXPORT DATA and profits at any stage of duly met obligations.

INCENTIVE & FACILITIES
. 100% ownership.
. 100% IMPORT EXPORT DATA & profits.
. No personal income tax
. No corporate tax for 12 years renewable.
. No currency restriction
. No restrictions on entry & stay permits.
. Cost effective labour supply.
. Freedom of labour recruitment.
.Abundant & cost effective raw material and production resources.

MAJOR SFZ ACTIVITIES
Trade
Import of varied commodities and goods for wholesale and retail distribution through the duty free and other outlets and shops in all major towns of Sudan.

Managing a Bond Area
Export of raw material and other Sudanese products such as: groundnuts, sesame and other oil seeds. cotton, wood products, water-melon seeds, vegetables & fruits, edible oils, animal fodder, meat and livestock.

Fairs and Exhibitions:
Organizing of local and international fairs including the annual International Fair of Khartoum in addition to participation and representation in fairs organized abroad.

Hotels and Catering:
To build and manage hotels and recreation facilities and to provide various catering services.

FAIRS AND EXHIBITIONS
The SFZ Fair Grounds was opened early in 1978 and is considered as one of the best exhibition facilities in Africa and the Middle East. SFZ was able to organize outstanding international and local exhibitions during the year.

The Fair Location:
The 475,000 square metres Fair Grounds lies on the western bank of the Blue Nile in eastern

Khartoum. It is about seven kilometres from the city centre and the International Airport, The SFZ main offices are located within the Fair Grounds.

The Pavilions:
The Fair has three pavilions of international standard each with an area of 1800 square metres. Additional covered spaces can be provided at short notice if the need arises. The open exhibition area covers more than 40,000 square metres.

Annual Fairs:
. The International Fair of Khartoum-
. Slates of Sudan Fair,
. Khartoum Information Technology Exhibition.
. Sudan Industrial Fair.
. Sudan Agricultural Fair.
. Eid Consumer Fair.
. School & Family Needs Fair.

THE RED SEA FREE ZONE

Name of Project:	The Red Sea Free Zone.
Location:	38 kms to the South of Port Sudan town.
Area:	600 kms – 26 kms are prepared as a first stage.
Date of Inauguration:	February 2000.
Cost of the implementation of the first stage:	US$ 12 millions.
Total Operating Investments:	US $ 45 millions.
The Investment Map:	Includes Several activities; such as: 41% Industrial Activities. 15% Commercial Activities. 44% service Activities. The preparation of export industries comes at the top of the set objectives.
The operating investments in the Zone:	- The number of licences granted to investors is 415 licences. The commercial system forms a ratio of 80%. These include the import, export, re-export, and transit trade to neighbouring states. - The total invested area is 600,000 m^2. - The industrial activity started to assume an important role, by the entry of some companies in the plastic products industry and some Sudanese exports processing industries; such as, gum Arabic and oil seeds (like sesame).For increasing the investment capacities, Dubai Islamic Bank implemented depots, by an area of 40,000m^2, at high quality specifications.
Contact Address:	The Sudanese Free Zones and Markets Co. The General Administration for Free Zones,
Internet site:	www.sudanfreezones.com

GARRI (AL-GAILI) FREE ZONE

Name of Project:	Garri (Al-Gaili) Free Zone
Location:	70 Kms North of Khartoum the Capital
Area:	26 kms^2 near the main station of petroleum refining. The infrastructures are complete.
Date of Inauguration:	End of December 2004

Cost of the implementation of the first stage:	US$ 9 millions.
The Available Investment Opportunities:	- Industrial investment and assembly industries. - Supporting services., logistic centres and distribution services. - Food industries trade centres. - Light transformational industries. - Packing and packaging requirements industry. - Petrochemicals and plastic products industry. - Financial and consultancy services.
Contact Address:	The Sudanese Free Zones and Markets Co. The General Administration for Free Zones, Tel: 249-183-481814/481811.
Internet site:	www.sudanfreezones.com

THE FREE PORT PROJECT

Name of Project:	The Free Port Project
Location:	Red Sea State
Objectives:	Expansion of sea transport vessels
Current Situation:	- A study and preliminary indicators have been completed for the establishment of the port. - Specialized bodies have been contacted for preparing the technical and economic feasibility study; together with the detailed and comprehensive plant.
Contact Address:	The Sudanese Free Zones and Markets Co. The General Administration for Free Zones, Tel: 249-183-481814/481811.
Internet site:	www.sudanfreezones.com

MINISTRY OF FINANCE & NATIONAL ECONOMY

The Ministry of Finance and National Economy is the principal competent agency assigned the functions and responsibilities for managing and directing the national economy to achieve its goals and objectives within the federal system of rule and market-oriented economy enshrined in the country's philosophy, strategy and programs.

MAIN FUNCTIONS & RESPONSIBILITIES OF THE MINISTRY:

- **Overall Functions:**

Play a major role in the economic front to spawn socio-economic resilience and economic health through:

- Upgrading the economic capacities of the country through designing intellectual policies and instruments capable of stimulating resource mobilization.
- Liberalizing the national economy from various forms of restrictions and distortions inhibiting economic activities and competitiveness,
- Realizing a balanced national socio-economic development,
- Allocating economic resources in a way that raises standards of living, generates prosperity and engenders gracious livelihood,
- Building and maintaining a strategic food grains stock and achieve food security, and.

- Serving as a custodian of the public funds.

Management of the National Economy:

- Formulating development strategies, programs and policies in order to achieve economic growth and development.
- Introducing modern scientific techniques and methodologies of macro-economic modelling, analysis, review and monitoring mechanisms necessary for improving economic management and performance and rational use of resources.
- Spearheading the national development process.
- Monitoring economic progress and performance in view of the rapidly changing international environment and remove impediments to impeccable strategic path to growth and development with transformation.

FINANCIAL & ECONOMIC PLANNING:

- Ensuring coordination and integration between financial and economic management and development planning and improvising coherent policies and procedures required to achieve the desired objectives and targets thereof.
- Maintaining effective institutional mechanisms and modalities to ensure coordination and consolidation between development plans and programs at the Federal, State, Local and scrotal levels in order to realize national objectives.
- Developing and maintaining effective monitoring and evaluation systems to analyze Federal and State plans and programs in a comparative fashion.

FINANCIAL MANAGEMENT:

- Drawing and executing financial, monetary and developmental policies, plans and strategies.
- Introducing modern techniques and systems for budget preparation and management.
- Developing standards and regulations to ensure optimum utilization of national resources.
- Developing sound policies and appropriate instruments and measures to restore financial balance through increased revenues and rational use of public expenditure and ensuring that such expenditure is fairly distributed and in accordance with priorities.

FINANCIAL & ACCOUNTING CONTROL:

- Developing appropriate policies that sharpen the institutional structure of the financial and accounting systems and introducing requisite rules and regulations to ensure and realize effective custody of public funds.
- Strengthening the accounting system and applying modern techniques to ensure accurate recording of public assets and financial resources in systematic registers.
- Developing and upgrading human and administrative capacities of accounting and internal audit.

EXTERNAL FINANCE & ECONOMIC COOPERATION :

- Drawing strategies, policies, modalities and procedures for external financial cooperation and granting final approval of external cr agreements.
- Upgrading capacities and skills in the fields of management, implementation and loan negotiation and efficiently deal with external economic agencies.
- Effectively represent the country in the annual meetings of international and regional financial and economic institutions.

SUDAN DEVELOPMENT CORPORATION

ADDRESS:

Sudan Development Corporation
SDC Building Complex
Street 21 Al Amarat (New Extension) Khartoum
P.O.Box 710
Khartoum –Sudan
Cables :DECORP
Telex :24078 SDC SD
Tel. :472186-472195(10 Lines)
Fax : 249-11-472148

ESTABLISHMENT DATE : March 1974 (Act Mo. 93)
AUTHORIZED CAPITAL : US $ 500 million
PAID UP CAPITAL : US $ 200 million
LEGAL STATUS : An autonomous Corporate body,
Financially independent, and wholly owned by
The Government of Sudan.
LINE OF BUSINESS: SDC is the leading National Development Finance
Institution (MDFI) in the country.

OBJECTIVES:

To identify, formulate, prepare, appraise, implement, and monitor and evaluate joint-venture projects between Sudanese and foreign technical and financial parties in various sectors particularly agriculture, industry and services.

To act as catalyst by combining in joint-venture projects local funds and entrepreneurship with foreign appropriate technology and capital for the acceleration of socio-economic development of Sudan.

To provide finance, technical and management skills to technically sound, financially feasible and economically viable new and existing projects/compantíes in both public and private sectors.

SALIENT FINANCIAL FEATURES AS AT 31 DECEMBER 1995:

Total assets: US $ 133.9 million
Total Investment Portfolio: 104 projects/companies
Total Value of the Portfolio: 126.9 million.
Total Equity/Musharaka
Investment: US $ 53.2

MANAGEMENT & ORGANIZATION:

Board of Directors:
Eng. Al Saeed Osman Mahgoub - Chairman
Dr. Mohamed Kheir El Zubair - Member
Eng. Monier Yousif El Hakim -Member
Mrs. Bedour Osman Abu Affan - Member
Mr. George Moris Lomoro -Member
Dr. Babiker Mohamed Tom -Member
Mr. Khogali Abu Bakr -Member
Mr. Abdalla Ali Abdalla -Member
Mr. Nasr El Din Mohamed Omer -Member
Mr. Mahmoud Yousif Ismail -Secretary

TOP MANAGEMENT:

NAME	NATIONALITY	ACADEMIC QUALIFICATION	STATUS	DEPT./SECTION
Dr. Mohamed Kheir EL Zubair	Sudanese	Ph.D. Degree	Managing Director	
Mr. Awad Abdalla Higazi	Sudanese	M.Sc.Degree	Project Director	Project
Mr. Farouk Mohamed Abderahman	Sudanese	M.Sc.Degree	Manager	Project-Preparation
Mr. Abdalla Karamalla Babiker	Sudanese	B.Sc.(Hon).Degree	Manager	Follow-up
Mr. Stephen Pitya Lako	Sudanese	M.Sc.Degree	Manager	Planning Research & Foreign Relation
Mr.Nafee Mahmoud Hamid	Sudanese	M.Sc.Degree	Manager	Administration
Mr. Nasr El din Satti Badi	Sudanese	Accounting Experience	Manager	Finance
Mr. Ibn El-Haj Mohamed Salih	Sudanese	M.Sc.Degree	Manager	SDC Building Complex

STATUS AND OWNERSHIP

Sudan Development Corporation (SDC), established in 1974, is the leading financial institution involved with investment and the provision of finance for development in the Sudan. SDC, as defined by its Act, is an autonomous corporate body having perpetual succession, a common seal, and may sue and be sued in its own name.

Authorized Capital = U.S.$500 Million
Paid Up Capital = U.S. $200 Million
SDC is wholly owned by the Government of the Sudan and is managed by a Board of Six Directors.

OBJECTIVE

I. Contribute to the promotion and acceleration of the economic development of the Sudan through the provision of financial and technical assistance to new and existing revenue-bearing projects/companies.

II. Encourage the participation of capital and skills - domestic and foreign - for the economic development of the Sudan with the objective of contributing directly or indirectly to the increase in earning and / or saving of foreign exchange through export promotion or import substitution.
III. Initiate and encourage the extension of technical and managerial assistance in the promotion and development of revenue-bearing projects, whether or not such projects shall be financed by SDC.
IV. Act as a coordinating agent in projects or joint ventures; by providing local currency components of the financing and / or entrepreneurship and supplementing the appropriate technology and foreign finance from Arab, Asian and other international sources.

FUNCTIONS

In pursuance of its objectives the Corporation may:
I. Promote and identify opportunities in new development projects in the Sudan.
II. Invest directly in any project, which proves to be financially sound, commercially viable and technically feasible.
III. Provide administrative, technical and financial assistance for the development, expansion or operatin of projects/companies.
IV. Assist in streamlining the operation of existing development projects to achieve optimum utilization of planned capacities.

INVESTMENT CRITERIA

Sudan Development Corporation within the context of its investment policy :-
I. Manages its participations and capital assets in accordance with the principles of sound business practice within the framework of national development policies.
II. Uses its best endeavours to attract foreign finance and mobilize internal financial resources.
III. Seeks to diversify its portfolio of investment among different economic sectors and endeavours to extend its range of activity to cover the different regions of the country.
IV. Extends its assistance to revenue-bearing projects and companies in the fields of agriculture, industry, agro-industry, mining and services.
V. Accords priority to projects aiming at import-substitution and export promotion.
VI. Participates only in projects, which prove through feasibility studies and appraisal reports, to be technically feasible, commercially viable, economically sound and contribute to the development of the National Economy.
VII. Renders assistance only to projects, which demonstrate the availability of competent management and the commitment of adequate finance including cost over-runs.

FINANCIAL POLICY

I. SDC requires sponsors to make sufficient contribution to the financing of projects to ensure their commitment to the success of the projects.
II. SDC conducts its operations on a self-sustained and profitable basis.
III. SDC normally acquires a share in the equity capital of any one project.
IV. SDC shareholding shall not exceed 40% of the total capital of the project.
V. SDC may dispose of its shares or fade out its investment in any one project whenever if deems appropriate.
VI. The total amount of SDC's financial assistance in the form of equity, guarantees and other forms, to any one project shall not exceed 50% of the total cost of the project and 10% of the net worth of the Corporation.
VII. Loans shall be repayable in the currency or currencies in which they are extended or in any other currency or currencies acceptable to SDC,
VIII.SDC shall make adequate provisions against potential losses and build up reserves to a level

consistent with sound financial practices taking into account the size and quality of its portfolio of equity participation, loans and guarantees. Within these limitations, SDC shall seek to pay fair dividends to the Government while maintaining satisfactory prospects for the continuation of a sound liquidity situation in local and foreign currencies.
IX. SDC shall not bear the risks resulting from foreign exchange fluctuations in respect of loans. The borrower(s) shall bear the costs of such risks.
X. SDC shall not incur or permit any of its subsidiaries to incur any long-term debt from outside sources whereby the total indebtedness of SDC and all its subsidiaries exceeds three times the capital and reserves of SDC and its subsidiaries.
XI. SDC shall seek to obtain the best return on its short-term investments while reasonably diversifying their maturities in accordance with financial projection.
XII. SDC shall be reimbursed for all its preinvestment expenses.

FINANCIAL ASSISTANCE

SDC provides loans and other forms of financial assistance as follows ;-
a) Equity Participation in Project Capital.
b) Islamic Modes of Finance.
Murabaha - Financial assistance in which a client desirous of purchasing equipment, goods, raw materials etc., requests the financial institution to acquire these items on his behalf at cost and sells them to the client on a cost-plus negotiable profit margin basis. Capital and profit will be payable on terms and conditions to be agreed upon.

Musharaka (Participation) - Financial assistance, which is formally a limited partnership, whereby both the financial institution and the customer provide capital for a specific project. Another possibility is the participation of the financial institution in an existing enterprise by means of a capital contribution. The pro-rata distribution of profits between the financial institution and the customer is subject to a contract between the parties. Losses are shared by the partners in direct proportion to their capital contribution. The financial institution may participate in the management of the venture but it may also waive this right.

Musharaka is based on either permanent or diminishing participation. In the latter form the participation of the financial institution diminishes through time.

Leasing - This is a mode of financial assistance under which production and/or services facilities are provided by SDC and leased to the client on terms and conditions to be agreed upon. Normally, this includes rentals, operational costs and maintenance charges to be paid by the client.

Guarantees - In certain circumstances the Corporation may further assist a project by acting as a guarantor within the limits of total finance indicated above.

THE ROLE OF SDC

In addition to the financial assistance listed above, the Corporation plays a leading role in all stages of the project cycle including the operational stage. The continuous support of the corporation may include:

I. Assistance during the negotiation stages to ensure that the project company will be structured on a sound economic, financial and legal basis.
II. Participation on the Board of Directors of these project companies.
III. Participation in the promotion, formulation, establishment and commissioning of these project

companies-
IV. Provision of contracts inside and outside the Sudan to facilitate and expe implementation of projects.
V. Spearheading of reappraisal and market surveys and studies during the operational stage.
VI. Monitoring and reviewing of operations throughout the project life,
VII. Provision of technical assistance to new or operational projects whether or not financed by SDC.

RELATIONS WITH FOREIGN INSTITUTIONS

SDC maintains a wide network of relationships with foreign finance institutions, which permits it to serve as a link between Sudanese project sponsors and foreign technical or management partners, investors and financial sources.

THE LOCAL SPONSOR

I. Several projects co-financed by the Corporation are initiated by local sponsors seeking assistance. In cases where a project is identified by the Corporation, one of the first steps is to find a suitable local sponsor. Such a local sponsor may be an individual, a group of individuals, partnership, or a corporate body.
II. The local sponsor should be ready to participate in the development of the project and ultimately to become the owner of the project.
III. In cases where 3 project is initiated by a local sponsor, he / she must submit a preferability study outlining the principal characteristics of the proposed project, on the basis of which the corporation shall decide the further steps to be taken.
IV. The local sponsor will also be expected to assist the technical partner in planning the project and to acquire a reasonable stake in the share capital of the project company to be established

FEES AND CHARGES

Financial assistance is advanced at a profit margin determined from time to time by the Board of Directors.

Fees chargeable by SDC include: "Murabaha" margin; an investigation fee of 1/2 percent charged on total financial assistance to a project; a commitment fee of 1 percent payable on the undisbursed portion of a loan; guarantee fees at a rate to be determined by the Board of Directors; charges in respect to technical assistance are determined on the basis of mutual agreement.

LEGAL DOCUMENTS

a) All financial assistance rendered by SDC should be evidenced by authenticated documents.
b) SDC assists projects implemented by enterprises having distinct legal entity.
c) Subject to the type of assistance rendered, any of the following legal documents are required wherever relevant: Memorandum and Articles of Association; Certificate of Registration; Shareholder's Agreement; "Murabaha" Agreement; "Musharaka" Agreement; Lease Agreement; Loan Agreement; Technical Cooperation Agreement; and Management Agreement.

Security To protect its own financial position, SDC shall take adequate security measures towards any loan, murabaha, or guarantees and in this respect shall ascertain that any of the following requirements for collateral security are fulfilled:-

a) First mortgage on the borrower's registered property including land, buildings, machines and other fixed assets and / or a lien on the floating assets.
b) Bank guarantee from a reputable bank acceptable to SDC or counter guarantee.
c) In addition SDC may in its absolute discretion: Demand collateral security from a third party or a counter guarantee; Earmark certain present or future assets of the borrower as security with regard to the claims of the Corporation;
Demand post-dated cheques.

HOW TO APPROACH THE CORPORATION FOR SUPPORT

Initial contacts with the Corporation should be made by way of a formal letter supported by: Prefeasibility study on the marketing, technical and financial aspects of the project; Name of the applicant's bankers and, if a company or a Partnership, the Registration Certificate, Memorandum and Articles of Association or Partnerships Deed; Licences, permits and concessions which will be available to the project; Audited accounts for previous years if any. (for existing companies); Other information and documents SDC may deem necessary.

EL-NILEIN INDUSTRIAL DEVELOPMENT BANK GROUP:

P.O. Box 1722
KHARTOUM - SUDAN
Tels: 780082-773939-780750
Tlx: 22456-22243
Fax: 780776

NIDBG is a pioneering developmental banking institution in financing industrial development projects in all sectors (food industry, chemical industry, textile, construction materials, medicines, engineering workshops etc.)

1- The group extends its funding services through all Islamic formulas of financing.

2- Special concern and easy funding terms are extended to the small scale, rural handicraft, and productive families industries.

3- Through its branches spreading in all the states of the Sudan, the group presents its advanced banking and investment services the country- wide in realization of the balanced comprehensive development goal, besides its branches in the United Arab Emirates (UAE).

4- NIDBG is the only banking institution which has introduced the automatic teller system, and work is currently underway to generalize the system in all the group's branches.

5- The group presents comprehensive investment projects for the expatriates, and developing the export sector.

6- Our correspondents network covers the biggest capitals of the world.

The group's affiliated company (the Industrial Bank;s Company) provides production inputs and equipment to craftsmen and the small scale producers and productive families with the aim of stabilizing the price and encouraging the productive sectors.

8- NIDBG following incorporation of former Nilein Bank and the Sudanese Bank for Industrial Development, has become more capable of realizing the comprehensive industrial development.

9- NIDBG is the only bank in Sudan that has branches outside the country.

10- NIDBG has capital contributions in many of the regional financing institution and companies (funding program), Arab trade, Arab financial services company and Kenana Sugar Company .

11- NIDBG has broad relation with much of the regional and international development financing institutions.

(NIDBG The Pioneering Name in Banks' World).

The NIDBG Was constituted on the 8th of March 1993 as a consequence of a merger process between the Nilein Bank and the previous industrial Bank of Sudan. The new organ embodies the mission of the two banks, respectively commercial banking and development banking.

THE GROUP OBJECTIVES:

1- Mobilizing internal and external resources in the development process.
2- Providing financial assistance for industrial sector.
3- Providing technical assistance for industrial enterprises.
4- Supporting small-scale industries both financially and technically.
5- Providing finance to different economic sectors in Sudan.
6- Providing banking services to enhance foreign trade.

THE GROUP ACTIVITIES:

The group performs all the activities of commercial bank among which are:
- Accepting different kinds of deposits.
- Opening letters of cr and issuing letters of guarantee.
- Dealing in foreign exchange.
- Extending cr to different economic sector.
- Establishing correspondent network with foreign banks and in international financial institutions.

THE GROUP NETWORK OF BRANCHES:

NIDBG Comprises about 42 banking branches inside Sudan and one branch in Abu Dhabi abroad. These branches provide all banking activities.

THE CORRESPONDENTS NETWORK:

The group enjoys a wide range of correspondents all over the world, the network intensively correspondents covers the different parts of the world and assists in promoting foreign trade in Sudan.

THE NIDBG'S MAIN SUBSIDIARY:

The group has its own subsidiary company, the industrial Bank company for development and trade . The company tended to support industrial enterprises, both large scale and small scale. Within its activities, the company also work in the field of foreign trade, it is engaged in the import and export of goods.

General features of the group:

Authorized capital	ls. 10.000.000.000
Paid- up capital	ls. 7.000.000.000
Number of branches	42

Planned branches 8
Number of employees 2000
Finally the NIDBG seeks to extend cooperation with all institution and corporation ... etc, in different fields of banking activities, hoping that this cooperation would develop the mutual interest of all parties.
All correspondents should be sent to the following address:

NILEIN INDUSTRIAL DEVELOPMENT BANK GROUP,
P.O BOX 1722
KHARTOUM SUDAN
TELEX ; 22456 - 22243, FAX : 780776
PHONE : 771992 - 780750 - 780082
TELEGRAPH ADDRESS : NILEIN BANK OR SENAIE

AGRICULTURE BANK OF SUDAN

Head office : Al Mugran area, to the west and Gamhoriya Avenu.
P.O.Box : 1263
Tel : 777432 – 770150 – 779413
Fax : 778296
Tel : 22610
The Bank's capital is L.S 2 billion. It has 114 branches spreading at the state levels.
The Bank welcomes its clients and presents them its quick and advanced services:

1. Opening of accounts in foreign currencies which allow the opportunity of depositing and withdrawing along with easy procedures.
2. Saving facilities in local and foreign currencies with high satisfactory returns, at hand deposit, saving accounts and investment deposits.
3. Buying and selling of foreign currencies and providing legal banking facilities.
4. Financing of internal and external trade, issuing of Bank cheques and cr statements and opening of cr document.
5. Correspondents all over the world.

Distinguished services for the expatriates.

INVESTMENT

Investment is a renewed economic activity governed by the renewed ambitions of man, with the changing demands of life and with its unstable conditions.
due to the availability of information, the world has become one village with resources competitively sought by big, international companies.

These companies seek the best conditions for the investment of their funds, especially that the development of stock markets and the increase in their number, along with the diversity of high technology contributed to ensuring a quick turnover.
Sudan realized the need for investment, now that the country has great potentialities, and its unexploded resources prevail its wide area. These resources included crude oil, valuable minerals,

arable land and conducive atmospheric conditions secured by its tropical location.
Sudan also realized the necessity of providing an investment atmosphere with the most stable conditions to attract investors who are no larger barred by barriers of time and place.

So it (SUDAN) hastened to regulating and encouraging investment, now and kept coping with its quickening pace.

Promotion for investment now comes on top of economic researchers' concern, and has even become the most important marketing factor in the field of economic infrastructure.
Sudan was successfully during the previous decade in promoting investment in the various fields and scored notable successes on the investment domain.
Sudan enacted in 1999 a law for the regulation and encouragement of investment and determined privileges and guarantees.

The law exempted strategic investment from direct fax. And granted non-strategic investment a tax exemption not exceeding five years.
It also cut short investment procedures and determined where each procedure can be carried out to save time.

The law further stated that no state nor local duties should be imposed on any commercial investment project.
Investment is guaranteed against nationalization and confiscation as investors are entitled to restore their investment after obtaining an agreement from the authority that issued the license. they can hence get their funds and profits accruing from the investment.

Widened during the 1990s and included agriculture, industry, animal production, electricity, oil and minerals.

Multi-national companies entered Sudan and competition started owing to Sudan's adoption of the economic liberalization policy.
The stability of this policy, along with the government trend towards modernizing the structure of the Sudanese economy to cope with developments, at the international level boosted the channel of investment in the country. Globalization led to a radical change in the economic dealings.

Some of the most prominent fields of investment in Sudan include projects of infrastructures, electricity, water, strategic projects, heavy petro-chemical projects, along with projects of rehabilitation, modernization, expansion, implementation of quality programmes and international standard specifications.

The investment in oil prosecution was widely undertaken to attract local and foreign investment.

Many international companies embarked on the prospecting , refinement and transportation of oil.

The oil transportation sector received the concern of local investors rather than investment in the field of oil storage and other concomitant oil-production industries.
In the field of processing industries, greater concern was given to this sector on the domain of investment.

Many industries based on the local agricultural raw materials were adopted and promoted. Such being the case, sugar, meat, animal production and cotton industries became popular. This is in addition to the spread of small-scale industries throughout the country. Sudanese expatriates were even inclined to invest in many investment projects and contributed to the establishment of passenger and goods transportation companies under the umbrella of this attractive investment atmosphere.

INDUSTRY

The Arab Authority for Development and Investment, an Arab financing institution based in Sudan, set up many factories.

The production of this factory reached 3646 tonnes of starch and 3556 tonnes of glucose.

The factory faces some difficulties in marketing and administration. However, it enjoys some preferential privileges owing to the registered office agreement of the Arab authority for Development and Investment.
Sudan achieved self-sufficiency in biscuit industry as the production rate of operating factories increased. Whereas, modern factories were established enjoying some preferential privileges due to an act issued for encouraging investment. This is in addition to the availability of industrial inputs such as sugar, flour and wheat.

FLOUR MILLS

The flour industry brings in an added value of 100 million dollars. It also satisfies the increase in the rate of animal production.

The production of flour mills amounts to 254,000 tonnes annually.
Despite the competition of imported flour, the production of the local mills remains of good quality, especially after modernizing the operating mills

LEATHER INDUSTRY

Sudan is distinguished by its prominence in the field of animal resources, which led to the flourishing of leather industries.
Sudan is considered one of the largest hide-exporting countries.
In the wake of hide abundance, tanning industry emerged in Khartoum and wad Medani as a modern industry that brought in heard currency to the country.

It is an industry with good specifications and requires special technical skills.

The tanning industry contributed to the promotion and up-grading of leather industries.

Hide is also used in presents given to foreigners and tourists.
The tanning industry shows the quality of leather industries. It is derived from the skin of reptiles, wild animals, sheep and goats.
Sudan benefited from modernizing the tanning industry.
It carried out a programmed for promoting this industry with the UNIDO international Organization losses when animals are slaughtered and skinned

OIL INDUSTRY

The oil industry began as early as the 20th century. The availability of the agricultural inputs contributed the promotion and modernization of this industry.

The oil industry had a primitive start and soon it was modernized and promoted. It nearly satisfies the country's need of local consumption.

Sudan has bout 76 oil factories whose production capacity is estimated at about 3 million tonnes of oil.

The oil industry sector was burdened with high tax and customs duties imposed on oil seeds and plant oil.
Owing to the growing consumption of oil, local investment in this field was successful and contributed towards satisfying the need of rural areas.
Local oil presses prevailed many villages due to the availability of oil seeds derived from peanut, sunflower and sesame

INDUSTRY AND INVESTMENT

Sudan as other less developed countries contred its concern since independence in 1956 on the industry sector, especially the processing industries, considering the fact that industry is the modern sector expected to mobilize the rational economy of the country and achieve balances economci and social development to put the country on a par with the developed countries.

The first national government.
Issued after indepencence the first law to encourage and regulate investment. In the process of time, That law progressed to include, not only the ifnvestmoent sector, but also other non-industrial sectors.
The ten-year plan (1961-1970) centred its efforts on the development ans promotion of the indnstry sector to raise its contribution to the gross National Product (GNP) from 4% to 16% by the end of 1970 Sudan was still promoting that plan by enhancing its industrial prospects.
It also contributed, as part of the developing countries, to the preparation of the First Industrial Sevelopment Decade in Africaf 1980-1990 and the Second Industrial SýDevelopment Decade 1990-2000 as it proposed for promotion many industrial projects.

In its more towards modernizing and developing industry, Sudan was still facing unending challenges represented in poor infra structure including roads, bridges, electrical power, insufficent frained cadre, inadequate sources of firance and equpment. This is in addition to the galloping rate of inflation, the burder of tax increase imposed on industrial products and the bureaucracy of the fgovernment ergan dominating the industry sector.

FOOD INDUSTRIES

The food industries sector includes various fields most important of which is the sugar industry due to its success and the availablity of its means of production.

It is known that sugar industry is widely adopted in the middle of the country, particularly in kennana and asalaya projeits on the White Nile, sennar and AL-geneid on the Blue Nile and Khashm Al-Girba project on Atbara River. This is in addition to sWhite Nile sugar project at Al-Kawa.
The technical and economic feasibiflity studies for all these projects have been completed.

When the white Nile sugar factory starts full operation, Sudan will become the fifth largest sugar-producing country in the world, and the second largest in Africa, trailing Sauthy Africa in this field.

OFFSHORE INDUSTRY, GOVERNMENTAL AND RELATED ORGANISATIONS IN SUDAN

Institute of Energy Research
PO Box 2649, Khartoum
Sudan
Tel: +249 11 80 137

Ministry of Energy, National Energy Administration
PO Box 2087, Khartoum
Sudan
Tel: +249 11 75 595

Sudan Exploration and Production Authority

PO Box 2986, Khartoum
Sudan
Tel: +249 11 79 366
Fax: +249 11 73 663

BANKING SYSTEM CONTACTS

There are many commercial and specialized banks, which have branches in 26 states. Also there are foreign exchange bureau's (Sirafat). The exchange rates are determine according to the demand and supply factors (market forces).

The banks in the Sudan:

Bank of the Sudan Tel: 778064-778594 Fax: 778547

1st) Governmental Banks

Bank of Khartoum
Tel: 779924-770198-780137
Fax: 772880-774528

Sudanese Saving and Social Development
Tel: 774358- 775157

SPECIALIZED BANKS

Elnilein Industrial Development Group Bank

Tel: 7712109-771984-773939
Fax: 774686-772638

Agricultural Bank of Sudan

Tel: 777401-776975-770150-774049
Fax: 779081-778296

Farmer's Commercial Bank

Tel: 774960-783005-779836
Fax: 779907

Animal Resources Bank

Tel: 472025-472026-449383
Fax: 471533

3rd) Private Sharing Banks

Tadamon Islamic Bank
Tel: 781709-771505-771845
Fax: 771073

Elbaraka Bank
Tel: 783962-784911-780688
Fax: 788948

Omduman National Bank
Tel: 770400-777221-7770360779306
Fax: 770392

Elgharb Islamic Bank
Tel: 779583-777110-779583-788472-772529

Faisal Islamic Bank
Tel: 773566-773401-774716-781848-772800
Fax: 781830

Ialamic Co-operation and Development Bank
Tel: 775234-775366-774081-780505-777706
Fax: 777715

Islamic Bank of Sudan
Tel: 780759-780142-774554-774552
Fax: 779545

Sudanese - Saudi Bank
Tel: 781708-775049-776700
Fax: 771505

Sudanese French Bank

Tel: 770403-778600-773794-779542
Fax: 771740-773696

ElShamal Islamic Bank
Tel: 774728-779078-782190-782186
Fax: 773585-774277

Almashriq Bank
Tel: 779840-778777
Fax: 772743
Customs

Customs Tariff structure For Imports To Sudan
Products imported to Sudan are Subject to four banks to tariff rate a follows (in 2001)

Rate	Example of products
0%	Rice, rentals, computer system of accessories, animal production inputs
6%	Raw matenals, capital goods, pharmaceuticals, fertilizers.
20%	Intermediate goods foodstuffs.
40%	Household machinese, passenger cars, Tobacco cement, Sugar

EXILE DUTINGOR IMPORTS

The following products are subject to excise duty in addition to the import tariff rate.

Product	Exile Rate
Crenate	25%
Saloon cars	40%
Pickup cars	40%
Tobacco and cigarettes	200%
Mineral water softdrinks	10%
Parts	10%
Sugar	10%

VAT on Imports

All imports to Sudan are subject to VAT with 10% except the following products.
(1) Agricultural inputs (seeds, fertilizers, and presticides)
(2) Cultural inputs papers for printing News papers of magazines and printing equipment's.
(3) Capital goods

Export Duties
All produced of Sudan origin when exported to any country are not subject to any export duty with the exception of raw hides of skins which are subject to 15% export duty. All exports are exported from the VAT.

SSMO

SUDANESE STANDARDS AND METROGY ORGANIZATION
P.O. Box: 13574 Khartoum Fax: 774852 Tel: (249)-11-775247
E-mail: ssmo@Sudantel.net

SSMO IN BRIEF LEGAL IDENTITY AND FOUNDATION:

Sudanese Standards & Metrology Organization low was issued in 1992 and indorsed by the National Assembly
SSMO Headquarters based in Khartoum where it opeates the following offices:

States Office:

1. Port sudan Harbour Office
2. Al Obied Office
3. Al Gedarif Office
4. SSMo s Objectives
5. Protection of consumer
6. Protection of National Economy
7. Promotion of efficiency and maintining quality control of local product
8. Training the required cadre to run the job related to standard.
9. Awarding certificates for imports and exports according to standard requirements
10. Linking Sudan's Stardards & metrology with international and regional Organizations
11. Linching orientation to enlighten the public and local institution.

For the first is to realize which of the best quality and for later must have to follow the total quality management.

SSMo Facilities. Head Quarter Khartoum:

1. cereal lab
2. Dairly lab
3. Mineral water lab
4. Paints lab
5. High performance liquid
6. Chromatography lab
7. Microbiology lab
8. Gas chromatography lab.
9. Analysis and Hall marking of Gold and precious Metal lab.
10. Port Sudan lab.

Information Center(1.c)

SSMO information center in Khartoum work in coordination to exchange up-to-date with international and regional standards & metrology organizations such as ISO, CODEX, ARSO & ADIMO in additions SSMO coordinates with British, Japan, India, Australia, South Africa, Germany, Saudi Arabia and Tunisia, In the field of standards in these respected countries. Further.

More, in response to the requirements and needs of integration with world to boost business however SUDAN adopted as active policy to restore quality control system related to regional and international standards organization. As a result Sudan has obtained the fully accred membership of the following

1. CODEX
2. ISO
3. ARSO
4. ASMO
5. International Institute for Standards and Metrology of Islamic countries based in Turkey
6. Mycotoxin lab
7. Microbiology lab.
8. Gas chromatography lab
9. Analysis and Hall marking of Gold and Precious Metal lab.
10. Port Sudan lab

SCIENTIFIC RESEARCH

SSMocooperates with Sudanese Universities and scientific research center to make technical standards data of commodities which needed. Blow are number of researches conducted by SSMO collaboration with universities and research centers.

1. GUM Arabic (Hashab) and rest of Sudanese gum varieties
2. All Karkdi varieties (the process includes picking, drying and packing methods)
3. aflatoxins and ocratoxins researches on groundnuts Cakes and grain
4. Poultry and animal seeds industry in Khartoum
5. Promotion of local bricks including up grading of a hand used machine.
6. Promotion of jaguar Sugar and its applications in local industry
7. Using of solar energy for drying vegetable and fruits.
8. Use of solar energy for production distilled water
9. separation of impurities from the drinking water
10. Improvement of town bus to the standard required
11. Promotion of hides and skins production.

INVESTMENT 30 REASONS TO INVEST IN THE SUDAN

1. Investors should not miss the privilege to invest in Sudan, the largest country in Africa and the Middle East, and number ten in size in the world, with its unmatched investment opportunities in all Sectors.

2. Sudan is a country with great potentialities whether in form of the extensive uncultivated farmland or the plentiful water resources, differing climatic zones; its huge animal wealth and limitless natural pastureland, forests or the mineral wealth, particularly its large oil reserves, which have not been fully exploited yet. The diversities in wealth are an added advantage.

3. There are countless and various investment opportunities in the different economic sectors such as the agricultural sector, the industrial sector, energy and mining and in fields of economic services. There are also investment opportunities in the fields of air, and road transport, warehousing and the infrastructure sectors. In all these areas the Investment Authority will do the homework and finalize necessary steps on behalf of the investor.

4. With its abundant resources and immense potential, investors in the Sudan are assured of great benefits and successful partnerships.

5. In addition to the availability of raw material, Sudan is home to the most secure and stable environment. It is an ideal climate for investors and businessmen.

6. An unprecedented investment Encouragement Act enacted with its huge incentives and privileges.

7. There are well-identified economic, social and investment plans and sectoral programmes embodied in the "Comprehensive National Strategy for the Sudan".

8. The most recent reformatory steps taken by the state have freed investment in Sudan from all restrictive acts. The Sudanese economy is a market-driven economy, and there is a rapid shift towards privatization in all sectors.

9. Stable policies, easy access to all cities, quick movement to the different parts of the country.

10. With its strategic location, Sudan is a gateway to African and Middle-Eastern markets and beyond.

11. All procedures pertaining to investment in Sudan are prompt and of a simple nature. There shall be facilities, adequate assurances and incentives for both the investor and the invested capital without any hindrances.

12. Transactions in hard currency shall not be restricted, and there shall be an extraordinary freedom of trade with the outside world and at the national level; assured flexibility in the pricing policies.

13. Availability of a highly trained and qualified manpower in the agricultural, industrial, mining, energy and the economic services sectors.

14. The banking sector in Sudan is firmly established and banking services are accessible in all the states of the country. Moreover there are some specialized banks which are solely devoted to spur investment and development to greater efficiency in particular fields. There are also some state-owned institutions and private companies that finance investment activities. Partners to all are invited.

15. Big market at home and abroad to the nine neighbouring countries. The unique geographical location of the country makes it an ideal marketing center and traverse point for supplying neighbouring countries with commodities and services.

16. Cheap labour.

17. Organized business sector ready for joint ventures.

18. Examples of success stories in local and foreign direct investment such as the giant projects in sugar, telecommunication and oil can be emulated.

19. More than thirty universities and research centers as reservoir for highly trained and qualified personnel.

20. Sudan is the largest and key member of the Common Market for East and South Africa (COMESA), in addition to its membership in other international, regional and sub-regional economic and financial institutions. Sudan is also party to regional and international investment protection regimes.

21. Advanced telecommunication networks... easy access to and from Sudan to any place in the world.

22. Affordable destination with easy air connections to and from Sudan to Africa, the Middle East, Europe and beyond.

23. Different varieties of hotel services with affordable prices for tourists and investors.

24. Roads, seaports and airports connecting the national capital with the regional states and production centers.

25. Enchanting locations... the Nile which is the longest river in the world-the confluence in Khartoum of the Blue and White Niles- the Sahara desert, the mountains and the valleys with unmatched scenery... Wealth in wildlife and game viewing□The country is an ideal destination for tourists and filmmakers.

26. An investment regime that does not discriminate between foreigners and nationals; complete ownership with guarantees against any form of nationalization or confiscation.

27. Well-established stock markets as well as insurance and re-insurance companies.

28. Easy and quick visa procedure.

29. The country is well known for the traditions of hospitality and warmth of its people.

30. Pleasant climate in most parts of the year including the Merranean, poor savannah, rich savannah and equatorial.

The historical, deep-rooted, cordial and warm relations that characterize Indo-Sudanese ties for thousands of years is an added incentive, indeed a solid foundation of economic, trade and investment relations.

SUDAN ECONOMIC POTENTIAL & DEVELOPMENT PROSPECTS

Sudan is an Afro-Arab country of multi-ethnic, multi-cultural and multi-lingual society. It enjoys a remarkable strategic location in the center of the African continent that marks a melding point between Arabs and sub-Saharan peoples. The country shares extensive boarders with nine countries of Northern, Central, Eastern and Western Africa. Such juxtaposition engenders a mix of trade, culture, social, ethnic and other human ties built through history.

The country enjoys a total area of 2.5 million km^2, the largest in Africa. It extends from the hot arid North to West tropics in the South with diversified ecosystems that provide immense fertile land of about 80 million hectares (about 20% of this land space is cultivated), natural pastures of about 24 million hectares, forest area of about 64 million hectares and the remaining land is desert or semi-desert. Considerable water resources is available from the River Nile and its tributaries, seasonal streams and rains with annual amount of 109 billion m^3 of water in addition to the underground water underlay the Nubian Sand-Stone Aquifer which is one of the the largest water reservoirs in the world of estimated potential rechargeable 29 billion m^3 of water. Sudan also enjoys a long coastal line at the Red Sea.

Current estimates put the population in excess of 30 million with estimated annual growth rate of 2.6% and a population density of 10.2 per km^2, though this figure masks wide variation with respect to effective population density on arable land which exceeds 50 persons per km^2. About 67% of the population live in rural areas while 33% live in urban areas. The demographic characteristics of the country indicate a young population structure with the number of population under 15 years accounts for about 45% of total population, according to the last Census of 1993. Total estimated labor force accounts for 9 million with increasing female participation in economic activities. Unemployed people represent about 15% of the total labor force. Employment structure since 1996 is dominated by agriculture followed by services, industry, transport and construction with 55%, 10%, 5%,6% and 3% respectively. Broad agriculture and rural sector espouse about 77% of the labor force.

Agriculture remains the leading sector in the economy with an estimated contribution of 45% of GDP, and 85% of export earnings before the year 2000. The main export commodites are livestock (having potential animal wealth of about 128 million heads of sheep, goats, cattle and camels), sesame, groundnuts, cotton, vegetables, fruits, sugar and gum Arabic. Oil exports started in August and refined oil products and natural gas in July 2000.

In addition to its natural, agricultural and animal resources, Sudan abounds with potential mineral wealth of which petroleum, now exploited, is the most important with commercially proven and prospects for additional reserves. Gold mining and exports are on a rising trend while numerous minerals such as iron ore, copper, mica, zinc, chromate and manganese together with non-ferrous resources such as plaster, lime and black sand are also available in appreciable quantities and potentially tradable. This could pose a real base for industrial development.

The industrial sector still depends on agricultural raw materials inputs such as vegetable oil, sugar cane, cotton, hides, skins etc.. With more development of these natural resources agro-industrial potential investment opportunities will thrive and encourage manufacturing of agricultural-related means of production required for improving productivities of both plant and animal sectors.

PEACE AND SOCIO-ECONOMIC STABILITY:

The daunting civil strife inflicting the South continues to impend national security and the very texture of the society in its various political, economic and social fabrics. The ramification of this war, flaring over since 1950s, has a devastating impingement not only at the war fields but on other areas in the form of influx of displaced people with the consequences of wide spread of poverty and pauperism. However, the quest for peace continues to be the main concern of the Government with commitment to building confidence through devolution of power and wealth sharing among all the States particularly the Southern States.

The Government has assiduously engaged in efforts to end the war. It believes that stopping the war is a moral obligation to unravel the human tragedy of the people of the South and restore economic, social and security situations. The Government has announced its readiness to make peace through preparing the climate for talks, announcing repeatedly a ceace-fire from one side, granting general amnesty for all those who carried arms against the Government and agreeing on Operation Life-line to safe the citizens exposed to hunger and diseases. Since 1989, the Government and the rebels have entered into more than twelve rounds of talks outside the framework of IGAD Initiative. In a parallel line to the external mediation, the Government has doubled its efforts to achieve peace from-within. In April 1997 the Khartoum Peace Agreement was signed between the Government and a number of Southern rebel factions. This agreement recognizes for the first time in contemporary Sudan the right of self-determination for the South. It was followed by Fashoda and the Nuba Mountains Agreements. These agreements feature in the Permanent Constitution. A recent development was the signing of the new Nuba Mountains Agreement with the main rebel stream following the United States special envoy initiative. It is expected that with the successful implementation of this agreement the peace process will continue to cover the South.

ISSUES OF GOVERNANCE:

The Sudan Government is committed to adhere to the basic human rights enshrined in the divine laws and international covenants, ensuring the supremacy of society and its legitimate right to developing own indigenous democracy and peaceful exchange of power among the various partisan movement within the Federal System and united Sudan. Enforcing peace, restoring security and the rule of law, building confidence among all people and ensuring fair distribution of wealth and power are the main policy agenda of the Government. However, the rehabilitation of society's political, social and economic infrastructure are basic issues necessary to achieve peace, decent livelihood, fairness and justice together with fostering democracy among all citizens having different social, ethnic, religious and cultural background without discrimination.

REGIONAL AND INTERNATIONAL COOPERATION

Sudan is a member of a number of regional and international organizations of which the following are the most important with respect to economic, financial, investment and trade flows:

- Member of the the Arab League and its Economic and Social Council.
- Member of IMF, WB/IDA.
- Member and Founder of the Arab Monetary Fund.
- Member and host country of the Arab Bank for Economic Development in Africa.
- Member and host country of the Arab Corporation for Agricultural Investment and Development.

Member of the Arab Investment Guarantee Agency.

- Member of the Inter-Arab Trade Development Agreement (now called the larger Arab Free Trade Zone).

- Member and founder of the Organization of African Unity.
- Member and founder of the Common Market for Eastern and Southern Africa and its Preferential Trade Bank. Trade has been liberalized within this market following the abolition of custom duties between member states.
- Member of the Islamic Conference Organization and its affiliates.
- Member of the Islamic Development Bank.
- Member of the African, Caribbean and Pacific Group and the European Union (ACP/EU).
- Member of the African Development Bank.
- Member of the International Fund for Agricultural Development.
- Member of Food Agricultural Organization.

Sudan has managed to normalize its relations with international, regional and bilateral financial institutions. In this respect, the IMF's declaration that Sudan is a cooperative country has been a major incentive for Sudan to continue its efforts to normalize relations with other financial institutions. Most of them resumed their financial activities with the Sudan particularly the Arab funds and the OPEC Fund. Presently Sudan is witnessing a remarkable flow of technical missions from the world Bank, Arab funds, China, Russia, Malaysia, Turkey, Egypt, the Gulf states, Iran and others. Financial agreements for financing major projects in the fields of electricity, agriculture, irrigation, health and education were signed including crs to the private sector from available financial windows of external financial institutions.

EFFORTS TO JOIN THE WORLD TRADE ORGANIZATION (WTO):

Sudan has presented its offer to join the WTO since 1994. Measures have been taken to meet the requirements of membership terms and conditions especially in the fields of economic, trade and investment liberalization and revision of laws and regulatory framework.

IMPORTANT GOVERNMENT AND BUSINESS CONTACTS IN SUDAN

IMPORT AGENTS

Through the Commercial & Industrial Associations:

- Sudanese Businessmen & Employers Federation
- Sudanese Chambers of Industries Association
- Union of Chamber of Commerce
- Chamber of Small Industries & Crafts Union.
- Customs Tariff Structure for Imports to Sudan

VAT ON IMPORTS

All import to Sudan is subject to VAT with 10% except the following products.
(1) Agricultural inputs (seeds, fertilisers, and pesticides)
(2) Input papers for printing newspapers or magazines and printing equipment.
(3) Capital goods

EXPORT DUTIES

All produce of Sudanese origin when exported to any country are not subject to any export duty with the exception of raw hides of skins which are subject to 15% export duty. All exports are exempted from the VAT.

EMBASSIES OF THE SUDAN

ALGERIA

Embassay of the Republic of The Sudan
8, Shara baski Brond,
El Yanabia, Beir Murad Reis,
Algiers, Algeria,
Tel: (2132) 566-623/566-616,
Fax: (2132) 693-019,
TLX: 662145

AUSTRIA

Embassay of the Republic of The Sudan
Reisner Str., 29/5,
1030 Wien,
Vienna, Austria.
Tel (+431-7102343, 7102344)
Fax: (+431-7102346) Tlx: 114385 E-mail: Sudan-emabassy-vienna@aon.at

AZERBAIJAN

Embassay of the Republic of The Sudan
P.O. Box 65,
Paco Azerbaijan,
Tel 994-456/020-767

BELGIUM

Embassay of the Republic of The Sudan
12 Avenue Franklin D. Roosvelt,
1060, Brussels, Belgiuum,
Tel: (322) 647-9494/647-5159,
Fax: 648-3499,
TLX: 24370 .

CANADA

Embassay of the Republic of The Sudan
457, Laurier Avenue East,
Ottowa, Ontario,
Canada K1N 6R4,
Tel: (613) 235-4000/235-4999,
Fax: 235-6880.

CENTRAL AFRICAN REPUBLIC

Embassay of the Republic of The Sudan
Avenue de l'Independence,
P.O. Box 1351,
Bangui, Central African Republic,
Tel (23661) 615-011.

CHINA

Embassay of the Republic of The Sudan
Building # 27, San Li Tuin,
Beijing, China,
Tel: (8610)532-375/532-3329
Fax: (8610)532-1280.
e-Mail:mission.sudan@itu.ch

CZECH REPUBLIC

Embassay of the Republic of The Sudan
Malostranske Nabrezi no. 1,
110 00 Praha 1, Czech Republic.
Tel: (422) 536-547.

DJIBOUTI

Embassay of the Republic of The Sudan
Iron House, IE12,
P.O. Box 4259,
Tel: (253) 356-404,
Fax: (253) 356-662.

EGYPT

Embassay of the Republic of The Sudan
3 Ibrahim St. Garden City,
Cairo, Egypt,
Tel: (202) 355-7705, 7925/354-5043/354-0582/354-5658/ 354-0364
Fax: 354-2693.

ETHIOPIA

Kerkos Kelly,
P.O. Box 1110,

Addis Ababa, Ethiopia,
Tel (2511) 515-241,
Fax 517-030/518-141.
e-Mail:sudan.embassy@telecom.net.et

FRANCE

Embassay of the Republic of The Sudan
56 Avenue Montaigne,
75008, Paris, France,
Sudan Embassay in France Website

Tel. : (331) 422-55-573
Fax 456-36-673.
e-mail:ambassade-du-soudan@wanadoo.fr

GERMANY

Botschaft der Republik Sudan.
Koblenzer Strasse 107.
53177 Bonn. Germany
Sudan Embassay in Germany Website

Tel.: (+)49 (0)228 933700. Fax: (+)49 (0)228 335123
e-mail:Botschaft@sudan-embassy.de

INDIA

Embassay of the Republic of The Sudan
M. 14, N.D.S.E., Part 11,
New Delhi, 110049, India,
Tel: 644-0434/644-0336
Fax: 9111-688-3758.

INDONESIA

Embassay of the Republic of The Sudan
Jakarta, Indonesia,
Tel (6221) 521-2099
Fax (6221) 521-2077.,br>

IRAN

Embassay of the Republic of The Sudan
Hotel, Room 1021-1024,
P.O. Box 1526,
Teheran, Iran.
Tel: (9821)297-211/297-212, Fax: (9821)295-008/ 437-8931, Tlx: 213372.

IRAQ

Embassay of the Republic of The Sudan
El Mansoura, Sharia El Malouk,
Station 601, Shariia 11,
House 41,
Baghdad, Iraq
Tel: (9641) 542-4889 TLX: (9641) 213374.

ITALY

Embassay of the Republic of The Sudan
Via Lazzaro Spallanzani 24,
00161 Roma, ITALY.
Tel: (396) 440-3609, 440-3071
Fax: (396) 440-4377/440-2358

TLX: 610302.

JAPAN

Embassy of the Republic of The Sudan
Obana House,
2-7-11, Shirogane,
Minato-Ku,
Tokyo (108), JAPAN.
(8133) 3280-3161, 3280-3162, 3280-3163, Fax 3280-3164, Tlx J73876.

JORDAN

Embassy of the Republic of The Sudan
P.O. Box 3305, Area no. 13135
Square no. 22,El Malfuf Eastern Oman mountain,
St. of Maviada,
Amman, Jordan,br>
Tel: (9626)644-251/644-252,
Fax: (9626)644-187
TLX: (9626)23941 5450.

KENYA

Embassy of the Republic of The Sudan
Minet I.C.D.C. Building Mamlaka, Nyrere Road, ,br> P.O. Box 48784,
Nairobi, Kenya,
Tel: (2542) 720-854
Fax: (2542)722-253.

KOREA

Embassy of the Republic of The Sudan
653-24, Hannam-dong - Yongsa-ku,
Seoul, Korea (South),
Tel: (822) 793-8692/ 792-0358, 749-1090 Fax: (822) 793-8693,
TLX: K25936 .

KUWAIT

Embassy of the Republic of The Sudan
P.O. Box no. 1076,
Safaa, Kuwait.
Tel: (965) 251-9299 Fax: (965)251-9382.

LEBANON

Embassy of the Republic of The Sudan
Verdun Street - Minkara Building
Beirut, Lebanon
Tel: (9611) 353270
Fax: (9611) 353271.

LIBYA

Embassy of the Republic of The Sudan
68 Mohamed Ali Mosadak Street, Tripoli, LIBYA.
Tel: (21821) 753-87/600-968/600-709
Fax: (21821) 607-611.

MALAYSIA

Embassy of the Republic of The Sudan

Kuala Lampur, Malaysia,
Tel: (603) 456-9104, Fax: (603) 293-9732/456-8107.

MOROCCO

Embassy of the Republic of The Sudan
5 Rue Ghomara Ave. Souissi
Rabat, Morocco,
Tel: (2127)752-863, Fax: (2127)752-865.

NAMIBIA

Embassy of the Republic of The Sudan
Johanna Albrecht Street no. 6,
P.O. Box 3708,
Windhoek West, Namibia,br> Tel: (2461) 228-544
Fax 228-617.

NETHERLANDS

Embassy of the Republic of The Sudan
81 Laan Copes Van Cattenburch,
2585, EW, The Hague, Netherlands
Tel: (3170) 360-5300/ 346-3704/362-0939

Fax: (3170) 361-7975,
Tlx: 32213 SUDANI NL.

NIGERIA

Embassy of the Republic of The Sudan
28 Kofo Abayomi Street, Victoria Island,
P.O. Box 2428,

Lagos, Nigeria,
Tel: (2341) 615-889/617-311, Fax: (2341) 615-945.

OMAN

Embassay of the Republic of The Sudan
P.O. Box 3971, P.C. 112
Shatti Al-Qurum, Bildg #31 Muscat, sultanate of Oman
Tel: +968-697-875, +968-697543
Fax: +968-699-065
E-Mail: suanimt@gto.net.om

PAKISTAN

Embassay of the Republic of The Sudan
203, Ramna 6/3, P.O. Box 1041,
Islamabad, Pakistan
Tel (9251) 212-142/213-294/212-142
Fax (9251) 820-172
TLX 5617 SUDIS PK.

QATAR

Embassay of the Republic of The Sudan
Al-Hilal Street,
P.O. Box 2999,
Doha, Qatar,
Tel: (974) 423-007 / 008
Fax: (974) 351-366
TLX: (974) 4707.

ROMANIA

Embassay of the Republic of The Sudan
Str. Brincutel no. 11, Sector 1,
Bucharest, Romania
Tel: (401) 611-4968

Fax: (401) 211-1217.

RUSSIAN FEDERATION

Embassay of the Republic of The Sudan
Moscow, UL Povarskaya 9
RUSSIA
Tel:(7095)290-3732/290-3713
Fax: 290-3985
Email:sudanimos@moscow.portal.ru

SAUDI ARABIA

Embassay of the Republic of The Sudan
Shara 30,
P.O. Box 94337,
Riyadh 11693, Saudi Arabia
Tel (9661) 488-7979/488-7396/488-7388/488-7478
Fax 488-7729
TLX 406844

Consulate : Jeddah : TEL: 9662 6476003 - 9662 6471090 - Priv. 6478728-

SOMALIA

Embassay of the Republic of The Sudan
Makka El Mukarrama Avenue, P.O. Box (552)
Mogadisho, SOMALIA

SOUTH AFRICA

Embassay of the Republic of The Sudan
Pretoria, South Africa
Tel (2712) 320-153 Fax (2712) 342-4539/24539.

SWEDEN

Embassay of the Republic of The Sudan
Drottninggatan 81A, Solna,
Tel. : (468)208041/201241/201621
Fax (468)201621,
Tlx 12609 SudStkk.

SWITZERLAND

Embassay of the Republic of The Sudan
49 Avenue Blanc, 1202
Geneva - P.o. Box 335, 1211,
Geneva 19, Switzerland , TEL: (4122) 731-26-63/6
Fax 731-26-56 ,
TIX 414124 SUDN CH.

SYRIA

Embassay of the Republic of The Sudan
Shara El Karama
El Jahiz Garden, no. 4/86
Damascus, Syria
Tel 330-447/247-046/334-797
Fax 330-247-238
TLX 330-412155

TANZANIA

Embassay of the Republic of The Sudan
64 Upanga Road,
P.O. Box 2266,
Dar Es Salam, Tanzania,
Tel (25551)32-022/46-509/32-023.

CHAD

Embassay of the Republic of The Sudan
N'Djameina, Chad,
Tel (235) 513-497.

TUNISIA

Embassay of the Republic of The Sudan
30 Africa Avenue,
Tel (2161) 238-544/238-917,
Fax 750-884.

TURKEY

Embassay of the Republic of The Sudan
ANKARA G.O.P. KOZA SOK. NO. 51
Tel. : (0312) 4413884/ 85 - Amb. Dir. : 4416378
Fax : (0312) 4413886 - Telex : 46719 SD.

UGANDA

Embassay of the Republic of The Sudan
Parliament building, Fourth Floor,
P.O. Box 3200,
Tel (25641) 43-518/58-971.

UNITED ARAB EMIRAES

Embassay of the Republic of The Sudan
Abu Dhabi, United Arab Emirates, Hamdan Avenue,
P.O. Box 4027,
Abu Dhabi, UAE, Tel (9712) 822-7502/727-334,
Fax 780-836.
Sudembii@emirates.net.ae.

UNITED KINGDOM

Embassay of the Republic of The Sudan
3 Cleveland Row, St. James,

London SW1A 1DD, England,
TEL: (44171) 839-8080
Fax 839-7560.

UNITED STATES OF AMERICA

Embassay of the Republic of The Sudan
2210 Massachusetts Avenue,
N.W., Washington, D.C. 20008, TEL:(202) 338-8565 Fax:(202) 745-2615/667-2406,

PERMANENT MISSION : NEW YORK, UNITED STATES OF AMERICA,

655 Third Avenue Suite 500-10
New York, N.Y. 10017
Tel. (212) 573-6033,
Fax (212) 573-6160.

EMBASSAY OF THE REPUBLIC OF THE SUDAN AND PERMANENT MISSION TO THE UNITED NATIONS AND INT'L ORGANIZATIONS

REISNER STRASSE 29/5 A-1030 Vienna.
TEL: (+431)7102343, 7102344
FAX: (+431)7102346
Telex: 114385 SUDAN

YEMEN

Embassay of the Republic of The Sudan
P.O. Box 517,
Sanaa, Yemen,
Tel (9672) 265-231.

CONGO

Embassay of the Republic of The Sudan
83 Avenue des Treis, Kinshasa-Gombe,
P.O. Box 7347.
Kinhasa, CONGO

ZAMBIA

Embassay of the Republic of The Sudan
Lusaka, Zambia

Tel (2601) 215-570/292-868
Fax (2601) 40-653
TLX: 40653 SEMLUN ZA.

ZIMBABWE

Embassay of the Republic of The Sudan
4 Pascoe Avenue, Belgravia,
Harare, Zimbabwe,
Tel (2634) 732-586.

STRATEGIC AND PRACTICAL INFORMATION FOR CONDUCTING BUSINESS

ECONOMY & ECONOMIC DEVELOPMENT

Cooperation between Sudan and the IMF continues within the framework of a medium-term staff-monitored program (MTSMP) for the period of 1999-2001. The MTSMP is based on the government's economic recovery strategy and builds on the progress achieved in the implementation of the 1997-98 annual staff-monitored programs (SMP), including in reducing financial imbalances, strengthening taxation, improving public expenditure management, financial deepening, exchange rate unification, foreign trade liberalization, and privatization.

The objective of the MTSMP is to lay a solid foundation for sustained economic growth through a further improvement in the macroeconomic situation supported by implementation of structural reforms to enhance resource allocation and encourage private sector activity. The program establishes medium-term targets of annual real growth of 5-6 percent, a reduction in average inflation to 5 percent, a further narrowing of the current account deficit, and a substantial buildup of gross usable reserves.

In 1999, the Sudanese authorities broadly achieved the macroeconomic objectives of the first annual program under the MTSMP. Based on solid performance of rainfed and non-traditional crops, livestock, and the new oil sector, growth is estimated to have reached about 6 percent. Tight fiscal and monetary policies allowed the government to successfully reduce inflationary pressures and to bring the average inflation rate down, for the third consecutive year, to 16 percent. After averaging about 8 percent of GDP in recent years, the external current account deficit contracted to 3.5 percent of GDP (excluding interest due and public transfers) as higher than projected oil prices helped to offset the weaker performance of traditional exports. By end-1999 the Bank of Sudan (BOS) doubled its usable foreign exchange reserves, to US$53 million, exceeding the target by US$6 million.

Structural reforms moved forward in 1999 and early 2000. The tax authority has finalized preparations for the June 1, 2000 start date for the Value Added Tax (VAT). Implementing regulations for the revised Investment Encouragement Act have been passed. Exchange market reforms continue. The BOS has introduced instruments for indirect monetary management, although their monetary impact remains limited. The BOS has announced a new bank restructuring strategy and is addressing the issue of nonperforming loans.

Despite the progress achieved, the overall economic situation remains fragile and susceptible to exogenous shocks. Determined policy implementation by the government is needed if the objectives of the MTSMP are to be met. Public expectations and political pressures for immediate use of oil revenues are high. However, the oil revenue windfall by itself will not be enough to sustain even required increases in spending, such as in the social and development sectors. For the near future, Sudan will remain a predominantly agricultural economy, facing financing shortages, a deteriorated infrastructure, recurrent problems with flooding, an inappropriate institutional framework in the irrigated sector, and a secular decline in world commodity prices. The banking system is weak, with many banks undercapitalized, and is not capable of supporting private sector growth. Poverty, especially in the South, is extremely high. Finally, Sudan's external debt, estimated at US$24 billion at end-1999 and most of it in arrears, is unsustainable.

Against this background, the program for 2000 aims at cementing the macroeconomic gains of the previous years, while expanding the breadth and depth of the structural reforms. Real GDP growth is targeted to reach 6.5 percent. New oil revenue will allow the government to reduce its borrowing from the BOS and leave more room for cr to the private sector. The resulting lower monetary expansion will help to relieve inflationary pressures and to achieve the 9 percent end-of-year inflation target. In line with expected improvements in the balance of payments, Sudan's gross usable reserves will increase by US$45, doubling the level at end-1999. On the structural side, the program pursues the goal of strengthening the budget by introducing a VAT and improving expenditure management through establishing accounts classification compatible with international standards.

The government intends to start automatic adjustments of domestic oil prices in line with international prices. Financial sector reforms include bank consolidation and restructuring, enforcing capital adequacy requirements, reduction of nonperforming loans, and further development of indirect monetary management instruments. The program also envisages a wide range of other structural reforms, such as further trade and exchange market liberalization and privatization. The government has committed to US$60 million in payments to the IMF in 2000. The authorities are also working with the World Bank to develop policies that would eventually enhance the social safety net, strengthening health and education systems and reducing poverty.

EXECUTIVE BOARD ASSESSMENT

Executive Directors noted the progress achieved by Sudan over the past three years in stabilizing the macroeconomic situation, moving forward the structural reform agenda, and improving relations with crors against a background of a difficult domestic and international environment. Directors generally considered that Sudan's performance under the staff-monitored program (SMP) in 1999 had been satisfactory both in terms of policy implementation and payments to the Fund. Nevertheless, they noted that the overall macroeconomic policy stance had not yet succeeded in reducing inflation adequately, and there had been delays in implementing some of the key reforms. Looking ahead, Directors urged the authorities to consolidate and sustain the improvement in the macroeconomic situation, to push forward their agenda of structural reforms in order to enhance confidence and the expansion of the private sector, and to ensure careful management of Sudan's new oil resources. Directors also emphasized the contribution that a peaceful resolution of the armed conflict would make to poverty alleviation and improvements in social indicators.

In considering the outlook for 2000, Directors urged the authorities to be vigilant against the possible reversal of the recent improvements in the inflation rate and to proceed with caution in implementing the program by minimizing central bank financing of the budget and restraining expenditure as needed to keep inflation on track. Directors strongly emphasized the importance of ensuring that higher oil revenues not undermine budgetary discipline, and, in this regard, they welcomed the commitment to use excess oil revenues to reduce net borrowing from the Bank of Sudan. Moreover, they cautioned against increasing entitlement programs, which would be difficult to unwind should oil prices weaken. Directors also noted the need to continue to broaden the tax base and improve collection of non-oil revenue. In this connection, they welcomed the indication that the VAT will be put in place as planned on June 1. Directors underscored that cuts in nonproductive, and especially military expenditures would greatly facilitate the achievement of social objectives consistent with overall strength in the fiscal position.

Directors observed that no major pressure on the exchange rate was evident, despite the virtual stability in the rate in recent months. However, in view of the many challenges and risks facing Sudan's economy and the still low level of international reserves, Directors encouraged the authorities to allow the exchange rate to move flexibly in response to market forces and not to allow any perception to develop in the market that the rate was effectively fixed. In this regard, Directors considered that efforts should be stepped up to further develop the interbank foreign exchange market. Directors encouraged the authorities to closely monitor developments in external competitiveness, and, in particular, to avert any threat of oil-induced strength in the exchange rate undermining the competitiveness of the non-oil sector.

Directors welcomed the recent measures taken by the Bank of Sudan to strengthen the financial and banking sector, including the recent unification of the reserve requirements on domestic and foreign currency deposits, and urged the authorities to continue their program on an accelerated basis. They drew attention to the recent decline in cr to the private sector, observing that its reversal—in line with the program—would be an essential prerequisite for future economic growth. To that end, Directors agreed with the package of measures prepared by the authorities to address this problem, including the updating of laws to remove impediments to the extension of cr, strengthening provisioning and compliance with prudential regulations, and improving performance with respect to loan recovery. Directors encouraged the provision of Fund technical assistance to assist the authorities in these areas.

In other structural reform areas, Directors were encouraged by the measures taken recently—in particular, the approval of the implementing regulations for the Investment Encouragement Act—but urged the authorities to avoid any further delays in implementation. Directors were concerned with the continuing delays in adjusting petroleum product prices and recouping the remaining losses of the Sudan Petroleum Company. They stressed that it would be important for the authorities to utilize the agreed automatic petroleum price mechanism. Directors advised the authorities to move to full market liberalization in the petroleum product sector as quickly as possible.

The commitment to transparency in the oil sector to date was welcomed, and Directors strongly urged the authorities to build on this by full public disclosure of oil revenue data and periodic internal audits.

Taking a longer-term perspective, Directors were in general agreement with the medium-term macroeconomic targets for the SMP, noting that these were based on continued structural reforms across many sectors, and in particular the financial and agricultural sectors. At the same time, they recognized the risks to the program from structural weaknesses in the economy, such as low investment in physical and human capital, deteriorating infrastructure in the agricultural sector, and an unsustainable debt burden.

Directors noted Sudan's adherence to the schedule of payments to the Fund through April 2000, and urged the authorities to continue this performance. Welcoming the continued improvement in relations with external crors, they also urged that further progress be made toward an eventual resolution of Sudan's external debt problem.

Directors welcomed the authorities' intention to strengthen the statistical database, especially regarding monetary statistics where some problems had emerged.

Sudan: Selected Economic and Financial Indicators, 1996-1999

	1996	1997	1998	1999
	(Annual changes in percent)			
Domestic economy				
Real GDP growth	4.0	6.7	5.0	6.0[1/]
End-of-period CPI inflation	114.2	32.0	7.9	17.0
Average CPI inflation	132.8	46.7	17.1	16.0

	(In percent of GDP)				
Financial variables					
Total revenue		6.3	6.6	7.9	8.5
Total expenditure		9.8	7.4	8.6	9.3
Current expenditure		9.2	6.8	7.8	8.0
Capital expenditure		0.6	0.6	0.8	1.3
Overall balance (cash)		-3.5	-0.7	-0.7	-0.9
Broad money (change in percent)		6.5	37.0	29.6	24.6
Reserve money (change in percent)	81.8	34.3	29.4	35.1	
	(In millions of U.S. dollars)				
External sector					
Exports, f.o.b.		620	594	596	780
Imports, c.i.f.		-1,547	-1,580	-1,925	-1,412
External current account balance 2/	-579.6	-330	-338	-236	
In percent of GDP		-7.6	-4.0	-3.9	-2.4
Real effective exchange rate (change in percent)		6.7	22.0	-25.8	18.8

Sources: Data provided by the Sudanese authorities, IMF staff estimates.
1/ Preliminary
2/ Excluding interest due, public transfers, and oil pipeline imports.

[1]Under Article IV of the IMF's Articles of Agreement, the IMF holds bilateral discussions with members, usually every year. A staff team visits the country, collects economic and financial information, and discusses with officials the country's economic developments and policies. On return to headquarters, the staff prepares a report, which forms the basis for discussion by the Executive Board. At the conclusion of the discussion, the Managing Director, as Chairman of the Board, summarizes the views of Executive Directors, and this summary is transmitted to the country's authorities. In this PIN, the main features of the Board's discussion are described.

THE ECONOMY IN THE EARLY AND MID-1990S

The Economy of Sudan continued to be in disarray in 1994. The principal causes of the disorder have been the violent, costly civil war, an inept government, an influx of refugees from neighboring countries, as well as internal migration, and a decade of below normal annual rainfall with the concomitant failure of staple food and cash crops.

The economic and political upheavals that characterized Sudan in the 1980s have made statistical material either difficult to obtain or unreliable. Prices and wages in the marketplace fluctuated constantly, as did the government's revenue. Consequently, information concerning Sudan's economy tends to be more historical than current.

In the 1970s, economic growth had been stimulated by a large influx of capital from Saudi Arabia and Kuwait, invested with the expectation that Sudan would become "the breadbasket" of the Arab world, and by large increments of foreign aid from the United States and the European Community (EC). Predictions of continuing economic growth were sustained by loans from the World Bank and generous contributions from such disparate countries as Norway, Yugoslavia, and China. Sudan's greatest economic resource was its agriculture, to be developed in the vast arable land that either received sufficient rainfall or could be irrigated from the Nile. By 1994 Sudan had not yet claimed its full water share (18.5 billion cubic meters) under the 1959 Nile Waters Agreement between Egypt and Sudan.

Sudan's economic future in the 1970s was also energized by the Chevron Overseas Petroleum Corporation's discovery of oil on the borderlands between the provinces of Kurdufan and Bahr al Ghazal. Concurrently, the most thoroughly researched hydrological project in the Third World, the Jonglei Canal (also seen as Junqali Canal), was proceeding ahead of schedule, planned not only to provide water for northern Sudan and Egypt, but also to improve the life of the Nilotic people of the canal zone. New, large agricultural projects had been undertaken in sugar at Kinanah and cotton at Rahad. Particularly in southern Sudan, where the Addis Ababa accords of March 27, 1972, had seemingly ended the insurgency, a sense of optimism and prosperity prevailed, dashed, however, when the civil war resumed in 1983. The Khartoum government controlled these development projects, but entrepreneurs could make fortunes through the intricate network of kinship and political relations that has traditionally driven Sudan's social and economic machinery.

In the early 1970s, public enterprises dominated the modern sector, including much of agriculture and most of large-scale industry, transport, electric power, banking, and insurance. This situation resulted from the private sector's inability to finance major development and from an initial government policy after the 1969 military coup to nationalize the financial sector and part of existing industry. Private economic activities were relegated to modern small- and medium-scale industry. The private sector dominated road transport and domestic commerce and virtually controlled traditional agriculture and handicrafts.

In the 1980s, however, Sudan underwent severe political and economic upheavals that have shaken its traditional institutions and its economy. The civil war in the south resumed in 1983, at a cost of more than £Sd11 million per day. The main participant in the war against government was the Sudanese People's Liberation Army (SPLA, the armed wing of the Sudanese People's Liberation Movement (SPLM)), under John Garang's leadership. The SPLA made steady gains against the Sudanese army until by 1992 it controlled nearly one-third of the country.

The dearth of rainfall in the usually productive regions of Sahel and southern Sudan added to the country's economic problems. Refugees, both Sudanese and foreigners from Eritrea, Ethiopia, Uganda, and Chad, further strained the Sudanese budget. International humanitarian agencies have rallied to Sudan's aid, but the government rejected their help.

When Jaafar an Nimeiri was overthrown in April 1985, his political party disappeared, as did his elaborate security apparatus. The military transitional government and the democratically elected coalition government of Sadiq al Mahdi that succeeded the exiled Nimeiri failed to address the country's economic problems. Production continued to decline as a result of mismanagement and natural disasters. The national debt grew at an alarming rate because Sudan's resources were insufficient to service it. Not only did the SPLA shut down Chevron's prospecting and oil production, but it also stopped work on the Jonglei Canal.

On June 30, 1989, a military coup d'état led by Colonel (later Lieutenant General) Umar al Bashir overthrew the government of Sadiq al Mahdi. Ideologically tied to the Muslim Brotherhood and dependent for political support on the Brotherhood's party, the National Islamic Front, the Bashir regime has methodically purged those agencies that dealt primarily with the economy--the civil service, the trade unions, the boards of publicly owned enterprises, the Ministry of Finance and Economic Planning, and the central bank. Under Bashir's government, Sudan's economy has been further strained by the most severe famine of this century, the continuation of the war in the south, and a foreign policy that has left Sudan economically, if not politically, isolated from the world community.

ECONOMIC DEVELOPMENT BACKGROUND

Historically, the colonial government was not interested in balanced economic growth and instead concentrated its development efforts on irrigated agriculture and the railroad system throughout the Anglo-Egyptian condominium. Incidental government investment had gone mainly into ad hoc projects, such as the construction of cotton gins and oilseed-pressing mills as adjuncts of the irrigation program. A limited amount of rainfed mechanized farming, similarly on an ad hoc basis, had also been developed during World War II.

After the war, two development programs-- actually lists of proposed investments--were drawn up for the periods 1946-50 and 1951-55. These plans appear to have been a belated effort to broaden the country's economic base in preparation for eventual Sudanese independence. Both programs were seriously hampered by a lack of experienced personnel and materials and had little real impact. Independently, the private sector had expanded irrigated agriculture, and some small manufacturing operations had been started, but only three larger industrial enterprises (meat and cement plants and a brewery) had been constructed, all between 1949 and 1952. As a result, at independence the new Sudanese government's principal development inheritance was the vast irrigated Gezira Scheme (also seen as Jazirah Scheme) and Sudan Railways.

Not until 1960 did the new government attempt to prepare a national development plan. Since that time, three plans have been formulated, none of which has been carried through to completion. Work on the first of these, the Ten-Year Plan of Economic and Social Development, for the fiscal years 1961-70, began in late 1960, but the plan was not formally adopted until September 1962, well over a year after its scheduled starting date. The total ten-year investment was set at £Sd565 million, at the time equivalent to more than US$1.6 billion. The private sector was expected to provide 40 percent of the amount. Unfortunately, the goals were overly ambitious, and the government had few experienced planners.

The plan as prepared was not adhered to, and implementation was actually carried out through investment programs that were drawn up annually and funded through the development budget. Projects not in the original plan were frequently included. Investment was at a high rate in the first years, well beyond projections, and a number of major undertakings had been completed by mid-plan, including the Khashm al Qirbah and Manaqil irrigation projects, a sugar factory at the former site, another at Al Junayd irrigation project, and the Roseires (also called Ar Rusayris) Dam.

As the 1960s progressed, a lack of funds threatened the continuation of development activities. Government current expenditure had increased much faster than receipts, in part because of the intensification of the civil war in the south, and government surpluses to finance development vanished. At the same time, there was a shortfall in foreign investment capital. The substantial foreign reserves held at the beginning of the plan period were depleted, and the government resorted to deficit financing and foreign borrowing. The situation had so deteriorated by 1967 that implementation of the Ten-Year Plan was abandoned. Sudan's international cr worthiness became open to question.

Despite major financial problems, real economic gains were nevertheless made during the Ten-Year Plan, and per capita income rose from the equivalent of US$86 in 1960 to about US$104 at the end of the decade. Late in the 1960s, the government prepared a new plan covering FY 1968 to FY 1972. This plan was discarded after the military coup led by Nimeiri in May 1969. Instead, the government adopted a Five-Year Plan of Economic and Social Development, 1970-74. This plan, prepared with the assistance of Soviet planning personnel, sought to achieve the major goals of the May revolution (creation of an independent national economy; steady growth of prosperity; and further development of cultural, education, and health services) through socialist development.

During the plan's first two years, expenditures remained low, affected largely by uncertainties that stemmed from the civil war. After the war ceased in early 1972, the government felt that the plan failed to provide for transportation improvements and large-scale productive projects. In 1973, the government therefore established in the Interim Action Program, which extended the original plan period through FY 1976. New objectives included the removal of transportation bottlenecks, attainment of self-sufficiency in the production of several agricultural and industrial consumer items, and an increase in agricultural exports.

To accomplish these goals, proposed public sector investment increased from £Sd215 million to £Sd463 million (however, actual expenditures during the five years, excluding technical assistance, were £Sd250 million). Private sector projected investment was estimated at £Sdl70 million originally, but the nationalizations carried out in 1970 and 1971 discouraged private investment in productive undertakings. Foreign private capital investment became negligible, and domestic private capital was put mostly into areas considered less subject to takeover, such as service enterprises, housing, traditional agriculture, and handicrafts.

The denationalizations since 1972 resulted in increased private foreign investment in development. The final investment total during the first five years was considerably above the original plan projection. The plan failed to achieve its goal of a 7.6 percent annual growth rate in gross domestic product, however, and was extended to 1977.

From FY 1973, after introduction of the Interim Action Program, through 1977, development expenditures grew to more than 1 billion Sudanese pounds. The government initiated several irrigation projects at Rahad, Satit southeast of Khashm al Qirba, Ad Damazin, and Kinanah; and established factories at Sannar, Kinanah, at Shandi on the Nile northeast of Khartoum, Kusti, Kaduqli, Nyala, and Rabak on the White Nile south of Khartoum. Roads between Khartoum and Port Sudan were paved with tarmacadam. Excavation began on the Jonglei Canal. Chevron discovered oil. The original plan called for almost half of investment to be provided by surpluses in the central government budget. Although this assumption appeared highly optimistic in view of the modest surpluses attained during the last half of the 1960s, tax revenues did increase as projected.

Earnings from public corporations, however, fell short of projections, and growth in government current expenditures greatly exceeded revenue growth. As a result, not only were there no surpluses in the public sector, but the government had to borrow from the Bank of Sudan to cover the current expenditure account. Foreign capital, although abundant, also did not equal the spending on development, and, contrary to the expectations of the plan's drafters, the government had to resort to domestic borrowing to proceed with project implementation.

In early 1977, the government published the successor Six- Year Plan of Economic and Social Development, 1977-1982. Its goals and projections also appeared optimistic because of the worsening domestic economic situation, which was marked by growing inflation. The inflation stemmed in large part from deficit development financing (printing money), increasing development costs because of worldwide price rises, and rising costs for external capital. During the plan's second year, FY 1978, there was no economic growth as the deficit development financing in the mid- and late 1970s led the Sudan into a deepening economic crisis. At the same time, external debt pressures mounted, and Sudan failed to meet its scheduled payments A substantial cutback in further development expenditures became unavoidable. The result was an abandonment of Six-Year Plan projections, a restriction of expenditures generally to the completion of projects under way, improvement of the performance of existing operational projects, elimination of transport constraints, and a series of short-term "rolling" programs that particularly emphasized exports.

In October 1983, the government announced a three-year public investment program, but efforts to Islamize the economy in 1984 impeded its implementation, and after the Nimeiri overthrow in April 1985, it was suspended. In August 1987, an economic recovery program was initiated. This program was followed, beginning in October 1988, by a three-year recovery program to reform trade policy and regulate the exchange rate, reduce the budget deficit and subsidies, and encourage exports and privatization. There was little possibility for early economic recovery offered by the military government of General Umar al Bashir that took office on June 30, 1989. The government's economic policies proposed to Islamize the banking system, but foreign business interests viewed this measure as a disincentive to do business in Sudan, because no interest would be paid on new loans.

Furthermore, Islamic banks and other economic supporters of the regime were to be granted disproportionate influence over the economy, which led to widespread resentment among other sectors. Finally, the government did not go far enough to satisfy the International Monetary Fund or other major crors that it had sufficiently reduced subsidies on basic commodities, thus reducing its budget deficit. Bashir had announced an economic recovery program in mid-1990, but in 1991 its results were still awaited.

The late 1970s had seen corruption become widespread. Although always present, corruption never had been a major characteristic of the Sudanese economic scene. The enormous sums that poured into Sudan in the late 1970s from the Arab oil- exporting countries, the United States, and the European Community, however, provided opportunities for the small clique that surrounded Nimeiri to enrich themselves. This corruption fell into three principal categories: embezzlement of public funds, most of which left the country, agricultural acquisition schemes, and investment in the mercantile sphere.

The most common ways of embezzling public funds were acquiring liquid assets from banks or government agencies, selling the state's assets, selling state land, and smuggling. The siphoning off of liquid assets usually required the connivance of a high government official. Between 1975 and 1982, more than 800 cases were reported of embezzlement of, on the average, more than £Sd1,000. In one case, principal bank officials embezzled £Sd3 million; another bank made a loan of £Sd200 million to a businessman whose business was fictitious.

State property sold by embezzlers included gasoline and medicines. State officials also sold real estate in residential areas at below the market price. An impressive residence would then be built on the property for rental to diplomatic officials or executives of multinational companies. In the past, small operators penetrating the vast and unpatrolled borders of Sudan carried out smuggling, but in the late 1980s it became a vast and sophisticated business. Of the smuggling operations uncovered, one involved £Sd2.5 million in cloth, another £Sdl million in matches, and a third £Sd0.5 million in automobiles.

Another highly profitable form of corruption was the selling of state farmlands, each about 30,000 *feddans* (1 *feddan* is equivalent to 0.42 hectares). Mechanized Farming Corporation (MFC) officials sold large numbers of *feddans* at low prices to senior officials in Khartoum; many of the latter exploited the land for profit at the expense of the peasantry and caused profound ecological deterioration.

As corruption ran rampant during the late 1970s until Nimeiri was overthrown, commercial companies, particularly in the export- import trade, profited through their influence on public policy and through special permits they received. The Islamic institutions that dominated Sudanese banking facilitated this corruption. These banks, of which the most important was the Faisal Islamic Bank, possessed privileges not enjoyed by Sudanese national banks, such as exemption from taxation and the right to transfer profits abroad. An example of the combination of political power and financial capital was the Islamic Development Company. Established in 1983 as a limited shareholding company with an authorized capitalization of US$1 billion, the company was chartered to invest in agriculture, industry, services, construction, and Islamic banks. In practice, it concentrated on the export-import trade, where high profits could be made quickly and easily, in contrast to the slow returns of agricultural development projects.

The board of directors consisted of ten persons, four Sudanese and six foreign nationals, mostly Saudis, including a son of the late King Faisal ibn Abd al Aziz Al Saud. Of the Sudanese, three belonged to the National Islamic Front, and the fourth was the son of the leader of the Khatmiyyah, a Muslim religious group associated with the National Unionist Party. All had connections with Islamic banks and the Sudanese parliament. Their purpose was to strengthen the Islamist movement's economic power by tying their commercial enterprise to the state in order to achieve a privileged position in the marketplace. They accomplished this aim by granting shares valued at US$100,000 to founding members and to prominent persons, ranging from the republic's president to wealthy Muslim businessmen.

Between 1978 and 1985, agricultural and industrial production had declined in per capita terms. Imports during much of the 1980s were three times the level of exports. By 1991 the value of the Sudanese pound against the dollar had sunk to less than 10 percent of its 1978 value, and the country's external debt had risen to US$13 billion, the interest on which could be paid only by raising new loans.

Two reasons for this decline were the droughts and accompanying famine occurring in the 1980s and 1991, and the influx of more than 1 million refugees from Eritrea, Ethiopia, Chad, and Uganda, in addition to the persons displaced by the continuing war in southern Sudan who were estimated to number between 1.5 million and 3.5 million. Nevertheless, the decline in Sudan's agricultural and industrial production had begun before these calamities. Few development projects were completed on time and those that were failed to achieve projected production. After 1978 the GDP steadily fell so that the vast sums of money borrowed could not be repaid by increased productivity. Sudan found itself in a cycle of increasing debt and declining production.

These economic problems had two fundamental causes. First, in planning little thought was given to the impact of any one project on the whole economy and even less to the burden such huge projects would place on a fragile infrastructure. Some ministries undertook projects by unilaterally negotiating loans without reference to the Central Planning Agency. Second, remittances by Sudanese laborers in the Persian Gulf (thousands of workers were based in Kuwait and Iraq, until many of them were expelled) placed a stress on Sudan's economy, because the government was forced to relax its stringent currency controls to induce these workers to repatriate their earnings. Such funds were largely invested in consumer goods and housing, rather than in development projects.

AGRICULTURE, LIVESTOCK, FISHERIES, AND FORESTRY

In the early 1990s, agriculture and livestock raising were the main sources of livelihood in Sudan for about 61 percent of the working population. Agricultural products regularly accounted for about 95 percent of the country's exports. Industry was mostly agriculturally-based, accounting for 15 percent of GDP in 1988. The average annual growth of agricultural production declined in the 1980s to 0.8 percent for the period 1980-87, as compared with 2.9 percent for the period 1965-80. Similarly, the sector's total contribution to GDP declined over the years, as the other sectors of the economy expanded. Total sectoral activities, which contributed an estimated 40 percent of GDP in the early 1970s, had fluctuated during the 1980s and represented about 36 percent in 1988. Crop cultivation was divided between a modern, market-oriented sector comprising mechanized, large-scale irrigated and rainfed farming (mainly in central Sudan) and small-scale farming following traditional practices that was carried on in the other parts of the country where rainfall or other water sources were sufficient for cultivation.

Large investments continued to be made in the 1980s in mechanized, irrigated, and rainfed cultivation, with their combined areas accounting for roughly two-thirds of Sudan's cultivated land in the late 1980s. The early emphasis on cotton growing on irrigated land had decreased. Although cotton remained the most important crop, peanuts, wheat, and sugarcane had become major crops, and considerable quantities of sesame also were grown. Rainfed mechanized farming continued to produce mostly sorghum, and short-fiber cotton was also grown. Production in both subsectors increased domestic supplies and export potentials. The increase appeared, however, to have been achieved mainly by expanding the cultivated area rather than by increasing productivity. To stimulate productivity, in 1981 the government offered various incentives to cultivators of irrigated land who were almost entirely government tenants. Subsistence cultivators produced sorghum as their staple crop, although in the northerly, rainfed, cultivated areas millet was the principal staple. Subsistence farmers also grew peanuts and sesame.

Livestock raising, pursued throughout Sudan except in the extremely dry areas of the north and the tsetse-fly-infested area in the far south, was almost entirely in the traditional sector. Because livestock raising provided employment for so many people, modernization proposals have been based on improving existing practices and marketing for export, rather than moving toward the modern ranching that requires few workers.

Fishing was largely carried out by the traditional sector for subsistence. An unknown number of small operators also used the country's major reservoirs in the more populated central region and the rivers to catch fish for sale locally and in nearby larger urban centers. The few modern fishing ventures, mainly on Lake Nubia and in the Red Sea, were small.

The forestry subsector comprised both traditional gatherers of firewood and producers of charcoal--the main sources of fuel for homes and some industry in urban areas, and a modern timber and saw milling industry, the latter government owned. Approximately 21 million cubic meters of wood, mainly for fuel, were cut in 1987. Gum Arabic production in FY 1986-87 was about 40,000 tons. In the late 1980s, it became in most years the second biggest export after cotton, amounting to about 11 percent of total exports.

LAND USE

By 1991 only partial surveys of Sudan's land resources had been made, and estimates of the areas included in different landuse categories varied considerably. Figures for potentially arable land ranged from an estimate of 35.9 million hectares made in the mid-1960s to a figure of 84 million hectares published by the Ministry of Agriculture and Natural Resources in 1974. Estimates of the amount actually under cultivation varied in the late 1980s, ranging from 7.5 million hectares, including roughly 10 or 11 percent in fallow, to 12.6 million hectares.

Substantial variations also existed in land classified as actually used or potentially usable for livestock grazing. The ministry and the United Nations Food and Agriculture Organization (FAO) have classified about 24 million hectares as pastureland. The 1965 estimate of land use classified 101.4 million hectares as grazing land, and in 1975 an ILO-United Nations Development Programme (UNDP) interagency mission to Sudan estimated the total potential grazing land at between 120 million and 150 million hectares.

Forestland estimates also differed greatly, from less than 60 million hectares by staff of the Forestry Administration to about 915 million hectares by the Ministry of Agriculture and Natural

Resources and the FAO. Dense stands of trees only covered between 20 million and 24 million hectares of the total forestland. Differences in land classification may have been accounted for by use of some woodland areas for grazing and some traditional grazing lands for raising crops. Given the dearth of rainfall during the 1980s and early 1990s, the ecological damage from mechanized farming, and the steady march of desertification, discrepancies in these statistics had little meaning in 1991.

It was generally agreed, however, that in the late 1980s Sudan still had a substantial amount of land suitable for future cropping. The ILO-UNDP mission believed that two-thirds of the potential area for livestock grazing, however, was already in use. In addition to land suitable for cultivation and livestock grazing, Sudan also had about 76 million to 86 million hectares of desert. Additionally, an area of about 2.9 million hectares was covered by swamps and inland water, and about 280,000 hectares were occupied by urban settlements and other man-made features.

LAND TENURE

The right to own property, to bequeath it to heirs, and to inherit it was established by the Permanent Constitution of 1973; this right was suspended in 1985. Sudan had long had a system of land registration through which an individual, an enterprise, or the government could establish title to a piece of land. Such registration had been extensive in northern Sudan, especially in Al Khartum, Al Awsat, and Ash Shamali provinces. Before 1970 all other land (unregistered) belonged to the state, which held ownership in trust for the people, who had customary rights to it. In 1970 the Unregistered Land Act declared that all waste, forest, and unregistered lands were government land. Before the act's passage, the government had avoided interfering with individual customary rights to unregistered land, and in the late 1980s it again adhered to this policy.

The government owned most of the land used by the modern agricultural sector and leased it to tenants (for example, the Gezira Scheme) or to private entrepreneurs, such as most operators of large-scale mechanized rainfed farming. In the late 1980s, however, the great area of land used for pasture and for subsistence cultivation was communally owned under customary land laws that varied somewhat by location but followed a broadly similar pattern. In agricultural communities, the right to cultivate an area of unused land became vested in the individual who cleared it for use. The rights to such land could be passed on to heirs, but ordinarily the land could not be sold or otherwise disposed of. The right was also retained to land left in fallow, although in Bahr al Ghazal, Aali an Nil, and Al Istiwai there were communities where another individual could claim such land by clearing it.

Among the transhumant communities of the north, the rights to cultivated land were much the same, but the dominant position of livestock in community activities had introduced certain other communal rights that included common rights to grazing land, the right-of-way to water and grazing land, the right to grass on agricultural land unless the occupier cut and stacked it, and the right to crop residues unless similarly treated. In the western savannas, private ownership of stands of *hashab* trees could be registered, an exception to the usual government ownership of the forests. But dead wood for domestic fuel and the underlying grass were common property. Water, a matter of greatest importance to stock raisers, was open to all if free standing, but wells that had been dug and the associated drinking troughs were private property and were retained by the digger season after season. In northern Sudan, especially in the western savanna where increasing population and animal numbers have placed pressure on the land, violations of customary laws and conflicts between ethnic groups over land rights have been growing. Resolution of these problems has been attempted by local government agencies but only on a case-by-case basis.

IRRIGATED AGRICULTURE

In 1991 Sudan had a large modern irrigated agriculture sector totaling more than 2 million hectares out of about 84 million hectares that are potentially arable. About 93 percent of the irrigated area was in government projects; the remaining 7 percent belonged to private operations. The Nile and its tributaries were the source of water for 93 percent of irrigated agriculture, and of this the Blue Nile accounted for about 67 percent. Gravity flow was the main form of irrigation, but about one-third of the irrigated area was served by pumps.

The waters of the Nile in Sudan have been used for centuries for traditional irrigation, taking advantage of the annual Nile flood. Some use of this method still continued in the early 1990s, and the traditional *shaduf* (a device to raise water) and waterwheel were also used to lift water to fields in local irrigation projects but were rapidly being replaced by more efficient mechanized pump systems. Among the first efforts to employ irrigation for modern commercial cropping was the use of the floodwaters of the Qash River and the Baraka River (both of which originate in Ethiopia) in eastern Sudan to grow cotton on their deltas. This project was started in the late 1860s by the Egyptian governor and continued until interrupted by the turbulent period of the 1880s, leading to the reconquest of the country by the British in 1899. Cultivation was resumed in 1896 in the Baraka Delta in the Tawkar area, but in the Qash Delta it only resumed after World War I. Between 1924 and 1926, canals were built in the latter delta to control the flood; sandstorms made canals unfeasible in the Baraka. Between the 1940s and the 1970s, various projects were developed to irrigate land. In 1982 both deltas yielded only one crop a year, watered by the flood. Adequate groundwater, however, offered the eventual possibility of using pump irrigation from local wells for additional cropping or for supplementing any flood shortages.

The drought that affected Sudan in the 1980s was a natural disaster that had a crushing effect on the country's irrigation systems. In 1990-91, for instance, water was so scarce in the Tawkar area that for the first time in 100 years the crops failed.

As of 1990, the country's largest irrigation project had been developed on land between the Blue and White Nile rivers south of their confluence at Khartoum. This area is generally flat with a gentle slope to the north and west, permitting natural gravity irrigation, and its soils are fertile cracking clays well suited to irrigation. The project originated in 1911, when a private British enterprise, Sudan Plantations Syndicate, found cotton suited to the area and embarked on what in the 1920s became the Gezira Scheme, intended principally to furnish cotton to the British textile industry. Backed by a loan from the British government, the syndicate began a dam on the Blue Nile at Sannar in 1913. Work was interrupted by World War I, and the dam was not completed until 1925. The project was limited by a 1929 agreement between Sudan and Egypt that restricted the amount of water Anglo-Egyptian Sudan could use during the dry season. By 1931 the project had expanded to 450,000 hectares, the maximum that then could be irrigated by the available water, although 10,000 more hectares were added in the 1950s. The project was nationalized in 1950, and was operated by the Sudan Gezira Board as a government enterprise. In 1959 a new agreement with Egypt greatly increased the allotment of water to Sudan, as did the completion in the early 1960s of the Managil Extension on the western side of the Gezira Scheme. By 1990 the Managil Extension had an irrigated area of nearly 400,000 hectares, and with the 460,000 hectares eventually attained by the original Gezira Scheme, the combined projects accounted for half the country's total land under irrigation.

In the early 1960s, the government set up a program to resettle Nubians displaced by Lake Nubia (called Lake Nasser in Egypt), which was formed by the construction of the Aswan High Dam in Egypt. To provide farmland for the Nubians, the government constructed the Khashm al Qirbah Dam on the Atbarah River and established the Halfa al Jadidah (New Halfa) irrigation project. Located west of Kassala, this project was originally designed to irrigate about 164,000 hectares.

In 1982 it was the only large irrigation project in the country that did not use the waters of the Blue Nile or White Nile. The resettlement was effected mainly after completion of the Khashm al Qirbah Dam in 1964. Part of the irrigated area was also assigned to local inhabitants. The main commercial crops initially introduced included cotton, peanuts, and wheat. In 1965 sugarcane was added, and a sugar factory having a design capacity of 60,000 tons was built to process it. The project enabled 200,000 hectares of land to be irrigated for the first time. Heavy silting as well as serious problems of drainage and salinity occurred. As a result, by the late 1970s the reservoir had lost more than 40 percent of its original storage capacity and was unable to meet the project water requirements. These problems persisted in the early 1990s.

The multipurpose Roseires Dam was built in 1966 and power- generating facilities were installed in 1971. Both the water and the power were needed to implement the Rahad River irrigation project located east of the Rahad River, a tributary of the Blue Nile. The Rahad entered the Blue Nile downstream from the dam and during the dry season had an insufficient flow for irrigation purposes. Work on the initial 63,000 hectares of the project began in the early 1970s, the first irrigation water was received in 1977, and by 1981 about 80 percent of the prepared area was reported to be irrigated. (In May 1988, the World Bank agreed to provide additional funding for this and other irrigation projects). Water for the project was pumped from the Blue Nile, using electric power from the Roseires plant, and was transported by an eighty-kilometer-long canal to the Rahad River (en route underpassing the Dindar River, another Blue Nile tributary). The canal then emptied into the Rahad above a new barrage that diverted the combined flow from the two sources into the project's main irrigation canal. Irrigation was by gravity flow, but instead of flat field flooding, furrow irrigation was used, because it permitted more effective use of machinery.

In the 1920s, private irrigation projects using diesel pumps also had begun to appears in Al Khartum Province, mainly along the White Nile, to provide vegetables, fruit, and other foods to the capital area. In 1937 a dam was built by the Anglo-Egyptian condominium upstream from Khartoum on the White Nile at Jabal al Awliya to regulate the supply of water to Egypt during the August to April period of declining flow. Grazing and cultivated land along the river was flooded for almost 300 kilometers. The government thereupon established seven pump irrigation projects, partially financed by Egypt, to provide the area's inhabitants with an alternative to transhumance.

This irrigation project eventually proved successful, making possible large surpluses of cotton and sorghum and encouraging private entrepreneurs to undertake new projects. High cotton profits during the Korean War (1950-53) increased private interest along the Blue Nile as well, and by 1958 almost half the country's irrigated cotton was grown under pump irrigation. During the 1960s, however, downward fluctuations in world cotton prices and disputes between entrepreneurs and tenants led to numerous failures of pump irrigation projects. In 1968 the government assumed ownership and operation of the projects. The government established the Agricultural Reform Corporation for this purpose, and the takeover began that year with the larger estates. Subsequently, as leases expired, the corporation acquired smaller projects, until May 1970 when all outstanding leases were revoked. A considerable number of small pump operations that developed on privately owned land, chiefly along the main Nile but also on the Blue Nile, continued to operate.

Since the 1950s, the government has constructed a number of large pump projects, mostly on the Blue Nile. These have included the Junayd project on the right bank of the Blue Nile east of the Gezira Scheme. This project, with an irrigated area of about 36,000 hectares, went into operation in 1955 to provide an alternative livelihood for nomadic pastoralists in the area. It produced cotton until 1960, when about 8,400 hectares were converted to sugarcane. A sugar factory built to process the crop (with a potential capacity of 60,000 tons of sugar a year) opened in 1962. In the early 1970s, the Japanese-assisted As Suki project, also of 36,000 hectares, was established upstream from Sannar to grow cotton, sorghum, and oilseeds. In the mid-1970s, the government constructed a second project near Sannar of about 20,000 hectares. In addition to cotton and other crops such as peanuts, about 8,400 hectares of the area were devoted to raising sugarcane. The cane-processing factory, with a design capacity of 110,000 tons of sugar a year, opened in 1976. Several smaller Blue Nile projects added more than 80,000 additional hectares to Sudan's overall irrigated area during this time.

In the 1970s, when the consumption and import of sugar grew rapidly, domestic production became a priority, and two major pump-irrigated sugar plantations were established on the White Nile in the Kusti area. The Hajar Asalaya Sugar Project, begun in 1975, had an irrigated area of about 7,600 hectares. The sugar factory, completed in 1977, had a potential annual capacity of 110,000 tons. The Kinanah Sugar Project, which had almost 16,200 hectares under irrigation in 1981 and had a future potential of over 33,000 hectares, was one of the world's largest sugar-milling and refining operations. In 1985-86 production reached more than 330,000 tons a year. This project, first proposed in 1971, was beset with funding problems and overruns that increased overall costs from the equivalent of US$113 million estimated in 1973 to more than US$750 million when the plant opened officially in early 1981.

The Kinanah Sugar Project, unlike the country's four other government-owned sugar projects, was a joint venture--among the governments of Sudan, Kuwait, and Saudi Arabia, and the Arab Investment Company, the Sudan Development Corporation, Kinanah Limited, and the AAAID, including local Sudanese banks. An initial trial run in the 1979-80 cane season produced 20,000 tons of sugar. Yield increased to an estimated 135,000 to 150,000 tons the following season. Production at the Hajar Asalaya factory did not get under way until the 1979-80 season because of cane and sugar-processing difficulties. Problems have also affected the other three state sugar factories, but as a result of proposed World Bank management, the output total of these four government operations for the 1984-85 season improved to nearly 200,000 tons. Output declined to 159,000 tons in 1985-86 because of the drought. In 1989 sugarcane production reached 400,000 tons.

RAINFED AGRICULTURE

Cultivation dependent on rainfall falls into two categories. Most Sudanese farmers always have relied on rainfed farming. In addition to these traditional farmers, a large modern mechanized rainfed agriculture sector has developed since 1944-45, when a government project to cultivate the cracking clays of central Sudan started in the Al Qadarif area of Ash Sharqi Province, largely to meet the food needs of army units stationed in the British colonies in eastern Africa (present-day Kenya, Tanzania, and Uganda).

An average of about 6,000 hectares a year was cultivated between 1945 and 1953, producing chiefly sorghum, under a sharecropping arrangement between the government and farmers who had been allocated land in the project. These estates proved costly, however, and in 1954 the government began encouraging the private sector to take up mechanized farming in the area, a policy that continued after Sudan gained independence in 1956. Under the new approach, the government established several state farms to demonstrate production methods and to conduct research. Research activities have been very limited, however, because of staffing and funding problems, and the farms have been operated essentially as regular production units.

The private sector response was positive, and by 1960 mechanized farming had spread into other areas of the cracking clay zone in Ash Sharqi and Al Awsat provinces. The government set aside rectangular areas that were divided into plots of 420 hectares (later raised in places to 630 hectares) each. Half of these plots were leased to private farmers, the other half left in fallow. After four years, the originally leased land was to be returned to fallow and the farmer was to receive a new lease to an adjacent fallow area. When the demand for land grew faster than it could be demarcated, areas outside the designated project limits were taken over by private individuals. The four-year lease proved unpopular because it meant new investment in clearing land every four years, and apparently much of the worked land continued to be cultivated while fallow land was also placed under cultivation. By 1968 more than 750,000 hectares were being cultivated, of which it was estimated that more than 200,000 hectares constituted unauthorized holdings. The average agricultural production growth rate declined, however, from 2.9 percent in the period between 1965 and 1980, to 0.8 percent in the period between 1980 and 1987, the latest available figures. Reportedly, for the 1992-93 season, the Ministry of Agriculture and Natural Resources planned for about 7.3 million hectares of food crops to be planted, with about 1.6 million hectares planted in the irrigated sector and about 5.7 million hectares in the rain-fed areas.

The investment requirements for mechanized farming favored prosperous cultivators, and eventually most farms came to be operated by entrepreneurs who raised capital through mortgageable property or other assets in the urban centers. Through arrangements with other individuals, these entrepreneurs frequently managed to control additional plots beyond the legal limit of two. Their ability to obtain capital also permitted them to abandon depleted land and to move into newly demarcated uncleared areas, a practice that had a deleterious impact upon the environment, deprived the indigenous inhabitants of work opportunities, and increased desertification. In 1968, to expand the operator base and to introduce more control over land allocation, crops, and farming methods, the government established the Mechanized Farming Corporation (MFC), an autonomous agency under the Ministry of Agriculture and Natural Resources. From 1968 through 1978, the IDA made three loans to the government to enable the MFC to provide technical assistance, cr for landclearing and machinery, and marketing aid to individual farmers and cooperative groups. The MFC also became the operator of state farms.

In the late 1970s, about 2.2 million hectares had been allocated for mechanized farming, and about 420,000 hectares more had been occupied without official demarcation. About 1.9 million hectares in all were believed to be under cultivation in any one season. Of the officially allocated land, more than 70 percent was held by private individuals. Private companies had also begun entering the field, and some allocations had been made to them. State farms accounted for another 7.5 percent. About 15 percent of the total allocated land was in MFC-IDA projects.

The largest proportion of mechanized farming was in Ash Sharqi Province, 43 percent; the next largest in Al Awsat Province, 32 percent; and about 20 percent was in Aali an Nil Province. Mechanized farming had also been initiated in southern Kurdufan Province through a project covering small-scale farmers in the area of the Nuba Mountains, but under a different government program. Proposals also have been made for MFC projects using mechanized equipment in other areas of southern Kurdufan (some have already been tried) and southern Darfur provinces. There were serious feasibility problems in view of competition for land and conflicts with traditional farming practices, difficult soil conditions, and the probable negative effect on the large numbers of livestock of nomads.

Only a few crops had been found suitable for cultivation in the cracking clay area. Sorghum had been the principal one, and during the early 1980s it was planted on an average of about 80 percent of the sown area. Sesame and short-fiber cotton were also grown successfully but in relatively smaller quantities, sesame on about 15 percent of the land and cotton on about 5 percent. Soil fertility has reportedly been declining because of the continued planting of sorghum and the lack of crop rotation. Yields have apparently decreased, but in view of the area's greatly varying climatic conditions and the uncertain production data, definitive conclusions on trends appeared premature.

LIVESTOCK

In the early 1990s, drought caused a dramatic decline in livestock raising in Sudan, following a period in the early 1980s when livestock provided all or a large part of the livelihood of more than 40 percent of the country's population. Livestock raising was overwhelmingly in the traditional sector, and, although initial steps had been taken to improve productivity and develop market orientation, for the modern monetized economy the sector represented largely a potential asset. In 1983 Sudan's more than 50 million animals comprised the second largest national herd in Africa, next in size to that of Ethiopia.

An FAO estimate in 1987 indicated that there were about 20.5 million cattle, 19 million sheep, 14 million goats, and 3 million camels. Other animals included 660,000 donkeys, 21,000 horses, a small number of pigs (kept by such non-Muslim peoples as the Nuba) and 32,000 chickens. By 1991 these numbers had been reduced by perhaps one-third by the drought of 1990-91; the August 1988 floods in the south, described as the worst in Sudan's history; and the ravages of civil war in the south. Poultry was raised mainly by farm families and villagers. A small modern sector consisted of limited government commercial operations and a few semicommercial private ventures.

Sudanese cattle are of two principal varieties: Baqqara and Nilotic. The Baqqara and two subvarieties constituted about 80 percent of the country's total number of cattle. This breed was found chiefly in the western savanna regions and in fewer, although significant, numbers farther to the east from Aali an Nil to Kassala in Ash Sharqi. The Nilotic, constituting approximately 20 percent of all cattle, were common in the eastern hill and plains areas of southeastern Al Istiwai, which were free of the tsetse fly, and in those parts of the Bahr al Ghazal and Aali an Nil lying outside the tsetse-fly zone. Because of periodic rinderpest epidemics, the total number of cattle was relatively small until about 1930, when it stood at an estimated 2 million. A vaccination program begun about that time and mass inoculations during the succeeding decades resulted in a great increase in numbers, which by 1970 had reached about 12 million. In the vast areas used by pastoral herders (estimated to be 80 million to 100 million hectares), cattle husbandry was conducted in an economic, cultural, and social context that had evolved over generations.

This included an emphasis on increasing herd size as an investment for future family security. Small surpluses (usually bulls) were available for subsistence use, exchange, or sale for local consumption or export. Cattle were also used for marriage payments and among the Nilotes for rituals. Numbers of cattle also helped to establish or increase status and power in a social system in which cattle were the measure of wealth.

Most Nilotic cattle were kept by transhumant groups. Migrations , related to the wet and dry seasons, usually did not exceed 150 to 160 kilometers. The majority of the Baqqara strain of cattle belonged to the Baqqara Arabs. The latter were largely nomadic, but since at least the early 1900s had a settled base on which crop cultivation was practiced. The farmers, their relatives, or their agents moved the cattle over traditional migratory routes northward during the rainy season and southward to the area of the Bahr al Arab as the dry season progressed. Migrations in either direction might amount to 400 kilometers. The expansion of mechanized rainfed agriculture in the region used by the Baqqara, continued government efforts to enlarge the cultivated area, and pressures on the land from the growing population have gradually reduced grazing areas. At the same time, traditional cultural forces have brought about a steady increase in cattle numbers.

The result has been increasing overstocking and pasture depletion until the outbreak of civil war in 1983 and the devastating droughts of the 1980s and early 1990s decimated not only the Nilotic herds but livestock throughout Sudan. Many families and indeed whole ethnic groups who have traditionally survived on their cattle, sheep, goats, or camels, lost all of their herds and were forced to migrate to the Three Towns (Omdurman, Khartoum, and Khartoum North) in search of sustenance.

Sheep were herded chiefly by transhumants in Darfur and Kurdufan. Large numbers were found in the drier areas at greater elevations than the usual cattle zone. Several breeds were raised, but the predominant and preferred one was the so-called desert sheep, which had both good weight and good milk yield. Villagers in Al Awsat also raised large numbers of sheep, mostly on a nonmigratory basis. Fodder was obtained from crop residues on irrigated and rainfed farms and from vegetation along the rivers and canals. Goats, of which there were three principal breeds (desert, Nubian, and Nilotic), were found throughout the country south of the northern desert areas. They were raised mainly by sedentary families for milk and meat. Goat meat, although less popular than mutton, formed part of the diet of most families, particularly those having low incomes. Goat milk was an important source of protein, and many families in urban areas kept a few goats for their milk.

Camels were largely concentrated in the desert and subdesert regions of northern Darfur, northern Kurdufan, and southern Ash Sharqi. They were kept almost entirely by nomadic and seminomadic peoples, for whom the animal represented the preferred mode of transport. Camels were also important for milk and for meat. Camel ownership and numbers were sources of prestige in nomadic societies.

FISHERIES

Sudan's total production of fish, shellfish, and other fishing products reached an estimated 24,000 tons per year in 1991, the latest available yearly figures. This compared with estimates of a potential yearly catch exceeding 100,000 tons. The principal source of fish was the Nile River system. In central and northern Sudan, several lakes and reservoirs have been formed by the damming of the river and its branches: the 180-kilometer section of Lake Nubia on the main Nile in Sudan and the reservoirs behind the Roseires and Sennar dams on the Blue Nile, the Jabal al Awliya Dam on the White Nile, and the Khashm al Qirbah Dam on the Atbarah tributary of the main Nile. These bodies of water accounted for about 11,000 tons of fish against a calculated potential of about 29,000 tons.

Production from Lake Nubia through 1979, the latest figures available in 1991, was only 500 tons a year, or about one-tenth of the estimated potential. Inhabitants around the lake, which had formed gradually in the 1960s, had no previous experience in fishing, and the first significant commercial exploitation of the lake's resources had been undertaken by the government's Fisheries Administration. In 1973 a private company also started operations. In the mid- and late 1970s, an ice plant and a cold storage facility were built at Wadi Halfa with assistance from China. China also furnished thirty-five two-ton fishing vessels, a number of transport launches, and other fishing equipment. Cooling plants were constructed at Khartoum and Atbarah to hold fish that were brought from Wadi Halfa by railroad. Although ice was used in the shipments, substantial loss occurred, especially during the hotter months. To what extent fish production from the lake and availability to consumers were increased by these new facilities was not known in 1991.

The largest potential source of freshwater fish was southern Sudan whose extensive river network and flooded areas in As Sudd were believed able to provide 100,000 to 300,000 tons annually on a sustained basis. Statistics on actual production were unavailable in 1991; much was consumed locally, although limited quantities of dried and salted fish were exported to Zaire where it was in great demand.

The country's second source of fish, the Red Sea coastal area, was relatively unexploited until the late 1970s. Annual production toward the end of the decade amounted to about 500 tons of fish, shellfish (including pearl oysters), and other marine life. In 1978 the British Ministry of Overseas Development began a joint project with the government Fisheries Administration to raise output by making boats, motors, and equipment available to fishermen. Included was an ice plant built at Sawakin to furnish local fishermen with ice for their catch. By 1982 the project was well advanced, and about 2,000 tons of fish were taken annually. A sustained catch of 5,000 tons might eventually be possible.

FORESTRY

Since the early 1900s, extensive areas of woodland and forest have been converted to agricultural use. Large amounts of land classifiable as woodland have been cleared in the development of large-scale mechanized rainfed farming in Ash Sharqi and Al Awsat states, and smaller amounts in Aali an Nil and southern Kurdufan states. Although Sudan had a large quantity of natural forest, by 1994 much of it remained almost totally unexploited. In the late 1970s, FAO estimated that the country's forests and woodlands totaled about 915,000 square kilometers, or 38.5 percent of the land area.

This figure was based on the broad definition of forest and woodland as any area of vegetation dominated by trees of any size. It also included an unknown amount of cleared land that was expected to have forest cover again "in the foreseeable future." An estimate in the mid-1970s by the Forestry Administration, however, established the total forest cover at about 584,360 square kilometers, or 24.6 percent of the country's land area. More than 129,000 square kilometers (about onequarter) of this amount were located in the dry and semiarid regions of northern Sudan. These forests were considered valuable chiefly as protection for the land against desertification, but they also served as a source of fuel for pastoral peoples in those regions.

The continued population pressure on the land has resulted in an accelerated destruction of forestland, particularly in the Sahel, because charcoal remained the predominant fuel. The loss of forestland in the marginal areas of the north, accelerated by mechanized farming and by drought, resulted in a steady encroachment of the Sahara southward at about ten kilometers a year in the 1980s.

The productive forest extended below the zone of desert encroachment to the southern border. It included the savanna woodlands of the central and western parts of the country, which were dominated by various species of acacia, among them *Acacia senegal*, the principal source of gum arabic. Gum arabic was Sudan's second largest export product, accounting for 80 percent of the world's supply. It is nontoxic, noncalorific, and nonpolluting, having no odor or taste. It is used widely in industry for products ranging from mucilage (for postage stamps) to foam stabilizers to excipient in medicines and dietetic foods. In 1986-87 Sudan produced more than 40,000 tons marketed through the Gum Arabic Company. In the late 1980s the drought severely curtailed production.

The principal area of productive forest and woodland, however, was in the more moist southern part of the country. Covering an area of more than 200,000 square kilometers and consisting mainly of broadleaf deciduous hardwoods, it remained largely undeveloped in 1990. Timber processed by government mills in the area included mahogany for furniture and other hardwoods for railroad ties, furniture, and construction. Domestic production of timber fell far short of local needs in the 1970s, and as much as 80 percent of the domestic requirement was met by imports.

Plantations established by the government Forestry Administration in the mid-1970s totaled about 16,000 hectares of hardwoods and 500 to 600 hectares of softwoods, most were in the south. They included stands of teak and in the higher elevations of the Imatong Mountains, exotic pines. Eucalyptus stands had also been established in the irrigated agricultural areas to serve as windbreaks and to supply firewood. A gradually increasing forest reserve has been developed, and by the mid1970s it covered more than 13,000 square kilometers. Additional protection of forest and woodland areas was provided by several national parks and game reserves that encompassed 54,000 square kilometers in the mid-1970s.

Since 1983 the civil war virtually halted forestry production in southern Sudan, from which came the overwhelming amount of forestry products. According to FAO estimates, however, in 1987 Sudan produced 41,000 cubic meters of sawn timber, 1,906,000 cubic meters of other industrial roundwood, and more than 18 million cubic meters of firewood. Each of these categories showed a substantial increase from production levels in the 1970s. The insatiable demand was for charcoal, the principal cooking fuel, and the one major forest product not dependent upon the south. Because wood of any kind could be turned to charcoal, the acacia groves of the Sahel have been used extensively for this purpose, with a resulting rapid advance of deforestation. To improve government forestry conservation and management policy, as well as the issue of land use, in 1990-91 plans were underway to establish a forestry resource conservation project, funded and cofinanced by several international development agencies and donors.

MANUFACTURING

The development of modern manufacturing received little direct encouragement in Sudan during the condominium period. British economic policies were aimed basically at expanding the production of primary products, mainly cotton, for export. Imports and traditional handicraft industries met the basic needs for manufactured goods. Indirectly, however, the vast Gezira Scheme cotton-growing project induced the construction of ginneries, of which more than twenty were in operation by the early 1930s. A secondary development was the establishment of several cottonseed oil-pressing mills. During World War II, small import substitution industries arose, including those manufacturing soap, carbonated drinks, and other consumer items. These operations did not survive the competition from imports after the war's end. Foreign private interests invested in a few larger enterprises that included a meat-processing factory, a cement plant, and a brewery, all opened between 1949 and 1952.

At independence the Sudanese government supported an industrial development policy to be effected through the private sector. To facilitate this process, Khartoum adopted the Approved Enterprises (Concessions) Act of 1956, to encourage private Sudanese and foreign investment. The act placed few restrictions on foreign equity holdings. By 1961, however, the government had concluded that the private sector lacked interest or funds to establish enterprises important to the national economy, and so it entered the manufacturing field. The first government project was a tannery opened that year, and this was followed in 1962 by a sugar factory. In 1962 Khartoum formed the Industrial Development Corporation (IDC) to manage government plants.

During the decade, several additional government enterprises were built, including a second sugar factory, two fruit and vegetable canneries, a date-processing plant, an onion-dehydrating plant, a milk-processing plant, and a cardboard factory. During this time, the private sector also made substantial investment, which resulted in factories making textiles and knitwear, shoes, soap, soft drinks, and flour. Other private enterprises included printing facilities and additional oil-pressing mills. Among the largest private undertakings was the foreign-financed and foreign-built oil refinery at Port Sudan, which opened in 1964. Well over half the private sector investment during the decade came from foreign sources.

Government participation in the manufacturing sector increased dramatically after the 1969 military coup and the adoption of a policy aimed at placing the country's economic development in government hands, although private ownership continued. During 1970 and 1971 Khartoum nationalized more than thirty private enterprises. In 1972, however, to counter the drop in foreign private investment that followed, Nimeiri announced that private capital would again be accorded favorable treatment, and the government passed the Development and Promotion of Industrial Investment Act of 1972, containing even more liberal provisions than precoup legislation.

As the economy remained dependent on private capital, as well as capital investment from developed nations, the government incorporated further incentives for the favorable treatment of such capital in a 1974 revision of the industrial investment act, and added provisions against arbitrary nationalization. Moreover, in 1972 Khartoum denationalized some enterprises nationalized earlier, and returned them to their former owners under an arrangement for joint government-private ownership. One of the largest of these enterprises was the Bata Shoe Company, which was returned in 1978 as a reorganized joint company in which Bata held a 51 percent interest and the government 49 percent. The most successful such enterprise, however, was the Bittar Group, which in 1990 had become the largest undertaking in Sudan. Begun in the 1920s, nationalized in 1969 but returned to its owners in 1973, it has diversified into products ranging from exports of vegetable oils to imports of wheat, sugar, and insecticides. The firm has been active in a wide range of projects involving agriculture, electricity, and such industrial products as household and office equipment, soap, and detergents.

Throughout the 1970s, the government continued to establish new public enterprises, some state-owned, others in conjunction with private interests, and some having foreign government participation, especially by the Arab oil-producing states. The new plants included three sugar factories, among which was the Kinanah sugar-milling and refining factory; two tanneries; a flour mill; and more than twenty textile plants. A joint venture with United States interests built Sudan's first fertilizer plant south of Khartoum, which was in operation by 1986. Private investment continued, particularly in textiles. About 300 million meters of cloth were produced annually in the 1970s, but output fell to 50 million meters in 1985. In 1988, the textile industry functioned at about 25 percent of capacity. The latter figure reflected the effects of the civil war, the dearth of hard currency for spare parts to maintain machinery, and the debt crisis.

Since independence Sudan's modern manufacturing establishment has emphasized the processing of agricultural products and import substitution. The production of foodstuffs, beverages, and clothing has accounted for a large part of total output. Significant import substitution industries included cement, chemicals, and dry battery manufacture; glass-bottle-making; petroleum refining; and fertilizer production. In the late 1980s, estimates of the contribution of modern manufacturing to GDP varied from about 7 to 8 percent a year, including mining (compared to about 2 percent in 1956). Employment in the sector had risen during that period from possibly 9,000 in 1956 to 185,000 in 1977, including wage earners in government enterprises. Almost three-quarters of large-scale modern manufacturing was located in Al Khartum, attracted by market size, higher per capita income, better transportation and power infrastructure, and access to financial and government services.

Total manufacturing output, however, had not met expectation by the end of the 1970s and steadily declined in the 1980s. Overall output in some subsectors had grown as new facilities began operating, but the goal of self-sufficiency had generally not been attained. Shortages of domestic and imported raw materials, power failures, transportation delays, lack of spare parts, and shortages of labor ranging from qualified managerial staff and skilled workers to casual laborers had been drawbacks to effective operations and increased output. Losses of skilled labor and management to the Persian Gulf states have been particularly debilitating. In the 1980s, many factories operated below capacity--frequently at well under 50 percent of their potential. In some instances, low production also was related to poor project planning.

For example, the government cannery at Kuraymah in Ash Shamali was already constructed when scientists found that the surrounding farming area could not produce the quantity of crops the plant could process. The milk-processing facility at Babanusah south of Khartoum had a similar record of poor planning. Efforts to improve the transportation and power infrastructure, whose deficiencies have been major contributors to the manufacturing problems, and rehabilitation of existing plants were among the basic goals of the 1977-82 Six-Year Plan of

Economic and Social Development. That plan was never effectively implemented. Some progress has been reported, but in 1990 the production problems faced earlier by manufacturing persisted.

MINING

In 1992 the mining industry accounted for less than 1 percent of the total GDP. A wide range of minerals existed in Sudan, but the size of reserves had not been determined in most cases. The discovery of commercially exploitable quantities of petroleum in the late 1970s offered some hope that the sector would play an increased role in the economy in the future. However, from February 1984, some months after concessions were allotted, oil exploration operations had been suspended in the south, where the largest deposits were located, as a result of the region's security problems. Nonhydrocarbon minerals of actual or potential commercial value included gold, chrome, copper, iron, manganese, asbestos, gypsum, mica, limestone, marble, and uranium. Gold had been mined in the Red Sea Hills since pharaonic times. Between 1900 and 1954, several British enterprises worked gold mines in the area, and extracted a considerable quantity of the metal--one mine alone reportedly produced three tons of gold between 1924 and 1936. Gold also has been mined along the borders between Sudan and Uganda and Zaire, but not in commercially profitable amounts. During the 1970s, the government's Geological Survey Administration located more than fifty potential gold-producing sites in different parts of the country. Several joint ventures between the Sudanese Mining Corporation, a government enterprise, and foreign companies were launched in the 1980s; these undertakings produced gold at Gebeit and several other mines near the Red Sea Hills beginning in 1987. In 1988, about 78,000 metric kilograms of gold ore were mined in Sudan. In late 1990, Sudan and two French mining companies formed a joint venture company to exploit gold reserves in the Khawr Ariab wadi in the Red Sea Hills.

Chrome ore was mined in the Ingessana Hills in Al Awsat. In the late 1970s, output was reportedly more than 20,000 tons a year, of which more than four-fifths were produced by the Ingessana Hills Mines Corporation, a subsidiary of Sudanese Mining Corporation. A private operation produced the remainder. The ore was exported, chiefly to Japan and Western Europe. In the 1980s, the establishment of ferrochrome processing facilities had been discussed with Japanese interests, but the estimated 700,000 tons of reserves were insufficient for profitable longterm operations. By 1983, when the civil war brought a halt to all production in the Ingessana Hills, chrome production had declined about 50 percent to only 10,000 tons per year. In 1988, production of chromium ore was estimated at 5,000 metric tons. Asbestos had also been found in the Ingessana Hills area. It was reportedly of good commercial grade, and mining possibilities were under study by a Canadian subsidiary of the United States firm of Johns-Manville. A small pilot extraction plant had been built, but larger scale operations were dependent on locating adequate reserves and on the ending of the civil war.

Large gypsum deposits, estimated to contain reserves of 220 million tons, were found along the Red Sea coast. Reportedly of high purity, the ore was mined mainly north of Port Sudan. In the late 1980s, about 20,000 tons were produced annually, about 6,000 tons by the Sudanese Mining Corporation and the remainder by private operations. Gypsum was used mostly in the production of cement. Limestone, found in substantial quantities in Sudan, was mined both for use in making cement and for other construction materials. Marble was also quarried for the latter purpose.

There has been some commercial mining of mica, exploitable deposits of which had been located in Ash Shamali Province by a UN mineral survey team between 1968 and 1972. The Sudanese Mining Corporation produced about 1,000 tons of scrap mica in FY 1978, but output reportedly slumped thereafter to about 400 tons annually. Manganese and iron ore, of which several large deposits exist in different parts of the country, have been mined at times but only on a small basis by international standards. There were more than 500 million tons of iron ore deposits in the

Fodikwan area of the Red Sea Hills, and beginning in the late 1980s a project had been planned to produce between 120,000 and 200,000 tons a month. Exploitation of Sudan's mineral deposits, however, depended in large part on foreign companies willing to undertake such risks in the face of the country's mounting problems, and on international market factors.

Uranium ores have been discovered in the area of the Nuba Mountains and at Hufrat an Nahas in southern Kurdufan. Minex Company of the United States obtained a 36,000-square-kilometer exploratory concession in the Kurdufan area in 1977, and the concession was increased to 48,000 square kilometers in 1979. Uranium reserves are also believed to exist near the western borders with Chad and Central African Republic. Another potential source of mineral wealth was the Red Sea bed. In 1974 officials established a joint Sudanese-Saudi Arabian agency to develop those resources, which included zinc, silver, copper, and other minerals. Explorations below the 2,000-meter mark have indicated that large quantities of the minerals are present, but as of 1990 no actual extraction had been undertaken.

ENERGY SOURCES AND SUPPLY

In the early 1990s the chief sources of energy were wood and charcoal, hydroelectric power, and imported oil. Wood and charcoal were principally used by households for heating and cooking. Substantial quantities of wood fuels, amounting to roughly onefifth of the country's annual consumption, were also used by commercial operations--chiefly baking and brickmaking and, to a lesser extent, tobacco curing. Some use was also made of other vegetable matter including sugarcane bagasse, which met a significant part of the energy needs of the sugar mills, and cotton stalks, used locally by households. Consumption of wood and charcoal has continued to increase as the population has grown, and some concern has been voiced at the gradual depletion of forest and woodland resources serving the large towns. Overuse of the sparser vegetation in the semidesert grazing areas reportedly was resulting in some fuel deficiencies in those regions, as well as in desertification.

The country's hydroelectric potential has been only partially exploited. Major undeveloped hydropower sources existed at the several cataracts on the main Nile downstream from Khartoum. Natural gas was discovered in the early 1960s along the Red Sea coast in a fruitless search for petroleum. In the mid-1970s, further quantities were found during additional oil explorations, but development was not considered at the time to be commercially feasible. In October 1988, Sudan announced that natural gas production would start in one year; presumably this would come from the 85 billion cubic meters of gas reserves Chevron had earlier estimated. The 1979 and later petroleum discoveries in southern and southwestern Sudan added a new potential domestic energy source. However, these deposits to date have yielded little oil because petroleum companies, such as Chevron, had suspended oilfield explorations in these regions because of the civil war. Sudan had no known deposits of coal or lignite as of the early 1990s.

ELECTRIC POWER

The only sizable area of the country having electric power available to the public was the central region along the Blue Nile from Khartoum south to Ad Damazin. The central region in the early 1990s accounted for approximately 87 percent of Sudan's total electricity consumption. The area was served by the country's only major interconnected generating and distributing system, the Blue Nile Grid. This system provided power to both the towns and the irrigation projects in the area, including the Gezira Scheme. Another small, local, interconnected system furnished power in the eastern part of the country that included Al Qadarif, Kassala, and Halfa al Jadidah. The remaining customers were in fewer than twenty widely scattered towns having local diesel-powered generating facilities: Shandi, Atbarah, and Dunqulah in the north; Malakal, Juba, and Waw in the south; Al Fashir and Nyala in Darfur; Al Ubayyid and Umm Ruwabah in Kurdufan; a few towns along the White Nile south of Khartoum; and Port Sudan. About fifty other urban centers in outlying regions, each having populations of more than 5,000, still did not have a public electricity supply in 1982, the latest year for which statistical information was available. Rural electrification was found only in some of the villages associated with the main irrigation projects.

Approximately 75 percent of the country's total electric power was produced by the Public Electricity and Water Corporation (PEWC), a state enterprise. The remaining 25 percent was generated for self-use by various industries including foodprocessing and sugar factories, textile mills, and the Port Sudan refinery. Private and PEWC electricity generation increased about 50 percent in the 1980s, to an estimated 900 gigawatt hours in 1989 in attempts to counter frequent cuts in electric power. PEWC also handled all regular electricity distribution to the public. In 1989 PEWC power stations had a total generating capacity of 606 megawatts, of which about 53 percent was hydroelectric and the remainder thermal.

The largest hydroelectric plant was at Roseires Dam on the Blue Nile; it had a capacity of 250 megawatts. Other hydroelectric stations were located at the Sennar Dam farther downstream and at Khashm al Qirbah Dam on the Atbarah River; the latter was part of the small power grid in the Al Qadarif-Kassala area. The Sennar and Roseires dams were constructed originally to provide irrigation, Sennar in 1925 and Roseires in 1966. Electric-power generating facilities were added only when increasing consumer demands had made them potentially viable (Sennar in 1962 and Roseires in 1971), yet power generation in Sudan has never satisfied actual needs.

The Blue Nile Grid, in addition to its Roseires and Sennar hydroelectric plants, had thermal plants at Burri in eastern Khartoum, where work on a 40-megawatt extension began in 1986, and in Khartoum North, where a 60-megawatt thermal station began operation in 1985. In the late 1980s, two additional stations producing 40 to 60 megawatts each were under consideration for Khartoum North.

The demand for electricity on the Blue Nile system increased greatly in the late 1970s, and power shortages have been acute from 1978 onward. Shortages have been blamed in part on management inefficiency and lack of coordination between the PEWC and irrigation authorities and other government agencies. Demand continued to grow strongly during the 1980s as development projects were completed and became operational and the population of the Three Towns increased dramatically. New generating facilities were completed in 1986 under the Power III Project, almost doubling generating capacity in the Blue Nile Grid. The project included work on the Roseires units, funded by IDA, and on the Burri and Khartoum North installations, funded by the British Overseas Development Administration. In 1983, recognizing the need for more electricity the government began seeking support for the Power IV Project to be funded by the World Bank, the African Development Bank, and the Federal Republic of Germany (West Germany) to bring the entire electrical system up to its full generating capacity. The plan was later scaled back from the initial cost of US$100 million and renamed Power V Project.

PETROLEUM USE AND DOMESTIC RESOURCES

In 1982 roughly four-fifths of the nation's energy requirement for industry, modern agriculture, transportation, government services, and households (in addition to wood fuel, charcoal, and the like) was provided by imported petroleum and petroleum products. Approximately 10 percent of these imports were used to generate electricity. Foreign exchange costs for oil imports rose dramatically after 1973 and by 1988 amounted to almost 46 percent of earnings from merchandise exports. Dependence on external sources might lessen when the security situation permits Sudan's domestic petroleum resources to be exploited.

The search for oil began in 1959 in the Red Sea littoral and continued intermittently into the 1970s. In 1982 several oil companies were prospecting large concessions offshore and on land from the Tawkar area near the Ethiopian border to the northern part of the Red Sea Hills. No significant discoveries were reported. In 1974 Chevron, a subsidiary of Standard Oil Company of California, began exploration of a 516,000-square-kilometer concession (later reduced to 280,000 square kilometers by voluntary relinquishment) in southern and southwestern Sudan. Drilling began in 1977, and the first commercial flow was obtained in July 1979 at Abu Jabirah in southern Kurdufan Province. In 1980 major finds were made at the company's Unity Field near Bentiu in Aali an Nil Province, where further drilling by early 1981 had brought in forty-nine wells having a combined flow of more than 12,000 barrels a day.

The company has estimated this field's reserves at from 80 to 100 million barrels, but exploration farther south placed the reserves at more than 250 million barrels. Other oil companies--including some from the United States, Canada, and France--have also obtained concessions, and by 1982 almost one-third of Sudan had been assigned for exploration. Oil exploration and production have been hampered, however, by the almost total lack of infrastructure and by the civil war in the south of the country. Chevron had found small aircraft and helicopters essential for transport, the latter for moving portable rigs and equipment and for general use during the rainy season when all roads and locally constructed air strips were washed out.

The domestic processing of crude petroleum began in late 1964 when the Port Sudan oil refinery went into operation. The refinery, which was financed, built, and managed by the British Petroleum and Royal Dutch Shell companies--from July 1976 as a joint equal shareholding project with the government--had a capacity of about 21,440 barrels per day. Its capacity was well in excess of Sudan's needs at the time it was built, and refined products were exported. Local demand had quintupled by 1990, well beyond the plant's capacity. As a result, more than one-third of the gas oil (used in diesel motors and for heating) and well over two-fifths of the kerosene required for domestic use had to be imported. A substantial quantity of other products refined by the plant in excess of Sudan's own needs were exported.

The domestic petroleum discoveries led to intensive discussion within the government concerning the establishment of a new refinery. Southern Sudan pressed for construction near the oilfields in the south, but it was decided finally to locate the refinery at Kusti on the White Nile about 315 kilometers south of Khartoum. In August 1981, the White Nile Petroleum Company (WNPC) was set up by the central government as a subsidiary of the Sudanese National Oil Company to handle the undertaking. The government held a two-fifths share in WNPC, Chevron Overseas Petroleum Corporation another two-fifths, and the International Finance Corporation the remaining one-fifth. Plans called for a 550-kilometer pipeline to be built from the oilfields to the new refinery. By early 1982, however, the estimated costs of the refinery and pipeline had risen to at least the equivalent of US$1 billion as against an earlier project allotment of about one-third that figure.

The Kusti refinery was predicated on production for domestic consumption. Its estimated capacity (in early 1982) of between 15,000 and 25,000 barrels a day would meet only part of Sudan's overall requirements, however, and the quality of the petroleum would restrict economic production to certain products, so the Port Sudan refinery would have to continue operating. In view of the greatly increased cost estimates of the new plant, the World Bank in 1982 undertook a study of an alternative plan that might be more attractive to foreign capital. Under this plan, the proposed pipeline would run to Port Sudan, and an extension to the existing refinery would make it possible to export surplus refined products and even earn foreign-exchange crs. Contracts were let for the construction of the pipeline, but the government canceled them in September 1986. Further seismic studies were undertaken in the swamps (As Sudd) of Aali an Nil, but all of Chevron's exploration and development activities came to an abrupt end in February 1984 when guerrillas from the southern Sudanese insurgent group known as Anya Nya II attacked the main forward Chevron base across the Bahr al Ghazal River from Bentiu, killing four Chevron employees. Chevron immediately terminated its development program and, despite repeated demands by successive Sudanese governments, has refused to return to work its concession until the safety of its personnel can be guaranteed by a settlement of the Sudanese civil war. Total, the French oil company, shut down its operations several months later.

The Nimeiri government pressured foreign oil companies to resume exploration and drilling and hoped to encourage them to do so in part by forming the National Oil Company of Sudan (NOCS) in a joint venture with Saudi Arabian entrepreneur Adnan Khashoggi. After Nimeiri was overthrown, the new government dissolved NOCS but continued to press companies to renew work. As a result, Chevron stated in late 1987 that it would begin a sixty-day, twowell drilling program in southern Kurdufan in 1988, but postponed this because of the spread of civil war. Several other foreign companies indicated an interest in petroleum exploration in 1988, following the completion of a three-year World Bank study of Sudan's hydrocarbon potential. The minister of energy and mining had announced in May 1987 that Sudan's confirmed oil reserves totaled 2 billion barrels, with an estimated 500 million barrels recoverable.

TRANSPORTATION AND COMMUNICATIONS

Sudan's transport infrastructure in 1990 included an extensive railroad system that served the more important populated areas except in the far south, a meager road network (very little of which consisted of all-weather roads), a natural inland waterway--the Nile River and its tributaries--and a national airline that provided both international and domestic service. Complementing this infrastructure was Port Sudan, a major deep-water port on the Red Sea, and a small but modern national merchant marine. Additionally, a pipeline transporting petroleum products extended from the port to Khartoum.

Only minimal efforts had been expended through the early 1980s to improve existing and, according to both Sudanese and foreign observers, largely inefficiently operated transport facilities. Increasing emphasis on economic development placed a growing strain on the system, and beginning in the mid-1970s a substantial proportion of public investment funds was allocated for transport sector development. Some progress toward meeting equipment goals had been reported by the beginning of the 1980s, but substantial further modernization and adequately trained personnel were still required. Until these were in place, inadequate transportation was expected to constitute a major obstacle to economic development.

RAILROADS

The country had two railroads. The main system, Sudan Railways, which was operated by the government-owned Sudan Railways Corporation, provided services to most of the country's production and consumption centers. The other railroad, the Gezira Light Railway, was owned by the Sudan Gezira Board and served the Gezira Scheme and its Manaqil Extension. Railroads dominated commercial transport, although competition from the highways has been increasing rapidly. The preeminence of the railroad system was based on historical developments that led to its construction as an adjunct to military operations, although the first line, built in the mid-1870s from Wadi Halfa to a point about fifty-four kilometers upstream on the Nile River, was initially a commercial undertaking. This line, which had not proved viable commercially, was extended in the mid-1880s and again in the mid-1890s to support the Anglo-Egyptian military campaigns against the Mahdiyah. Of little other use, it was abandoned in 1905.

The first segment of the present-day Sudan Railways, from Wadi Halfa to Abu Hamad, was also a military undertaking; it was built by the British for use in General Herbert Kitchener's drive against the Mahdiyah in the late 1890s. The line was pushed to Atbarah during the campaign and after the defeat of the Mahdiyah in 1898 was continued to Khartoum, which it reached on the last day of 1899. The line was built to 1.067-meter-gauge track specifications, the result apparently of Kitchener's pragmatic use of the rolling stock and rails of that gauge from the old line. This gauge was used in all later Sudanese mainline construction.

The line opened a trade route from central Sudan through Egypt to the Merranean and beyond. It became uneconomical, however, because of the distance and the need for transshipment via the Nile, and in 1904 construction of a new line from Atbarah to the Red Sea was undertaken. In 1906 the new line reached recently built Port Sudan to provide a direct connection between Khartoum and ocean-going transport.

During the same decade, a line was also built from Khartoum southward to Sannar, the heart of the cotton-growing region of Al Jazirah. A westward continuation reached Al Ubayyid, then the country's second largest city and center of gum arabic production, in 1911. In the north, a branch line was built from near Abu Hamad to Kuraymah that tied the navigable stretch of the Nile between the fourth and third cataracts into the transport system. Traffic in this case, however, was largely inbound to towns along the river, a situation that still prevailed in 1990.

In the mid- and late 1920s, a spur of the railroad was built from Taqatu Hayya, a point on the main line 200 kilometers southwest of Port Sudan, southward to the cotton-producing area near Kassala, then on to the grain region of Al Qadarif, and finally to a junction with the main line at Sannar. Much of the area's traffic, which formerly had passed through Khartoum, has since moved over this line directly to Port Sudan.

The final spurt of railroad construction began in the 1950s. It included extension of the western line to Nyala (1959) in Darfur Province and of a southwesterly branch to Waw (1961), southern Sudan's second largest city, located in Bahr al Ghazal Province. This essentially completed the Sudan Railways network, which in 1990 totaled about 4,800 route kilometers.

Conversion of Sudan Railways to diesel fuel started in the late 1950s, but a few mainline steam locomotives continued in use in 1990, serving lines having lighter weight rails. Through the 1960s, the railroads essentially had a monopoly on transportation of export and import trade, and operations were profitable. In the early 1970s, losses were experienced, and, although the addition of new diesel equipment in 1976 was followed by a return to profitability, another downturn had occurred by the end of the decade. The losses were attributed in part to inflationary factors, the lack of spare parts, and the continuation of certain lines characterized by only light traffic, but retained for economic development needs and for social reasons.

The chief cause of the downturn appeared to have been loss of operational efficiency. Worker productivity had declined. For example, repair of locomotives was so slow that only about half of the total number were usually operational. Freight car turnaround time had lengthened considerably, and the reported slowness of management to meet growing competition from road transport was also a major factor. The road system, although generally more expensive, was used increasingly for low-volume, high-value goods because it could deliver more rapidly--two or three days from Port Sudan to Khartoum, compared with seven or eight days for express rail freight and up to two weeks for ordinary freight. At the end of the 1980s, moreover, only 1 to 2 percent of freight trains arrived on time. The gradual erosion of freight traffic was evident in the drop from more than 3 million tons carried annually at the beginning of the 1970s to about 2 million tons at the end of the decade. The 1980s also saw a steady erosion of tonnage as a result of a combination of inefficient management, union intransigence, the failure of agricultural projects to meet production goals, the dearth of spare parts, and the continuing civil war.

Despite the rapidly growing use of roads, the railroads have remained of paramount importance because of their ability to move at lower cost the large volume of agricultural exports and to transport inland the increasing imports of heavy capital equipment and construction materials for development, such as requirements for oil exploration and drilling operations. Efforts to improve the rail system reported in the late 1970s and the 1980s included laying heavier rails, repairing locomotives, purchasing new locomotives, modernizing signaling equipment, expanding training facilities, and improving locomotive and rolling-stock repair facilities. One project would double-track the line from Port Sudan to the junction of the branch route to Sannar, thus in effect doubling the Port Sudan-Khartoum rail line. Substantial assistance has been furnished for these and other stock and track improvement projects by foreign governments and organizations, including the European Development Fund, the Development Finance Company, the AFESD, the International Development Association, Britain, France, and Japan. Implementation of much of this work has been hampered by political instability in the 1980s, debt, the dearth of hard currency, the shortage of spare parts, and import controls. Railroads were estimated in mid-1989 to be operating at less than 20 percent of capacity.

The Gezira Light Railway, one of the largest light railroads in Africa, evolved from tracks laid in the 1920s' construction of the canals for the Gezira Scheme. At the time, the railroad had about 135 route kilometers of 1.6096-meter-gauge track. As the size of the project area increased, the railroad was extended and by the mid-1960s consisted of a complex system totaling 716 route kilometers. Its primary purpose has been to serve the farm area by carrying cotton to ginneries and fertilizers, fuel, food, and other supplies to the villages in the area. Operations usually have been suspended during the rainy season.

ROADS

In 1990 Sudan's road system totaled between 20,000 and 25,000 kilometers, comprising an extremely sparse network for the size of the country. Asphalted all-weather roads, excluding paved streets in cities and towns, amounted to roughly 3,000 to 3,500 kilometers, of which the Khartoum-Port Sudan road accounted for almost 1,200 kilometers.

There were between 3,000 and 4,000 kilometers of gravel roads located mostly in the southern region where lateritic road-building materials were abundant. In general, these roads were usable all year round, although travel might be interrupted at times during the rainy season. Most of the gravel roads in southern Sudan have become unusable after being heavily mined by the insurgent southern forces of the Sudanese People's Liberation Army (SPLA).

The remaining roads were little more than fair-weather earth and sand tracks. Those in the clayey soil of eastern Sudan, a region of great economic importance, were impassable for several months during the rains. Even in the dry season, earthen roads in the sandy soils found in various parts of the country were generally usable only by motor vehicles equipped with special tires.

Until the early 1970s, the government had favored the railroads, believing they better met the country's requirements for transportation and that the primary purpose of roads was to act as feeders to the rail system. The railroads were also a profitable government operation, and road competition was not viewed as desirable. In the mid-1930s, a legislative attempt had been made to prevent through-road transport between Khartoum and Port Sudan. The law had little effect, but the government's failure to build roads hindered the development of road transportation. The only major stretch of road that had been paved by 1970 was between Khartoum and Wad Madani. This road had been started under a United States aid program in 1962, but work had stopped in 1967 when Sudanese-United States relations were broken over the June 1967 Arab-Israeli War. United States equipment was not removed, however, and was used by government workers to complete the road in 1970.

Disillusionment with railroad performance led to a new emphasis on roads in a readjustment of the Five-Year Plan in 1973--the so-called Interim Action Program--and a decision to encourage competition between rail and road transport as the best way to improve services. Paving of the dry-weather road between Khartoum and Port Sudan via Al Qadarif and Kassala was the most significant immediate step; this included upgrading of the existing paved Khartoum-Wad Madani section. From Wad Madani to Port Sudan, the road was constructed in four separate sections, each by different foreign financing, and in the case of the Wad Madani-Al Qadarif section, by direct participation of the Chinese. Other section contractors included companies from Italy, West Germany, and Yugoslavia. The last section opened in late 1980.

Other important road-paving projects of the early 1980s included a road from Wad Madani to Sannar and an extension from Sannar to Kusti on the White Nile completed in 1984. Since then the paved road has been extended to Umm Ruwabah with the intention to complete an all-weather road to Al Ubayyid. Paradoxically, most truckers in 1990 continued to pass from Omdurman to Al Ubayyid through the Sahelian scrub and the *qoz* to avoid the taxes levied to use the faster and less damaging paved road from Khartoum via Kusti.

A number of main gravel roads radiating from Juba were also improved. These included roads to the towns southwest of Juba and a road to the Ugandan border. In addition, the government built a gravel all-weather road east of Juba that reaches the Kenyan border. There it joined an all-weather road to Lodwar in Kenya connecting it with the Kenyan road system. All these improvements radiating from Juba, however, have been vitiated by the civil war, in which the roads have been extensively mined by the SPLA and the bridges destroyed, and because roads have not been maintained, they have seriously deteriorated.

Small private companies, chiefly owner-operated trucks, furnished most road transport. The government has encouraged private enterprise in this industry, especially in the central and eastern parts of the country, and the construction of allweather roads has reportedly led to rapid increases in the number of hauling businesses. The Sudanese-Kuwaiti Transport Company, a large government enterprise financed largely by Kuwait, began operations in 1975 with 100 large trucks and trailers. Most of its traffic was between Khartoum and Port Sudan. Use of road transport and bus services is likely to increase as paved roads are completed south of Khartoum in the country's main agricultural areas.

INLAND WATERWAYS

The Nile River, traversing Sudan from south to north, provides an important inland transportation route. Its overall usefulness, however, has been limited by natural features, including a number of cataracts in the main Nile between Khartoum and the Egyptian border. The White Nile to the south of Khartoum has shallow stretches that restrict the carrying capacities of barges, especially during the period of low water, and the river has sharp bends. Most of these southern impediments have been eliminated by Chevron, who as part of their oil exploration and development program dredged the White Nile shoals and established navigational beacons from Kusti to Bentiu.

A greater impediment has been the spread of the water hyacinth, which impedes traffic. Man-made features have also introduced restrictions, the most important of which was a dam constructed in the 1930s on the White Nile about forty kilometers upriver from Khartoum. This dam has locks, but they have not always operated well, and the river has been little used from Khartoum to the port of Kusti, a railroad crossing 319 kilometers upstream. The Sennar and Roseires dams on the Blue Nile are without locks and restrict traffic on that river.

In 1983 only two sections of the Nile had regular commercial transport services. The more important was the 1,436-kilometer stretch of the White Nile from Kusti to Juba (known as the Southern Reach), which provided the only generally usable transport connection between the central and southern parts of the country. Virtually all traffic, and certainly scheduled traffic, ended in 1984, when the SPLA consistently sank the exposed steamers from sanctuaries along the river banks. River traffic south of Kusti had not resumed in mid- 1991 except for a few heavily armed and escorted convoys.

At one time, transport services also were provided on tributaries of the White Nile (the Bahr al Ghazal and the Jur River) to the west of Malakal. These services went as far as Waw but were seasonal, depending on water levels. They were finally discontinued during the 1970s because vegetation blocked waterways, particularly the fast-growing water hyacinth. On the main Nile, a 287-kilometer stretch from Kuraymah to Dunqulah, situated between the fourth and third cataracts and known as the Dunqulah Reach, also had regular service, although this was restricted during the low-water period in February and March. Transport facilities on both reaches were operated after 1973 by the parastatal (mixed government and privately owned company) River Transport Corporation (RTC). Before that they had been run by the SRC, essentially as feeders to the rail line. River cargo and passenger traffic have varied from year to year, depending in large part on the availability and capacity of transport vessels. During the 1970s, roughly 100,000 tons of cargo and 250,000 passengers were carried annually. By 1984, before the Southern Reach was closed, the number of passengers had declined to less than 60,000 per year and the tonnage to less than 150,000. Although no statistics were available, the closing of the Southern Reach had by 1990 made river traffic insignificant.

Foreign economists have characterized the RTC's operations as inefficient, a result both of shortages of qualified staff and of barge capacity. The corporation had a virtual monopoly over river transport, although the southern regional government had established river feeder transport operations, and private river transport services were reported to be increasing until the resumption of the civil war. Despite its favored position, the RTC and its predecessor (SRC) experienced regular losses that had to be covered by government appropriations. In the late 1970s, the corporation procured new barges, pusher-tugboats, and other equipment in an effort to improve services, but this attempt proved useless because of the warfare that had continued from 1983.

MARINE PORTS AND SHIPPING

In 1993 Sudan had only one operational deep-water harbor, Port Sudan, situated on an inlet of the Red Sea. The port had been built from scratch, beginning in 1905, to complement the railroad line from Khartoum to the Red Sea by serving as the entry and exit point for the foreign trade the rail line was to carry. It operated as a department of SRC until 1974 when it was transferred to the Sea Ports Corporation, a newly established public enterprise set up to manage Sudan's marine ports. Facilities at the port eventually included fifteen cargo berths, sheds, warehouses, and storage tanks for edible oils, molasses, and petroleum products. Equipment included quay, mobile, and other cranes, and some forklift trucks, but much of the handling of cargo was manual. There were also a number of tugboats, which were used to berth ships in the narrow inlet.

During the early 1970s, port traffic averaged about 3 million tons a year, compared with an overall capacity of about 3.8 million tons. Exports were somewhat more than 1 million tons and imports about 2 million tons; about half of the latter was petroleum and petroleum products. By the mid-1970s, stepped up economic development had raised traffic to capacity levels. In 1985, however, largely as a result of the civil war, exports were down to 663 thousand tons (down 51 percent from the previous year) and imports were 2.3 million tons (down 25 percent from the previous year). Physical expansion of the harbor and adjacent areas was generally precluded by natural features and the proximity of the city of Port Sudan. However, surveys showed that use could be increased considerably by modernization and improvement of existing facilities and the addition of further cargo-handling equipment.

In 1978, with the assistance of a loan from the IDA, work began on adding deep-water berths and providing roll-on-roll-off container facilities. A loan to purchase equipment was made by a West Germany body. The first phase was completed in 1982, and the second phase began in 1983, aided by a US$25-million World Bank cr. One of the major improvements has been to make the port more readily usable by road vehicles. Developed almost entirely as a rail-serviced facility, the port had large areas of interlacing railroad tracks that were mostly not flush with surrounding surfaces, thereby greatly restricting vehicular movement. Many of these tracks have been removed and new access roads constructed. Much of the cleared area has become available for additional storage facilities.

In the early 1980s, the Nimeiri government announced a plan to construct a new deep-water port at Sawakin, about twenty kilometers south of Port Sudan. Construction of a new port had long been under consideration in response to the projected growth of port traffic in the latter part of the twentieth century. A detailed study for the proposed port was made by a West German firm in the mid-1970s, and plans were drawn up for three general cargo berths, including roll-on-roll-off container facilities, and an oil terminal. Major funding for the port, known as Sawakin, was offered in 1985 by West Germany's development agency Kranstalt für Wiederaufbau and the DFC. After the Nimeiri government repeatedly postponed work on the port, the German government allocated the funds instead for purchase of agricultural inputs. Once work resumed, however, Sawakin port opened in January 1991, and was capable of handling an estimated 1.5 million tons of cargo a year.

A national merchant marine, Sudan Shipping Line, was established in 1962 as a joint venture between the government and Yugoslavia. In 1967 it became wholly government owned. From the initial two Yugoslav-built cargo vessels, the line had grown by the mid-1970s to seven ships, totaling about 52,340 deadweight tons. During 1979 and early 1980, eight more ships were added, including six built in Yugoslavia and two in Denmark. In 1990 the merchant marine consisted of ten ships of 122,200 deadweight tons. The Yugoslav vessels were all multipurpose and included container transport features. The Danish ships were equipped with roll-on-roll-off facilities. Sailings, which had been mainly between Red Sea ports and northern Europe, were expanded in the late 1980s to several Merranean ports.

COMMUNICATIONS

Domestic telecommunications in Sudan were sparse, and the system suffered from poor maintenance. In 1994 the country had only 73,000 telephones, two-thirds of which were in the Khartoum area. Telex was available in the capital. A domestic satellite system with fourteen ground stations, supplemented by coaxial cable and a microwave network, linked telephone exchanges and broadcast facilities within the country. Eleven cities had amplitude modulation (AM) radio stations, and Khartoum, Atbarah, and Wad Madani had television stations with broadcasts in Arabic seven hours nightly.

The country had an estimated 6 million radio receivers and 250,000 television sets in 1994. International telecommunications were modern and provided high-quality links to the rest of the world. A satellite ground station near the capital working with the International Telecommunications Satellite Corporation's (Intelsat) Atlantic Ocean satellite permitted direct dialing of telephone calls between Sudan and Europe, North America, and parts of Africa. In addition, a second satellite ground station was linked to the Arab Satellite Communications Organization's (Arabsat) pan-Arab communications network. The Arabsat network was used for live television broadcasts, news exchanges, and educational programming among the members of the League of Arab States (Arab League).

OIL AND GAS SECTOR[1]

ENERGY OVERVIEW

Proven Oil Reserves: 262.1 million barrels
Oil Production : 209,000 barrels per day (bbl/d) **:** 219,000 bbl/d
Oil Consumption : 36,000 bbl/d
Net Oil Exports : 173,000 bbl/d
Natural Gas Reserves: 3 trillion cubic feet (tcf)
Natural Gas Production: None
Natural Gas Consumption: None
Electric Generation Capacity : 500 megawatts (60% thermal, 40% hydroelectric)
Electricity Generation: 1.760 billion kilowatthours (kwh)
Electricity Consumption: 1.637 billion kwh

ENVIRONMENTAL OVERVIEW

Minister of Tourism & Environment: Tagani Adam Tahir
Total Energy Consumption : 0.07 quadrillion Btu* (<0.1% of world total energy consumption)
Energy-Related Carbon Emissions : 1.2 million metric tons of carbon (<0.1% of world total carbon emissions)
Per Capita Energy Consumption : 2.3 million Btu (vs. U.S. value of 355.8 million Btu)
Per Capita Carbon Emissions : 0.04 metric tons of carbon (vs. U.S. value of 5.5 metric tons of carbon)
Energy Intensity: 5,300 Btu/$1990 (vs U.S. value of 13,900 Btu/$1990) **
Carbon Intensity: 0.09 metric tons of carbon/thousand $1990 (vs U.S. value of 0.22 metric tons/thousand $1990)**
Sectoral Share of Energy Consumption: Transportation (12.2%), Industrial (8.7%), Residential (74.0%), Commercial (5.1%)
Sectoral Share of Carbon Emissions: Transportation (65.2%), Industrial (16.9%), Residential (14.2%), Commercial (3.7%)
Fuel Share of Energy Consumption : Oil (85.6%), Natural Gas (0.0%), Coal (0.0%)
Fuel Share of Carbon Emissions : Oil (100.0%), Natural Gas (0.0%), Coal (0.0%)
Renewable Energy Consumption: 278 trillion Btu* (67% increase from 1997)
Number of People per Motor Vehicle: 100 (vs. U.S. value of 1.3)
Status in Climate Change Negotiations: Non-Annex I country under the United Nations Framework Convention on Climate Change (ratified November 19th, 1993). Not a signatory to the Kyoto Protocol.
Major Environmental Issues: Inadequate supplies of potable water; wildlife populations threatened by excessive hunting; soil erosion; desertification.
Major International Environmental Agreements: A party to Conventions on Biodiversity, Climate Change, Desertification, Endangered Species, Law of the Sea, Nuclear Test Ban, Ozone Layer Protection and Whaling.

* The total energy consumption statistic includes petroleum, dry natural gas, coal, net hydro, nuclear, geothermal, solar and wind electric power. The renewable energy consumption statistic is based on International Energy Agency (IEA) data and includes hydropower, solar, wind, tide, geothermal, solid biomass and animal products, biomass gas and liquids, industrial and municipal

[1] *With the completion of a major oil export pipeline in July 1999, Sudanese crude oil production and exports has risen rapidly over the past two years. Also, Sudan became an exporter of refined petroleum products, following the inauguration of the Khartoum Oil Refinery in June.*

wastes. Sectoral shares of energy consumption and carbon emissions are also based on IEA data.
**GDP based on EIA International Energy Annual 1998

OIL AND GAS INDUSTRIES

Major Oil Fields (Production - bbl/d): Heglig/Unity (200,000-220,000), Adar (10,000)
Oil Refineries (Capacity - bbl/d): Khartoum (50,000 bbl/d), El Gily (50,000 bbl/d), Port Sudan (21,700 bbl/d)
Major Foreign Oil Company Involvement: Agip, China National Petroleum Corp. (CNPC), Gulf Petroleum Corp. (GPC), Lundin Oil Corp., Exxon Mobil, National Iranian Gas Company (NIGC), OMV, Petronas, Royal Dutch/Shell, Talisman Energy, TotalFina Elf, Trafigura Beheer B.V.

Sudan gained its independence from Egypt and the United Kingdom in 1956. The current government, led by General Omar Hassan Ahmad al-Bashir, came to power in 1989 after overthrowing a transitional coalition government. A new constitution was promulgated on January 1, 1999. Multi-party presidential and parlimentary elections were held in December 2000, and President Bashir and his party won an overwhelming victory, tainted by a boycott by all main opposition parties.

Despite considerable natural resources, Sudan is among the world's (and region's) poorest countries. Traditionally, its economy has been mainly agricultural - a mix of subsistence farming and production of cash crops such as cotton and gum arabic. With the start of significant oil production (and exports) beginning in late 1999, however, Sudan's economy is changing dramatically, with oil export revenues now accounting for around 70% of Sudan's total export earnings. Sudan no longer relies on expensive imported oil products, which has helped the country's trade balance, while foreign investment has started to flow into the country (as of July 2001, total foreign investment stood at $7 billion). The country's currency, the dinar, has remained relatively stable since 1999, at around 257 dinars per U.S. dollar (recently it fell to 264 dinars per U.S. dollar). Sudan's economy shows signs of turning the corner after many years of poor performance.

Sudan's economic performance has been strong over the past few years. In 2000, the country's real GDP grew by 7.2%, with estimated growth of 5.5% in 2001 and forecasted growth over 5% in 2002 as well. Meanwhile, inflation has slowed dramatically over the past few years, from an average 110% between 1991 and 1996 to 16% in 1999, an estimated 6% in 2001, and a forecast 9% in 2002. Exports have grown sharply since 1999, and the merchandise trade balance has turned from negative to positive. In May 2000, the International Monetary Fund (IMF) expressed its satisfaction with Sudan's implementation of a structural reform and macroecomic stabilization program, adopted in 1997. As part of this program, Finance Minister Abdel-Rahim Hamdi -- a strong advocate of economic reform, appointed in February 2001 -- announced in July 2001 that Sudan was aiming to accelerate and broaden the country's privatization program. The government also is moving to cut costs, reduce subsidies (i.e., subsidies on gasoline and benzene were cut sharply in November 2001) and support to state-owned enterprises (SOEs), and raise revenues in order to bring the budget closer into balance.

In part due to its entry into world oil markets as an exporter, Sudan is becoming more engaged in the global economy. In February 2000, Sudan opened its Red Sea Free Trade Zone, designed to encourage foreign direct investment, and in March 2000, Sudan publicly repeated its desire to join the World Trade Organization. Since the end of 1999, Sudan has signed various trade and investment agreements with Bahrain, Egypt, Ethiopia, Iraq, Kuwait, Saudi Arabia, and Syria.

Despite its economic progress, Sudan still faces developmental obstacles, including a limited infrastructure and an external debt in 2000 of around $16 billion, representing a debt-to-GDP ratio of about 128%. Furthermore, the government remains embroiled in the long-running conflict with rebel movements in the south of the country, inhabited primarily by non-Muslims. This costly and bloody conflict has, over the past two decades, claimed (directly or indirectly through famine) as many as 2 million Sudanese lives. Finally, Sudan's new reliance on oil export revenues makes the country vulnerable to world oil price fluctuations, such as the sharp fall in oil prices since September 2001.

The United States imposed economic sanctions against Sudan in November 1997, prohibiting trade between the two countries, as well as investment by United States businesses in Sudan. At the time, Secretary of State Madeleine Albright stated that the sanctions were intended to "deprive the regime in Khartoum of the financial and material benefits of U.S. trade and investment, including investment in Sudan's petroleum sector." In February 2000, the Clinton administration broadened the sanctions to include a prohibition against U.S. citizens and companies conducting business with the Greater Nile Petroleum Operating Company (GNPOC), an international consortium of petroleum companies currently extracting oil from Sudan. The sanctions, however, do not apply to the foreign individual parent companies of GNPOC, which includes Calgary-based Talisman Energy. In October 2000, the United States continued its efforts to isolate Sudan by successfully lobbying African nations to deny Sudan a regional seat on the United Nations Security Council. Since the September 11, 2001 terrorist attacks on New York and Washington, however, U.S.-Sudanese relations appear to have improved somewhat, as the United States attempts to encourage Sudanese cooperation in the war against terrorism.

OIL

As of January 2001, Sudan's estimated proven reserves of crude oil stood at 262.1 million barrels. Crude oil production averaged 209,000 barrels per day (bbl/d) during 2001, and has been rising steadily since the completion of a vital pipeline in July 1999; oil production for 2002 is forecast to reach 219,000 bbl/d. By 2003, oil output could reach 290,000 bbl/d or higher, with plans to reach 450,000 bbl/d by 2005. In August 2001, in recognition of Sudan's growing significance as an oil exporter, OPEC granted the country observer status at OPEC meetings.

Petroleum exploration in Sudan began in the early 1960s. The activity was originally concentrated offshore in the Red Sea. The only significant offshore discovery was Chevron's Suakin gas discovery in 1976. Chevron's exploration in the 1960s and 1970s led to several oil finds in southern Sudan near the towns of Bentiu and Malakal. Chevron abandoned its concessions in Sudan in 1990, due to their location in an area where fighting was taking place between government and rebel forces. The French firm, Total, also suspended its onshore exploration activities, but retained the rights to its concessions. The Sudanese government sub-divided Chevron's concessions into smaller exploration blocks, and Canadian independent Arakis Energy (Arakis) acquired the portion of Chevron's concession north of the town of Bentiu in 1993.

GREATER NILE OIL PROJECT

Arakis began development of the Heglig and Unity fields within its concessions, and started production on a small scale (around 2,000 bbl/d) in 1996; this oil was processed and consumed within Sudan. The remote location of the field, aproximately 930 miles from the Red Sea coast, meant that it would require a very substantial capital investment to transport the oil to a seaport. To attract the necessary capital and spread the risks, Arakis entered into a consortium in December 1996 with GNPOC, consisting of the China National Petroleum Corporation (CNPC)(40%), Petronas of Malaysia (30%), Sudanese national firm Sudapet (5%), and Arakis (25%, and the field operator). Construction on the pipeline from the fields to an export terminal near Port Sudan began in May 1998 on an accelerated schedule. Originally built to move 150,000 bbl/d, the pipeline has a current capacity of 250,000 bbl/d and can be expanded to 450,000 bbl/d. Heglig and Unity reportedly produced around 220,000 bbl/d in September 2001.

Arakis' involvement in Sudan, even after the formation of the GNPOC consortium raised $700 million, remained hindered by a lack of capital. U.S. sanctions against Sudan prevented investment in the project by U.S. corporations and persons, and the high-risk nature of investment in Sudan also had an effect. In the end, Arakis agreed to be purchased by another Canadian independent, Talisman Energy, for $277 million in Talisman stock, in October 1998. The Talisman acquisition provided an infusion of capital which allowed the project to be completed on schedule in 1999. In July 1999, the pipeline began filling with crude, and the first cargo of "Nile Blend" departed the export terminal in early September 1999.

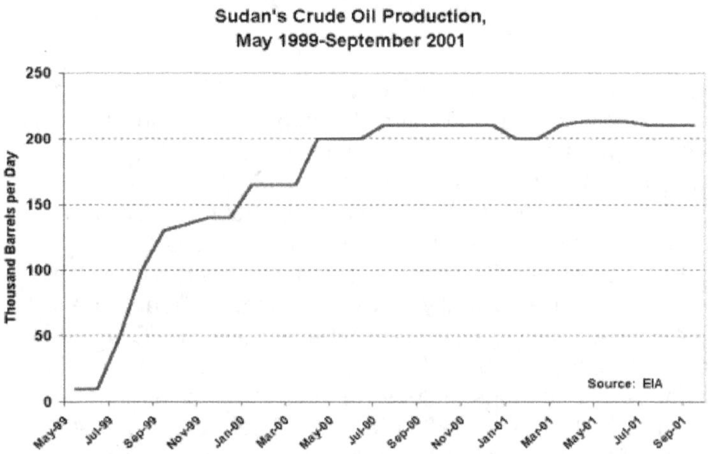

PRODUCTION

The fields in the Muglad area produce crude oil with a 33° to 42° API range, with only 0.5% sulfur content. The crude is highly parafinnic, which requires heating to maintain flow in the pipeline. Recoverable reserves from the Heglig and Unity fields have been estimated at around 300 million barrels. The area around these two fields also is suspected to contain oil, but estimates of reserves vary. The Swedish firm, Lundin Oil (partly bought out by Talisman in June 2001), reported a discovery at the "Thar Jath 2" exploration well in the adjacent Block 5A in March 2001, with oil flows of 2,000 bbl/d. Petronas, the Austrian firm OMV, and Sudapet have minority stakes in the block. In July 2000, Petronas was awarded a 40% share in Block 5B, and in October 2000, Petronas agreed to raise Sudan's oil output by 50,000 bbl/d by mid-2002. The increased production will result from Petronas' development of two untapped oil fields in Monga and Bambo in the Mujlad Basin of western Sudan, plus the construction of three additional oil pumps along the pipeline. In March 2001, OMV announced that it had found oil at its exploratory well, "Thar Jath 1."

Sudanese officials announced in June 2000, plans to begin oil exploration in northwest Sudan, the Blue Nile Basin in southeastern Sudan, and the Red Sea area in eastern Sudan. Oil exploration in Sudan previously was limited largely to the central and south-central regions, which, according to Khartoum officials, represent only 15% of the national oil reserves. Sudanese Energy Ministry representatives place estimated total reserves in the country at 3 billion barrels and estimated proven reserves at 700 million barrels. Government spokesmen said that unnamed Japanese, European and Middle East companies had expressed interest in the new oil concessions.

In March 2000, Canada-based Fosters Resources Ltd. signed an Exploration and Production Sharing Agreement with the government of Sudan to develop, in cooperation with a consortium of Arab and Sudanese companies, the concession covering the majority of the Melut Basin in

Central Sudan. One group, led by Fosters' affiliate, the Melut Petroleum Company, was granted 46% of the concession, while the other group, made up of Qatar's Gulf Petroleum Corporation (GPC) and smaller Sudanese companies, also received a 46% share. The remaining 8% is controlled by Sudapet. The concession area incorporates Adar Yeil field, where GPC is already producing 5,000 bbl/d. Fosters was forced to withdraw from the project, however, when its financial backing fell through in May 2000. Fosters cited pressure from human rights groups concerned about Sudan's human rights record as the reason for its investors' abandonment of the project. The Sudanese government signed a new production agreement for the concession in November 2000, granting GPC 46%, CNPC 23%, the Sudanese company Al Thani 23%, and Sudapet 8% (now in a consortium called Petrodar) to manage development of blocs 3 and 7 in the Melut basin.

Development of Sudan's oil resources has been highly controversial. Numerous international human rights organizations have accused the Sudanese government of financing wide-scale human rights abuses with oil revenues, including the mass displacement of civilians living near the oil fields. The Sudan People's Liberation Army (SPLA), the main southern rebel group, has declared that it considers oil installations a "legitimate military target," as oil development has provided the Sudanese government the financial resources to expand its war effort. In November 2001, southern rebels claimed to have ambushed an army convoy traveling near GNPOC facilities, and stated that such attacks would continue until "oil exploration, exploitation and development come to a halt." In August 2001, an attempt by rebels to blow up Sudan's oil export pipeline was thwarted, but rebels claimed to have killed 42 government soldiers in an attack earlier in the month, and also to have inflicted "extensive damage" to oil facilities at Heglig. The government and a representative of Talisman Energy both denied the latter claim. Rebels also claimed to have launched a successful attack on oil facilities in Bentiu in mid-October 2001, but this claim also was refuted by the government. In June 2001, Sudan's Foreign Minister (Mustafa Osman Ismail) said that the Sudanese government was prepared to share oil revenues with southern rebels if they gave up their armed struggle.

Broadened U.S. sanctions imposed against GNPOC in February reportedly had little impact on production or distribution of Sudanese oil. Talisman insisted that the corporate structure of its Sudanese oil venture effectively insulated the company's U.S. activities, thereby protecting U.S. shareholders from the penalties associated with violations of the U.S. sanctions. Despite the Canadian government's findings in February 2000 that oil revenues were exacerbating the Sudanese civil war, Canadian Foreign Minister Lloyd Axworthy declined to impose sanctions against Talisman or Sudan. As of November 2001, Talisman, which reportedly has considered selling its holdings in Sudan, appeared to be increasing oil output in the country and, in general, looking more likely to continue its operations there. In September 2001, the U.S. Congress delayed consideration of the "Sudan Peace Act," which would toughen U.S. policy towards Sudan, including imposition of possible additional sanctions on oil companies like Talisman operating in Sudan.

REFINING AND DOWNSTREAM

With the June 2000 opening of the 50,000-bbl/d Khartoum Oil Refinery in the Jayli area, 30 miles north of Khartoum, Sudan became self-sufficient in all petroleum products except for jet fuel. The Khartoum refinery, built and jointly operated by CNPC, produces benzene and butane gas for domestic consumption and export, as well as gasoline for local consumption. A portion of the surplus gas eventually will be used in the production of electricity, according to Khartoum officials. The Khartoum refinery is expected to save the Sudanese government over $100 million per year in refined petroleum product imports. Following the opening of the Khartoum refinery, the price of gasoline was reduced considerably throughout the country and the price of gas cylinders, which Sudanese use for cooking, dropped from $5.30 to $2.60.

In August, 2000, the Sudan's National Petroleum Company (NPC) announced plans to lay pipelines to supply Eritrea and Ethiopia with petroleum derivatives from the Khartoum refinery. If approved, the pipelines would pass through Sudan's Gezira, Sennar and Gedaref states. NPC is also studying the feasibility of running another pipeline to export crude oil from the Adaryel oil fields in southern Sudan to Ethiopia. In June 2001, Sudan agreed to provide Ethiopia with 85% of its oil requirements beginning in 2002. Sudan also appears to have begun exporting oil to fellow members of COMESA (the Common Market for Eastern and Southern Africa), including another neighbor, Kenya. Under COMESA, trade within the zone is not subject to tariffs, which means that Sudanese oil likely will be cheaper for COMESA members than other alternatives. In November 2001, Sudan reportedly expressed willingness to supply Uganda with oil at a low price.

Sudan has two other refineries, with the largest in Port Sudan. The Port Sudan facility has a current capacity of 21,700 bbl/d. Sudanese officials announced in July 2000, however, plans to expand the Port Sudan capacity by 70%. A petroleum products pipeline runs from the Port Sudan refinery to Khartoum. A smaller facility located in central Sudan near El Obeid has a capacity of 10,000 bbl/d.

ELECTRICITY

Sudan currently has installed electric generation capacity of 500 megawatts (MW), managed by the state owned National Electricity Corporation (NEC). Of this, around 60% is accounted for by thermal (mainly oil) and 40% by hydropower. Hydroelectric power generation varies greatly over time, however, according to rainfall patterns. The main generating facility is the Roseires dam located on the Blue Nile approximately 500 kilometers (315 miles) southeast of Khartoum. Roseires has an installed capacity of 280 MW, but output varies greatly as water levels on the river rise and fall through the year.

Sudan's total electricity generation was 1.760 billion kilowatthours (kwh) in 1999. Two interconnected electric grids exist -- the Blue Nile grid and the Western grid. Much of Sudan, however, is not served by the electric grids, and blackouts and brownouts are common. Some towns outside the two grids are served by their own small-scale diesel-fired plants.

Faced with a power shortage, Sudan has plans to add additional generating capacity. The largest projects are the proposed Kajbar and Merowe hydroelectric facilities in northern Sudan. The Kajbar Dam, located at the Nile's second cataract, is currently under construction, and will have a 300-MW capacity. An agreement to finance the Kajbar project was signed between Sudan and China in September 1997.

Under terms of the agreement, China is financing 75% of the project (approximately $200 million) and Sudan is to provide the remaining 25%. Environmental groups have expressed concern about Kajbar Dam, citing potential damage both to the Nile ecosystem and to the culture of the displaced Nubian residents of the area. The Merowe facility, if it is built, would have a capacity of 1,000 MW, and would be built at the Nile's fourth cataract. Egypt has not voiced major objections about the issue of Nile water diversion, which Sudan's hydroelectric projects would entail. In August 2001, the Merowe project received a boost when several Arab development funds (i.e., the Arab Fund for Economic and Social Development) pledged a total of $780 million to the project. In another development, in May 2001, China's Harbin Power Engineering Co. Ltd. reportedly signed a $140 million contract with Sudan to build a power plant, transmission line, and transformer station in Sudan.

On April 29, 1998, Minister of Energy and Mining al-Jaz signed two agreements with NCD of the Netherlands to develop three electric generating facilities. The facilities would have a capacity of 10 MW each. Other small electric power projects planned for Sudan include: two, 10-MW thermal units are to be built at the Khartoum oil refinery; four small diesel units are planned for eastern Sudan; and power turbines are to be installed at the Jebel Awlia Dam on the White Nile, south of Khartoum.

In other electricity-related news, the director of the NEC said in April 2001 that Sudan and Ethiopia had agreed to link their power grids. A related report in April 2001 indicated that Ethiopia had agreed to export power to Sudan (and Djibouti).

Sources for this report include: Africa Oil and Gas; Agence France Presse, CIA World Factbook 2001; CountryWatch.com; Dow Jones Interactive; Economist Intelligence Unit ViewsWire; International Market Insight Reports; International Monetary Fund; MBendi; Panafrican News Agency; Petroleum Economist; Petroleum Intelligence Weekly; Suna News Agency; U.S. Energy Information Administration; World Markets Online

INVESTMENT SYSTEM IN THE SUDAN

With its large size and varied climatic zones stretching from the lush vegetation of the equatorial south to the arid deserts of the north, Sudan is endowed with huge natural as well as human resources as follows:

1. Extensive stretches of cultivable land estimated at 200 million fertile feddans.

2. A huge livestock wealth, among the top largest in Africa and estimated to be over 116 million head of camels, cattle, sheep and goats. There are also more than 200 million feddans of forest, bushes and natural pastureland.

3. Great water-supply reserves in forms of rain waters, rivers, surface and underground water reservoirs.

4. Huge deposits of mineral wealth which have not yet been fully explored, exploited or utilized, such as gold, silver, chromium, asbestos, manganese, gypsum, mica, iron, lead, uranium, zinc, copper, cobalt, granite, marble, in addition to petroleum and natural gas.

5. Sudan is now an oil-producing country. The first shipment of Sudanese oil sailed to the international market on 30th August, 1999. Investment in the oil and energy sectors is a top priority in the country.

6. In Sudan, there is a surfeit of qualified manpower in the agricultural, industrial and economic services sectors. There are specialized research centres in food industries, leather and tanneries, weaving industry, oceanography and marine science, administrative sciences besides numerous institutes for banking, accountancy and computer studies, constituting a solid basis for successful interaction with the latest developments in science and technology.

Present Investment Climate in Sudan
The government is making serious efforts to create conditions to attract foreign investment to Sudan. Some of the important steps taken by it in this direction are as follows:

1. A three-year economic salvation programme (1990-1993) was formulated whereby several reforms were introduced, including abrogation of state monopoly of agricultural and industrial products, the economic services sector and marketing. The state has also withdrawn from some public sector corporations and institutions.

2. Radical changes in Investment Acts and Laws that regulated all economic activities has lifted all the curbs on private sector participation.

3. Economic, trade and financial policies supportive of the country's move towards a market-driven economy have also been adopted. These include:

i) Lifting of major consumer-goods subsidies.
ii) Freeing the Sudanese Dinar vis-a-vis other international currencies.
iii) Removing control on the prices of agricultural and industrial commodities to provide incentives to producers and encourage growth.
iv) Abrogation of the former import license system, except with the defrayal and preferential trade countries.
v) Abrogation of the mandatory declaration of hard currencies carried by travellers, who are now allowed to carry any amount of hard currencies in whatever form.
vi) Lifting of all restrictions on the movement of hard currency accounts. Now the client is allowed to feed such accounts by all possible methods of payment.

4. Promulgation of a new Investment Encouragement Act, 2000, the older 1990 Act and the ammended one of 1988.

The Investment Act consolidates the legal base for investment and while aiming at promoting and encouraging investment activities, endeavours to ease, unify and simplify procedures for foreign investors.

Salient Features of the Investment Encouragement Act, 1999
1. The Act encourages investment in the following sectors: agricultural (animal and crop), industrial, energy, mining, transport, warehousing, tourism, marine resources, information technology, health, education, electricity, roads, ports, water, communication, environment, storage, housing, contracting, basic infrastructure, economic services, etc.

2. It encourages investment in projects that endeavour to evolve alternatives for the country's main imports and projects that depend, to a large extent, on local raw materials for their inputs.

3. It grants the following incentives to investors:
i) Exemption from business profit taxes for not less than 10 years effective from the year that follows commercial production or commencement of activities.

ii) Total exemption from taxes and custom duties, and any other fees, as may be levied on imports during the period of exemption of the project.

iii) Total or partial exemption from customs and excise or any other duties pertaining to imports related to the project's requirements.

iv) Production and consumption tax cuts.

v) Foreign capital investors may transfer their profits and initial financing costs or debts provided that all the legally binding commitments pertaining to the project are met and settled. The transfer shall be in the original currency or currencies the capital was transacted in.

vi) Import of raw materials for project in whatever quantities without being restricted by the procedures of importers/ exporters registrars.

vii) Freedom of movement, residence or transfer of the project's expatriate employees is guaranteed in accordance with the prevailing laws.

4. Some of the most significant guarantees of the investment Act are:
i) The investor's project shall not be liable to nationalization or confiscation, whether totally or partially.

ii) The project's funds shall not be distrained, seized, freezed, confiscated, provisionally seized or sequestrated.

iii) Remittance of invested capital in its currency or currencies of origin in case the project has not started, or in case the project got liquidated or disposed off wholly or partially, provided that all legally binding commitments are met.

iv) Sudan is one of the signatories to several international and regional bodies concerned with investment disputes. The Act also stipulates ways and means and procedures for the settlement of any legal dispute that might arise.

5. Projects shall be granted licenses and/or privileges, facilities, guarantees as set in the Act, unless after submission of a technical and economic feasibility study of the project and a preliminary approval is obtained.

The Investment Authority
The Ministry of Investment has been established as the ministry responsible for setting up, advertising and publicizing for investments in Sudan.

It is also responsible for the creation of an ideal investment climate that attracts national and foreign capital in Sudan and removal of all obstacles to capital inflows. It is the body that draws encouraging investment policies, simplifies procedures for investors, issues licenses of investment projects and the relevant facilities and guarantees, follows up the actual execution of the proposed projects, prepares investment maps and saves the investors the trouble of data collecting by providing them with all the necessary information and data. The ministry shall also follow up all procedures of the investment licensing with relevant government circles on behalf of the investor.

The Investment Ministry enjoys close relations with local, regional and international corporations and organizations concerned with investment such as the Arab Organization for Investment Guarantee, the International Investment Guarantee Agency, the United Nations Industrial Development Organization (UNIDO) and other regional and international grouping and institutions of which Sudan is a part.

Privatization
Some of the major economic policies pertain to freeing the Sudanese economy from bureaucratic control and ensure let it be a market-driven entity. Besides, more open policies towards the private sector are recommended and implemented.

Under the aforesaid guidelines, the state monopoly over agriculture, industry, economic services, internal and external marketing sectors have already been abrogated, and the government has actually begun to pull out from many public sector corporations, establishments and companies operating in these fields.

The government has made radical amendments in all acts and lifted restrictions on investments and economic activities so as to encourage greater private sector participation in all sectors.

The government has also placed some state assets and public sector companies on the block for sale, partnership or transfer. Some of these units operate in the agricultural and industrial sectors (spinning and weaving, ready-made clothes, food industries and tanneries), others are in the services sector (hotel keeping, transportation, communication and telecommunication services) and some are trading and marketing corporations.

Certain guidelines are strictly observed throughout the privatization processes such as competitive bidding, prior publicity for sale, transparency so as to ensure justice and fair play.

Licensing and Facilitation Procedures for Investment:
1. The investor shall submit an economic "feasibility study of the project.

2. The investor shall file applications for licensing, privileges or facilities for an investment project against payment of prescribed fees. The form shall be issued by the investor's services section in the ministry.

3. The Investment Ministry shall review the application form and consult the competent technical organs if necessary.

4. Upon receipt of the provisional approval from the Ministry of Investment regarding the particular project, the investor shall then register a business name or company whose activities shall be limited to its specific field of licensing only.

5. Upon approval of the business name of company, the investor shall submit all the relevant documents to the Ministry in order to obtain the license covering the facilities granted and location of the plot where the premises of the project in question shall be sited.

6. Upon completion of all licensing procedures and issuance of the license, the investor may then import the project's requirements in accordance with "an itemized requisition list" which the Ministry must consent to in advance.

7. The Ministry shall then contact the customs authorities upon clearance of the project's imported items through the custom's co-ordinator in the Ministry.

8. The Ministry shall also contact the taxation authorities to exempt the project from tax duties in accordance with the granted privileges.

It is to be reiterated again that the Ministry follows up all procedures with the relevant government bodies on behalf of the investors.

ECONOMY AND INVESTMENTS REGULATIONS

FOREIGN DIRECT INVESTMENT

Investment in Sudan has witnessed remarkable progress in terms of efficiency, performance and investment laws. Investment laws are in continuos improvement and amendment since first Investment Encouragement Act of 1956 till the new Act of 1999.

Efforts has gone far to streamline and simplify project approval and procedures and by identifying projects by providing preliminary feasibility and final feasibility studies.

- Free Zone areas were created in Suakin (600 square km) in the Red Sea coast, and in Khartoum North.

- Bonded warehouses were allowed in all parts of the country.

EIGHTEEN STRATEGIC REASONS FOR INVESTMENT IN SUDAN:

1. Cheap labour.
2. Availability of raw materials, land, water.
3. Liberalisation of market, removing price controls, currency floating.
4. Big market (ten countries neighbouring) + 29 million Sudanese.
5. Member of COMESA (Common Market for East & South Africa) with tax reductions and preference, ACP groups, new grand Arabs free trade area under progress & LDC member with preferences in EU and world markets.
6. Skilled labour, 22 universities research institutions (Agriculture, Animal Resource, Industrial Research & Consultant food research centre, health research & training ... etc.)
7. Continental Climate: from 3c to 48c, (Desert, Merranean, Savannah,Equatoria).
8. Investment law: gives all incentives without discrimination between foreigners & nationals in joint venture, partnership, complete ownership with guarantee against any form of nationalisation or confiscation.
9. As LDC in WTO Sudan will benefit from the preference hi Access to markets without barrier and reduced taxes for its products and benefit from rise in food prices due to elimination of subsidies in other countries.
10. Infrastructure : 7000 Km of rail, asphalt roads connecting most regional capitals and production areas to Khartoum, and sea ports, 6 international airports and 22 regional airports, 2000 km of river steamers service.
11. Telecommunication: advanced telephone & fax service through privatisation of sector.
12. Baking service: 32 commercial & specialized Banks with 800 branches.
13. Twelve insurance companies and reinsurance companies.
14. Stock market with 30 registered joint stock companies out of 140 in the country.
15. Organized business sector ready for Joint venture.
16. Success Projects of foreign investment like Kenana Sugar, Eriab gold (French) Daewoo (Korea) and Many investing in oil may be incentive for others to invest in Sudan.
17. Peace Agreements to end the civil war which started in 1995 with many
18. fighting groups and negotiation with SPLA under IGAD.

Economic reforms stressing on development of infrastructure

- Privitzation
- Export oriented policies
- Encouragement of micro, small and medium scale enterprises
- Encouragement of women to enter business by forming and supporting organizations of business women.

A. INVESTMENT IN AGRICULTURE:

Total arable land is about 200 million feddan (4200 sqm) and only 30 million feddan is cultivated.

Investment needed welcomed in :

1. wheat production.
2. Sorghum (Dura).
3. Oil seeds (sesame, groundnut, sunflower).
4. Fruits (mango, banana, Juava, lemon, strawberry, pineapple (ananas), grapefruit.
5. Vegetables (tomato, through out the year and 9 months ill the central regions, greenbeans, okra, cucumber, potatoes, onion, garlic, spices, legumes, lentils.
6. Beekeeping to produce honey .
7. Organic fruits and vegetables (alluvial soil along the Nile Banks and deltas of wadi-Toker, El Gash etc.), makes the soil fertility very high and makes very big potentiality for production of organic fruits and vegetables to meet the rapid growing demand which will reach 10 % of European food consumption within the coming 10 years.

LIVESTOCK

50 million feddan of pasture land ill addition to crop residue and oil cakes make cost of feeding very cheap. 106 million heads of cattle, sheep, goats and carriers producing only 3 million tons of milk and less than one million ton of meat. Also Sudan is very rich in wild life and there are investment opportunities for modem farms for ostriches, antelopes, crocodiles etc.

Investment is welcomed in:

1. Modern farms to fatten and produce meat, milk, wool etc.
2. Slaughter houses to export meat.
3. Milk factories, to provide fresh milk, milk products for local and export.
4. Investment in transport facilities for life animal and refrigerated means for meat and milk products.
5. Fisheries (Nile perch) in the Nile, lake Nubia, Red Sea Poultry.
6. Animal fodder.
7. Drugs and vaccines.
8. Improvement of quality of the natural herds by introducing new breeds crossbreeding to improve milk and meat production.

MINING

Potentiality:

Sudan has vast mineral deposits that have not been exploited, mineral deposits which are discovered in different parts of the country are waiting for local and foreign investors which include;

1. Gold (now exported by joint French/Sudanese Eriab company-8 tons per annum.
2. Silver, iron ore, chromate, mica, silica, gypsum, granite, marble, chinaclay, manganese, asbestos, trauna (costic soda), talc and lime stone, copper, zink, lead, cement (production 500.000 toils and tons, and consumption above 1.5 million tons).
3. Small quantities of mica, chromate, asbestos and marble are exported ill addition to gold.

d. Energy

Potentiality:

One of the bottlenecks in Sudan is shortage of energy as fuel for all uses and electricity. River Nile with many cataracts and waterfalls, strong winds, agricultural by -products, sun, forests covering 200 million feddans, all these sources give excellent opportunity for investment in those areas:

1. Petrol and gas production.
2. Hydro-electric projects (micro, small and big)
3. Solar energy for lighting, heating, irrigation wind power for irrigation
4. Wind power for irrigation
5. Water turbines for irrigation from the Nile.
6. Biomass.
7. Charcoal from agricultural by-products.
8. Coal.

FIELDS FOR INVESTMENT IN INDUSTRY

The biggest investments in Sudan was in edible oil with capacity of 600 thousand tons, soap, textile and sugar industry and the share of industry is 16% in GDP (1994/1995).

1. Joint venture **in** rehabilitation of (edible oil mills, leather industry, textile etc..).
2. New sugar factories.
3. Oil productions (petrol and gas).
4. petrochemical.
5. Fertilizers: urea (demand 500.000 tons).
6. Tomato paste & syrup (9 months tomato season).
7. Fruit juice & concentrates, dried fruits : mango, juava, lemon, grapes, papaya, dates, strawberry, and pineapples.
8. Yeast (from sugar by products, dates).
9. Leather products.
10. Dehulling of sesame seed.
11. Spray dry for gum Arabic and guar gum.
12. Packing industry: cardboard, plastic, glass and sacks for grains.
13. paper industry: from dates tree, agricultural by products and forests.
14. compressed earth brick machines.
15. pharmaceutical products and medical equipments.

Sudan Oil Production : self sufficiency & export in 1999

Oil exploration started in Sudan in late fifties and in seventies oil was discovered in Sudan. After the withdrawal of Chevron Overseas many other international companies started oil exploration in Sudan specially after 1992. Now there are many companies working in exploration and productions and construction of pipe lines.

Oil deposits till now is estimated by two billion barrels.

Companies working in oil development:

1. The Canadian Arakis Energy Corporation, and International Petroleum of Canada (I PC).
2. Malaysian Petronas Oil company.
3. China National Petroleum.

4. Qatar National Petroleum.
5. Sudanese National Petroleum.
6. Chinese company to construct 1100 km of pipe line.
7. German company to construct 500 km of pipe line.
8. Some other companies in preparation and development from Russia, Iran.. etc.
9. Now oil production due to limitation of transport and refineries is around 17 thousand barrels per day after the construction of the pipe line and refineries oil exportation will start in 1999.

What Oil Production Means to Sudan?

The Oil importation bill is above 400 million US Dollar taking 66 % of export earnings and by oil production this amount will be released for development. Oil means production of electricity, asphalt for roads, fertilizer for agriculture, packing industry for export, fuel for irrigation pupms, for transport. 011 production will push Sudan economy upward by increasing production iii all sectors in addition to providing capital goods, spare parts ... etc. to economy which was mainly hampered by energy shortage and by of hard currency.

Giant consortium of 1.2 billion us signed:

In March 1997, the group of companies working in Sudan come to an agreement on setting up against partnership to extract Sudan's oil reserve for commercial use. The consortium which s16,.iied a 25 years long agreement is pooling together u$ 1.2 billion to pump out 150,000 BPD of oil by 1999 with exploration continuing for new discoveries.

Gas Discovered:

Huge gas deposits was also discovered in the Red Sea Coast Waiting investment for production.

SUDAN EXPORTS

Sudan export many products mainly agricultural and agricultural processed goods:

- Cotton, Cotton yarns, Cotton Waste,
- Gum Arabic raw and semi processed - guar gum, lubban.
- Sesame seed, groundnuts, sunflower,
- Edible oils, oil cakes and meal, sorghum (Dura)
- Livestock, meat semi-processed leather,
- Gold, mica, marble, asbestos, chromium, fruits (mango, grapes,
- guava, lemon, banana, dates, Galia melon etc.)
- Vegetables (onion, garlic, beans, spices),
- Fresh vegetables (green beans),
- Medical herbs (senna pods, henna... etc.),
- Hibiscus flowers, melon seeds,
- Sugar & molasses ... etc.

INVESTMENT LAWS AND REGULATIONS

INVESTMENT REGULATIONS

1. These Regulations may be cited as the, " Investment Encouragement Regulations, 2000 " amended2003 , and shall come into force, as from the date of signature.

Revocation and saving

2. The Investment Encouragement Regulations, 1990 shall be revoked; provided that all the licences and measures, taken there under, shall remain in force, until revoked, or amended .

Interpretation

3. In these Regulations, :-

(a) the words and phrases, set out therein, and interpreted in the Investment Encouragement Act,1999 , shall have the same meanings assigned therein thereto ;

(b) unless the context otherwise requires, :-

"Act", means the Investment Encouragement Act,1999 ;

"Federal project", means every project, the site of the facilities of which extends for more than one state, a foreign investment, or joint with foreign parties, works under licences from foreign companies, or established, under a special agreement, with the Republic of the Sudan, or that the project is established on investment in the federal natural resources;

"State project", means, other than the federal project, such project, as the site of the facilities of which may be in the state, and works according to a licence granted, in accordance with the provisions of the Act, and these Regulations, in the state.

Objects of encouragement of investment

6. This Act targets encouragement of investment into such projects, as may achieve the objects of the development policy, and the investment initiatives, on the part of the Sudanese and non-Sudanese private sector, the co-operative, mixed and public sector. Without prejudice to the generality of the foregoing, it aims at encouragement of investment into the projects of any of the fields set out in section7 .

Fields of investment

7. This Act encourages investment, into the fields of agricultural, animal and industrial activities, energy and mining, transport, communication, tourism and environment, storage, housing, contracting, infrastructure, economic, administrative and consultative services, information technology, education, health, water and culture and information services and any such other field, as the Council of Ministers may specify.

Discrimination between projects prohibited

8.(1) For the purposes of this Act, no discrimination shall be made between invested money, by reason of its being local, Arab or alien, or by reason of its being public, private, co-operative or mixed sector.

(2) No discrimination shall be made between such similar projects, as may be specified by the regulations, with respect to granting privileges or guarantees.

Branch I

Strategic projects

9.(1) Investment, in the following fields, shall be deemed strategic investment, namely :-

(a) relating to infrastructure, roads, ports, electricity, dams, communications, energy, transport, contracting business, education, health and tourist and information technology services and water projects;

(b) relating to extraction of subterranean and deep seas wealth;

(c) agricultural, animal and industrial production;

(d) crossing more than one state;

(e) any such other fields, as the Council of Ministers may prescribe.

(2) The regulations shall specify the strategic projects in the fields provided for in sub-section (1).

Exemption from taxes

10.(1) Subject, to the provisions of section19 , and without affecting any privileges, as may have been granted to any of the investment projects, in accordance with such conditions and safeguards, as may be in use :-

(a) the strategic project, specified in the regulations, shall after its registration, in accordance with the organizing laws, enjoy exemption from the business profits tax for a period of ten years, the effect of which shall commence, as of the date of commercial production, or practice of activity;

(b) the Minister may grant the non-strategic project exemption from the business profits tax, for a period, not exceeding five years, the effect of which shall commence, as of the date of commencement of commercial production, or practice of activity .

(2) Notwithstanding the provisions of sub-section (1)(a), the Council of Ministers, upon a recommendation, from the Minister, may extend the exemption of strategic and non strategic projects, as to such conditions and safeguards, as the regulations may specify.

Exemption from customs duties

11.(1) Subject, to the provisions of section19 , each of such strategic and non-strategic projects, as may be spcified in the regulations, after registration thereof, in accordance with the laws organizing the same, shall enjoy such customs privileges, as the Council of Ministers may prescribe.

(2) Notwithstanding the provisions of sub-section (1), customs privileges shall, with respect to cars, salon cars, box cars and station wagons, be granted as the regulations may specify.

(3) The Council of Ministers may, upon the recommendation of the Minister, amend the prescribed customs privileges, as he may deem fit.

Project granted the privileges of allocation

of land and depreciation account

12. The Minister may grant such strategic and non-strategic projects, as may be specified in the regulations :-

(a) the land necessary for the strategic project free of charge, and at the encouragement price for the non-strategic project, in co-ordination with the bodies concerned, from such lands, as may have been planned by the competent bodies;

(b) the privilege of depreciation account of the assets, as to such renewal value, as may be specified by the regulations, and in accordance with the circuits of operation work;

(c) deeming any such loss, as may have occurred, during the period of exemption, provided for in sections10 , as if it is such loss, as may have occurred during the last year of such period.

Grant of privileges to State projects

13. The State Minister may grant such state project, as may be specified in the regulations, the following privileges :-

(a) total, or partial exemption, from such taxes and fees, as may be levied by a state, or local law, for a period not exceeding five years; provided that he may, upon the approval of the State Council of Ministers, extend such exemption for another similar period;

(b) any such other state taxes, or fees, as may subsequently be levied on the project;

(c) allocation of the land necessary for the state project, at the encouragement price , in co-ordination with the bodies concerned, from the lands allocated by the competent bodies.

State projects granted federal privileges

14.(1) The Minister, upon the recommendation of the State Minister, may grant a state project the privileges provided for in section11 .

(2) The State Minister, upon delegation by the Minister, may grant a state project the privileges, provided for in section11 , as to such conditions and safeguards, as the Minister may deem fit.

No taxes or fees levied on federal projects

15. No state, or locality shall levy any state, or local taxes, fees or rates, on any investment project federally licensed, during the period of the tax exemption, provided for in sections 10 and11 , save in consideration of such services, as may be of public nature, performed by the state, or the locality.

Preference privileges

16.(1) The Minister, upon the approval of the Minister of Finance, and in consultation with the Competent Minister may grant preference privileges to such projects, as may satisfy any of the following features :-

(a) direct investment towards the least developed areas;

(b) assist in the development of export capabilities of the country;

(c) contribute to achievement of integrated rural development;

(d) create great chances of work;

(e) strive to encourage charitable trust;

(f) strive to develop scientific and technological research;

(g) re-invest the profits thereof.

(2) For the purposes of sub-section (1), privileges mean any of the privileges provided for in section10 , or11 , with respect to the size, extent, or term thereof, as the regulations may specify.

Branch III

Guarantees

Investment guarantees

17.(1) An Investor shall enjoy the following guarantees :-

(a) the non-nationalization, or non-confiscation of his project, non- acquisition of all, or part of the estates of the project thereof, or his investments, for public interest, save by law and in consideration of just compensation;

(b) the non-attachment, non-confiscation, non-custody or non-sequestration of the property of his project;

(c) the re-remission of the invested money, in case of the non-execution of the project, at the outset, liquidation, or disposal of the same, in any of the ways of disposal totally, or partially, in the currency, in which it has been imported; on condition of satisfying all the obligations legally due thereon, and in the case of non- execution of the project, at the outset, machinery, equipment, apparatuses, means of conveyance and other requisites, which have been imported for the project, may be re-exported, whenever all the obligations, mentioned in this paragraph have been satisfied;

(d) the remission of the profits and the cost of financing for the foreign capital, or loans, in the currency in which the capital or loan has been imported, at the date of accrual, after payment of the obligations legally due on the project;

(e) the import of such raw materials, as the project may need, and the export of the products thereof, after the automatic registering , of the investment project, onto the Exporters and Importers Register.

(2) For the purposes of paragraph (c) of sub-section (1), the invested capital shall be specified in foreign currency ; and the elements of the capital in kind shall be evaluated by the customs authorities by the customs certificate of value (CCV) , or the import form (IM).

Privileges and guarantees of

the project protected

18. Notwithstanding the provisions of any other law, no administrative body shall refrain from implementing the Privileges and guarantees, granted under the provisions of this Act.

Investor licensed to establish a project

19.(1) Subject to the provisions of section4 , no person shall establish any project, in the Sudan, save after obtaining a licence therefor, from the Minister, or the State Minister, as the case may be, in accordance with the provisions of this Act.

(2) Subject to the provisions of sub-section (1) , no licence shall be granted, for mixed or foreign investments, by states, save after approval of the Minister.

Feasibility study of the project presented

20. No project shall be granted licence, nor shall it be granted any such privileges and guarantees, as may be set out in this Act, save after presenting a technical and economic feasibility study of the project.

Grant of licence and privileges requested

21. An application, for the grant of licence, for any project, or of any of the privileges provided for in this Act, shall be presented, on the prescribed form as follows :-

(a) strategic and non-strategic federal projects, to the Ministry;

(b) strategic and non-strategic state projects, to the State Minister.

Grant of licence

22.(1) The Ministry, or the State Ministry shall, upon receipt of a satisfied licence application, for any project, transfer the application to the federal Competent Minister, or the State Minister, as the case may be, within one week, to obtain the primary approval of establishing the project.

(2) The federal Competent Minister, or State Minister, as the case may be, shall determine the application for primary approval, and send the same, to the Ministry, or State Ministry, as the case may be, within seven days, of the date of receipt of such application.

(3) In case of not sending the primary approval, in the period provided for in sub-section (2), the Minister, or the State Minister, shall determine the application, after lapse of such period.

(4) In all cases, the Minister, or the State Minister, as the case may be, shall determine the licence application, within a period not exceeding thirty days , of the date of receipt of the satisfied application, from the Investor.

(5) Every applicant, for licence, shall be entitled to grievance, to the Federal, or State Council of Ministers, as the case may be, against the non-determination of his application, in accordance with the provisions of sub-section (1), to determine his grievance, within the period of one month, of the receipt of the satisfied grievance.

Land allocated for the project delivered

23. The Federal, or State Competent authority, shall deliver the land allocated for the project, within a maximum period of one month, of the date of granting the licence.

Conditions of the continued enjoyment

of the licence and privileges

24. No Investor shall take any of the following measures, during the period of validity of the licence and privileges, granted under the provisions of this Act, without obtaining a written approval , from the Minister, or the State Minister, as the case may be, the measures being to :-

(a) conduct any amendment, or alteration, of the size of the project, or the object for which the licence has been granted, or transfer the project, from the place thereof prescribed in the licence;

(b) use, or sell any of the equipment, machinery , apparatuses, materials or spare parts, with respect to which privileges have been granted, for any other purpose, other than the purpose, for which the licence has been granted;

(c) change the purpose of use of the land allocated for the project, sell, mortgage or hire the same totally, or partially.

Duties of the Investor

25. The Investor shall :-

(a) commence executing the project, within a maximum period of twelve months, of the date of receipt of the land, unless such period has been extended, on the part of the Minister, or the State Minister, for any such period, as he may deem fit;

(b) submit, to the Minister, the Competent Minister and the State Minister, periodical reports, every six months, during the period of validity of privileges, on the progress of the operation of executing the project, up to the date of commencement of production, or practice of activity;

(c) keep regular books, and maintain records, whereon shall be entered the assets of the project exempted from customs duties, and the exempted imported materials;

(d) present, to the Minister, the Competent Minister and the State Minister, annually, during the period of validity of the privileges, a copy of the annual accounts of the project, approved by a certified auditor;

The Investor contravening the

provisions of this Act

26.(1) An Investor shall be deemed to have committed a contravention of the provisions of this Act, where he :-

(a) contravenes the provisions of sections19 , 24 and25 ;

(b) delivers false, or misleading information , or uses such unlawful methods, as may result in obtaining any benefit, in accordance with the provisions of this Act, for himself, or any other person;

(c) suspends the project, without reasonable cause;

(d) contravenes the laws of the country, in such way, as may endanger the security and safety thereof.

(e) Contravenes licence condition.

(2) Without prejudice to any such penalty, as may be provided for in any other law, the Minister, or the State Minister, as the case may be, may in case of commission, by the Investor, of any of the contraventions, provided for in sub- section(1), impose any of the following sanctions, in accordance with the size of the contravention and the circumstances of commission thereof, and the extent of such damages, as may affect the national economy :-

(a) warning him, to remove the grounds of the contravention, if the same is required, within such period, as he may specify;

(b) decrease the period of any of the privileges granted to the project, or the size thereof;

(c) not granting him any of the privileges and guarantees provided for in this Act;

(d) total, or partial revocation of the privileges, and the same shall result in binding the Investor to restitute the value of the material benefit gained thereby, from obtaining any previous privileges, where gaining such benefit results, from occurrence of the ground which led to the issue of the decision of revocation;

(e) revocation of the licence, and the same shall result in acquisition of the land granted to him under the provisions of this Act.

(3) An Investor in respect of whom a decision, under the provisions of sub-section (2), has been passed may submit his grievance, to the Federal, or State Council of Ministers, as the case may be, within one month, of the date of his being notified of the decision, and the decision, in this respect, shall be final; provided that this provision shall not prevent the Investor from access to courts.

The ministerial committee

27. The Council of Ministers, upon the recommendation of the Minister , may constitute a ministerial committee under the chairmanship of the Minister, and membership of the Minister of Finance and the Competent Minister, and the regulations shall specify the functions thereof.

Constitution of the committee

of commissioners

27A. The Minister shall constitute the committee of commissioners, from a chairman and a number of members, representing the competent bodies, having a relation to investment, from the ministries and competent government units; provided that the post of any of them shall not be less than the head of the unit, or whoever may deputize therefor, and shall fully be officially authorized, by the body which he represents, and the committee shall include representatives of the private sector.

Functions of the Committee

28.(1) The Committee of Commissioners shall have the following functions, to :-

(a) consider the extent of compatibility, by strategic projects, with the priorities of investment, in the strategic fields;

(b) consider the needs, by strategic projects, to infrastructure and basic services, needed by the project, and the extent of availability, or possibility of providing the same;

(c) consider the needs of the project, to manpower and the specialized one, procured from abroad, in accordance with the prevailing laws;

(d) achieve the sector investment plans, by the approved and proposed investment projects;

(e) co-ordinate, between the Ministry, and the Competent Ministries, and the states, in every such thing, as may concern investment projects, especially on the map of investment lands.

(2) The Committee may call any person, or body of competence, upon discussing any such subject, as may fall within the competence of such Committee, and he shall not be entitled to vote.

Functions of federal ministries

29. Federal ministries, having connection with investment, shall have competence, as to the following :-

(a) specify priorities, and lay down the investment policies, at their ministries;

(b) prepare sector investment maps;

(c) approve, on point of principle, the establishment of the project, upon such primary feasibility study, as may be transferred thereto, by the Ministry; provided that the final feasibility study of the project shall be presented to the Ministry ;

(d) follow-up the execution of the projects concerning the Competent Ministry, and submit periodical reports, as the Minister may require.

State Investment

30. An investment Act in the states shall be promulgated, by a state law, as to the form of Federal Investment Encouragement Act,1999 .

Among the efforts which aim at promoting foreign investment, the government has established free zones which include:

1 - Suakin Free Zone

2 - Aljaily Free Zone.

THE FREE ZONES AND FREE MARKETS LAW1994

This law represents the legislative framework for the establishment and operation of free zones and markets in Sudan. The rules resultant from this law represent the organizational framework for operating and managing free zones in Sudan.

Advantages of investment in free zones:

Industrial, commercial or service investments which are licensed to be established in the free zones enjoy the following advantages:

a- Exemption of the projects from profits tax for a period of 15 years, renewable for an extra period dependant on the decision made by the concerned minister commencing from the 1 year period of grace which follows the year of commencement of production.

b- Salaries of expatriates working in projects within the free zones will be exempted from the personal income tax

c- Exemption of products imported into the free zone or exported abroad from all customs fees and taxes except service fees and any other fee imposed by the board of the Sudan Free Zones Company.

d- Real estate establishment inside the free zones area are exempted from all taxes and fees

e- Invested capital and profits are transferable from Sudan to abroad through any bank licensed to operate in the free zone.

f- Exemption of products of industrial projects established in the free zones from customs fees; depending on materials used and local costs incurred in production, provided that the value be estimated by a committee assigned for this purpose by the board of the Sudanese Free Zones Company.

□ • **Guarantees (rule10)**

Money invested in the free zones may not be frozen, confiscated, or arrested

- **Transiting (rule15)**

With respect to agreements binding on the government of Sudan, goods transiting, waiting to be transferred to other countries may be stored in the free zones under the supervision of the customs police available at the inlets and outlets of the free zones.

- **Rent (rule16)**

The company has the right to rent its land and buildings according to the terms it agrees upon and without being bound by any other law

PROCEDURAL STEPS FOR INVESTMENT TRANSACTIONS :

APPLICATION FOR A NEW LICENSE

1 .Provide 2 copies of the technical and economic feasibility studies

2.A copy of the company registration and a certificate of establishment if the owner is a specified company

3.Fill in the form prepared for that purpose after paying an application fee of 15 , 800dinars (fifteen thousand eight hundred dinars)

4.Pay the application fee

5.The study is then transferred to the concerned ministry to obtain the technical agreement for establishment of the project

6.Issue a primary consent to the project

7.Register a name for the project with the Delegate Commercial Registrar in the Ministry of Investment

8.Issue a final license for the project acceding with followed rules

9.Please submit an agency agreement authorized by a lawyer if the project is to be supervised by someone other than the owner or in the case of companies

Application for Activity Change

Firstly: the conditions

1. the new activity must be an encouraged activity
2. no planning, environmental or health impediment should exist

Second: required documents

1. a copy of the license for the first activity
2. a copy of the business name
3. a valid ownership certificate or rental contract

4. application to the administration

Third: the procedures

1. payment of the application fees
2. the application is transferred to the specialized sector for analysis
3. after the consent is issued a new business name should be registered for the new activity at the Delegate Commercial Registrars department.
4. the license of the new activity is issued after payment of required legal fees

ADDITION OF A PRODUCTION LINE TO AN EXISTING PROJECT

First: the conditions

1. the main line must be readily executed and is working in an acceptable manner
2. the availability of a suitable area for the new line
3. the new should not oppose the old line in any technical or planning manner

Second: required documents

1. a copy of the license granted to the first line
2. a copy of the business name
3. an ownership certificate or rental contract

Third: procedures

1. payment of the application fees
2. obtain approval from the concerned technical party
3. transfer the application to the concerned sector for examination, issue consent and then transfer the consent to the Commercial Registrar to add a new line to the original business name
4. Issue a license or decision after payment of the required fees

TRANSFER OF OWNERSHIP

First: the conditions

1. execution of the project to a reasonable extent not less than60 % of the required structures
2. it is not possible to transfer empty land granted in accordance with the investment encouragement act

Second: required documents

1. submit a valid ownership certificate of the transferred project
2. a copy of the projects license
3. a copy of the business registration
4. a primary concession contract from a recognized legal body
5. an application to the ministry for acceptance of the concession

Third: procedures

1. payment of application fees
2. transfer of the application to the specialized sector for examination
3. a field visit to the project by the monitoring department and preparation of a report explaining the execution of the project
4. the application will be transferred to the ministry's legal consultant to ascertain the legality of the proceeding
5. consideration of the application in agreement or disagreement; incase of agreement the project is registered with the Delegate Commercial Registrar in the ministry
6. issue a final license to the owner and a new business name

FORMING OR ENDING A PARTNERSHIP

As long as the purpose of involving a new partner is fully executing the project then agreement to this will be issued after the following documents are submitted:

1. a copy of the business registration
2. a copy of the license
3. a valid ownership certificate
4. a partnership contract ratified by a legal body
5. an application to the administration requiring the transaction

MORTGAGING THE PROJECT FOR FINANCE

First: the conditions

1. the project must be executed to an extent allowing the mortgage of the buildings not the granted land
2. a letter from a bank clarifying the purpose of finance which must be for the operation or execution of the project

Second: required documents

1. a copy of the license
2. a copy of the business registration
3. a valid ownership certificate
4. a banks letter of finance

Third: procedures

1. payment of application fees
2. transfer the application to the concerned sector
3. a field visit is executed by the monitoring department and a report is prepared showing the extent of execution
4. the documents are revised by the ministry's legal counsel
5. consideration of the application and making the decision concerned

General rules

First: cars and other transport means are not allowed except after the capital equipment is imported

Second: the project is not granted a tax exemption for more than 10 years except after the project is proven a strategic one with a capital of 10 million dollars and a budget audited by a legal auditor

Third: capital equipment has become an automatic concession with 0 customs and does not need any exemption

Fourth: rehabilitating the industrial projects now enjoys a constant percentage for business profits which is10 % instead of30 %

INDUSTRY AND MINING PROJECTS

Processing Gum Arabic

Introduction:

Gum Arabic is one of the most important cash-generating export crop in Sudan. It is one of the best of its type in the world. The project aims at processing gum Arabic, locally, to improve exports and benefit from the value-added.

- The sites producing gum Arabic in Sudan:
- - Kordofan region 49 .3%
- - Kassala region 24 .4%
- - Darfur region 23 . 4%
- - White and Blue Nile region 2 .9%
- The proposed sites for erecting the project:
- Near the production collection regions.
    - The productive capacity: 4000 tons per year.
    - Methods of gum Arabic processing:
    - The mechanical method.
    - The method of sprinkle drying.
    - The mechanical Method:
    - Preliminary cleaning unit.
    - Air cleaning and sorting unit
    - Breaker.
    - Refining mill and granules production mill.
    - Conveyor belts.
    - Packing unit with weighing machine.
    - Quality control laboratory.
    - Electrical control panel.
- The sprinkle Drying Method Equipment
    - Dissolving container.
    - Sifters with various openings.
    - Sedimentation cylinder and the solution concentration cylinder.
    - Drying and spraying unit.
    - Cylinder drying unit.
    - Solar energy unit for heating water.
    - Cleaning and sorting unit.
    - Quality control laboratory.

Area : Estimated at 800 m^2; as follows:-
$144m^2$ Production hall.

280m^2 First cleaning shed.
48m^2 Second cleaning shed
250m^2 Stores
75m^2 Offices + utilities
Invested capital : US $6 .628.032
Operating capital : US $192 .247
Fixed Assets : US $150 .735
Net profits : US $843.561
Profitability : 10 %

Period of Re-imbursement : 2 years
Raw Materials : gum Arabic – packing materials (Jute sacks)

Contact Address:
Investment Department,
Federal Ministry of Industry
Tel :0249183777770

The Processing of Basic Chlorine

The Sudan is distinguished by its Red Sea shore, which provides salt. This encourage the establishment of a basic chlorine plant for the production of the following:-

- Caustic Soda: which is used in numerous industries, such as, textiles, industrial detergents, soap, edible oil refining and other industries which benefit from the characteristic of bleaching of the caustic soda.

- Chlorine: Which is used in many fields; such as, the water purifying and sterilization networks, the sewerage system networks and several other uses which benefit from the characteristic of chlorine as a disinfectant and insecticider.

- Hydrochloric acid (HCL): which is widely used as a multi-purpose acid. It is also used in large quantities for purifying the calcium carbonates from the bottom of oil wells and in petroleum refineries.

- Sodium hypochlorine: Which is used in the Weaving and spinning industry; and other purposes which benefit from its characteristic as a bleacher and pesticider.

- Productive capacity:
  - • Caustic soda 5 tons/day.
  - • Chlorine 5 tons/day.
  - • Hydrochloric acid 5 tons/day.
  - • Sodium Hypochlorine 5 tons/day.
  - \- Invested capital US $2 .700.000
    - Raw materials:
    - Sodium chloride.
    - Phosphoric acid.
    - Soda dust.
    - Hydrochloric acid.
    - Electricity.
    - Man-power:
  - 35(direct and direct labour).

- - Area of plant: 6560 m^2.
    - Location : It is preferred that the project shall be close to salt sources (i.e. Eastern Sudan.).
    - Project's Product users:
    - Edible oil plants..
    - Petroleum fields.
    - Weaving and spinning plants.
    - Water distribution networks.
    - **The average imported amounts during the last three years:-**
- 2000tons

- **Contact Address:**

The Investment Department,
Federal Ministry of Industry,
Tel:777770 183 0249

Assembly and manufacture of

Solar Energy Equipments

God endowed the Sudan with a climate of less clouds and much sunshine throughout the year, therefore the Sudan is considered an ideal place for the system of transferring the light of the sun to electricity.

The Invested capital: 673653000 Sudanese Dinar
Machineries and Equipments:

- Assembly of Solar cells.
- Liquid batteries.
- Tools and Equipments.

Total cost of Machineries and Equipments:
122,000, 000Sudanese Dinar
Cost of raw materials for One Operational year:
150,000, 000Sudanese Dinar
Recovery Period: Two years
Contact Address:
Department of Investment ,
Federal Ministry of Industry
Tel: 0249183777770

Calcium Carbonate Manufacture

Introduction:

The lime stone is composed of the matter of calcium carbonate which could be grinded and purified for the extraction of pure powder of calcium carbonate, which is used in filling the plastic pipes and the plastic utensils, and also it is used in the production of insecticides and tooth paste, in addition to its use in cultivation and animal husbandry.

The proposed productive capacity: 20 ton/day.

The Investment Capital: 1 ,500, 000US Dollar.

The raw materials: Lime stone

The volume of employment: 450 direct and indirect employees.

The establishment area: The total area of the project is35 , 000m^2.

The Location: It is preferable to establish the project near the areas where the raw materials are available and they are: Gabalain province, 'Gabalain 'town' Atbara town, Sennar, Jabal Marra and any areas where the lime stone is discovered.

The Users of the Production:

a. Plastic pipes production Factories.
b. Plastic house utensils production Factories.
c. Insecticides poweder production factories.
d. Tooth paste production factories.
e. The farmers.

Average of the Imported quantities during the last three years:214tons
Contact address: Investment Department:
The Federal Ministry of Industry,
Tel: 0249183777770

Concentrated Feed Manufacture

Introduction: The concentrated feed are protein and hydrocarbonic materials produced from the agricultural and processing remains and they wore divided into:

- Animal feed: They use the residues of legumes. Couch grass straw, Durra reeds, rice straw, residues of oil seeds like cotton seed, peanuts husks sesame sunflower, beans and the retuse of sugar factories such as Mollas, bugas and cane heads.

- Poultry feed: Contains fish powder, meat and bones powder and other animal remains like blood in addition to some materials used in Animal feed.

The targeted market: To cover the local market and exportation to the African and Arab countries.
The Productive capacity:
The proposed: 15, 000ton/year
The invested capital: estimated USD 1 ,550,000
The raw materials: Oil cake of cotton seed, wheat bran, bugas, Molas, pea-nuts husk, Dhura stalks, Calcium carbonates,
Table salt and vitamins.
The Premises area: 2200 m^2
The Working force: 35 direct and indirect workers.
Average of imported quantities during the last three years:3503tons
Contact Address: Investment Department
Federal Ministry of Industry.
Tel :0249183777770

GOLD PROCESSING PROJECT

Umm Nyardi Mine

Location: North Wadi Half town
Annual Mining Capacity:
The Project target the mining and processing of 700 Kilograms annually.
Investment Costs: about USD 90 millions, Annual costs of production. USD2 . 5millions.
Annual Sales Returns: USD 7 million, net profits : USD4 .5millions.
Financial indicators: Net profits ratio to sales :64 %
Capital Recovery Period : about two years.
Contact Address: Investment Department
River Nile State
Tel :0211822557

Glass Production Project

Location of the Project: Mattama Area
Mining capacity: 150ton/per day
Project sales returns : Amounts to 17 , 4million us Dollar.
Annual Production costs for the entire project:
Amounts to9 . 1million us Dollar
Financial indicators: Net profits ratio to the sales:52 %, Net profits ratio to the investment37 %
Capital recovery period: Two years

Contact Address: Investment Department
River Nile State.
Tel :0211822557

Iron Extraction Project

The proposed Location: Bigrawiyya area
Raw materials: The raw iron belt which was formely expolcted by the pharaohs exist in the Bigrawiyya belt area with quantities not less than
750 million tons.
The targeted productive capacity: amounts to USD 100 millions.
Annual cost of production: amount to USD 362 million
Sales returns: amounts to USD 550 million
Annual net profits: amount to USD 100 million.
Financial indicators:
Net profits ratio to Sales :34 %
Net profits ratio to investment :100 %
Capital recovery period: One year
Relative advantages of the project: Electricity is considered the principal element in the costs of production as the project needs annually 3000 megawatt/hour.
The establishment of Kajbar reservoir will make available the electrical energy to this project.
Note: The establishment of the project requires the execution of geological surveys to determine the reserve volume.
Contact Address: Investment Department,
River Nile State:
Tel : 0211822557

Ceramic and Porcelain Production Project

Location of the project: South Matamma.
The targeted productive capacity:
The project aims to produce3 , 000 m^2 annually.
Cost of Investment: The volume of the required investment is estimated around31 , 7millions US Dollar.
The return of the project's annual sales: 63million US Dollar.

Costs of Production: A sum of 48 , 9million US Dollar.
Annual net profits:14 . 1million US Dollar.
Financial indicators:
Net profits ratio to sales :17 . 4
Net profit ratio to investments :32 .2%.
Internal return average : 39 .6%
Capital Recovery Period: 3 years
Contact Address: Investment Department
River Nile State,
Tel:0211822557

Cement Production Project

The proposed Location: Five factories will be established as follows:

Two factories in west Berber area.
One factory in Abu Hamad area.
One factory in Ebiediyya area.
One factory in Atbara town.
The designed productive capacity for each project:
Each project aims to produce325 , 000ton cement/year.
Investment for each project:
The Total investment cost: 55, 1 million US Dollars.
The annual project sales, ' for each project'.

The project gross return when it works with full capacity:
29 . 2million US Dollar.

Annual cost of production: 10. 2US Dollar.
Annual total profit for the project : 19million US Dollar
Financial Indicators:
Net profits ratio to the Sales =65 %
Net profits ratio to the investment =35 %
Period of capital Recovery: Three year
Contact Address : Investment Department,
River Nile State
Tel :0211822557

Mica Production Project

Location of Project: El-Shriek – River Nile State
Targeted productive capacity : 200ton/day.
Investment Costs :2 . 5million US Dollar.
Annual Sales return : 1. 2million US Dollar
Costs of Production: 0. 6million US Dollar.
Net profits ratio to the Sales =34 %
Net profits ratio to the investment =100 %
Capital recovery period: 3 years
Contact Address : Department of Investment
River Nile State
Tel :0211822557

IMPORTANT PRACTICAL INFORMATION FOR STARTING BUSINESS

COMPANY REGISTRATIONREGISTRATION

1	Submit application for preliminary approval to Registrar and reserve company name	3 days	SDG 120
2	Notarize memorandum and articles of association	2 days	SDG 350
3	Notify taxation chambers	1 day	SDG 55
4	Register with commercial registry	4 days	Stamp duty and other application/administrative fees (see comment)
5	Conduct site inspection	2 days	no charge
6	Apply for tax identification number	1-2 days	SDG 5
*7	Register for VAT	2 days (simultaneous with previous procedure)	no charge
8	Register with labor authorities	14 days	SDG 192
9	Enroll employees for social security	3-7 days	SDG .25
10	Make a company seal	2 days	SDG 40

* Takes place simultaneously with another procedure.

REGISTRATION REQUIREMENTS

Procedure 1.

Submit application for preliminary approval to Registrar and reserve company name

Time to complete:

3 days

Cost to complete:

SDG 120

Name of Agency:

Comment:

The application for the business name registration is filled stating the name of the owner/ owners whether a company or a natural person, and stating the nature of the Business Name. The memorandum and articles of association and three proposed names must be attached to the application. The application shall then be submitted to the business names registrar after attaching the required stamps, the Business Names Registrar will then study the application and make sure that there are no similar names and issue a Business Names Registration Certificate. The name approval and the preliminary approval for establishing a company must be granted in 3 days.

Procedure 2.

Notarize memorandum and articles of association

Time to complete:

2 days

Cost to complete:

SDG 350

Name of Agency:

Comment:

The memorandum and articles of association and Form C2, the declaration of compliance, must be notarized the preliminary approval at a lawyers' office. The notarized documents are then submitted to the registrar for final approval. Muslim companies must also obtain a Zakat clearance certificate before notarizing the documents at no cost.

Procedure 3.

Notify taxation chambers

Time to complete:

1 day

Cost to complete:

SDG 55

Name of Agency:

Comment:

Before applying for final approval and registration, the company must submit a preliminary approval to the Taxation Chamber with the memorandum and articles of association, which should be stamped by the Chamber in acknowledgement of the notification.

Procedure 4.

Register with commercial registry

Time to complete:

4 days

Cost to complete:

Stamp duty and other application/administrative fees (see comment)

Name of Agency:

Comment:

Fee schedule for stamp duties:
SDG 55 for workers' association stamp duty.
SDG 4 for lawyers' association stamp duty.
SDG 425 for registry fees (0.25% of the nominal Capital for registration fees).
SDG 28 Certificate stamp

Procedure 5.

Conduct site inspection

Time to complete:

2 days

Cost to complete:

no charge

Name of Agency:

Comment:

As of 2005, a Companies' Registry representative must visit the proposed place of business to confirm its existence. therefore, before delivering the certificate of incorporation, a registry representative may visit the registered office to confirm its existence. It is now also mandatory for the company to obtain and post a signboard outside its place of business.

Procedure 6.

Apply for tax identification number

Time to complete:

1-2 days

Cost to complete:

SDG 5

Name of Agency:

Comment:

The following documents are required to apply for a tax identification number:
- Shareholder information.
- Memorandum and articles of association (notarized).
- Certificate of incorporation (two copies).
- Completed registration forms.

Procedure 7.

Register for VAT

Time to complete:

2 days (simultaneous with previous procedure)

Cost to complete:

no charge

Name of Agency:

Comment:

The company registers for VAT in the same building but at a separate department. It is not mandatory to register at the same time.

Procedure 8.

Register with labor authorities

Time to complete:

14 days

Cost to complete:

SDG 192

Name of Agency:

Comment:

The company must deposit the basic work and penalties regulations with the competent labor office.

Procedure 9.

Enroll employees for social security

Time to complete:

3-7 days

Cost to complete:

SDG .25

Name of Agency:

Comment:

The company must resister itself before the Social Insurance Fund. the required documents for this procedure are:
- Copy of Company Certificate of Incorporation and Memorandum and Articles of Association.
- Completed registration form.

At the same time, the company registers its employees for the social Insurance, registration procedure is free of charge, and the required documents for this procedure are:
- List with employees names and salaries
- Completed registration form.

Procedure 10.

Make a company seal

Time to complete:

2 days

Cost to complete:

SDG 40

Name of Agency:

Comment:

The cost to make a company seal depends on the kind of material used. Costs vary and are as low as SDG 40.

DOING BUSINESS IN SUDAN

ANNUAL INDICATORS

	2003	2004	2005	2006	2007	2008	2009 (est)
GDP at market prices (US $ bn)	17.6	21.5	27.5	36.7	50.7		
Real GDP growth (%)	5.1	5.2	9	11.8	10.2	6.5	3
Consumer price inflation (%)	6.5	8.3	8.5	7.2	8	18	10
Population (mn)	33.6	34.5	37	39	40	40	40
GDP per capita US$ PPP	499	590	720	1,000	1,250	2,200	
Exports of goods fob (US$ bn)	2.57	3.77	4.82	5.96	8.88	11.67	
Imports of goods cif (US$ bn)	2.53	3.58	5.94	8.07	8.3	9.35	
Current-account balance (US$ bn)	-0.955	-0.871	-3.013	-5.109	-3.812	-2.1	
Reserves excl gold (US$ bn) year end	0.529	1.338	1.869	1.660	1.4		
Total external debt (US$ bn)	24.2	26.3	27.7	28.2	29	34	35
Exchange rate (av) Sudanese Pound: US$	2.6	2.6	2.4	2.2	2.05	2.20	2.40

Net international reserves in mid-2009 were less than one month of imports.

Main exports: Crude oil, sesame, livestock, cotton, gum arabic

Main imports: Machinery and Equipment, manufactures, transport equipment, chemicals, cereals

2008 GDP = Agriculture (31%, Industry 35%, Services 34%)

Sudan's main sources of imports in 2008 were China, India, Saudi Arabia, Egypt, Japan, France, Italy, UK.

Despite its substantial natural resources (including 200 million acres of arable land of which only a fifth is presently exploited) Sudan is still classified as a Least Developed Country (LDC).

Doing business with Sudan is exciting, rewarding and uncertain. Most major projects need some kind of financing (preferably concessional). However, we advise commercial prudence and Indian exporters and investors should stay in touch with the Embassy.

Exports should be ONLY against full advance payment or letters of credit confirmed by first class international banks.

The 2008 Corruption Perceptions Index of Transparency International ranks Sudan as one of the most corrupt countries in the world – 173/180 (at the same level as Afghanistan and below Zimbabwe) while the World Bank ranks Sudan at 151/155 countries in its 2008 "Ease of Doing Business" Report.

Notwithstanding the negative perceptions, we encourage Indian companies to explore commercial possibilities in Sudan.

As this country develops, there will be opportunities for Indian companies in railways, roads, automobiles, power generation, telecommunications, water treatment, human resource development, agriculture, pharmaceuticals and IT. Import demand is surging as reconstruction moves into high gear.

PATTERN OF BILATERAL TRADE

(In US$ million)

YEAR	INDIA'S EXPORTS	INDIA'S IMPORTS	TRADE BALANCE
1998	63.36	26.51	(+) 36.85
1999	63.81	5.46	(+) 57.44
2000	77.54	5.46	(+) 72.08
2001	87.72	9.24	(+) 78.48
2002	104.62	5.93	(+) 98.69
2003	115.96	33.17	(+) 82.79
2004	197.10	27.90	(+) 169.20
2005	317.84 (+61%)	30.77	(+) 287.07
2006	599.04	20.00	(+) 579.04
2007	546.50	16.43	(+) 530.07
2008	886	182.3	(+) 703.70
2009	624.50	194.78	(+) 429.72

The Mission's target for 2009 is a 50% increase in India's exports

To give a sustained focus to India-Sudan trade relations, the Mission's commercial policy since October 2005 is a non-exclusive ***five-plus-one*** *policy. The five priority sectors in which India can respond to Sudan's developmental requirements are infrastructure, agriculture, human resource development, information & communications technologies, and small & medium industries. The "plus-one" is commercially viable investment in the energy sector (oil, electricity, gas). To achieve this, the Embassy has a Target and Introduce Programme (TIP) from January 2006 under which one new Indian export is introduced into Sudan every semester.*

TARIFF AND NON-TARIFF ISSUES

In 1992, Sudan abolished most export and import licensing requirements. It has also eliminated most export taxes although some have been reintroduced from May 2009 (especially in raw materials) following the country's poor economic situation.

Importers must present an import declaration, commercial invoice certificate of origin, quarantine license (where necessary), Sudanese Standards and Metrology organization (SSMO) requirements or other documents for specific type of goods, and completion of bank formalities. Importers must pay the required duties, taxes and fees and receive an official release for the goods.

SETTING UP OF OFFICES/FIRMS/COMPANIES FOR TRADE AND MANUFACTURING PURPOSES

A request is made to the Union of Chambers of Commerce and the Ministry of Foreign Trade conveying the intent to establish offices or firms/companies, etc. There are no special rules for renting office spaces or residential accommodation or hiring of local staff.

WTO

Sudan applied to join the WTO in 1994 and had completed the basic fact-finding stage of negotiations but is unlikely to be given entry to WTO while US sanctions are in place.

FORMS OF DOING BUSINESS IN SUDAN

A business may be a sole trader, partnership, registered limited liability company (private or public), or branch in the Sudan of a foreign registered company. The significant advantage of forming a local company is limited liability status.

A company can have 100% foreign shareholding if it does not engage in commerce (import and export).**To trade, it must have majority Sudanese shareholding.**

Tax concessions under the Investment Encouragement Act are being phased out under IMF pressure.

FOREIGN EXCHANGE REGULATIONS

The draconian "Dealing in Foreign Exchange Control Act", 1979 (introduced when Sudan had no reserves) has given way to a system free of restrictions on payments and transfers for current international transactions. However, intensified US sanctions since 2007 inhibit dollar denominated transactions at present.

Visitors can bring in any amount of foreign currency. Private financial transfer firms such as UAE Exchange can presently remit up to US$ 3,000 per transaction.

In practice, repatriation of foreign capital and profits (dividends) requires the approval of the Central Bank and tax clearance certificates.

IMPORT REGULATIONS

The importer should be registered with the Ministry of Foreign Trade.

Permission may be granted for temporary import of machinery and plant without customs duty against a letter of guarantee to the Customs Department. At the time of re-export, the difference in value of the goods at the time of import and subsequent re-export is calculated and custom tariff levied.

Sudan is founding member of the 20 member COMESA (Common Market for Eastern and Southern Africa) and all imports from and exports to member countries are exempt from customs duties.

ENCOURAGEMENT OF INVESTMENT ACT 1999 (AMENDED IN 2001, 2002, 2003, 2006, 2008)

The Act provides for specific additional benefits to encourage investment and classifies investment into strategic and non-strategic. Significant features include:

- 1-3 year profit tax holiday
- No discrimination for being of local, Arab or foreign origin in the public or private sector
- Level playing field for analogous projects in terms of privileges and guarantees
- Permission to expatriate staff to remit their post-tax savings
- Carry forward of losses incurred during the exemption period
- Customs exemption for strategic projects
- Land free (strategic projects) or at concessional rates (non-strategic projects)
- Transfer of profits and the cost of finance in the currency of import
- No need for a local partner

INVESTMENT GUARANTEES

In theory, there are several investment guarantees:

- Real estate (property) shall not be nationalized, expropriated or confiscated
- Moneys shall not be seized, impounded, frozen or sequestered
- Invested funds are remittable
- Profits and import costs arising from the invested capital are remittable
- Machineries, equipments, instruments, transport means etc can be re-exported

A social insurance scheme requires contributions from both employees and employers. Expatriate staff, if they receive part or whole of their salaries in the country (irrespective of whether they enjoy tax exemption) are also subject to social insurance.

BANKING

While North Sudan conforms to shariat banking laws, the South follows conventional banking norms.

FREE ZONES

There are two free zones: Suakin on the Red Sea near Port Sudan and Garri near Khartoum. The 1994 Free Zones and Markets Act permits fill possession for foreign investors, exemption from income tax for non-nationals working in the free zones, tax exemption for companies, free capital and profits transfer, no restrictions on entry and residence visas.

PREFERRED SECTORS FOR PRIVATE INVESTMENT

a) Meat processing

b) Jam, juice and tomato-paste concentrates

c) River and rail transport

d) Food processing

e) Grain silos

f) Water bottling plants

g) Refrigerated warehouses

h) Gum Arabic cultivation

i) Poultry farming

j) Animal husbandry

k) River transport

l) Roads and bridges

m) Sugar

n) Meat and fish processing

o) Wood industries

p) Rice cultivation

q) Forest development

r) Apiculture

s) Telecom services

t) Hotels and resorts

u) Airports

TAXATION

Sudan has direct and indirect taxation. The direct tax system comprises personal income tax, business profit tax, land tax, and capital gains tax. Indirect taxation includes value added tax, development tax and customs duties.

The Government of Sudan has double taxation avoidance agreements with various countries including India.

SOUTH SUDAN

The semi-autonomous region of Southern Sudan offers huge opportunities for the intrepid businessperson and risk taker. After over four decades of civil war, it needs everything. India became the first Asian country to open a Consulate General in Juba (capital of South Sudan) in October 2007.

The January 2005 Comprehensive Peace Agreement offers South Sudan a self-determination referendum in January 2011 with unity and secession as the options.

For further information contact the Embassy of India in Khartoum. We respond to all email commercial queries within eight working hours.

Address	61, Africa Road, Mailing Code 11111, P O Box 707, Khartoum II (Sudan)
Telephone	Country Code 249, Khartoum City Code 1 8357 4001, 8357 4002, 8357 4003, 8357 4004
Fax	8357 4050/1
Email	**ambassador@indembsdn.com** **commercial@indembsdn.com**
Website	www.indembsdn.com
Local Time	IST (-) 2$^{1}/_{2}$ Hours
Working Hours	0830 to 1700 Hrs (Sunday through Thursday)

TRAVEL TO SUDAN

US STATE DEPARTMENT SUGGESTIONS

WARNING (Issued December 12, 2000): The Department of State warns U.S. citizens against all travel to Sudan because of the unstable security situation throughout the country. In addition to the ongoing civil war that affects both southern and eastern Sudan, the government of Sudan's control over its police and soldiers may be limited.

The government of Sudan continues to conduct a bombing campaign against rebel forces in southern Sudan. In addition, there has been rebel activity in and around Kassala, in eastern Sudan. Following a rebel incursion in Kassala in early November 2000, the government of Sudan authorities arrested an American relief worker in that area on suspicion of espionage and severely beat him. As a result of the rebel activity, the United Nations ordered all its personnel operating in Kassala to evacuate the area in and around the city. Other non-governmental organizations operating in Kassala evacuated their personnel as well.

The United States has no permanent diplomatic presence in Sudan because of concerns regarding the government of Sudan's ability to ensure adequately the safety of U.S. officials. While U.S. officials elsewhere in the region make periodic visits to Sudan, their ability to provide consular services, including emergency assistance, is severely limited.

U.S. citizens in Sudan are urged to consider their personal security situations in determining whether to remain in the country. Those who remain in Sudan should keep a low profile and stay alert to changing developments. Avoid large crowds and other situations in which anti-American sentiments may be expressed.

COUNTRY DESCRIPTION: Sudan is a large, developing country in northeastern Africa. Tourism facilities are minimal. The capital is Khartoum.

ENTRY REQUIREMENTS/REGISTRATION WITH LOCAL POLICE: A passport and visa are required. Americans citizens should apply for a Sudanese visa in a third country. Visas cannot be obtained in the United States, or at the Sudanese airport, or at the Sudanese border. Travelers must pay an airport departure tax in U.S. dollars or Saudi riyals or, if they have residence permits in Sudan, in Sudanese pounds. The Sudan Relief and Rehabilitation Association requires travelers to opposition-held areas of southern Sudan to obtain a travel permit at its office in Nairobi.

Travelers to Sudan are required to register with police headquarters within three days of arrival. Travelers must obtain police permission before moving to another location in Sudan and must register with police within 24 hours of arrival at the new location. These regulations are strictly enforced. Even with proper documentation, travelers in Sudan have been subjected to delays and detention by Sudan's security forces, especially when traveling outside Khartoum. Authorities expect roadblocks to be respected.

For further information on entry requirements and registration with local police, please contact the Embassy of the Republic of Sudan, 2210 Massachusetts Avenue, N.W., Washington, D.C. 20008; telephone (202) 338-8565 to 8570. Overseas, inquiries may be made at the nearest Sudanese embassy or consulate.

TRADE RESTRICTIONS: On November 4, 1997, President Clinton signed an Executive Order imposing comprehensive financial and commercial sanctions against Sudan, prohibiting U.S. transactions with Sudan. Travelers intending to visit Sudan, despite the Travel Warning, should contact the Department of the Treasury, Office of Foreign Assets Control (OFAC), Office of Compliance, regarding the effect of these sanctions; telephone 1-800-540-6322 or 202-622-2490; web site http://www.treas.gov/ofac/.

SAFETY AND SECURITY: Travel in all parts of Sudan, particularly outside Khartoum, is potentially hazardous. Civil war persists in the southern Sudan provinces of Upper Nile, Bahr El Ghazal, and Equatoria, and has spread to the eastern Sudan provinces of Blue Nile, Red Sea, and Kassala, along the Ethiopian and Eritrean borders. Banditry and incursions by southern Sudanese rebels are common in western Sudan, particularly in Darfur Province along the Chadian and Libyan borders, where a state of emergency exists. The land border with Egypt (ferry from Aswan to Wadi Halfa) has been reopened. Transportation between Eritrea and Sudan is currently halted. The Sudan People's Liberation Army controls all border crossings from Kenya and Uganda.

CURFEW: The curfew in Khartoum has been lifted. However, persons who are outside between midnight and 5:00 a.m. are subject to document searches at police checkpoints. Hotel officials and local police can inform visitors whether a curfew is in effect in other localities.

CRIME: Petty crime and thievery occur. Travelers should exercise caution at the airport, in markets and at public gatherings.

The loss or theft abroad of a U.S. passport should be reported immediately to local police and to the nearest U.S. embassy or consulate. The pamphlets, *A Safe Trip Abroad* and *Tips forTravelers to Sub-Saharan Africa*, provide useful information on personal security while traveling abroad and on travel in the region in general. Both are available from the Superintendent of Documents, U.S. Government Printing Office, Washington, D.C. 20402, via the Internet at http://www.access.gpo.gov/su_docs, or via the Bureau of Consular Affairs home page at http://travel.state.gov.

MEDICAL FACILITIES: Medical facilities in Sudan are extremely limited.

MEDICAL INSURANCE: U.S. medical insurance is not always valid outside the United States. U.S. Medicare and Medicaid programs do not provide payment for medical services outside the United States. Doctors and hospitals often expect immediate cash payment for health services. Uninsured travelers who require medical care overseas may face extreme difficulties.

Please check with your own insurance company to confirm whether your policy applies overseas, including provision for medical evacuation, and for adequacy of coverage. Serious medical problems requiring hospitalization and/or medical evacuation to the United States can cost tens of thousands of dollars. Please ascertain whether payment will be made to the overseas hospital or doctor or if you will be reimbursed later for expenses that you incur. Some insurance policies also include coverage for psychiatric treatment and for disposition of remains in the event of death.

Useful information on medical emergencies abroad, including overseas insurance programs, is provided in the Department of State's Bureau of Consular Affairs brochure, *Medical Information for Americans Traveling Abroad*, available via the Bureau of Consular Affairs home page or autofax: (202) 647-3000.

OTHER HEALTH INFORMATION: Information on vaccinations and other health precautions may be obtained from the Centers for Disease Control and Prevention's international travelers hotline at telephone 1-877-FYI-TRIP (1-877-394-8747), fax 1-888-CDC-FAXX (1-888-232-3299), or via the CDC's Internet site at http://www.cdc.gov.

TRAFFIC SAFETY AND ROAD CONDITIONS: While in a foreign country, U.S. citizens may encounter road conditions that differ significantly from those in the United States. The information below concerning Sudan is provided for general reference only and may not be totally accurate in a particular location or circumstance.

Safety of Public Transportation: Poor
Urban Road Conditions/Maintenance: Poor
Rural Road Conditions/Maintenance: Poor
Availability of Roadside Assistance: Poor

Road conditions are hazardous due to unpredictable local driving habits, pedestrians and animals in the roadway, and the lack of basic safety equipment on many vehicles. Roads are narrow and poorly maintained. Only some major highways are paved. Roads in southern Sudan may be impassable during the rainy season, while roads in the north can be quickly covered with shifting sand at anytime during the year. Nighttime driving throughout the country is dangerous and should be avoided if possible because vehicles often operate without lights or park in the road without warning. Ambulance and road emergency services are available in major urban areas, but the are extremely limited or unavailable elsewhere in the country.

Public transit is limited except in and between major urban areas. Passenger facilities are basic and crowded, especially during rush hours or seasonal travel. Schedules are unpublished and subject to change without notice. Vehicle maintenance does not meet the same standards as those in the United States or other Western countries. There is regular passenger train service from Khartoum to Wadi Halfa and Port Sudan. Inter-city bus service between major cities is regular and inexpensive. Intra-city bus service in the major urban areas is generally regular, but most buses and bus stops are unmarked. Taxis are available in the major cities at hotels, tourist sites and government offices. Public transit service to medium-size communities in the interior usually is limited to irregularly scheduled mini-buses. Most rural communities in the interior have no public transit.

U.S. citizens are subject to the laws of the country in which they are traveling. Traffic laws and custom in Sudan are substantially different from those in the United States. In Sudan, one drives on the right side of the road. There is no government agency specifically responsible for road safety, nor is there any regime to regularly inspect vehicle maintenance or safety. Seat belts and/or infant seats are not required. Many vehicles do not have seat belts or other safety equipment that is standard in the United States or other Western countries. Traffic on the right has the right of way. Right turns on a red light are prohibited. Speed limits are not posted. The legal speed limit for passenger cars on inter-city highways is 120 KPH (70 MPH), while in most urban areas it is 60 KPH (35 MPH). The speed limit in congested areas and school zones is 40 KPH (24 MPH).

All motor vehicle operators are required to purchase third-party liability insurance from the government. Nonetheless, many local drivers carry no insurance. Persons involved in an accident resulting in death or injury are required to report the incident to the nearest police station or official as soon as possible. Persons found at fault can expect fines, revocation of license, and jail sentences depending on the nature and extent of the accident. Penalties for persons convicted of driving under the influence of alcohol are strict, and convicted offenders may expect fines, jail sentences, and corporal punishment.

U.S. citizens may use their U.S. issued driver's licenses up to ninety days after arrival. After that, they must present either an "International Driving Permit" (IDP) or obtain a Sudanese driver's license. There are no restrictions on vehicle types, including motorcycles and motorized tricycles. Motorcycles, however, are relatively rare because of public perceptions that the highways are too dangerous for them.

The government of Sudan does not publish traffic statistics. The last reported instance of an American citizen injured in a traffic accident in Sudan was in 1996.

For additional general information about road safety, including links to foreign government sites, please see the Department of State, Bureau of Consular Affairs home page at http://travel.state.gov/road_safety.html. For specific information concerning Sudanese driving permits, vehicle inspection, road tax and mandatory insurance, please contact the Sudanese Embassy in Washington, D.C.

AIR TRAVEL: As there is no direct commercial air service by local carriers at present, nor economic authority to operate such service between the United States and Sudan, the U.S. Federal Aviation Administration (FAA) has not assessed the Sudan's Civil Aviation Authority for compliance with international aviation safety standards for oversight of Sudan's air carrier operations. For further information, travelers may contact the Department of Transportation within the U.S. at telephone 1-800-322-7873, or visit the FAA Internet home page at http://www.faa.gov/avr/iasa/. The U.S. Department of Defense (DOD) separately assesses some foreign air carriers for suitability as official providers of air services. For information regarding the DOD policy on specific carriers, travelers may contact the DOD at telephone (618) 229-4801.

Unforeseen circumstances such as sandstorms and electrical outages may cause flight delays. The Khartoum International Airport arrival and departure procedures are lengthy. Passengers on international flights should allow three hours for pre-departure security and other processing at the airport. Passengers for domestic flights should be at the airport at least two hours before flights. Domestic flights, including those to and from Port Sudan, Dongola and Juba, are subject to change or cancellation without notice.

CURRENCY REGULATIONS: A currency declaration statement is required upon arrival and departure from Sudan. Visitors who attempt to exchange money at unauthorized banking institutions or on the black market risk arrest and/or loss of funds. Please note restrictions on transactions with Sudan contained in the section on Trade Restrictions. Some visitors to Sudan have experienced difficulty exchanging U.S. dollar denomination instruments -- such as travelers' checks or cr cards -- due to U.S. economic sanctions.

PHOTOGRAPHY RESTRICTIONS: A permit is required before taking photographs anywhere in Khartoum, as well as in the interior of the country. Photographing military areas, bridges, drainage stations, broadcast stations, public utilities and slum areas or beggars is prohibited.

INFRASTRUCTURE: Disruptions of water and electricity are frequent. A new telecommunications system is in the process of being installed.

CRIMINAL PENALTIES: While in a foreign country, a U.S. citizen is subject to that country's laws and regulations, which sometimes differ significantly from those in the United States and may not afford the protections available under U.S law. Penalties for breaking the law can be more severe than in the United States for similar offenses. Persons violating Sudanese laws, even unknowingly, may be expelled, arrested, or imprisoned. Penalties for possession, use, or trafficking in illegal drugs in Sudan are strict, and convicted offenders can expect jail sentences and fines.

CHILDREN'S ISSUES: For information on international adoption of children, international parental child abduction, and international child support enforcement issues, please refer to our Internet site at http://travel.state.gov/children's_issues.html or telephone (202) 736-7000.

EMBASSY LOCATION/REGISTRATION: U.S. citizens traveling to Sudan, despite the Travel Warning, are encouraged to register with local employees at the U.S. Embassy in Khartoum located at Sharia Ali Abdul Latif, and to obtain updated information on travel and security in Sudan. The mailing address is P.O. Box 699, Khartoum; telephone (249)(11) 774-700 and 774-611; fax 774-137. The U.S. consular officer can be contacted via the Consular Section in Khartoum or directly at the U.S. Embassy in Cairo; telephone (20)(2) 795-7371; e-mail: consularcairo@state.gov. The workweek in Cairo and Khartoum is Sunday through Thursday. Information on services available for residents of Sudan may be found on the U.S. Embassy Cairo's web site: http://usembassy.egnet.net/sudan.htm.

IMPORTANT INFORMATION TO TRAVELLER TO SUDAN

VISAS & PERMITS

Entry visas are required by almost all nationalities, and are valid usually for one month.

Evidence of a previous visit to Israel will result in a visa refusal.

Permits are required by visitors wishing to travel anywhere outside Khartoum, and can take upto 2 days to obtain. Visitors arriving in any town or city in the Sudan must register with the police on their arrival, and show the necessary paperwork.

For those wishing to visit archaeological and/or historical sites, permits are again required. These are often fairly expensive, and can be obtained from the Department of Antiquities in Khartoum.

The Tourist Information Office in Khartoum will issue visitors with a photography permit. This is essential for anyone wishing to take photographs anywhere in the country, and is issued together with a list of items which may not be photographed.

CURFEW

A curfew operated in most large cities and towns from midnight until 4am.

HEALTH AND VACCINATIONS

As a result of the war, there is a severe shortage of medicines, trained doctors and hospital equipment in the Sudan. Many serious diseases are common, particularly malaria, hepatitis, dysentery, and bilharzia.

All visitors are strongly recommended to take out a good health insurance policy before travelling. Recommended vaccinations are yellow fever, cholera, typhoid, tetanus and meningitis. Malaria is rife, so preventative medication -- such as Paludrine -- should be taken before, during and after your trip. A mosquito net and repellent cream are both essential, especially if you are travelling south of Khartoum.

Water is rarely safe to drink straight from the tap, even in the larger cities. Boiling all water or the use of water purification tablets or boiled water is strongly recommended. Snakes and scorpions can present their own problems! Visitors should keep a watchful eye.

COMMUNICATIONS

Postal, telephone and telegraph services are administered by the government. In Khartoum, the post office is open from 8:30am to 1pm and from 5:30 to 6:30pm every day except Friday. International mail, both in and out, is often very slow.

International telephone calls are relativly easy to make from major cities from any of the telemunication stores.

PUBLIC HOLIDAYS

All regular Islamic holidays and festivals are kept, with the following additions:

- 1st January: Independence Day, commemorating the birth of the Sudanese Republic in 1956.
- 30th June: Salvation Day, Commemorating the Salvation Government takeover of government from civillian rule
- 25th December: Christmas Day

SHOPPING

Weaponry, such as daggers and swords in leather sheaths, can be unearthed in the markets of Sudanese towns. Some local men still wear these as part of everyday attire, but this is becoming an increasingly rare sight. As an exotic souvenir, however, these weapons are an interesting purchase.

Ebony carvings are for sale in the souqs at Omdurman and Khartoum, as well as gold jewellery. In the western region, in and around the town of Mellit, shoppers can find attractive carpets and some beautiful pottery.

Those interested in world wildlife and ecology will do best to avoid such purchases as ivory goods, stuffed crocodiles and purses made from crocodile skin. Animals are being massacred in large numbers to provide these goods, and they are -- unfortunately -- on sale throughout the Sudan and in other parts of Africa.

ENTERTAINMENT

Cultural events in the Sudan are few and far between. At the end of Ramadan, however, during the Eid Al-Fitr, it is possible to find Sudanese bands performing in the larger towns. As Sudanese music is an interesting blend of Arabian and African, listening can be a pleasant experience.

SUDAN: LOCAL TRANSPORTATION

Roads

There are about 50,000km (31,080 miles) of roads in the Sudan, but most are unsurfaced dirt tracks which may become completely impassable after heavy rain. Paved highways, runs between Khartoum - Port Sudan, Atbara, Dongola, Gedarif.

Buses run between Khartoum, Kassala, Port Sudan, Gedarif. These boast air-conditioning, comfortable seats and shock absorbers, but most buses are a far cry from this class of transport. The vast majority have wooden bench seats, no shock absorbers and are very crowded and uncomfortable.

Travel by lorry is probably even more unpleasant, as the rear section must be shared with all kinds of cargo and livestock. It is also open to the elements, and is hot and dusty in the extreme. Travel by both bus and lorry is extremely slow, due to the poor condition of the roads and the inevitable breakdowns en route.

A slightly faster way of getting about is by Toyota Hilux pick-ups, known to the locals as 'boxes' (boksi, plural bokasi). These cost a little more than lorries or buses and, although not a great deal more comfortable, they will certainly get you to your destination in a much shorter time. Boxes are mostly used as local transport between villages, but some longer routes are available, notably a trans-desert route from Dongola to Karima and Karima to Atbara.

Many of the locals travel by camel (western and northern Sudan) or donkey (country-wide). Bicycles are rarely seen, due to poor road conditions.

In the larger urban areas -- Khartoum, Omdurman, Kassala and Port Sudan -- taxis are available, but fares are erratic, and travellers need to bargain before starting their trip.

Rail

The railway system in the Sudan is extensive, with about 5,500km (3,420 miles) of track linking most of the major towns and cities. It is, however, in a poor state of repair and is currently operating at about one-fifth of its capacity. Most of the railway system dates from Kitchener's offensive against the Mahdi in the 1890s, and is a narrow gauge, single track line.

There are three classes of travel on the Sudanese railway. First-class compartments carry six passengers, while no limit seems to be fixed on the numbers in second and third classes, so these can be very crowded. Some passengers even ride for free on the carriage roofs. This practice is not recommended, however, as accidents have been known to occur.

Air

The national carrier is the government-owned Sudan Airways, Other airline companies operate on local routes.

SUDAN: PLACES OF INTEREST

Khartoum and Omdurman

Khartoum is one of three sister cities, built at the convergence of the Blue and White Niles: Omdurman to the north-west across the White Nile, North Khartoum, and Khartoum itself on the southern bank of the Blue Nile.

Khartoum has a relatively short history. It was first established as a military outpost in 1821, and is said to derive its name from the thin spit of land at the convergence of the rivers, which resembles an elephant's trunk (khurtum). Khartoum grew rapidly in prosperity during the boom years of the slave trade, between 1825 and 1880. In 1834 it became the capital of the Sudan, and many explorers from Europe used it as a base for their African expions.

Khartoum was sacked twice during the latter half of the 19th century -- once by the Mahdi and once by Kitchener when the Mahdi was ousted. In 1898, Kitchener began to rebuild the city, and designed the streets in the shape of the British flag, the Union Jack, which he hoped would make it easier to defend. On the opposite bank of the Nile, North Khartoum was developed as an industrial area at about the same time.

Today's Khartoum is a quiet, unremarkable city. It has peaceful, tree-lined streets, and in some ways still bears the unmistakable mark of an outpost of the British Empire. Its expansion to accommodate a rapidly-growing population, however, has added very little in terms of charm or atmosphere.

Places to visit in Khartoum

National Museum. This contains antiquities and artefacts from several periods of Sudanese history and pre-history, including glassware, pottery, statuary and figurines from the ancient kingdom of Cush. Ancient Nubia's Christian period is well-represented, with frescoes and murals from ruined churches, dating from the 8th to the 15th century. The Museum's garden contains two reconstructed temples, which have been salvaged from the Nubian land flooded by Lake Nasser. These Egyptian temples of Buhen and Semna were originally built by Queen Hatshepsut and Pharaoh Tuthmosis III respectively. The temples have corrugated iron covers built over them to protect them from humidity during the wet season. The original concept was to roll back these covers during the dry season, but whether this ever happened or not is unclear. The covers are rusted into place and are now permanent and immovable!

Ethnographical Museum. This is a small museum which contains an interesting collection of items relating to Sudanese village life. These include musical instruments, clothing, cooking and hunting implements.

Places to visit in Omdurman

Souq. This is the largest in the Sudan, and has an interesting variety of goods on display. Ivory and ebony candlesticks are carved by market craftsmen, goldsmiths and silversmiths fashion all kinds of jewellery in their shop-fronts, and the atmosphere is lively and bustling. The best time to visit is on Friday mornings.

Camel Market. This is situated about 2km north of Omdurman's main souq. Animals are mostly brought from eastern or western areas of the Sudan.

Tomb of the Mahdi. On the death of the Mahdi in 1885, his body was entombed in a silver-domed mosque in Omdurman. This was completely destroyed by Kitchener in 1898, when the Mahdi's body was burned and his ashes thrown into the river. In 1947 the Mahdi's son had the mosque and tomb rebuilt. Not surprisingly, it is closed to foreigners, but can be viewed from the outside.

Beit al-Khalifa. This is situated opposite the Mahdi's tomb. Once the home of the Mahdi's successor, the house was built of mud and brick in 1887, and is now a museum. It contains relics from Mahdiyya battles, including guns, war banners and suits of mail. An interesting collection of photographs depicts the city of Khartoum at the time of the Mahdi's revolt and its subsequent occupation by the British.

El-Obeid

This is the capital city of the Kordofan region in Western Sudan, and was once the Mahdi's capital and political centre. Situated in the middle of a vast stretch of barren desert, it has a population of 200,000 people and is an important centre for the production of gum arabic. This substance is used in the manufacture of food thickening, ink and medicinal products, and is obtained from acacia trees.

The city experiences problems with its supplies of both electric power and water. Electricity from the city's own generators is erratic and power cuts are the norm. In such an arid desert environment, water supplies often dwindle and have to be brought in by truck from other areas.

The two souqs in the city deal mostly in meat and vegetables. There are also some tailor's shops where fabric can be purchased and clothes made to order.

There is little to interest the visitor in El-Obeid, apart from a small museum, which displays exhibits relating to ancient Sudanese history. Its Catholic cathedral is impressive, however, and is said to be one of the largest in Africa.

Port Sudan

Port Sudan is a harbour city, established by the British in 1905 as a seaport. Once a thriving export centre handling the country's raw commodities such as sesame, cotton and sorghum, it has now fallen into decay as a result of the ongoing war.

Today's city is badly in need of care and repair, although it is still possible to see beautiful lattice woodwork on the window-screens of older buildings, which provide a glimpse into the city's more prestigious past.

It was once possible to travel by boat from Port Sudan to Jeddah in Saudi Arabia, but passenger traffic, like commercial activity, has dwindled to the merest trickle. As a result, passenger services from the port are no longer in existence.

For visitors interested in Red Sea diving, this is still quite a good place to use as a base, and local hotels and dive shops can make the necessary arrangements.

Kassala

Kassala is situated in Eastern Sudan and has a population of 150,000. The city is built on the Gash River and is the power centre of one of the Sudan's traditional families -- the Khatmiya Brotherhood, which opposed the Mahdi family in the last century.

On the outskirts of the city live the Rashaida tribe, mostly inhabiting goatskin tents. They are a nomadic people who breed camels and goats, and are closely related to the Saudi Arabian Bedouin, having migrated from the Arabian Peninsula about 150 years ago. It is the mysteriously-veiled Rashaida women who make a great deal of the silver jewellery sold in the Kassala souq.

The souq is said to be one of Sudan's best, and sells a wide variety of the fruit for which Kassala is renowned. Grapefruit, pomegranates, oranges, bananas and melons are all for sale here, as well as local handicrafts, fabrics and the aforementioned silver jewellery.

Several kilometres outside Kassala are the curiously-shaped 'sugar-loaf' hills, known as the jebels. They can be seen on the horizon from the city and are the habitat of a tribe of baboons, which come down from the hills at sunset to drink at a nearby village well.

Kassala is also a favourite retreat for Sudanese honeymoon couples, and in the nearby village of Khatmiya, the same village well is a traditional place for newly-wed couples to drink. Water from the well is said to bring good luck and a fertile married life.

Suakin Island

The island is situated 58km south of Port Sudan and was once a major trading centre, particularly in the 19th century, during the boom years of slavery. As far back as the 10th century BC, Suakin was used by Pharaoh Rameses III as a trading port, but declined in importance after the close of the 19th century AD, and in 1905 was superseded in importance by Port Sudan.

Its unique architecture is made of coral, but these once-beautiful buildings, although restored by the Mahdi in 1881, are now in the final stages of crumbling away.

The island is linked to the mainland by means of a causeway.

Dongola

Once an important centre of power in ancient Nubia, the remains of the old northern-Sudanese city are being excavated by a Polish-led team -- a project that has been in operation since 1964.

The town is now noteworthy for its palm groves and its September date harvest, when young boys climb the palm trunks, carrying sharp knives in their teeth, to cut the clusters of dates. The fruit and vegetable souq here is a colourful sight, occasionally dealing in camels, which the desert nomads bring in for sale.

The Cushite temple of Kawa is situated on the eastern bank of the river. The ruins of this temple can be visited by taking a ferry across the river from the main town.

Karima

This northern-Sudanese market town has a population of about 15,000. The town itself is of little interest, but there are several ancient sites nearby which are worth a visit.

Just 2km south of the town is the 100-metre high Jebel Barkal, a hill which was regarded as sacred by the Egyptians of the 18th Dynasty. From its summit, there is an excellent view of the Nile. At its foot lies the Temple of Amun, second only in length to the famous Temple of Karnak. This was once surrounded by about six smaller temples, and ruins of these, together with statuary and hieroglyphics, make this an interesting Cushite site.

Lying west of the temple are the Jebel Barkal Pyramids, similar in style to those at Meroe.

Atbara

Located at the conjunction of the Atbara tributary, flowing down from Ethiopia, and the River Nile, Atbara is on two main railway routes: from Atbara to Port Sudan, and from Khartoum to Wadi Halfa.

The city has a population of 75,000 people. In 1898 it was the site of a battle between the British and the Mahdists, when 2,000 of the latter were wiped out by Kitchener. After the battle, British officials settled here, building colonial-style houses, which are now used as government offices.

The ruins of the Royal City of Meroe are located about 100km south of Atbara. Residence of the kings of Meroe between 592BC and AD350, the city shows strong Egyptian architectural influence. The ruined Temple of Amun is still standing, together with the remains several palaces and a swimming pool.

In the desert, about 5km to the east, stand the royal pyramids, where the dead kings of Meroe are buried.

Jebel Marra Mountains

This western-Sudanese mountain range is dominated by the second-highest mountain in the Sudan, known as Jebel Marra. This is an extinct volcano which rises to a height of 3071 metres.

At the base of the mountain range lies the town of Nyala, and this town forms a good starting point for an exploration of the surrounding mountainous countryside. It is a beautiful region of hills, rivers and orchards, and is an interesting spot for walking enthusiasts. There is a waterfall near the village of Quaila and some hot springs near the crater of the volcano itself.

El-Fasher

In the 18th century, El-Fasher was the main centre of the Fur Sultanate. The sultan's palace can still be seen in this western-Sudanese town, and is now a museum.

The town was also famous as the starting point of one of the most important camel caravan routes in Africa. Known as the Darb al-Arba'een, or Forty Days Road, this route carried ebony, spices, rich cloth, ivory and slaves from all parts of Africa to the Egyptian bazaars of Aswan and Asyut.

MAJOR HOTELS IN THE KHARTOUM AREA

ACROPOLE HOTEL , Khartoum, Sudan
Single: USD 45, *Double:* USD 55
AMBASSADOR HOTEL , Khartoum, Sudan
Sorry no Price List
ARAAK HOTEL , Khartoum, Sudan
Sorry no Price List
FRIENDSHIP PALACE , Khartoum, Sudan
Single: USD 110, *Double:* USD 130
GRAND , Khartoum, Sudan
Sorry No Price List
GREEN VILLAGE *, Khartoum, Sudan*
Sorry No Price List
KHARTOUM HILTON *, Khartoum, Sudan*
Sorry No Price List
LE MERIDIEN KHARTOUM *, Khartoum, Sudan*
Single: USD 130, Double: USD 160,
SUDAN *, Khartoum, Sudan*
Single: USD 48

SUPPLEMENTS

PROCEDURAL STEPS FOR INVESTMENT TRANSACTIONS

APPLICATION FOR A NEW LICENSE

1.Provide 2 copies of the technical and economic feasibility studies

2.A copy of the company registration and a certificate of establishment if the owner is a specified company

3.Fill in the form prepared for that purpose after paying an application fee of 15,800 dinars (fifteen thousand eight hundred dinars)

4.Pay the application fee

5.The study is then transferred to the concerned ministry to obtain the technical agreement for establishment of the project

6.Issue a primary consent to the project

7.Register a name for the project with the Delegate Commercial Registrar in the Ministry of Investment

8.Issue a final license for the project acceding with followed rules

9.Please submit an agency agreement authorized by a lawyer if the project is to be supervised by someone other than the owner or in the case of companies

APPLICATION FOR ACTIVITY CHANGE

Firstly: the conditions

1. the new activity must be an encouraged activity
2. no planning, environmental or health impediment should exist

Second: required documents

1. a copy of the license for the first activity
2. a copy of the business name
3. a valid ownership certificate or rental contract
4. application to the administration

Third: the procedures

1. payment of the application fees
2. the application is transferred to the specialized sector for analysis
3. after the consent is issued a new business name should be registered for the new activity at the Delegate Commercial Registrars department.

4. the license of the new activity is issued after payment of required legal fees

ADDITION OF A PRODUCTION LINE TO AN EXISTING PROJECT

First: the conditions

1. the main line must be readily executed and is working in an acceptable manner
2. the availability of a suitable area for the new line
3. the new should not oppose the old line in any technical or planning manner

Second: required documents

1. a copy of the license granted to the first line
2. a copy of the business name
3. an ownership certificate or rental contract

Third: procedures

1. payment of the application fees
2. obtain approval from the concerned technical party
3. transfer the application to the concerned sector for examination, issue consent and then transfer the consent to the Commercial Registrar to add a new line to the original business name
4. Issue a license or decision after payment of the required fees

TRANSFER OF OWNERSHIP

First: the conditions

1. execution of the project to a reasonable extent not less than 60% of the required structures
2. it is not possible to transfer empty land granted in accordance with the investment encouragement act

Second: required documents

1. submit a valid ownership certificate of the transferred project
2. a copy of the projects license
3. a copy of the business registration
4. a primary concession contract from a recognized legal body
5. an application to the ministry for acceptance of the concession

Third: procedures

1. payment of application fees
2. transfer of the application to the specialized sector for examination
3. a field visit to the project by the monitoring department and preparation of a report explaining the execution of the project
4. the application will be transferred to the ministry's legal consultant to ascertain the legality of the proceeding
5. consideration of the application in agreement or disagreement; incase of agreement the project is registered with the Delegate Commercial Registrar in the ministry

6. issue a final license to the owner and a new business name

FORMING OR ENDING A PARTNERSHIP

As long as the purpose of involving a new partner is fully executing the project then agreement to this will be issued after the following documents are submitted:

1. a copy of the business registration
2. a copy of the license
3. a valid ownership certificate
4. a partnership contract ratified by a legal body
5. an application to the administration requiring the transaction

MORTGAGING THE PROJECT FOR FINANCE

First: the conditions

1. the project must be executed to an extent allowing the mortgage of the buildings not the granted land
2. a letter from a bank clarifying the purpose of finance which must be for the operation or execution of the project

Second: required documents

1. a copy of the license
2. a copy of the business registration
3. a valid ownership certificate
4. a banks letter of finance

Third: procedures

1. payment of application fees
2. transfer the application to the concerned sector
3. a field visit is executed by the monitoring department and a report is prepared showing the extent of execution
4. the documents are revised by the ministry's legal counsel
5. consideration of the application and making the decision concerned

General rules

First: cars and other transport means are not allowed except after the capital equipment is imported

Second: the project is not granted a tax exemption for more than 10 years except after the project is proven a strategic one with a capital of 10 million dollars and a budget audited by a legal auditor

Third: capital equipment has become an automatic concession with 0 customs and does not need any exemption

Fourth: rehabilitating the industrial projects now enjoys a constant percentage for business profits which is 10% instead of 30%

BASIC TITLES ON SUDAN

Title
Sudan (North) Country Study Guide - Volume 1 Strategic Information and Developments
Sudan (North): How to Invest, Start and Run Profitable Business in Sudan (North) Guide - Practical Information, Opportunities, Contacts
Sudan (South) Country Study Guide - Volume 1 Strategic Information and Developments
Sudan (South): How to Invest, Start and Run Profitable Business in Sudan (South) Guide - Practical Information, Opportunities, Contacts
Sudan A "Spy" Guide - Strategic Information and Developments
Sudan A Spy" Guide"
Sudan Banking & Financial Market Handbook
Sudan Banking & Financial Market Handbook
Sudan Business and Investment Opportunities Yearbook
Sudan Business and Investment Opportunities Yearbook
Sudan Business and Investment Opportunities Yearbook Volume 1 Strategic Information and Opportunities
Sudan Business Intelligence Report - Practical Information, Opportunities, Contacts
Sudan Business Intelligence Report - Practical Information, Opportunities, Contacts
Sudan Business Law Handbook Volume 1 Strategic Information and Basic Laws
Sudan Business Law Handbook Volume 2 Investment and Trade Laws
Sudan Business Law Handbook Volume 3 Mining Laws and Regulations
Sudan Business Law Handbook Volume 4 Sharia and Islamic Laws
Sudan Company Laws and Regulations Handbook
Sudan Constitution and Citizenship Laws Handbook - Strategic Information and Basic Laws
Sudan Country Study Guide - Strategic Information and Developments
Sudan Customs, Trade Regulations and Procedures Handbook
Sudan Customs, Trade Regulations and Procedures Handbook
Sudan Diplomatic Handbook - Strategic Information and Developments
Sudan Diplomatic Handbook - Strategic Information and Developments
Sudan Ecology & Nature Protection Handbook
Sudan Ecology & Nature Protection Handbook
Sudan Ecology & Nature Protection Laws and Regulation Handbook
Sudan Economic & Development Strategy Handbook
Sudan Economic & Development Strategy Handbook
Sudan Energy Policy, Laws and Regulation Handbook
Sudan Energy Policy, Laws and Regulations Handbook
Sudan Energy Policy, Laws and Regulations Handbook
Sudan Export-Import Trade and Business Directory
Sudan Export-Import Trade and Business Directory
Sudan Foreign Policy and Government Guide
Sudan Foreign Policy and Government Guide
Sudan Healthcare Sector Organization, Management and Payment Systems Handbook - Strategic Information, Programs and Regulations

Title
Sudan Immigration Laws and Regulations Handbook - Strategic Information and Basic Laws
Sudan Industrial and Business Directory
Sudan Industrial and Business Directory
Sudan Internet and E-Commerce Investment and Business Guide - Strategic and Practical Information: Regulations and Opportunities
Sudan Internet and E-Commerce Investment and Business Guide - Strategic and Practical Information: Regulations and Opportunities
Sudan Investment and Business Guide - Strategic and Practical Information
Sudan Investment and Business Guide - Strategic and Practical Information
Sudan Investment and Business Guide - Strategic and Practical Information
Sudan Investment and Business Guide - Strategic and Practical Information
Sudan Investment and Trade Laws and Regulations Handbook
Sudan Land Ownership and Agriculture Laws Handbook
Sudan Mineral & Mining Sector Investment and Business Guide - Strategic and Practical Information
Sudan Mineral & Mining Sector Investment and Business Guide - Strategic and Practical Information
Sudan Mining Laws and Regulations Handbook
Sudan Oil & Gas Sector Business & Investment Opportunities Yearbook
Sudan Oil & Gas Sector Business & Investment Opportunities Yearbook
Sudan Oil and Gas Exploration Laws and Regulation Handbook
Sudan Recent Economic and Political Developments Yearbook
Sudan Recent Economic and Political Developments Yearbook
Sudan Recent Economic and Political Developments Yearbook
Sudan South Business and Investment Opportunities Yearbook Volume 1 Strategic Information and Opportunities
Sudan South Economic, Development Strategy and Programs Handbook
Sudan Starting Business (Incorporating) in....Guide
Sudan Taxation Laws and Regulations Handbook
Sudan Telecom Laws and Regulations Handbook
Sudan Telecommunication Industry Business Opportunities Handbook
Sudan Telecommunication Industry Business Opportunities Handbook
Sudan Transportation Policy and Regulations Handbook

NUCLEAR ENERGY SECTOR POLICY LIBRARY

(PRICE $149.95 each)

Argentina Nuclear Energy Sector Policy, Laws and Regulations Handbook
Armenia Nuclear Energy Sector Policy, Laws and Regulations Handbook
Belgium Nuclear Energy Sector Policy, Laws and Regulations Handbook
Brazil Nuclear Energy Sector Policy, Laws and Regulations Handbook
Bulgaria Nuclear Energy Sector Policy, Laws and Regulations Handbook
Bulgaria Nuclear Energy Sector Policy, Laws and Regulations Handbook
Bulgaria Nuclear Energy Sector Policy, Laws and Regulations Handbook
China Mainland Nuclear Energy Sector Policy, Laws and Regulations Handbook
Czech Republic Nuclear Energy Sector Policy, Laws and Regulations Handbook
Finland Nuclear Energy Sector Policy, Laws and Regulations Handbook
France Nuclear Energy Sector Policy, Laws and Regulations Handbook
Germany Nuclear Energy Sector Policy, Laws and Regulations Handbook
Hungary Nuclear Energy Sector Policy, Laws and Regulations Handbook
India Nuclear Energy Sector Policy, Laws and Regulations Handbook
Iran Nuclear Energy Sector Policy, Laws and Regulations Handbook
Japan Nuclear Energy Sector Policy, Laws and Regulations Handbook
Korea, Democratic People's Republic of Nuclear Energy Sector Policy, Laws and Regulations Handbook
Korea, Republic of Nuclear Energy Sector Policy, Laws and Regulations Handbook
Mexico Nuclear Energy Sector Policy, Laws and Regulations Handbook
Netherlands Nuclear Energy Sector Policy, Laws and Regulations Handbook
Pakistan Nuclear Energy Sector Policy, Laws and Regulations Handbook
Romania Nuclear Energy Sector Policy, Laws and Regulations Handbook
Russia Nuclear Energy Sector Policy, Laws and Regulations Handbook
Slovakia Nuclear Energy Sector Policy, Laws and Regulations Handbook
Slovenia Nuclear Energy Sector Policy, Laws and Regulations Handbook
South Africa Nuclear Energy Sector Policy, Laws and Regulations Handbook
Spain Nuclear Energy Sector Policy, Laws and Regulations Handbook
Sweden Nuclear Energy Sector Policy, Laws and Regulations Handbook
Switzerland Nuclear Energy Sector Policy, Laws and Regulations Handbook
Taiwan Nuclear Energy Sector Policy, Laws and Regulations Handbook
Ukraine Nuclear Energy Sector Policy, Laws and Regulations Handbook
United Kingdom Nuclear Energy Sector Policy, Laws and Regulations Handbook
United States Nuclear Energy Sector Policy, Laws and Regulations Handbook

WORLD ENERGY POLICY, BUSINESS & INVESTMENT OPPORTUNITIES LIBRARY

Price: $149.95 Each

Title
Albania Energy Policy, Laws and Regulations Handbook
Algeria Energy Policy, Laws and Regulations Handbook
Angola Energy Policy, Laws and Regulations Handbook
Australia Energy Policy, Laws and Regulations Handbook
Azerbaijan Energy Policy, Laws and Regulations Handbook
Bahrain Energy Policy, Laws and Regulations Handbook
Bangladesh Energy Policy, Laws and Regulations Handbook
Benin Energy Policy, Laws and Regulations Handbook
Brazil Energy Policy, Laws and Regulations Handbook
Brunei Energy Policy, Laws and Regulations Handbook
Cameroon Energy Policy, Laws and Regulations Handbook
Canada Energy Policy, Laws and Regulations Handbook
China Energy Policy, Laws and Regulations Handbook
Colombia Oil & Gas Sector Energy Policy, Laws and Regulations Handbook
Congo Energy Policy, Laws and Regulations Handbook
Congo, Dem. Republic Energy Policy, Laws and Regulations Handbook
Cote d'Ivoire Energy Policy, Laws and Regulations Handbook
Dubai Energy Policy, Laws and Regulations Handbook
Ecuador Energy Policy, Laws and Regulations Handbook
Egypt Energy Policy, Laws and Regulations Handbook
Equatorial Guinea Energy Policy, Laws and Regulations Handbook
Gabon Energy Policy, Laws and Regulations Handbook
India Energy Policy, Laws and Regulations Handbook
Indonesia Energy Policy, Laws and Regulations Handbook
Iran Energy Policy, Laws and Regulations Handbook
Iraq Energy Policy, Laws and Regulations Handbook
Kazakhstan Energy Policy, Laws and Regulations Handbook

Title
Kuwait Energy Policy, Laws and Regulations Handbook
Libya Energy Policy, Laws and Regulations Handbook
Malaysia Energy Policy, Laws and Regulations Handbook
Mexico Energy Policy, Laws and Regulations Handbook
Morocco Energy Policy, Laws and Regulations Handbook
Namibia Energy Policy, Laws and Regulations Handbook
New Zealand Energy Policy, Laws and Regulations Handbook
Nigeria Energy Policy, Laws and Regulations Handbook
Norway Energy Policy, Laws and Regulations Handbook
Oman Energy Policy, Laws and Regulations Handbook
Pakistan Energy Policy, Laws and Regulations Handbook
Papua New Guinea Energy Policy, Laws and Regulations Handbook
Papua New Guinea Oil & Gas Sector Energy Policy, Laws and Regulations Handbook
Peru Energy Policy, Laws and Regulations Handbook
Philippines Energy Policy, Laws and Regulations Handbook
Qatar Energy Policy, Laws and Regulations Handbook
Sri Lanka Energy Policy, Laws and Regulations Handbook
Romania Energy Policy, Laws and Regulations Handbook
Russia Energy Policy, Laws and Regulations Handbook
Saudi Arabia Energy Policy, Laws and Regulations Handbook
Sudan Energy Policy, Laws and Regulations Handbook
Suriname Energy Policy, Laws and Regulations Handbook
Syria Energy Policy, Laws and Regulations Handbook
Trinidad and Tobago Oil & Gas Sector Energy Policy, Laws and Regulations Handbook
Tunisia Energy Policy, Laws and Regulations Handbook
Turkey Energy Policy, Laws and Regulations Handbook
Turkmenistan Energy Policy, Laws and Regulations Handbook
Ukraine Oil & Gas Sector Energy Policy, Laws and Regulations Handbook
United Arab Emirates Energy Policy, Laws and Regulations Handbook
United Kingdom Energy Policy, Laws and Regulations Handbook
United Kingdom Oil & Gas Sector Energy Policy, Laws and Regulations Handbook
United States Energy Policy, Laws and Regulations Handbook
Venezuela Energy Policy, Laws and Regulations Handbook
Vietnam Energy Policy, Laws and Regulations Handbook
Vietnam Energy Policy, Laws and Regulations Handbook
Yemen Energy Policy, Laws and Regulations Handbook

www.ingramcontent.com/pod-product-compliance
Lightning Source LLC
LaVergne TN
LVHW080028210926
848481LV00011B/3130